SASHA POLAKOW-SURANSKY
THE UNSPOKEN ALLIANCE

"A harrowing account of a Mephistophelian bargain between two rogue states, told with indisputable facts—many of them new—and on-the-record interviews. No moralizing needed. Israel's twenty-year collaboration with South Africa betrayed its founding principles and, more tragically, anticipated the cynicism with which it conducts its Palestinian policy today."   —Seymour Hersh

"A compelling history. . . . All states engage in secret diplomacy, but Israel offers some of the most shocking examples. . . . Although he deplores Israel's ties to the apartheid regime, Polakow-Suransky has treated the handful of officials in the two countries implementing that alliance fairly, even empathetically."   *—Foreign Affairs*

"A deft, pacy and revealing account. . . . Admirably dispassionate."
—The Economist

"The extent to which these two countries began to rely on each other economically and militarily in the mid-1970s through the late 1980s has never been so fully fleshed out. . . . There are some striking revelations."   *—Forward*

"A tale of clandestine missions, surreptitious shipments, and elaborate political theater between two states perched precariously on the margins of both their continents and the Cold War."   *—National Review*

"A meticulously researched book that reads like a spy thriller."
—The Nation

"A careful, painful, hugely important book."
—Peter Beinart, author of *The Icarus Syndrome*

"Provocative. . . . Richly detailed. . . . Especially relevant today, as nuclear rivalries escalate in the Middle East, because it explains— calmly, methodically, and with full documentation—how Israel and South Africa helped each other build atomic bombs in secret."
—Stephen Kinzer, *The Daily Beast*

"Pathbreaking. . . . Remarkably revealing. . . . A wise, elegantly written, and strikingly fair-minded book which deserves the widest possible readership."
—Avi Shlaim, author of *The Iron Wall: Israel and the Arab World*

"Stands out because of the new material its author has dug up, which may be deemed to provide a measure of insight into ongoing and tricky proliferation issues." —*The New York Review of Books*

"Well researched, readable and . . . balanced." —*London Review of Books*

"Comprehensive. . . . A very important contribution in the study of modern and contemporary history for its wealth of material and the objectivity of its author. It is highly recommended for both academics and the general reader." —*The Middle East Journal*

"Fascinating. . . . A major, long-overdue study of the rise and demise of one of the most intriguing alliances of our time. Polakow-Suransky has written a masterfully researched history that reads like a thriller unraveling the secrets of an alliance between two embattled societies under siege." —Shlomo Ben-Ami, foreign minister of Israel, 2000–2001

SASHA POLAKOW-SURANSKY
THE UNSPOKEN ALLIANCE

Sasha Polakow-Suransky is an editor at *The New York Times* op-ed page. He was senior editor at *Foreign Affairs* from 2007 to 2011 and holds a doctorate in modern history from Oxford University, where he was a Rhodes Scholar from 2003 to 2006. His writing has appeared in *The American Prospect*, *The Boston Globe*, *The International Herald Tribune*, *The New Republic*, and *Newsweek*. He lives in Brooklyn.

THE UNSPOKEN ALLIANCE

*Israel's Secret Relationship
with Apartheid South Africa*

SASHA POLAKOW-SURANSKY

VINTAGE BOOKS

A DIVISION OF RANDOM HOUSE, INC.

NEW YORK

The Library of Congress has cataloged the Pantheon edition as follows:
Polakow-Suransky, Sasha.
The unspoken alliance : Israel's secret relationship with apartheid South Africa /
Sasha Polakow-Suransky.
p. cm.
Includes bibliographical references and index.
1. Israel—Relations—South Africa. 2. South Africa—Relations—Israel. 3. Israel—
Military relations—South Africa. 4. South Africa—Military relations—Israel. I. Title.
DS119.8.S6P65 2010
327.5694068—dc22
2009047156

Vintage ISBN: 978–0–307–38850–6

Author photograph © Michael Lionstar
Book design by M. Kristen Bearse

www.vintagebooks.com

146056540

In memory of Michael Bhatia,
who told me to write it.

Contents

ABBREVIATIONS AND TERMS

AAI	Afro-Asian Institute (Israel)
ADL	Anti-Defamation League
AEB	Atomic Energy Board (South Africa)
AIPAC	American Israel Public Affairs Committee
ANC	African National Congress
BOSS	Bureau of State Security (South Africa)
CSIR	Council for Scientific and Industrial Research (South Africa)
DIA	Defense Intelligence Agency (United States)
FNLA	National Front for the Liberation of Angola
GRU	Soviet Military Intelligence
IAEA	International Atomic Energy Agency
IAF	Israeli Air Force
IAI	Israel Aircraft Industries
IDF	Israel Defense Forces
IMF	International Monetary Fund
IMI	Israel Military Industries
ISSACOM	Israel–South Africa Interministerial Security Affairs Committee
MPLA	Popular Movement for the Liberation of Angola
MTCR	Missile Technology Control Regime
NP	National Party (South Africa)
NPT	Nuclear Non-Proliferation Treaty
NRL	U.S. Naval Research Laboratory
NSC	National Security Council (United States)
OAU	Organization of African Unity
OB	Ossewa Brandwag (Afrikaner nationalist group)
PLO	Palestine Liberation Organization
RSA	Republic of South Africa

SAAF   South African Air Force
SADF   South African Defence Force
SWAPO   South-West Africa People's Organization
UNITA   National Union for the Total Independence of Angola
WZO   World Zionist Organization

FREQUENTLY USED HEBREW TERMS AND ACRONYMS

Herut   Menachem Begin's right-wing political party, precursor to Likud
Histadrut Israeli public sector trade union
Irgun   Pre-1948 armed movement (Irgun Tzvai Leumi, National Military Organization)
Lakam   Council for Scientific Liaison (Israel)
Lehi   Pre-1948 armed movement (Lohamei Herut Yisrael, Fighters for the Freedom of Israel)
Malmab   Directorate of Security of the Defense Establishment
Mapai   Israel Workers Party, precursor to Labor Party
Mapam   United Workers Party
Mossad   Israeli Intelligence Service

THE UNSPOKEN ALLIANCE

PROLOGUE

ON APRIL 9, 1976, South African prime minister Balthazar Johannes Vorster arrived at the Yad Vashem Holocaust memorial in Jerusalem with full diplomatic entourage in tow. After passing solemnly through the corridors commemorating those gassed in Auschwitz and Dachau, he entered the dimly lit Hall of Remembrance, where a memorial flame burned alongside a crypt filled with the ashes of Holocaust victims. Vorster bowed his head as a South African minister read a psalm in Afrikaans, the haunting melody of the Jewish prayer for the dead filling the room. He then kneeled and laid a wreath, containing the colors of the South African flag, in memory of Hitler's victims. Cameras snapped, dignitaries applauded, and Israeli officials quickly ferried the prime minister away to his next destination.[1] Back in Johannesburg, the opposition journalist Benjamin Pogrund was sickened as he watched the spectacle on television. Thousands of South African Jews shared Pogrund's disgust; they knew all too well that Vorster had another, darker past.

In addition to being the architect of South Africa's brutal crackdown on the black democratic opposition and the hand behind many a tortured activist and imprisoned leader, Vorster and his intelligence chief, Hendrik van den Bergh, had served as generals in the Ossewa Brandwag, a militant Afrikaner nationalist organization that had openly supported the Nazis during World War II.*

The group's leader, Hans van Rensburg, was an enthusiastic admirer of Adolf Hitler. In conversations with Nazi leaders in 1940, van Rensburg formally offered to provide the Third Reich with hundreds of

---

* Afrikaners are white, Afrikaans-speaking South Africans descended from seventeenth-century Dutch, German, and Huguenot settlers. They account for approximately 60 percent of South Africa's white population.

thousands of men in order to stage a coup and bring an Axis-friendly government to power at the strategically vital southern tip of Africa. Lacking adequate arms supplies, van Rensburg's men eventually abandoned their plans for regime change and settled for industrial sabotage, bombings, and bank robberies. South Africa's British-aligned government considered the organization so dangerous that it imprisoned many of its members.

But Vorster was unapologetic and proudly compared his nation to Nazi Germany: "We stand for Christian Nationalism which is an ally of National Socialism . . . you can call such an anti-democratic system a dictatorship if you like," he declared in 1942. "In Italy it is called Fascism, in Germany National Socialism and in South Africa Christian Nationalism."[2] As a result of their pro-Nazi activities, Vorster and van den Bergh were declared enemies of the state and detained in a government camp.

Three decades later, as Vorster toured Yad Vashem, the Israeli government was still scouring the globe for former Nazis—extraditing or even kidnapping them in order to try them in Israeli courts. Yet Vorster, a man who was once a self-proclaimed Nazi supporter and who remained wedded to a policy of racial superiority, found himself in Jerusalem receiving full red-carpet treatment at the invitation of Israeli prime minister Yitzhak Rabin.

· · ·

PRIOR TO 1967, Israel was a celebrated cause of the left. The nascent Jewish state, since its creation amid the ashes of Auschwitz, was widely recognized as a triumph for justice and human rights. Leftists across the world, with the notable exception of those in Muslim nations, identified with the socialist pioneering spirit of the new nation. Africans welcomed Israeli development aid and voted in Israel's favor at the United Nations. Europeans for the most part supported the Jewish state, often out of socialist idealism or sheer guilt. Even Britain, which fought Jewish guerrilla organizations until the eve of Israel's independence in 1948, recognized the state of Israel in January 1949. Although the South African Jewish community became the largest per capita financial contributor to Israel after 1948, relations between the two countries' governments were cordial but chilly for much of the 1950s.

In the 1960s, Israeli leaders' ideological hostility toward apartheid kept the two nations apart. During these years, Israel took a strong and unequivocal stance against South Africa. In 1963, Foreign Minister Golda Meir told the United Nations General Assembly that Israelis "naturally oppose policies of apartheid, colonialism and racial or religious discrimination wherever they exist" due to Jews' historical experience as victims of oppression.[3] Israel even offered asylum to South Africa's most wanted man.

In addition to condemning apartheid, Meir forged close ties with the newly independent states of Africa, offering them everything from agricultural assistance to military training. Many African leaders accepted invitations to Israel and some, impressed with the Israeli army, decided to hire Israeli bodyguards. African states returned the favor by voting with Israel at the U.N. in an era when the Jewish state had few diplomatic allies. At the time, black American leaders such as Martin Luther King Jr. were also outspoken in their support of Israel, likening criticism of Zionism to anti-Semitism.[4]

Things began to change with Israel's stunning victory over its Arab neighbors in the Six-Day War of 1967, which tripled the size of the Jewish state in less than a week. The post-1967 military occupation of Egyptian, Jordanian, and Syrian territory and the settlement project that soon followed planted hundreds of thousands of Jews on hilltops and in urban centers throughout the newly conquered West Bank and Gaza Strip, saddling Israel with the stigma of occupation and forever tarring it with the colonialist brush.

Israelis did not take kindly to the colonial label. After all, Zionism had in many ways been an anti-imperial movement. The World Zionist Organization may have mimicked European colonial settlement tactics in the early 1900s, but by the 1940s Zionism's more extreme proponents were fighting to oust the British Mandate government in Palestine.[5] Consequently, many Israelis saw their independence as a postcolonial triumph akin to the successful liberation struggles of newly independent African and Asian countries and they bristled at any attempt to equate Zionism with European colonialism.

Conquest and expansion had not been part of the IDF's (the Israel Defense Forces) strategic planning for a war that it perceived as a defensive struggle for survival. Even Israel's leaders were shocked by the extent of their territorial gains in the Six-Day War. Indeed, before the shooting stopped, the first internal military memos proposed withdrawing almost completely from the newly acquired territories in exchange for peace with the Arab states.[6] Yet, as Arab negotiating positions hardened and religious Zionists and socialist idealists alike sought to redeem and settle the land, the occupation of the West Bank, Gaza, and the Sinai Peninsula slowly transformed Israel into an unwitting outpost of colonialism.

Aided by a healthy dose of Arab and Soviet propaganda, Israel's image as a state of Holocaust survivors in need of protection gradually deteriorated into that of an imperialist stooge of the West. As criticism of Israel mounted and Arab states dangled dollars and oil in the faces of poor African nations in the late 1960s and early 1970s, Third World countries increasingly switched allegiance. After the 1973 Yom Kippur War, all but a few African countries severed diplomatic ties with the Jewish state, and the Israeli government abandoned the last vestiges of moral foreign policy in favor of hard-nosed realpolitik.

It wasn't long before Israel initiated defense cooperation with some of the world's most notoriously brutal regimes, including Argentina's military dictatorship, Pinochet's Chile, and apartheid South Africa.

At its core, the Israeli–South African relationship was a marriage of interests and ideologies. Israel profited handsomely from arms exports and South Africa gained access to cutting-edge weaponry at a time when the rest of the world was turning against the apartheid state. For the next twenty years, a Janus-faced Israel denied its ties with South Africa, claiming that it opposed apartheid on moral and religious grounds even as it secretly strengthened the arsenal of a white supremacist government.

Israel and South Africa joined forces at a precarious and auspicious time. The alliance began in earnest after the October 1973 Yom Kippur War, and shared military and economic interests drove the relationship for the next three years. Though both countries were receiving varying degrees of support from the United States, neither enjoyed a defense pact with Washington and both were wary of relying too heavily on the Americans for their survival—especially in the early 1970s, when unconditional U.S. support for Israel was by no means assured. This alliance exposed Israel to great risks in the realm of public relations, especially when the Jewish state's legitimacy was already under attack at the U.N.

from pro-Palestinian groups and aligning itself with the hated apartheid regime threatened to tarnish its reputation further.

Rabin's Labor Party government, which ruled the country from 1974 to 1977, did not share the ethnic nationalist ideology of South Africa's rulers, but Israel's war-battered industries desperately needed export markets and the possibility of lucrative trade with South Africa was hard for Defense Minister Shimon Peres to resist. As Rabin, Peres, and a new generation of leaders inherited the party from David Ben-Gurion and Golda Meir, the conviction that compromising certain values was necessary for survival gained sway and socialist idealism gave way to realpolitik. During the Rabin years, South African arms purchases breathed life into the Israeli economy and Israeli weapons helped to reinforce the beleaguered and isolated apartheid regime in Pretoria.

The impact of their tryst was felt across the globe. As the Cold War spread south in the 1970s, Africa became an ideological battleground, pitting Angolan government troops and their Cuban allies against South Africa's formidable military machine, which owed its prowess in no small measure to Israel. The U.S. government feared that South Africa's white minority regime, driven by a siege mentality and militant anticommunism, might resort to the nuclear option when faced with Soviet proxies on its borders. The U.S. government had by 1970 accepted that Israel was a member of the nuclear club, but Washington worked tirelessly in the late 1970s to prevent South Africa from joining it. As hard as officials in Jimmy Carter's administration tried, their nonproliferation policy failed to prevent South Africa from acquiring the bomb soon after Carter left office, and subsequent U.S. administrations couldn't stop Israel from helping the apartheid state develop more advanced components of its nuclear arsenal.

These two isolated states formed an alliance that allowed South Africa to develop advanced nuclear missile technology and provided Israel with the raw material and testing space it needed to expand its existing arsenal of missiles and nuclear weapons. All of this occurred in the face of intense international criticism, surveillance by U.S. and Soviet intelligence agencies, and constant condemnation by the United Nations General Assembly.

This mutually beneficial relationship was forged outside the jurisdiction of international conventions such as the Nuclear Non-Proliferation

Treaty (NPT) and the Missile Technology Control Regime (MTCR), the cornerstones of Western efforts to prevent the spread of weapons of mass destruction. The two countries developed and improved their respective weapons systems under such secrecy that not even American intelligence agencies knew the full extent of their cooperation.[7]

The Israeli–South African relationship was not only about profit and battlefield bravado, however. After Menachem Begin's Likud Party came to power in 1977, these economic interests converged with ideological affinities to make the alliance even stronger. Many members of the Likud Party shared with South Africa's leaders an ideology of minority survivalism that presented the two countries as threatened outposts of European civilization defending their existence against barbarians at the gates.

Indeed, much of Israel's top brass and Likud Party leadership felt an affinity with South Africa's white government, and unlike Peres and Rabin they did not feel a need to publicly denounce apartheid while secretly supporting Pretoria. Powerful military figures, such as Ariel Sharon and Rafael (Raful) Eitan, drew inspiration from the political tradition of Revisionist Zionism—a school of thought that favored the use of military force to defend Jewish sovereignty and encouraged settlement of the biblical lands of Greater Israel, including the West Bank and the Gaza Strip. Sharon, Eitan, and many of their contemporaries were convinced that both nations faced a fundamentally similar predicament as embattled minorities under siege, fighting for their survival against what they saw as a common terrorist enemy epitomized by Nelson Mandela's African National Congress (ANC) and Yasser Arafat's Palestine Liberation Organization (PLO). The ANC may have never employed indiscriminate violence to the extent that the PLO did, but in the eyes of the generals in Tel Aviv and Pretoria, Mandela and Arafat were one and the same: terrorist leaders who wished to push them into the sea. And for the top brass in both countries, the only possible solution was tight control and overwhelming force.

Foreign Ministry officials in Israel did not always approve of close ties with South Africa, but it was the defense establishments—not the diplomatic corps—that managed the alliance. The military's dominance was so complete that the Israeli embassy in Pretoria was divided by a wall through which no member of the diplomatic corps was allowed to pass. Only when opponents of apartheid within the Israeli government sought to bring down that wall in the late 1980s did the alliance begin to crumble.

. . .

THE RESEARCH FOR THIS BOOK took place in a world where information and disinformation are equally important. Even decades after the fact, Israel remains extremely sensitive about keeping secret the details of its collaboration with a regime that is now universally condemned as immoral. Journalists and scholars who wrote on the Israeli–South African relationship during the 1980s suffered from a lack of access to key participants and official documents. As a result, the story they told, though partially accurate, was incomplete.[8] For the past six years, I have struggled to fill in the gaps by prying open bureaucratic doors, accessing highly restricted archives, and interviewing more than one hundred key players in both countries.

In Israel, dozens of people initially refused to speak with me. I traced former ambassadors to desert kibbutzim and elderly South African Jewish émigrés to designer apartments in the posh northern suburbs of Tel Aviv. From the offices of defense contractors to assisted living communities, I was treated to battlefield tales and old photo albums offering glimpses of a relationship that until now few government officials have dared to talk about.

In South Africa, retired military intelligence officials asked for my U.S. passport number and ran background checks before inviting me to their homes for interviews. Tracking down the key protagonists led me to sprawling rural farms and gated retirement communities. I met former defense ministers and generals for coffee in strip malls and over shots of brandy in Pretoria's bars. A Soviet spy who had sent some of South Africa's and Israel's most sensitive military secrets to Moscow invited me to his home on the windswept coast of the Cape Peninsula, where he now lives comfortably among the retired naval officers he once betrayed. Former employees of the arms industry giant Armscor and the nuclear scientists involved in building South Africa's atomic weapons were the most reluctant of all, but several eventually opened up. My family's roots in South Africa helped ease the suspicions of several octogenarian generals, who instantly became candid in the presence of someone they regarded as a fellow white South African in the hope that I would share their nostalgia for the old days.[9] Some saw the interviews as an opportunity to secure their place in history and were self-aggrandizing to the extreme; others guarded their secrets closely. I have therefore not relied exclusively on oral history.[10]

Accessing government and military archives was even more difficult. The South African authorities repeatedly rebuffed and then delayed my requests. But after sixteen months of waiting for documents, I managed to get my hands on over seven thousand pages of records from the South African Defense Ministry, the Foreign Ministry, and the defense contractor Armscor, including the Israeli side of the correspondence—but not before Israel's government did its utmost to prevent me from getting them.

In April 2006, the Israeli Defense Ministry intervened to block South Africa's release of a 1975 agreement outlining the planned military cooperation between the two countries, which is signed by Defense Ministers Shimon Peres and P. W. Botha. The Directorate of Security of the Defense Establishment (known by its Hebrew acronym Malmab) insisted that declassification of the 1975 document or any others would endanger Israel's national security interests. Fortunately, the South African Defense Ministry disregarded these protests. This is due in no small measure to the fact that the people whose records I sought are no longer in power in Pretoria. While the ANC government has not fully thrown open the doors to the apartheid government's archives, it is far less concerned with keeping old secrets than with protecting its own accumulated dirty laundry after sixteen years in power.

Israel, of course, is a different story. There, intense secrecy surrounding this relationship remains in force. The actions of Israeli administrations from the 1970s and 1980s are still regarded as state secrets, and many of the architects of the Israeli–South African alliance—including Israel's president as of this writing, Shimon Peres—remain in powerful positions. Even so, South African records pieced together with the oral testimony of retired high-level officials in both countries provide a startlingly clear, if incomplete, picture of the relationship.

This book does not equate Zionism with South African racism, as a 1975 United Nations resolution infamously did. Rather, I contend that material interests gave birth to an alliance that greatly benefited the Israeli economy and enhanced the security of South Africa's white minority regime. Yet ideology was a factor, too: while the relationship was driven by concrete economic interests, it would have begun far earlier and ended much sooner had it not been for the influence of ideology.[11]

As the Israeli-Palestinian conflict festers and the prospects for peace appear gloomier each day, it has become increasingly popular to compare the situation in Israel to the dying days of the apartheid regime in South Africa. This is not a new argument, but it is gaining traction in some circles as hopes fade for a two-state solution. During the 1980s, both the Israeli and South African governments were the targets of vicious criticism and international condemnation. In the end, apartheid South Africa collapsed while Israel survived, albeit as a fortress state mired in war. This was not surprising. As two leading South African academics wrote in 1979: "Israel solicits empathy because she stands for the minority right to live after experiencing the most systematic genocide in history. Israel can offer the Western world the continuous exorcism from fascism."[12] Apartheid South Africa, by contrast, had no such moral standing. The government's overt racism offended Western political sensibilities far more than Israel's occupation of Palestinian land, and American and European policymakers did not believe white South Africans deserved protection in the same way Jews did after the Holocaust.

Yet today, left-wing activists are attempting to paint Israel as a latter-day South Africa, erode its claim to a unique moral position, and question its legitimacy. By calling for boycotts and divestment from Israel, these activists are following the script that proved so effective for the anti-apartheid movement during the 1980s. And to their own detriment, Israel's leaders are playing their parts by building Israeli-only access roads, erecting countless military checkpoints, and expanding settlements in the West Bank.

Of course, Israel's leaders have a responsibility to protect their citizens, but the Israel they have created is a far cry from the "light unto the nations" that was once revered by the African liberation heroes and American civil rights leaders.

Countless authors have chronicled, with varying degrees of fairness, how the Jewish state betrayed its founding ideals, abandoned socialist Zionist principles, and saw its democratic soul corrupted by occupation after 1967. But Israel's domestic policies are only part of the story; its foreign policy, especially its ties with some of the world's most reviled regimes, also contributed to its moral decay and the rise of anti-Israel sentiment abroad. Israel's intimate alliance with apartheid South Africa was the most extensive, the most lucrative, and the most toxic of these pacts. Just as expanding settlements in the West Bank and Gaza eroded Israel's democratic values at home, arms sales to South Africa in the early 1970s marked the beginning of an era in which expediency trumped morality in Israeli foreign policy and sympathy for the conquered gave way to cooperation with the conqueror.

1

THE REICH THAT WASN'T

South Africa's Jews in the Shadow of Nazism

WHEN ARTHUR GOLDREICH, an eighteen-year-old Jew growing up in rural South Africa, left home in 1948 to fight for Israel's independence, he did so with pride and confidence. Goldreich was one of a few hundred Jews in a rural town filled with Afrikaners who hated the British and hoped for a German victory in World War II. His uncles had battled Hitler's armies in North Africa and Goldreich himself had fought off pro-Nazi classmates as he walked home from school. As a teenager, Goldreich—who would two decades later become the apartheid regime's most wanted man—followed the war religiously through the newspapers. A budding artist, he drew portraits of Allied heroes, including Winston Churchill, Joseph Stalin, and Chiang Kai-shek. But none of this prepared him for the images from Auschwitz and Buchenwald he saw after the war. Those pictures marked a turning point in his life. "I decided that studying architecture in South Africa was a luxury that I politically or morally . . . couldn't afford," he says. The struggle for a Jewish state appealed to Goldreich as a just anticolonial war on behalf of a nearly exterminated people. And so, along with four thousand other South African Jews, he signed up to fight.[1]

As Arab armies invaded the newly independent state of Israel in the spring of 1948 and Goldreich journeyed north to join the fight, South Africa's Jewish community remained on edge. They were a minority within a minority—a community of just over 100,000 constituting less than one percent of South Africa's population and a mere 4 percent of the country's ruling white minority.[2] For them, May 1948 was a month of great jubilation and terrible anxiety. Within a matter of weeks, both nations were transformed: the state of Israel declared its independence and an Afrikaner nationalist government, led by Daniel François Malan, came to power in South Africa.

Malan was trained as a minister in the Dutch Reformed Church and left South Africa in 1900 to pursue his doctoral studies in divinity. While his Afrikaner nationalist colleagues fought for independence from the British Empire in the Anglo-Boer War, Malan was studying at the University of Utrecht in the Netherlands. When he returned to South Africa in 1905, Malan was ordained as a minister and in 1915 he became the founding editor of the National Party's (NP) mouthpiece, *Die Burger*. Malan and his party became famous for making white supremacy and strict racial separation—a policy known as apartheid—the law of the land after 1948.

The Afrikaner nationalist ideology that would define South African politics for nearly five decades went beyond white supremacy, strictly enforced segregation, and vicious racism toward blacks; it also drew on dour Dutch Calvinist theology and a deep and abiding hatred of imperial Britain. Before the 1930s, however, it was not particularly anti-Semitic; in fact, Afrikaner nationalists drew heavily on Jewish history and symbolism. They imported the framework of the Old Testament wholesale to twentieth-century South Africa, branding the country a "new Israel" and elevating their defining national moment—the Great Trek of the 1830s, during which pioneering Afrikaners moved north into the interior of the country to seek independence from the British colonial government—to the status of a biblical exodus. With a heavy dose of political mythology, the Afrikaners portrayed themselves as chosen people destined to dominate the native "Canaanites," giving birth to a uniquely South African brand of Christian Nationalism.[3]

Beginning in 1918, the Broederbond, a secret society comprising much of the Afrikaner elite, spread the ideology of Christian Nationalism to schools, universities, and through the press,[4] purveying an explicitly ethnic definition of white South African identity, in which the Afrikaans language and culture were the central national traits. The Broederbond became an incubator of ideas and a launching pad for future NP leaders—both a policy think tank and a "ubiquitous political mafia."[5] In the coming years, gaining prominence as a member of the Afrikaner intelligentsia or joining the NP political elite would become virtually impossible without membership in the Broederbond.

As more Afrikaners moved to large cities such as Johannesburg, a nationalism that had always been defined primarily by grievances against Britain began to give way to a new focus on segregation and control of the black population. In 1924, more than two decades before apartheid became official state policy, James Barry Hertzog, a heroic Afrikaner general from the Boer War, defeated his fellow general Jan Smuts at the polls and became prime minister. Hertzog promised to restore Afrikaners' national pride and to make them the equals of Englishmen. Ten years later, as a worldwide depression took its toll on the South African economy and Hertzog's popularity, the prime minister extended an olive branch to his old rival Smuts and the two leaders formed a Fusion government under the banner of the United Party in 1934. A zealous younger generation of Afrikaner nationalists had no time for the gentle politics of compromise, however, and they abandoned Hertzog's moderation to form the Purified National Party under the leadership of Malan.[6] From the opposition benches in Parliament, the Purified Nationalists preached the gospel of Afrikaner self-reliance and espoused a platform that remained deeply hostile to imperial Britain.

Four years later, in 1938, the Broederbond's public front organized a centenary celebration of the Great Trek, unleashing an outpouring of nationalist sentiment and nostalgic kitsch. A procession of wagons departed Cape Town and slowly inched its way to Pretoria. For five months, crowds of folk-dancing farmers greeted the wagons as they rolled through rural towns. Men grew beards, streets were renamed for Afrikaner heroes, and young couples married in nineteenth-century Trekker garb.[7] The nationalist revival unleashed by the centenary exceeded the ideologues' wildest expectations. The Second Trek culminated in three days of ceremonies outside Pretoria, where 200,000 Afrikaners gathered as bonfires blazed on the hilltops surrounding the city. There, Reverend Malan told the crowd, "There is still a white race. There is a new volk. . . . You and your children will make history."[8] Ten years later, his electoral triumph would make apartheid the law of the land and satisfy the Afrikaners' long yearning for control of the state.

As fascism flourished in Europe during the 1930s, Malan's younger nationalist colleagues went north to study abroad. The future Ossewa Brandwag leader Hans van Rensburg was an open admirer of Hitler during his student days in Germany. As head of the German-Afrikaans Cultural Union, he was received in Berlin by Hermann Göring, Joseph

Goebbels, and Hitler himself.[9] Piet Meyer, another member of the Broederbond intellectual elite, led a 1934 Afrikaner National Student Union trip to Europe during which he went skiing with Rudolf Hess in the Alps and saw Hitler "close up."[10]

In addition to meeting top Nazi leaders, the Afrikaner students borrowed liberally from the great continental thinkers of the nineteenth century while absorbing the newer fascist ideas emanating from German universities. Romantic nationalists, who celebrated the revival of culture and literature in their Teutonic mother tongue, were particularly appealing to young Afrikaners seeking their own cultural and linguistic renaissance. From Johann Gottfried Herder, they took the idea of the nation as an organic *volk* with common traits and a specific "national genius" that would be hindered if diluted by outside influences.[11] From Johann Gottlieb Fichte, they borrowed the idea of an exclusive historical mission assigned to the German *volk*.[12] Fichte's belief that nations could only achieve their true potential when allowed to develop in isolation struck a powerful chord among Afrikaners seeking to rationalize racial segregation. The young students carried these concepts back to South Africa in the 1930s, where they proved particularly attractive to the men of the Broederbond, as did anti-Semitism.

Although racism toward blacks was an integral part of Afrikaner nationalist thought, explicit hostility toward Jews had never been a part of the Christian Nationalist worldview. Exposure to fascist ideas in Europe during the 1930s changed that. Nazism provided the Broederbond with precisely the sort of scapegoat it needed to rally poor, unemployed Afrikaners, who resented the ballooning Jewish population, which had grown from 47,000 in 1911 to over 90,000 by the late 1930s.[13] At the time, the Broederbond's influence as an elite intellectual movement was still limited; their new ideology was shared by the educated classes, but it had not yet succeeded in mobilizing the people. To gain power, the Afrikaner intelligentsia needed mass support. And in order to create a cohesive sense of national identity that included poor whites, it was essential for the educated elites to blur class differences among Afrikaners.[14] Anti-Semitism was the perfect glue.

Socially and intellectually steeped in Nazism, the students returning from Europe graduated into powerful positions in the Broederbond, their racist ideas endowed with a veneer of legitimacy by the rise of totalitarianism in Europe.[15] The Broederbond began to argue that Jews were the group that "stands in the way of the Afrikaner's economic prosperity," while denouncing "Jewish money power" and "British-Jewish capitalism."[16] The fictional villain Hoggenheimer—a fat, hook-nosed capitalist—soon became a fixture of political cartoons in South African newspapers. As Jews fled Nazi Germany, the Broederbond's leaders actively protested the influx of refugees and demanded quotas in the business world in order to protect Afrikaner jobs that were supposedly being usurped by Jews.[17] All of this scapegoating appealed to the Afrikaner poor and working classes, who began to blame Jewish immigrants for unemployment and other economic woes.

In fact, Jewish immigration had already slowed in the wake of a 1930 law designed to stop Eastern European Jews from flocking to South Africa, but anti-Semitic sentiment among Afrikaners continued to grow nonetheless.[18] In October 1936, when a ship carrying German Jewish refugees arrived in Cape Town's harbor, the newspaper editor and future prime minister Hendrik Verwoerd joined the Nazi-aligned Greyshirt movement in protest at the docks. And in 1939, South Africa's future foreign minister Eric Louw introduced yet another immigration bill in Parliament, declaring Jews "unassimilable." For his part, Malan blamed the country's ills on "the steely, calculating, greedy visage of Hoggenheimer."[19] He accused Jews of having "so robbed the population of its heritage that the Afrikander [sic] resides in the land of his fathers, but no longer possesses it," while pursuing a policy of neutrality toward Nazi Germany.[20]

Hitler's invasion of Poland on September 1, 1939, was the death knell for Hertzog and Smuts's Fusion government. Suddenly their United Party found itself riven by conflict between supporters of Smuts, who wished to join the Allied war effort, and followers of Hertzog, who, mindful of their Afrikaner constituents, refused to adopt an openly pro-British stance. Smuts prevailed in a narrow parliamentary vote, South Africa declared war on Germany, and Hertzog resigned in protest, clearing the way for Smuts to become prime minister.

When Hertzog crossed the aisle to join the Purified Nationalists, Malan offered the elder statesman leadership of the opposition. But Hertzog's moderation was unacceptable to Malan's more radical followers and the doubly defeated former prime minister eventually retired to his farm in the Orange Free State—a rural province in the country's Afrikaner heartland. Hertzog passed away on November 21, 1942, and with him the last hope for moderate Afrikaner politics was extinguished.[21]

As South African forces fought the Nazis in North Africa and Europe during the early 1940s, extremist factions to the right of Malan's Purified National Party were growing more popular. Louis Weichardt, an unrepentant anti-Semite, led the Christian National Socialist group known as the Greyshirts; Oswald Pirow, Hertzog's old defense minister, endorsed Nazi principles and launched a New Order movement; and Hitler admirer Hans van Rensburg led the most popular of these splinter movements: the Ossewa Brandwag.[22] Like many other extremist nationalist movements that have influenced right-wing political parties, the OB subtly pulled Malan's platform to the right.[23] Van Rensburg explicitly denounced Britain and its liberal tradition, declaring that "if democracy is not yet dead, it is in any case well on the way."[24] German diplomatic records reveal that in 1940 van Rensburg formally offered to provide the Third Reich with 170,000 OB members to help overthrow Smuts's government if Germany provided the arms. The OB leader gave the Nazis multiple options, suggesting that they fly weapons to South-West Africa or Southern Rhodesia and that his members then sabotage the South African railroad network and blow up the offices of English-language newspapers. The coup never materialized due to a lack of adequate supplies, so the OB turned to bombings of government buildings instead as well as the occasional bank robbery to fund its activities.[25]

A year later, the Germans hatched their own plans for a putsch in South Africa. A former South African Olympic boxer and Nazi sympathizer, Robey Leibbrandt, was transported on a German yacht to a remote area off the Atlantic coast and dispatched to assassinate Prime Minister Smuts and stage a coup. Leibbrandt had been working as a German agent and harbored such extreme views that even the OB's politics were too moderate for his liking. In the end, his extremism proved to be his downfall. OB leader van Rensburg feared that if Nazi victories continued in Europe and the coup succeeded, he might be passed over as a future leader of the South African Reich. Afraid of being eclipsed by Leibbrandt, van Rensburg leaked details of the plot to government officials, who lured the boxer spy into a police trap.[26] Still, even after Leibbrandt's capture, Afrikaner nationalists continued to enthusiastically support the Nazi war effort.

· · ·

AS HITLER'S FORCES suffered setbacks in North Africa, France, and on the Eastern Front and revelations of the Holocaust began to emerge, Malan decided to steer a more moderate course and focus on domestic politics. He distanced himself from the OB's Nazism and sought to bring its supporters under the exclusive control of his party.[27] In May 1948, Malan defeated Smuts by running a superior campaign and promising to shield white areas from *oorstroming* (inundation) by blacks, purge the government of communists, and improve the economic lot of the downtrodden Afrikaner. By depicting Smuts as a liberal darling of the international community who would end segregation and sell out white South Africans' interests, Malan prevailed and became prime minister.[28] He owed his victory in no small part to a young party operative named P. W. Botha, who corralled the right-wing splinter groups, including the OB, and unified them behind Malan.

As the rest of the world moved haltingly toward self-determination and decolonization, South Africa veered off in precisely the opposite direction, looking inward and shunning the international community. With his triumph over Smuts, Malan's dream of a white man's country was now within reach.

Not surprisingly, South Africa's Jews were terrified. Given the NP's recent history of anti-Semitism, the country's Jews—especially refugees from Nazi Germany—worried that they might once again find themselves targeted by an anti-Semitic government. "I can remember the fear that swept through the community," recalls the liberal journalist Benjamin Pogrund, who was a teenager at the time. "These were the guys who'd been detained during the war. Nazi lovers! Eric Louw was known as South Africa's Goebbels."[29] As a child refugee arriving in Cape Town from Nazi Germany in 1934, Harry Schwarz had looked out from the deck of a ship as anti-Semitic crowds protested against Jewish immigration. "If you read some of the stuff that somebody like Eric Louw said in Parliament," says Schwarz, who later became South Africa's ambassador to the United States, "you can't differentiate between that and what the Nazis said in Germany."[30] Indeed, in early 1945, four months before the fall of Berlin, Louw was still reassuring readers of his newspaper column that Hitler's Reich would prevail.

In the early 1950s, however, the tone in Pretoria began to change, eas-

ing the fears of the Jewish community. Having won an upset victory by a
small margin, and faced with the challenge of maintaining a minority
regime ruling over more than nine million disenfranchised nonwhite
South Africans, Malan needed every white vote he could get. He was
charting a new course, firmly rejecting the anti-Semitism of Louw and
the Ossewa Brandwag and broadening his vision of the NP to include all
whites.[31] The last vestiges of institutionalized anti-Semitism soon fell
away as the Transvaal Province branch of the NP, which included Johannesburg and Pretoria, finally allowed Jews to join the party in 1951.[32]
Under these circumstances, excluding Jews was simply bad politics.

When Parliament passed apartheid legislation formalizing the separation of races, Jews were left unaffected by the draconian new laws, which
included the Group Areas Act, the Bantu Education Act, and other
measures that stripped black, Asian, and Colored (mixed race) South
Africans of fundamental rights. Though they had feared persecution by
the state, South Africa's Jews were instead granted the privileges of
whiteness under apartheid. As South African professor Steven Friedman
notes, for the first time in history, "Jews were defined into the ruling
caste."[33] For immigrants from Nazi Germany and Czarist Russia, who
had suffered oppression, disenfranchisement, expulsion, and attempted
annihilation, gaining a berth on the ruling-class ship was a dramatic and
unexpected reversal of fortune.

Fears among Jewish South Africans subsided further in 1953 when
Prime Minister Malan went to Israel. For Malan, an ordained minister,
visiting the Holy Land had been a lifelong dream. Upon his return, he
voiced his admiration of the Jews' ability to maintain their national identity despite centuries of adversity and described the restoration of the
Jewish homeland in Palestine as a momentous historical event.[34] Warmer
relations between Afrikaners and Jews soon followed; as Pogrund recalls,
"Everyone realized they needed each other and they became friends."[35]

But even as South African Jews breathed a collective sigh of relief,
Israel's Zionist Labor government, led by David Ben-Gurion, began to
voice its opposition to apartheid policies. Laws mandating residential
segregation, restricting the movement of black citizens, and creating
separate and unequal educational institutions reminded Israeli leaders of
the Nuremberg Laws, which had institutionalized discrimination against
German Jews in the 1930s. Despite being a young state with few friends,
Israel vowed to oppose them.

Having defeated multiple Arab armies on the battlefield in 1948 and driven hundreds of thousands of Palestinian refugees into exile in neighboring states, Israel was facing a new challenge. The defeated Arab governments immediately began to organize against the Jewish state, seeking to delegitimize it in the diplomatic arena by recruiting newly independent countries to their cause, voting against Israel at every turn, and seeking to expel or exclude it from U.N. bodies.[36] Israel needed allies, and rather than turning to the racists in Pretoria, Ben-Gurion and Meir looked to the emerging nations of the Third World.

2

A LIGHT UNTO THE NATIONS

Israel's Honeymoon in Africa

Once I have witnessed the redemption of the Jews, my people, I wish also to assist in the redemption of the Africans.

—Theodor Herzl, *Altneuland*, 1902[1]

IN 1955, ISRAEL WAS INVITED to participate in a conference of independent Asian and African states in Bandung, Indonesia. But no sooner had the invitation been issued than Indian premier Jawaharlal Nehru withdrew it, much to Ben-Gurion's dismay. Nehru did so under pressure from Egypt, other Arab states, and Pakistan, all of whom threatened not to attend the conference if Israel did.

Throughout the mid-1950s Israel's relations with its Arab neighbors steadily deteriorated.[2] In July 1954, Britain signed an agreement with Egypt, agreeing to withdraw its forces from the Suez Canal Zone. In a botched effort to derail the accord, Israeli military intelligence set up a spy ring, planted explosives, and sabotaged public venues in Egypt. But one of the agents was caught, leading to twelve arrests, eight guilty verdicts, and two death sentences. In September, Israel attempted to sail an Israeli vessel, the *Bat Galim*, into the Suez Canal; the ship was seized and its crew imprisoned. On the northern front, five Israeli soldiers were captured several miles inside Syria's borders, and in January 1955, two Israelis driving tractors were murdered by Jordanians who had sneaked across the border. Ben-Gurion returned to the Defense Ministry in February 1955 and within a week launched a devastating reprisal: IDF paratroopers commanded by the young Ariel Sharon attacked Egyptian soldiers outside Gaza City, killing at least thirty-seven and escalating tensions with Egypt.[3]

A year after Bandung, Israel was excluded from the second Interna-
tionalist Socialist Conference in India, despite the strong socialist lean-
ings of Ben-Gurion's government.[4] Both moves came as a shock to
Israel's leaders and laid bare the Jewish state's diplomatic weakness in the
Third World. This lack of allies in Africa and Asia left Israel exposed and
vulnerable to the growing clout of the well-organized and vehemently
anti-Zionist bloc of Arab and Muslim countries at the United Nations.

With independence on the horizon for many African nations, the continent was an obvious target for an Israeli diplomatic offensive; building a
network of pro-Israeli leaders throughout Africa became a pet project of
the Mossad—Israel's intelligence agency. In the mid-1950s, Israel's relations with the United States were not particularly strong and Western
powers were at the time trying to convince Egypt to join a defense pact, a
hope that was soon extinguished by Egyptian president Gamal Abdel
Nasser's massive military buildup of Soviet weaponry and Moscow's
growing influence in the Middle East.[5] While allies in Africa could not
replace the patronage of a major Western power, Israel desperately
needed friends and the newly independent states of Africa and Asia, by
sheer force of numbers, were becoming increasingly powerful at the U.N.

Courting allies in Africa would not be easy, especially considering that
Israel's chief ally and arms supplier was a hated colonial power: France.[6]
Israel's French connection went back to the immediate postwar years,
when members of the Jewish underground had flocked to Paris to plan
anti-British attacks and liberate Palestine. These Zionist leaders met
with everyone from literary sympathizers, such as the cognac-guzzling
Arthur Koestler, to the Zionist philanthropists who congregated at the
Rothschilds' Parisian residence, and to the French bishops who wielded
clout at the Vatican. The postwar French government tolerated their
presence, realizing that the end of British control in Palestine would
strengthen its own hand in the Middle East.[7] Many of these government
officials were racked with guilt over the fate of French Jewry under the
Vichy regime; some gentiles with ties to the French Resistance possessed
an even deeper bond with the Jewish survivors of the Holocaust. One of
these Frenchmen was Abel Thomas, a young bureaucrat who would have
an enduring impact on Israel's defense establishment.

Thomas had served as a soldier in Charles de Gaulle's Free French army and survived the war. His younger brother, a French Resistance fighter, was murdered in the Buchenwald concentration camp in 1945 at the hands of Gestapo torturers. Thomas's natural affinity with the Jewish victims of the Holocaust made him a staunch supporter of Israel. A rising star in the Radical-Socialist Party, he became the chief of staff to Interior Minister Maurice Bourgès-Maunoury in 1955, a position that allowed him to play a major role in building France's postwar defense industry.[8] Thomas became Israel's key ally in the upper echelons of the French government and was instrumental in crafting the intimate French-Israeli relationship that developed in the late 1950s. Although he made an awkward first impression, striking the Israelis as unkempt and absentminded, Thomas soon became an indispensable link. His chief Israeli contact in Paris was a young technocrat named Shimon Peres.

Born Szymon Perski in 1923 in a Polish shtetl three miles by horse carriage from the nearest railroad station,[9] Peres immigrated to Palestine as an eleven-year-old. He left Tel Aviv after three years to attend school in the youth village of Ben-Shemen, where he studied under the Zionist intellectual and leader Berl Katznelson. Bookish to an extreme, Peres confesses to attempting to seduce his future wife by reading her passages of *Das Kapital* in the moonlight as a teenager.[10] Under the tutelage of Katznelson and later as an aide to Ben-Gurion, he tempered his adolescent Marxism and became a pillar of the Mapai Party establishment, the precursor to the modern Labor Party.[11] In 1953, before he turned thirty, Peres became director-general of the Defense Ministry and was sent to Paris to coordinate relations with the French military establishment.

Peres believed that securing a reliable arms supply should be the primary objective of Israeli diplomacy. He declared openly that "the conduct of foreign policy cannot be left to the foreign office alone," and proposed that the Defense Ministry take the lead role in managing relations with Israel's hostile neighbors and obtaining arms from its friends.[12] In this spirit, Peres created a parallel Foreign Ministry behind the back of Foreign Minister Golda Meir. Taking advantage of his perch at the Defense Ministry and the close personal relationship that gave him a direct line to Ben-Gurion, Peres simply circumvented traditional diplomatic channels and conducted arms deals with France on his own.

Peres was given access to high-level officials almost immediately thanks to introductions provided by Georges Elgozy, a glamorous Algerian-Jewish intellectual who socialized with literary luminaries such as André Malraux and Albert Camus and served as an adviser to the French prime minister.[13] But high-level hobnobbing did not translate into the arms supplies Peres sought right away. It was not until Peres met Thomas that genuine deals began to materialize.

The two men met for the first time in 1955 at a restaurant in Paris's tony 16th arrondissement, where Thomas promptly launched into a lengthy monologue about the need for France to aid Israel that ended with him proposing a back channel relationship between the two defense ministries, precisely the sort of arrangement Peres had hoped for. Soon afterward, Peres was introduced to Maurice Bourgès-Maunoury and other leading French government officials, including the prime minister, Guy Mollet. In April 1956, Peres's efforts yielded results for the first time. Over the objections of the Quai d'Orsay and without informing the Americans, Bourgès-Maunoury dispatched two dozen Mystère fighter jets to Israel. In June, Peres presented him with a wish list of weapons that the Israelis considered fantastical. To his great surprise, the French Defense Ministry approved it, resulting in a $70 million arms deal that included two hundred tanks and seventy-two more jets.[14]

Three months later, Egyptian president Nasser sent shock waves across the world by nationalizing the Suez Canal, the narrow waterway through which the bulk of Europe's and America's oil supply passed on a daily basis. This act set in motion a chain of events that would lure Israel into a risky war, strain its relationship with the United States, and forever alter the geography and balance of power in the Middle East.

Opened in 1869, the canal had been under London's control since 1882, when the British army occupied Egypt. Even after Egypt became a republic in 1953 and Britain agreed a year later to begin gradually withdrawing its troops from the Canal Zone, the Suez Canal Company still remained in the hands of British and French business interests. Nasser's move to nationalize it threatened the security of Western oil shipments, and Britain and France soon began to plot a military intervention, enlisting Israel to do the dirty work.

Bourgès-Maunoury, now the defense minister, arranged for Peres to meet with the French General Staff, whose members asked him how long Israel would need to conquer Sinai. Peres assured them it would take no more than two weeks.[15] In late October, Ben-Gurion and General Moshe Dayan convened at Sèvres with top British and French officials to plan the Suez campaign. British prime minister Anthony Eden feared a domestic backlash and damage to Britain's standing in the Arab world and refused to go to war if his government was seen as an aggressor. Eden eventually gave in, however, making crucial decisions about the war while suffering from biliary tract disease and heavily drugged on Drinamyl, a medication known to produce irritability and overconfidence.[16]

The French eventually persuaded the Israelis to launch the invasion and, with Eden's consent, all three countries moved forward. According to the Sèvres plan, Israel would conquer Sinai, Egypt would retaliate by moving into the Canal Zone, and the international community would demand that both withdraw. Israel would comply and Egypt would refuse, providing a justification for joint French and British intervention. And behind closed doors, in exchange for Israel's agreement to launch a unilateral invasion of Sinai, the French made a promise to Peres: France would finance the construction of a 10 megawatt nuclear reactor in Israel.[17]

Israel invaded on October 29 and, as planned, France and Britain demanded that both Egypt and Israel withdraw from Sinai. Israel agreed and Egypt refused, giving London and Paris the pretext they needed to invade.[18] But the superpowers were not pleased: the Soviets responded to Israel's invasion with a blunt nuclear threat, while U.S. president Dwight Eisenhower, fresh from reelection, demanded an immediate Israeli withdrawal.[19] Israel's adventure in Suez alongside the British and the French ended as a miserable failure.

Allying itself so closely with two colonial powers had seriously damaged Israel's already precarious position in the Third World, where many countries saw it as a pariah and made it the target of numerous international boycotts within the U.N. During the mid-1950s, nationalist movements blossomed and more and more countries broke free of their European colonial masters: France lost Vietnam in 1954, Tunisia and Morocco in 1956, and Ghana declared independence from Britain in 1957. As these African and Asian states fought for and attained their independence, Israel began to change tack and look for other allies. The United States' special relationship with Israel had not yet developed and rather than overtly aiding the hated French colonizers, the Jewish state began aggressively courting newly independent African nations.

· · ·

GOLDA MEIR FIRST VISITED Africa in 1958. Her trip began in Liberia—a nation established by freed American slaves in 1847 that identified with Israel due to their similar diaspora roots. Meir's Liberian hosts marveled at her nonchalant familiarity with the land of the Bible and in a rural village she was honored with the title of "Paramount Chief." After a ceremony involving male singers and dancers whirling around her, two hundred women of the Gola tribe whisked Meir away to a tiny, suffocating thatch hut, dressed her in brightly colored robes, and performed secret initiation rites while the prime minister's baffled security escorts waited nervously outside.[20]

From Liberia, the newly crowned Paramount Chief traveled to Ghana to celebrate the one-year anniversary of its independence. In Accra, Meir met with Ghanaian liberation hero Kwame Nkrumah and was invited to address other visiting African dignitaries on the topic of economic development. But rather than discussing agriculture, public health, and infrastructure, Meir found herself confronted by sixty skeptical men seated around a table. Black African leaders supported the struggle against French colonialism in the Arab nations of North Africa and deeply resented Israel's ties to France. The Algerian representative rose to demand how Israel could justify its ties with "a government that is fighting a ruthless and brutal war against my people . . . and that is the primary foe of the self-determination of the African people?"

The chain-smoking Meir paused, lit a cigarette, and replied coolly: "Our neighbors . . . are out to destroy us with arms that they receive free of charge from the Soviet Union. . . . The one and only country in the world that is ready . . . to sell us some of the arms we need in order to protect ourselves is France." She then put the question to her audience: "If you were in that position, what would you do?"[21]

Meir's bluntness killed the tension and her audience of skeptical statesman turned their focus to how Israel could help them. The Israelis had much to offer: many African countries had arid climates like Israel's and Israeli development experts were able to provide the farming and irrigation technology they needed. These African states were also in dire need of professional, well-trained armies. In return for economic aid and military training, Meir asked only for their friendship and diplomatic support.

Meir's 1958 visit to Africa was the first of many. In the years that followed, she became close friends with several African statesmen, feeling an affinity with them due to their common history of fighting for independence. "Independence had come to us, as it was coming to Africa, not served up on a silver platter but after years of struggle," she later wrote in her autobiography. "Like them, we had shaken off foreign rule; like them we had to learn for ourselves how to reclaim the land, how to increase the yields of our crops, how to irrigate, how to raise poultry, how to live together and how to defend ourselves."[22] In her eyes, Israeli aid to Africa fulfilled a dream of Zionism's founding father, Theodor Herzl, to assist in the redemption of the Africans.

Israel's charm offensive in Africa went hand in hand with a broader foreign policy initiative known as the "alliance of the periphery," whereby Israel sought close ties with countries just beyond the hostile Arab states surrounding it.[23] The brainchild of Mossad leaders Reuven Shiloah and Isser Harel, the periphery strategy was a crucial part of Israel's plan to check the expansion of Nasser's pan-Arabism as well as Soviet influence in the region.

By the late 1950s, Moscow had firmly entrenched itself as an enemy of Israel by supplying arms to Egypt and Syria. Meanwhile, Israel's requests for a formal defense pact with the United States had been repeatedly rebuffed by the Eisenhower administration. Harel saw alliances with an outer circle of states as the next best option. Turkey, Ethiopia, and Iran—strategically positioned, staunchly anticommunist, and fearful of pan-Arabism—were the main targets. Israel's leaders later forged close relationships with minority groups within enemy states as well, such as the Iraqi Kurds and the Lebanese Christians.[24]

Extending this approach further afield with the goal of courting additional allies, Israel launched technical assistance, police and intelligence training, and military aid programs throughout Africa in the early 1960s. By 1966, ten African countries were receiving military aid and Israelis were training young people and paramilitary groups in seventeen African nations. Unlike American and Soviet aid, Israel's did not come with ideological strings attached; Israel may have wanted support at the U.N. but it did not demand that African states take sides in the Cold War. African leaders saw Israel as a fellow small nation facing similar challenges, and appreciated the nonpatronizing attitude of their Israeli mentors.[25]

The Israeli diplomats and aid workers who fanned out across Africa were not Foreign Ministry bureaucrats, but socialist kibbutzniks. They were laid-back, sandal-wearing sabras,[26] who blended easily with statesmen and farmers alike. They were willing to work in the fields and sample local cuisine, in contrast to the more polished and distant European and American heads of mission who reminded Africans of the old colonial days. Several Israeli ambassadors became close confidants of African leaders. The Mossad ran training programs for new intelligence services throughout Africa, allowing them to break free of dependence on former colonizers for their security.[27]

Many African statesmen, especially those in francophone West Africa, had more personal reasons for supporting Zionism. Leaders such as Senegal's poet-president Léopold Senghor and Félix Houphouët-Boigny of the Ivory Coast had served as ministers in France and saw postwar Socialist prime minister Léon Blum, a Jew and a staunch Zionist, as their political mentor.[28] Ghanaian president Nkrumah also maintained a close relationship with Israel and was gaining influence at the Organization of African Unity (OAU), providing a counterweight to Egypt's anti-Israel rhetoric.

In contrast to these warm ties, Israel had a low-profile relationship with South Africa, and it was becoming increasingly strained. By 1960, Israel's blossoming relations with newly independent black African states and its strident denunciations of apartheid had put Jerusalem and Pretoria on a diplomatic collision course.

· · ·

ON THE MORNING OF March 21, 1960, a crowd of twenty thousand black South Africans gathered at the gates of a police station outside Johannesburg. The crowd had descended on the Sharpeville police department to protest the hated "pass laws" that required blacks to carry identification

listing their place of residence and employment at all times. Anyone failing to produce the document or traveling to a forbidden "white area"
where he or she was not employed faced immediate arrest. As tension
mounted, security forces tried to intimidate the crowd with low-flying
fighter jets overhead and armored cars on the ground. When the demonstrators refused to disperse, the police opened fire. Officers unloaded
over a thousand rounds of ammunition in less than two minutes, killing
sixty-nine people.[29] Many of the victims were women and children, several of them shot in the back as they fled.[30] The Sharpeville massacre
ignited the black opposition, led to the formation of the armed wing of
the African National Congress, and brought sustained international
media attention to South Africa for the first time. Demonstrators filled
central London, the Vatican condemned Pretoria, and Israeli diplomats,
along with those from many other countries, protested at the U.N.

As Israel's denunciations of South Africa grew louder, the South
African Jewish community—placated by Malan's embrace in the early
1950s—began to worry once again. Hendrik Verwoerd had replaced
Malan as prime minister in 1958 and his past as a fierce opponent
of Jewish immigration from Europe during the 1930s added to their
fears. South Africa's leading Jewish organization—the Jewish Board of
Deputies—feared an anti-Semitic backlash if it failed to remain on good
terms with the government of the day.

The board served as the primary public voice of the Jewish community and managed relations with the government in Pretoria. Its politics
reflected the views of the Johannesburg lawyers, doctors, and businessmen who dominated its ranks. They were not the sort of men who took
on the government. Aleck Goldberg, a prominent member of the board
from 1958 to 1990, recalls that National Party leaders were "annoyed
and taken aback" by Israel's criticism of South Africa. "They couldn't
understand it. It was a kind of slap in the face to what they thought were
gestures of friendship toward Israel and the Jewish community," says
Goldberg. Making matters worse was the fact that NP leaders seemed to
believe that South African Jews had the clout to influence Israeli foreign
policy at the U.N. Even if the board could have done so, Goldberg
insists that "being a very devoted Zionist community you would *never*,
under any circumstances, denounce Israel."[31] In 1961, however, the
Board of Deputies did just that.

In October of that year, African states opposing apartheid lashed out at Pretoria in the U.N. General Assembly. The South African government was represented on this occasion by the nemesis of South African Jewry, Foreign Minister Eric Louw. Israel voted with the African nations to censure South Africa and its leading anti-Semite before the eyes of the world.[32] Following the vote, Louw issued a radio statement calling on South African Jews to criticize Israel and express solidarity with South Africa. As much as they despised Louw, the Board of Deputies and its sister organization, the Zionist Federation, panicked and immediately denounced the Israeli government for denying Louw his basic freedom of speech and argued that Israel should have simply abstained from the vote, as other Western nations had.[33] In the eyes of Israel's leading diplomat in South Africa, Simcha Pratt, the Jewish community's reaction was disgraceful. "I saw before me panicky people, gripped by fear and without backbone," Pratt wrote to the Foreign Ministry in Jerusalem after meeting with Zionist Federation members.[34]

At that time, most Israeli government officials opposed apartheid on moral grounds, but a minority worried that such opposition might endanger the South African Jewish community.[35] Ben-Gurion himself doubted that the Jews in South Africa would be punished for Israeli policy and did not want to alienate his new African allies. After a contentious 1961 U.N. vote denouncing Pretoria, Israel's founding father declared to critics in the Knesset (parliament): "We knew the Jews there wouldn't suffer very much.... If there would have been *pogroms*—or if their lives were in danger—then we would have abstained, but we would not have voted in favour [of South Africa], certainly not. A Jew can't be for discrimination."[36]

Back in Johannesburg, the parochial board leaders failed to grasp Ben-Gurion's broader moral vision and saw Israel's actions only as a threat to the well-being of their community. In the end, Prime Minister Verwoerd's much feared retaliation against South African Jews was limited. His private secretary sent a letter containing veiled threats to a prominent Jewish citizen, and the Finance Ministry suspended special transfer privileges for South African Zionist organizations that raised money for Israel.[37] Jewish leaders in Johannesburg saw these restrictions on their ability to send money to Israel as a serious setback,[38] but their fears were overblown. In fact, most of the funds trapped in South Africa were eventually used by the Israeli government to buy an ambassadorial residence in Pretoria.[39] Israel continued to criticize apartheid, and the dreaded anti-Semitic backlash never materialized.

. . .

ON A VISIT TO AFRICA as foreign minister in the early 1960s, Golda Meir joined a busload of African dignitaries on a visit to Victoria Falls, along the border of newly independent Zambia and white-ruled Southern Rhodesia (now Zimbabwe). When the white Rhodesian soldiers invited Meir to visit the Rhodesian side of the falls but turned away her black colleagues, she declined. Meir was already revered by the leaders of Africa's anticolonial revolutions, and this act further cemented her reputation as a foe of racism and colonialism.[40]

Meir's strong line against apartheid was driven both by strategic considerations and by principle, and she was not afraid to publicly denounce South Africa's government. In 1963, Meir told the U.N. General Assembly that Israelis could not condone apartheid due to Jews' historical experience as victims of oppression and went on to pledge that Israel had "taken all necessary steps" to prevent Israeli arms from reaching South Africa, directly or indirectly.[41] That same year, Israel took a stand against apartheid in another international forum, this time at the founding convention of the Organization of African Unity in Ethiopia—a group that Israel feared would be co-opted by hostile Arab states. When Ben-Gurion addressed the assembled African dignitaries in Addis Ababa, the Jewish Board of Deputies in South Africa panicked once again, complaining, "One can understand that Israel has her own policies, but why should her Prime Minister go out of his way to harm this country?" South African Jewish leaders pleaded with Israeli diplomats to take a softer line; they viewed Israel's stand against apartheid not as principled opposition, but as "interference" in South Africa's domestic affairs and a threat to their own good relationship with the apartheid regime.[42] They felt the same way about members of their own Jewish community who dared to speak out against the government.

Three months after Ben-Gurion's OAU speech, the South African Jewish community found itself in the limelight once again when Arthur Goldreich and Harold Wolpe, a fellow Jew, were arrested and charged with conspiring to overthrow the government. Goldreich had stayed in

Israel for five years after going there to fight in the War of Independence, and he returned to South Africa in 1954 to pursue his studies in art and design. He was soon winning awards for his painting and emerging as one of the country's most talented young architects. But Goldreich was leading a double life; he was also a prominent figure in the underground struggle against the regime.

Goldreich's personal saga as South Africa's most wanted man began in 1961, when someone by the name of Mr. Jacobson began searching for a quiet, secluded farm in suburban Johannesburg. Claiming that he needed a place where an ailing family member could recover, Jacobson asked real estate agents to show him properties far from major thoroughfares and surrounded by trees. Finally, he settled on Liliesleaf Farm, a twenty-eight-acre plot with a four-bedroom house in Rivonia, fifteen miles north of downtown Johannesburg. But rather than handing over the house to his convalescing relative, Mr. Jacobson—whose real name was Michael Harmel—rented it to Goldreich and his family for 100 rand per month.[43]

Goldreich was the last person anyone in Pretoria would have expected of underground revolutionary activities. He deliberately cultivated the image of a high-society dandy. Clad in tweed and riding boots, he held dinner parties at the country house, joined the polo club, and when pressed by leftist friends to take a stand politically he claimed he preferred the good life to the struggle.[44]

Little did Goldreich's foppish friends and the security police in Pretoria know that the ANC's underground leader, Nelson Mandela, was living at Liliesleaf disguised as a domestic servant. Mandela used the alias David Motsamayi and spent his days taking out the garbage and making tea for black construction workers who looked down on him as a houseboy in blue overalls. Meanwhile, Goldreich made trips to Czechoslovakia and East Germany to study munitions and guerrilla warfare; he even visited Moscow and Beijing, where he spent four hours meeting with Deng Xiaoping in 1962.[45] Mandela later credited Goldreich with providing the ANC with much crucial military expertise: "[Arthur] was knowledgeable about guerrilla warfare and helped fill many gaps in my understanding," he wrote.[46]

Soon Michael Harmel—the faux Mr. Jacobson—and other leaders of the South African Communist Party began to visit Liliesleaf regularly, turning it into an "incubator for a revolution" where everyone from SACP head Joe Slovo to ANC leader Walter Sisulu would gather.[47] Having concluded that a purely nonviolent struggle could not succeed in a state where peaceful dissent was viewed as treason, the SACP and ANC began to plot a sabotage campaign targeting government installations and property. Mandela and Slovo were put in charge of forming a single armed movement: Umkhonto we Sizwe, or Spear of the Nation. Liliesleaf was their headquarters and Goldreich was seen as an especially valuable adviser given his battlefield experience during Israel's War of Independence.[48]

By July 1963, the police realized something was afoot in Rivonia. They staked out Liliesleaf and eventually raided the farm. Goldreich and Wolpe were arrested along with many other key ANC and SACP leaders and soon they all joined Mandela, who had been arrested eleven months earlier, behind bars. The arrests led to the infamous Rivonia trial, during which Mandela and other leading anti-apartheid figures such as Walter Sisulu, Denis Goldberg, and Govan Mbeki, the father of future president Thabo Mbeki, were sentenced to life in prison.

The prosecutor of the Rivonia defendants was Percy Yutar, a prominent member of the Jewish community. Yutar had grown up with seven siblings and went on to receive the first Ph.D. in law ever awarded by the University of Cape Town. As a student, he adorned his walls with images of robed, wig-wearing British legal giants and set his sights on a career as a judge. Despite his stellar academic achievements, the anti-Semitic legal establishment gave him menial work for much of his early career. After years of stoically enduring the slights of his academically inferior bosses, Yutar finally became a junior prosecutor. For an obsessive social climber with a chip on his shoulder, the Rivonia trial was the perfect opportunity to move up in government; by prosecuting enemies of the state— including several Jews like Goldreich and Wolpe—he could finally prove to anti-Semitic government officials that Jews were loyal citizens.[49] The Rivonia trial launched Percy Yutar's legal career, earned him the praise of apartheid regime leaders, congratulations from his synagogue's rabbi and the Board of Deputies, and the nickname "Dr. Persecutor" from his critics.[50]

But Goldreich and Wolpe never faced Yutar in the courtroom. They escaped from prison before the trial. After first failing to cut their way out of a cell with razors smuggled in to them in loaves of French bread, the two settled on bribing a white prison guard they had befriended. The guard was bored working the night shift at the Marshall Square prison in downtown Johannesburg and spent most of his time talking about cars and women with the inmates. When Goldreich and Wolpe offered him 4,000 rand, enough to buy the new Studebaker he dreamed of, the guard agreed to let them out a back door before knocking himself out and using his unconsciousness as an alibi.

The two men fled through the darkened streets of downtown Johannesburg, eventually reaching a suburban cottage, where they hid out for eight days. The fugitives then traveled 230 miles in the trunk of a car, dressed themselves as priests, and crossed the border into Swaziland. Posing as visiting English missionaries, they flew to Francistown in the British colony of Bechuanaland (now Botswana).

By the time Goldreich and Wolpe arrived in Francistown, hordes of journalists had already discovered their whereabouts and set up shop in their hotel. South African intelligence agents were close behind. On the morning that they were scheduled to leave on a passenger plane to Tanzania, Goldreich and Wolpe found their ride to freedom devoured by flames on the Francistown runway. For days afterward, no other commercial aircraft dared to land at the airport, for fear of sabotage by South African agents. The local police chief invited the fugitives to stay in jail rather than risk assassination in a hotel room. In the end, it was a correspondent for the American broadcaster NBC who bailed them out.[51]

Goldreich and Wolpe were flown to a U.N.-administered zone of the Republic of Congo and from there to Dar es Salaam on a plane chartered at NBC's expense in exchange for an exclusive interview.[52] Goldreich settled in London after his escape but soon moved to Jerusalem at the express invitation of the Israeli Foreign Ministry. He became the head of the world-famous Bezalel Academy's architecture department—and eventually of the Israeli anti-apartheid movement.

Back in Johannesburg, the board's leaders seized every opportunity to dissociate themselves from the escaped prisoners. Goldreich remembers that "they went to great lengths to say that I wasn't really a Jew, that I didn't observe. When I escaped they offered to pay additional money for the reward on my head."[53] The Afrikaans press focused obsessively on

Goldreich. An article entitled "Portrait of a Communist" ran in *Die Vaderland* denouncing Goldreich and declaring that the Jewish community had disowned him: "Jewish leaders in Johannesburg who are just as disturbed as others by the events of the past weeks, assure us that Goldreich, except at his circumcision, has never again been in a synagogue." *Dagbreek* published the article under a six-column headline "JEWISH BOARD CONDEMNS GOLDREICH AND CO.," just the sort of distancing the board wanted.[54]

The Jewish immigrants who had fled Russian pogroms and Nazi extermination continued to fear another round of persecution in their new homeland. But by 1961, South Africa's Jews were not in danger of a state-sponsored backlash—no matter what Goldreich or the Israeli government did to oppose apartheid.

After Goldreich settled in Israel, the Israeli government continued to speak out against apartheid and seek closer ties with black African nations while disregarding the grievances of South African Jews. Meanwhile, Arab states were attempting to woo African countries to their side with offers of aid, but most black leaders remained neutral, and some were openly hostile. The Arab slave trade in Africa was a not-so-distant memory and African statesmen did not appreciate being manipulated by wealthier Arab states. On one memorable occasion in 1960, during a U.N. debate on the Israeli-Palestinian conflict, a Saudi delegate accused African countries of "selling out" to Israel. This was too much for the delegate from Ivory Coast, who replied, "The representative of Saudi Arabia may be used to buying Negroes, but he can never buy us."[55] It appeared that Israel's Africa policy was working as planned.

Yet even as Israel was publicly pushing a highly moralistic policy at the U.N. and courting African allies, it was still maintaining some contact with South Africa through a low-level diplomatic mission in Pretoria and mutual friends in France. The early 1960s was a time of intense, if secretive, military cooperation between France and Israel. Despite the failed 1956 Suez campaign and the objections of Israel's African allies, the two military establishments remained close. France—which had a large defense industry and had always demonstrated a willingness to sell arms to controversial and isolated regimes—had also become South Africa's largest military aircraft supplier by the early 1960s. At the time, the South African government was well aware that growing opposition to apartheid might eventually lead to an arms embargo against Pretoria. The government was therefore eager to develop its own domestic defense industry and to buy any weapons the French were willing to sell.

South African diplomats were frustrated with Israel's public opposition to apartheid and believed that the French could help them smooth things over and convince Jerusalem to do business with Pretoria. Several of the most powerful political figures in France were openly pro-Israel, including the deputy speaker of the National Assembly, Raymond Schmittlein, and the renowned World War II general Pierre Koenig, for whom streets were named in Jerusalem.[56] Pretoria was especially interested in cultivating a relationship with Schmittlein because he was head of the French–South African friendship group in the National Assembly, was close to the Rothschilds and the Suez Finance Company, and had a direct line to Prime Minister Georges Pompidou and General Charles de Gaulle.[57]

Schmittlein had long advocated greater investment in South Africa and soon arranged for a team of high-level government officials and industrialists to visit South Africa and look into developing the country's infrastructure to facilitate arms production.[58] Privately, Schmittlein pledged to use the project "as a screen behind which substantial French military and other essential supplies could be made available to South Africa in the event of international sanctions."[59] The deal promised to benefit the French defense industry, which was a major employer and engine for economic growth; it was also an offer the isolated regime in Pretoria could not refuse.

As much as they resented Israel's increasingly harsh anti-apartheid rhetoric, the men in Pretoria were afraid to take action against Israel lest it endanger the flow of arms from France.[60] In 1963, as anti–South African rhetoric from Israel reached a fever pitch, with denunciations of apartheid coming from both Foreign Minister Meir and Prime Minister Ben-Gurion, the South African Foreign Ministry debated whether to sever ties with Israel. A top secret memo stressed that "our relations with France are of the utmost importance." More importantly, its author argued, French Zionists like Schmittlein would "play a leading role in the current negotiations regarding the delivery of weapons to South Africa."[61]

In the end, it was the Israelis who took the initiative and recalled their ambassador on September 15, 1963.[62] The South African government nonetheless remained extremely sensitive about offending the Israelis, and the Foreign Ministry stressed that Israel's low-ranking representative should be treated with all the usual diplomatic courtesies. Indeed, it was "strongly recommended . . . that he still be invited to all state functions such as the President's Garden Party . . . just like all the other heads of diplomatic missions."[63]

As Israel and South Africa were busy keeping up appearances, the French were helping Israel put the finishing touches on its first nuclear reactor in the desert town of Dimona.

3

THE ATOMIC BOND

The Israeli–South African Nuclear Connection

IN THE EARLY 1960S, soon after Israel and France broke ground in the Negev Desert, South Africa began to seek its own nuclear capability. But South Africa's role as a global nuclear heavyweight goes back much further, to the final days of World War II, when South Africa's emergence as one of the world's primary uranium producers suddenly made it a strategically vital ally for the United States.

Prior to World War II, uranium was not considered a commercially significant product, let alone a strategic asset. But as scientists in the late 1930s discovered its fissionable properties, strategists began to worry about uranium falling into German hands. At the time, the world's largest reserves were found in the Belgian Congo, specifically in the Shinkolobwe mine in the southern Katanga Province.

After Hitler's forces took control of Belgium in June 1940, U.S. president Franklin Roosevelt's advisers urged the Belgian mining company operating in Shinkolobwe to move all extracted uranium out of the region for safekeeping. Over one thousand tons were shipped across the Atlantic and stored in a warehouse on Staten Island. Five years later, those same minerals, enriched and reprocessed, exploded over Hiroshima and Nagasaki.[1] At the time, as historian Thomas Borstelmann notes, "few people in the world had any idea where the ingredients for this extraordinary power came from. The men of the Truman administration, however, knew that they had found the key to unprecedented power in the mines of southern Africa."[2]

As the Cold War arms race intensified, American planners worried about their excessive dependence on the Congolese mine and its finite supply. In order to fuel a massive nuclear buildup, finding new sources of uranium became a paramount concern. Two days after D. F. Malan's historic election victory in May 1948 ushered in the era of apartheid in South Africa, the British-American Combined Policy Committee on atomic energy development projected that South Africa would become the United States' primary source of uranium by 1952 and recommended signing import deals immediately in order to gain access to as much of it as possible. The State Department warned policymakers to "bear in mind the importance of South African uranium in all our future dealings with the Dominion."[3]

Anticipated dependence on South African uranium led the administration of Harry Truman to adopt an extremely soft policy toward the newly installed apartheid regime. South Africa became the eighth largest market for American products in 1948 in the midst of a postwar export boom. Pretoria was an especially favored customer as it paid for imports not in currency but in gold.[4] In 1950, South Africa agreed to produce and sell uranium ore to the United States and sent one of its air force squadrons, led by an ace pilot named Jan Blaauw, to fight on the American side in Korea.

Responding to this show of goodwill, an appreciative Secretary of State Dean Acheson assured South Africa's ambassador in Washington that Pretoria's requests for American arms would receive "the most sympathetic consideration."[5] Then, in 1957, the Eisenhower administration signed an agreement with the South Africans under the auspices of the American Atoms for Peace program—an effort to provide nuclear infrastructure, materials, and training to other countries in order to further the peaceful uses of atomic energy. Washington offered to provide South Africa with its first research reactor, SAFARI-1, at Pelindaba, outside Pretoria, and the highly enriched uranium needed to fuel it.[6] Two decades later, South Africa would have the bomb.

Israel, too, received a small research reactor from Washington under the Atoms for Peace program; but without its friends in France, Israel may have never become a nuclear power.

In October 1956, before Israel agreed to launch the invasion of Egypt that set off the Suez War, Shimon Peres had insisted that the French provide Israel with a nuclear reactor for research purposes. Defense Minister Maurice Bourgès-Maunoury, Foreign Minister Christian Pineau, and

Prime Minister Guy Mollet gave Peres a verbal commitment but no mention of a nuclear deal appeared in the Sèvres protocol signed by Britain, France, and Israel on the eve of the war.[7] Although some French officials believed it was intended solely for civilian purposes, Peres and his pro-Israel allies in the French defense establishment knew that the promised research reactor could make a far more significant contribution to Israel's nascent nuclear weapons program than the smaller 5,000 kilowatt reactor the United States had provided three years earlier.[8]

The Suez War may have been a failure for all three invading armies, but Israel still had its promise from the French. It would take another year before they sealed the deal. Bourgès-Maunoury, an enthusiastic supporter of Israel, succeeded Mollet as prime minister in 1957, but his government faced a crisis of confidence after only three months in office.[9] As the French administration faltered in September 1957, the Israelis feared that their nuclear program would collapse unless the reactor agreement was signed. Ben-Gurion began to panic.

Israel's scientific attaché in France told Shimon Peres to fly to Paris immediately to salvage the reactor deal.[10] By November, Bourgès-Maunoury's coalition government was crumbling and Peres began a furious round of lobbying, relying on all the contacts he had cultivated during his years as Israel's deputy defense minister and unofficial ambassador to the French military establishment. Abel Thomas, the man who had lost his brother to the Nazis and helped Peres craft the French-Israeli relationship, convinced the head of the French Atomic Energy Commission to go along with the plan; the approval of leading scientists satisfied former prime minister Mollet; and Mollet persuaded his successor, Bourgès-Maunoury, to close the deal. The French prime minister's signature on the pact was his last official act as head of state.

The agreement provided Israel with a 24 megawatt reactor that both parties knew was not going to be used exclusively for peaceful purposes.[11] While France agreed to supply some fuel for the new Israeli reactor being built in Dimona, the Israelis were forced to seek other sources of uranium to power their covert nuclear weapons program. They found a willing seller in Pretoria.

South Africa's status as a major nuclear player was well established by the late 1950s thanks to its key role as a uranium supplier to the United States. Pretoria sent representatives to international atomic energy meetings and played an influential role at the newly created International Atomic Energy Agency (IAEA) in Vienna. Other nations soon began to turn to South Africa for uranium as well, including Britain and Sweden. Only one of these new customers would end up acquiring the bomb covertly: Israel.

Initially, Pretoria refused to sell any uranium to Jerusalem due to the loose conditions the Israelis insisted upon. Most troubling was their opposition to South African inspections, which Israel believed would limit its sovereignty.[12] These were the days before the 1968 Nuclear Non-Proliferation Treaty (NPT) and mandatory IAEA safeguards, which subjected nuclear transactions between signatories to much closer international scrutiny.[13] At the time, contracting governments were left to sort out issues of peaceful use and inspections on their own, and Israel's demands made South Africa suspicious.

Pretoria was concerned that the Israelis "certainly possess the know-how to make a bomb and . . . there is considerable incentive for them to construct one"; Israel's close ties to black African states at the time did not endear it to South African diplomats either. For these reasons, they concluded that it was not in South Africa's interest to sell "anything but an insignificant quantity of uranium to Israel in this troubled year 1960."[14]

A year later, however, South Africa became a republic, loosening its ties to the British Commonwealth and reshuffling the Foreign Ministry's leadership. The new crop of diplomats was more open to a deal with Israel, and in 1962 the two countries finally signed an agreement. South Africa pledged to supply Israel with yellowcake—a uranium concentrate that, after extensive processing, can be enriched to make weapons-grade uranium or used to fuel nuclear reactors. The amount of yellowcake South Africa shipped to Israel—ten tons—was fairly small and both parties agreed that the shipment would be registered with the IAEA after delivery. The sale was duly reported to the Vienna agency in 1963.[15] Two years later, in 1965, the governments reached a formal bilateral agreement on safeguards.[16] It included detailed provisions forbidding the use of South African uranium for atomic weapons or weapons research and allowing South African inspectors to view the reactors used to process the material and their operating records.[17] Sealed three years before passage of the NPT—a treaty that neither Israel nor South Africa would sign due to their covert weapons programs—the uranium deal seemed as safe and secure as was possible to the atomic scientists and policymakers in Pretoria.

The 1965 agreement not only governed the ten tons sent to Israel, but envisioned a constant flow "for purposes of stockpiling and not for immediate use." The Israelis agreed to keep these future uranium shipments in sealed storage facilities and to allow one inspection by South Africa each year.[18] The IAEA was not mentioned anywhere in the detailed five-page document or in the letter signed by South African prime minister Hendrik Verwoerd attached to it; rather, regulation and inspection of the uranium in Israel would be the sole responsibility of the agency that had sold it: South Africa's Atomic Energy Board.

In the early 1960s, both Israel and South Africa were beginning to take the first tentative steps toward a nuclear weapons capability. This required both savvy sourcing and subterfuge. As Pretoria and Jerusalem sought to acquire the physical infrastructure and nuclear fuel needed to expand their respective programs, they had to deceive both their Western patrons and each other.

J. P. Hugo, the former administrator of the Atomic Energy Board's uranium enrichment program, recalls that the government decided that "we'll sell secretly to Israel because they'd felt the pulse of the Americans and British and others and had been turned down."[19] By the mid-1960s, Washington and London had found other uranium suppliers—namely Australia, Canada, and domestic supplies in the United States—and were no longer dependent on the increasingly vilified apartheid government for this crucial resource. Israel, on the other hand, needed uranium and South Africa was looking for new customers.

Sitting in his backyard in a leafy diplomatic enclave of South Africa's capital, Hugo explains that the initial ten-ton sale helped the Israelis to build uranium-tipped bullets capable of piercing tanks. Hugo remains proud of the project and keeps a replica of one of the foot-long Israeli shells on his desk at home, mounted on wood alongside a plaque bearing his name.

As Hugo explains, stringent safeguards were included in the agreement because he and other scientists at the Atomic Energy Board insisted on them. Hugo conducted an inspection himself in 1966 and recalls seeing the uranium in welded drums—evidence that it was not being used. He is confident that the South African uranium did not end up in Dimona, the heart of the Israel's clandestine nuclear weapons program; and in the mid-1960s it probably didn't. Instead, as predicted in the bilateral agreement, a growing stockpile of South African uranium began to build up in Israel. This stockpile would reach five hundred tons by 1976, when a South African minister of mines, enamored of Israel and facing near certain bankruptcy, would agree to lift the bilateral safeguards that had ensured its annual inspection and prevented its military use.

· · ·

OFFICIALLY, THE STATE OF ISRAEL does not acknowledge that it has nuclear bombs even though it is well known that the nation possesses a formidable arsenal of close to one hundred of the most advanced weapons.[20] This "opaque" policy is exemplified by the oft-repeated phrase that "Israel will not be the first nation to introduce nuclear weapons to the Middle East," which became the declared policy under Prime Minister Levi Eshkol during the crucial years 1963–66, when Israel was busy producing its first weapon and deceiving the United States about its level of nuclear advancement.[21] The definition of "introduce" was left deliberately vague to allow interpretations ranging from develop and build, to deploy and launch.[22]

Israel never debated the nuclear option openly in parliament and only a select group—Ben-Gurion's most trusted associates and the scientists involved—was privy to early discussions of Dimona. The divisions in this secret debate did not fall along predictable political lines. Instead, it pitted ambitious young technocrats set on the idea of going nuclear against those who preferred to invest the state's limited funds in conventional military power. By the early 1960s, many generals saw the nuclear and missile programs as fanciful. At a time when the army needed boots and bullets, they argued, the government was pouring all of its money into a project that many in the military regarded as "hallucinatory."[23] With a sufficient territorial cushion separating the Jewish state from its hostile neighbors, most generals believed, Israel would not need a nuclear deterrent. Arguing in favor of the bomb were Peres and Dayan.[24] With a nuclear deterrent, they insisted, the country's narrow nine-mile "waist" would no longer be such a dangerous liability. By openly declaring Israel's nuclear capability, it was unlikely that anyone would dare lay a finger on it.[25]

During the mid-1960s, diplomatic contact between Israel and South Africa was minimal. It was the Six-Day War of June 1967 that changed everything. In mid-May, Egyptian president Nasser unilaterally dismissed the U.N. peacekeeping force in the Sinai Peninsula as his troops built up their positions in the desert and the U.N. stood idly by.[26] Then, on May 22, Nasser closed the Straits of Tiran to Israeli vessels. The narrow maritime passage into the Red Sea was a commercial lifeline for Israel, and closure was seen in Jerusalem as a major provocation.

Without a security guarantee from Washington or the assent of the U.S. government, Israel launched a daring preemptive attack on the morning of June 5. As Egyptian pilots sat down to breakfast at 8:15 A.M. after returning from their morning patrols, more than two hundred planes—almost the entire Israeli Air Force—took off flying west just fifty feet above the Mediterranean, leaving the skies over Israel empty and exposed.[27] As the Israeli fighters banked south and ascended into the view of Egyptian radar, the Egyptian pilots on the ground ran to their planes. They were too late: in less than two hours, the Israeli Air Force destroyed thirteen Egyptian bases and 286 of the 420 aircraft in Nasser's arsenal. Israel's air force commander reported to IDF chief of staff Rabin that "the Egyptian Air Force has ceased to exist."[28] In less than a week, Israel proceeded to conquer the Jordanian West Bank, the Syrian Golan Heights, and take the entire Sinai Peninsula and the tiny Gaza Strip from Egypt, nearly doubling the amount of territory under its control. In the eyes of Israel's admirers in Africa, this stunning and unexpected victory marred its image as a socialist beacon and instead cemented its reputation as a colonial outpost aligned with the West.[29]

In 1969, the Harvard sociologist Seymour Martin Lipset declared that "Israel is now held to be a strong and rich nation, whereas the Arabs are weak, underdeveloped, poor."[30] The sentiments of radicals everywhere, he observed, were shifting to support the new Arab underdogs. The Old Left that had aggressively supported the creation of a Jewish state in 1948 had been replaced by a New Left that painted Israel as an imperialist aggressor. "The only way Israel can change it is to lose," wrote Lipset.[31]

In the United States, militant African-American groups targeted Israel in their publications, depicting it as a colonial aggressor and American Jews as economic oppressors of the black community. Israel's relations with African states gradually soured as well. The Arab attempt to brand Israel as a Western imperialist stooge was finally beginning to stick.

Arab countries soon redoubled their efforts to compete with Israel for influence over black African leaders. Wealthy Gulf states offered attractive aid packages to poor African nations in exchange for their support of the Palestinian cause. At the same time, the OAU began to throw its unequivocal support to the Palestine Liberation Organization. It didn't help that the apartheid government had lifted all restrictions on South African citizens wishing to transfer funds to Israel during the war, allowing South African Jews to raise $30 million for the Israeli war effort.

To add to the complications, the Suez Canal was closed for eight years in the wake of the Six-Day War as Egypt and Israel continued to fight in the Sinai Peninsula. East African states were hit hardest; close to a third of their dry cargo had been shipped through the canal. While these countries lost more than $100 million per year in export revenues, the Suez closure enriched their greatest enemy, apartheid South Africa, by diverting the bulk of international freight around the Cape of Good Hope. Israel's occupation of Egyptian territory and its consistent refusal to give back the Sinai led most African states to blame the Jewish state for the post-1967 canal closure.[32]

The reaction to Israel's victory in the Six-Day War was markedly different in South Africa. There, government officials and military officers clamored to visit Israel and learn from the victorious generals, leading the Board of Deputies' journal, *Jewish Affairs*, to declare proudly, "The destinies of the two countries are . . . so alike in a much more meaningful sense than any enemy propagandist could conceive."[33] The euphoria was not confined to the Jewish community. The South African press's attitude toward the Jewish state also warmed considerably as more and more white South Africans began to sense that they and the Israelis shared a common lot. The mouthpiece of the National Party government, *Die Burger*, declared, "Israel and South Africa . . . are engaged in a struggle for existence. . . . The anti-Western powers have driven Israel and South Africa into a community of interests which had better be utilized than denied."[34]

It was a remarkable change of tone. The same South African newspapers that had denounced Israel for taking in the escaped "terrorist" Arthur Goldreich four years earlier were now singing its praises. When Goldreich escaped from prison and chose to settle in Jerusalem, he had viewed Israel as a true light unto the nations.[35] Little did he know that merely a decade later he would find himself leading Israel's anti-apartheid movement, attempting in vain to convince his new government to cease its growing economic and military ties with the apartheid regime that had once imprisoned him and still kept his comrade Mandela behind bars.

· · ·

THE SIX-DAY WAR OF 1967 widened Israel's waist, giving it the territorial buffer the generals craved. A more comfortable strategic cushion between Israel and its enemies proved no obstacle to Israel's nuclear ambitions, however, nor did it stop the defense establishment from deceiving the international community—as it had done for years.[36]

During the 1960s, as Israel was working tirelessly to develop its nuclear capability, it succeeded in hiding the true capacity and output of Dimona from a succession of pro-Israeli American presidents, from John F. Kennedy to Richard Nixon.[37] The deception began in 1961, after Israel refused to allow International Atomic Energy Agency inspectors inside Dimona, claiming it would be an affront to Israeli sovereignty. Aware that Dimona existed, but uncertain of its level of advancement and ignorant of what exactly was happening there, the United States insisted on taking on the role of nuclear watchdog instead of the IAEA—agreeing to disguise the inspections by leading American nuclear experts as scientific exchanges out of respect for Israel's pride. The first inspection took place later that year; thanks to Israel's carefully curated visit, no evidence of a nuclear weapons program was found.[38]

This policy of deception caused major disagreements within the Israeli government and led to further tension between Golda Meir and younger Labor leaders such as Peres and Dayan. Meir feared that deceiving the Americans would backfire. She pushed her colleagues to simply tell Kennedy what she saw as the simple truth: Israel's existence was threatened and many of its citizens had almost been exterminated less than two decades before. After the Holocaust, who could deny the moral imperative or practical necessity of the Jewish state's right to defend itself by any means necessary?[39] As always, Meir's argument was not simply moral; she was also a savvy realist. "If we deny that Dimona exists, then we can't use it as a bargaining point, because it is impossible to bargain about something that doesn't exist," she told Foreign Ministry colleagues in 1963.[40]

After Kennedy was assassinated in November 1963, Israel found an even more willing friend in the White House. Lyndon Johnson had been told by his pious grandfather to "take care of the Jews," a compulsion heightened by Johnson's own biblical attachment to Israel. As a young congressman in the 1930s, he had arranged visas for European Jews and helped smuggle Jewish refugees with fake passports into Galveston, Texas.[41] Even so, Israel did not trust the United States enough to reveal its biggest secret. The Israelis continued to elaborately conceal their nuclear weapons production facilities, for years fooling inspectors sent from Washington into believing they were not producing plutonium at Dimona.[42]

During the Johnson administration, American arms sales were made conditional on both Israeli disclosures of all nuclear research activities in Dimona and ongoing U.S. inspections of the reactor. The Israelis made the most of these visits by distracting inspectors with days of "scientific research discussions," thereby limiting the amount of time the visitors could spend inside the Dimona complex. They insisted on scheduling the inspections on Saturdays, when most employees were off for the Jewish Sabbath, and refused to allow American inspectors to bring their own measuring instruments.[43] By denying unfettered access to the visiting U.S. scientists, the Israeli government bought itself valuable time and threw American intelligence agencies off the trail. While the CIA suspected that Israel was secretly developing nuclear weapons, it was unaware that Israeli scientists had managed to generate plutonium on their own.* Instead, intelligence analysts assumed that Israel was exclu-

---

* Early-generation nuclear weapons rely on the fission of weapons-grade uranium or plutonium. Both are ultimately derived from yellowcake, but the lengthy production cycle is different. Weapons-grade uranium is produced by enriching uranium hexa-

sively seeking enriched uranium supplies and that large amounts of nuclear fuel had been illegally diverted from the United States by Zalman Shapiro, the Orthodox Jewish owner of a nuclear fuel facility near Pittsburgh.[44]

The successful concealment of Dimona's true capabilities allowed Israel to finish producing the plutonium it needed for a bomb by late 1966. By the time of the Six-Day War, Israel had already finished building its first nuclear devices.[45] The Soviets were keenly aware that Israel had likely achieved a nuclear capability, and there are indications that they monitored Dimona closely from the air in May 1967, perhaps even drawing up plans to destroy it.[46] Following Israel's stunning victory in June, the government moved to expand its nuclear arsenal. It was then that the Americans finally found out the truth, and it came courtesy of one of the most celebrated and controversial figures in nuclear physics: Edward Teller.

Born in Budapest in 1908, Teller grew up in a neighborhood of eminent Jewish scientists, including Nobel laureate Paul Wigner and chain reaction pioneer Leo Szilard—both of whom would go on to play important roles in the Manhattan Project during World War II. Teller distinguished himself as a physicist, too, and went on to study with giants of the field, including Niels Bohr and Werner Heisenberg. In 1952, J. Robert Oppenheimer, the scientific director of the American nuclear program, joined Teller on a trip to Israel. There, the two men discussed atomic energy with Ben-Gurion, who was at the time weighing the merits of pursuing a nuclear option.

As the Cold War arms race escalated, many nuclear scientists became outspoken doves, but Teller veered to the right. During the McCarthy-era witch hunt, he alienated many of his colleagues by publicly questioning Oppenheimer's loyalty to America and casting doubt on others who objected to his hawkish views and his leading role in the design and development of the more powerful hydrogen bomb. In Israel, a country

fluoride, a processed form of yellowcake, to a level at which over 90 percent of the uranium is the highly fissionable U-235 isotope. Weapons-grade plutonium is produced by irradiating uranium fuel rods in an active nuclear reactor, removing these rods, and reprocessing them at a separate plant in order to produce plutonium rich in the isotope Pu-239.

threatened by Soviet-aligned Egypt, Teller's anticommunism was popular. He visited Israel often during the 1960s, lectured at Tel Aviv University, and formed a close friendship with fellow nuclear physicist Yuval Ne'eman.[47]

As a leading nuclear weapons expert, Teller sensed that Israel was building a bomb and he eventually broke the news to Ne'eman at an academic conference in upstate New York in late 1967. Teller sat down beside a tree trunk with Ne'eman and told him, "I am impressed by your high level, and I think that you have already finished." Teller shared Golda Meir's view that "the cat and mouse game" with the Americans was not healthy and let Ne'eman know that he intended to tell the CIA, but assured him that he would "explain that it is justified, on the background of the Six-Day War."[48] The CIA's science and technology gurus, still beholden to the diverted uranium theory, were reluctant to believe what Teller told them: that Israel had developed its own nuclear capability and that highly enriched uranium from the United States had nothing to do with it. Instead, Israel had fed yellowcake—obtained from South Africa and other sources—into its reactor, reprocessed the spent fuel rods at a well-concealed plant, and built bombs fueled by plutonium rather than enriched uranium.

Indeed, while the CIA and FBI were obsessively investigating Shapiro, Israel had successfully obtained two hundred tons of yellowcake in a 1968 Mossad smuggling operation.[49] Israel feared that buying uranium on the open market would arouse suspicion at the European nuclear regulatory body, EURATOM, and opted for a clandestine operation instead. The Mossad used a Liberian front company to purchase a ship, the *Scheersberg A*. In Antwerp, workers loaded the ship with a cargo of yellowcake—concealed in barrels marked "Plumbat," which is a lead derivative. Officials in Bonn helped Israel disguise the operation as a transaction between West German and Italian firms, reportedly in exchange for offers to aid the Germans with uranium enrichment technology. The Mossad fabricated a false Italian recipient for its cargo, declaring that a paint company in Milan would be receiving the shipment. But the ship never docked at its stated port of call in Genoa; when it reached Rotterdam, the crew was told that the ship had been sold to a new owner and they were dismissed. With a new Israeli crew on board, the *Scheersberg A* set sail for the eastern Mediterranean, bypassing Italy altogether. Off the coast of Cyprus, and under tight military supervision, its new crew transferred the secret cargo to an Israeli naval vessel. A few days later, as the uranium was unloaded in Haifa, the *Scheersberg A* arrived in the Turkish port of Iskenderun, empty and with several weeks of pages mysteriously missing from its logbook.[50]

For the South Africans, whose nuclear research reactor had gone critical three years before, in 1965, the Israeli model of nuclear ambiguity coupled with covert weaponization was enticing.* In order to gauge what it could get away with down the road, Pretoria was watching developments in the Middle East closely and, more important, observing the reactions of the superpowers.

Five years later, when Egypt launched a surprise attack on Sinai in October 1973, Israel's undeclared nuclear arsenal had grown to approximately a dozen weapons. Facing the real possibility of defeat, Israel seemed prepared to use them or threaten to do so in order to force Washington to intervene.[51] André Buys, a leading South African nuclear weapons engineer who served as manager of the facility where Pretoria's weapons were built, remembers hearing that Israel's nuclear threat had prompted U.S. aid during the Yom Kippur War. He admits that "the allegation probably subconsciously influenced our thinking. We argued that if we cannot use a nuclear weapon on the battlefield . . . then the only possible way to use it would be to leverage intervention from the Western Powers by threatening to use it."[52]

Buys is now a professor of engineering at the University of Pretoria. His small office on the quiet campus is a world apart from the secretive environment he worked in for most of his career. Back in the early 1970s, Buys and his colleagues were beginning work on a nuclear explosive device. The scientists involved in the program maintain to this day that their research was inspired by the Atoms for Peace program, which encouraged the production of so-called peaceful nuclear explosives for mining and construction purposes.[53] South Africa's Atomic Energy

---

* A nuclear reactor "goes critical"—supports a self-sustaining neutron chain reaction—when the number of neutrons produced by fission reactions equals the number of neutrons lost. This requires a sufficient amount of fissile material present in an appropriate geometric arrangement (a critical mass).

Board was well aware, however, that its country would soon be producing enough enriched uranium for a nuclear weapon, and they issued
a report recommending the development of various devices, many of
which were far too powerful for purely peaceful purposes.[54] A small team
of scientists, including Buys, was sent to work on the new designs at
Armscor's Somchem explosive and propellant facility near Cape Town.

For all their talk about peaceful commercial use, South Africa's leaders
were not naive, and it is inconceivable that the nuclear option on
the horizon did not cross their minds when the peaceful nuclear explosive research began. Indeed, Pretoria's refusal to sign the NPT in 1968
and its highly secretive nuclear research program reveal that a nuclear
weapons capability was in fact always the ultimate objective.[55]

4

THE RISE OF REALPOLITIK

The Yom Kippur War and Israel's Realignment in Africa

IN THE SPRING OF 1968, as thousands of French students inspired by Marx and Mao hurled Molotov cocktails at riot police in the boulevards of Paris, the Israeli and South African defense officials stationed in France were busy sharing blueprints for new weapons systems. The protesters were angry young idealists who, in the words of American historian Paul Berman, took to the Latin Quarter's streets "threatening vague unimaginable revolutions against . . . every conceivable thing that could be labeled a yoke on the neck of mankind."[1] And as they brought the city to a standstill, the Israeli admiral Mordechai Limon was quietly providing his South African colleagues with technical information about Mirage aircraft and illuminating bombs at an office off the Champs-Elysées.[2] At the time, their cooperation was still a well-kept secret, unknown to the throngs of student revolutionaries who filled the nearby streets.

Back in Israel, right-wing politicians were getting tired of Meir's and Ben-Gurion's continuing condemnations of South Africa. French president Charles de Gaulle had withdrawn his support for Israel after it ignored the old general's explicit advice and launched the Six-Day War—a move that severely jeopardized the Jewish state's arms supply. As France pulled back, South Africa's leaders and much of the white population cheered Israel on.

Knesset members Shmuel Tamir and Eliezer Shostak founded an organization called the Israel–South Africa Friendship League in 1968 to promote commercial ties between the two countries. Nearly a hundred Israeli firms joined the new group and the South African business community set up a parallel organization in Johannesburg. With the enthusiastic support of Israel's opposition leader, Menachem Begin, Shostak took his fight for closer ties with South Africa to the highest levels of government. In November 1968, he confronted Israel's foreign minister,

Abba Eban, on the Knesset floor, demanding that Eban instruct the Israeli U.N. delegation "once and for all, not to vote against the S.A. government in order not to further jeopardize the relations between our two states."[3]

Eban, Israel's most revered statesman on the international stage, refused to be bullied. He was born Aubrey Solomon in 1915 in South Africa. Eban's father died when he was a baby and his mother took him to England, where she remarried and began work as a translator for Zionist leaders in London. Aubrey took his stepfather's surname and eventually Hebraicized his first. A star student at Cambridge, he mastered ten languages, including Arabic and Farsi, and became a fixture at the Cambridge Union debating society. There he honed the oratorical skills that would later earn him praise from the likes of Henry Kissinger and John Foster Dulles. Eban served as an intelligence officer in the British army during World War II and eventually moved to Palestine in the mid-1940s, becoming Israel's first representative to the United Nations and its first ambassador to the United States. While Eban's refined Oxbridge English had been well received in the U.N. General Assembly, he faced harsher treatment back home in the Knesset.[4]

Eban reacted combatively when faced with Shostak's calls to normalize relations with the racist government of his native land. Shostak was suggesting "an essential change in Israel's policy towards racial discrimination," something Eban and his predecessor, Golda Meir, refused to countenance.[5] But the mood in Israel was changing; after the Six-Day War, completely shunning South Africa—one of the few states that had praised its victory—was becoming politically untenable. Within a year, the pro–South Africa lobby got its wish: Yitzhak Unna was sent to South Africa in February 1969 as Israel's consul-general, with the express goal of improving relations between the two countries.

Unna was born in Germany and immigrated to Palestine with his mother and sister in 1936, where they joined his father in a rat-infested Haifa apartment.[6] During World War II, he enlisted in the British army and saw action in places ranging from Jordan to Libya. It was in North Africa that Unna encountered South Africans for the first time. There, he met a South African warrant officer who refused to swim in the same pool with Unna's dark-skinned Yemenite Jewish comrade Shaul. The South African insisted that "all black bastards must get out." Shaul responded by punching him in the face.[7] At the end of the war, Unna met a South African once again on a ship home to Palestine; this time it was a violently anti-Semitic air force officer who was constantly drunk and eager to provoke the Jewish soldiers.[8]

Soon after the war, Unna joined the diplomatic corps, serving as a low-level embassy official in New York and Chicago and a counselor in London and Bonn. In New York, he frequented the United Nations, where he enjoyed sitting in on Security Council debates. During the Suez crisis of 1956, Unna witnessed a particularly vociferous exchange between American ambassador Henry Cabot Lodge and his Soviet counterpart, Arkady Sobolev, after Israel sent a ship through the Canal Zone to test Nasser's commitment to free passage through Suez. In a heated debate, Lodge defended Israel's right to sail through the canal while Sobolev denounced American imperialism and Zionist aggression. During a recess, Unna went to the delegates' restroom, where he stumbled upon the American and Soviet ambassadors casually joking around. He was shocked to hear Sobolev lamenting his need to defend Egypt—in perfect English. The lesson was a formative one for the young diplomat. "Listening to this friendly jocular conversation . . . after they had given the appearance of being at each other's throat a few minutes earlier, taught me that among diplomats official hostility did not necessarily have to imply personal animosity," Unna later wrote in his autobiography.[9] It was an art he would learn to emulate as his career progressed, allowing him to privately befriend those he publicly denounced.

Despite growing Soviet hostility toward Israel, Unna became friendly with several members of the Soviet mission during his posting in London. These contacts did not have great diplomatic value, but they did teach him how to drink. Because Unna arrived in London without his wife, he immediately became a target for KGB recruiters in the Soviet embassy, who saw a lonely man as easy to compromise with liquor and ladies. Unna found their overtures amusing and never fell for the trap. He would go drinking with the Russians, but only after stuffing himself with milk, sardines, and white bread—a formula that he maintains to this day will allow anyone to consume unlimited amounts of vodka without divulging state secrets to spies or prostitutes.[10]

When Unna arrived in South Africa in 1969, he caused a minor uproar in the Jewish community by attending a reform synagogue rather than one of the Orthodox congregations that dominated South African Jewish life. He made further waves when a leading Zionist Federation official caught him eating ham and eggs for breakfast—an act of dietary defiance that shocked many observant Jews.[11] Unna seemed to have an easier time forging ties with the NP government than with his fellow Jews. He promptly learned Afrikaans—a language that was not terribly difficult for him, given that German was his mother tongue—and insisted on reading all the local newspapers, including the pro-government Afrikaans press. His grasp of Afrikaans immediately endeared him to the apartheid regime's leaders, who rarely encountered a foreign diplomat who spoke in their native tongue. South Africa's ceremonial president, Jacobus Johannes Fouché, refused to believe Unna was a Jew because of his height and linguistic skills. "Listen to the bloody Jew, he speaks fluent Afrikaans," Fouché once exclaimed at a concert where Unna introduced the Israel Philharmonic Orchestra. Unna dismissed these slights as innocuous jokes that were "really a reflection of the affection they have for the Jews, the occasional manifestation of anti-Semitism notwithstanding."[12]

Unna's closest friend in the government was the former Ossewa Brandwag general Hendrik van den Bergh, who had since become the head of South Africa's intelligence agency, the Bureau of State Security, BOSS. Despite van den Bergh's wartime Nazi sympathies, the two got on well. Van den Bergh always stressed to Unna that Afrikaners had supported the Germans in World War II due to their long-standing hatred of the British. Although Unna was not completely convinced, this historical baggage had no impact on his good working relationship with van den Bergh, which allowed Unna to negotiate the release of several imprisoned Jewish anti-apartheid activists on the condition that they emigrate to Israel. Thanks to Unna's close ties with the upper echelons of the South African security forces, the contact between the military establishments that had begun a year before in France continued quietly.

Yet as the Israeli and South African military representatives in Paris forged closer ties with one another, Israel's relations with France were cooling off. In the wake of Algeria's independence in 1962, French president Charles de Gaulle had begun to play a dangerous double game: he sought closer ties with Arab states while remaining Israel's primary arms supplier. Washington had warmed to Israel during the Kennedy years and had begun to sell it major weapons systems such as the Hawk missile, but France remained paramount until the Six-Day War.[13] When Israel launched its preemptive strike on Egypt in June 1967, de Gaulle had taken it as a personal affront. In response, he ordered the French government to cease supplying Israel with Mirage aircraft and eventually placed an embargo on all weapons sales. Israel reacted by turning to the United States as its primary source for arms and milking midlevel French bureaucrats who remained sympathetic to Israel for any arms they could still get.[14]

The final straw came in 1969 when de Gaulle refused to deliver five missile boats that Israel had already purchased from France.[15] For the Defense Ministry officials in Tel Aviv, not following through on a signed contract was dishonorable and insulting. The Israeli Navy launched a daring covert operation in December to smuggle the boats out of Cherbourg harbor, spearheaded by Admiral Mordechai Limon, the Israeli Defense Ministry's chief representative in Paris and its point man on South Africa. Limon tricked the French government into believing that a Norwegian oil company had bought the ships, secured the cooperation of the shipyard's owner with a hefty sum of money, and ensured the silence of the local press with some more. As Cherbourg's residents sat down to dinner on Christmas Eve, Israeli Navy crews, who had entered France in civilian clothes posing as university students, boarded the ships.[16] High seas and gale force winds of over one hundred miles per hour nearly derailed the plan, but at 2:30 A.M. the winds subsided and the ships slipped away.[17] By the time the international scandal broke, they were in the middle of the Mediterranean, well on their way to Haifa.

Even after Cherbourg, many members of the French defense establishment remained loyal to Israel. Several lower-level defense officials had looked the other way during the Cherbourg affair,[18] and Israel's old friends in the French government soon found new ways to circumvent de Gaulle's embargo.

There was also still strong support for Israel within the French arms industry. In January 1970, an arms dealer using the name Mr. Jackel approached South Africa on behalf of the French arms manufacturer Dassault, claiming that the company was pro-Israeli and wished to continue selling weapons to the Jewish state. For these pro-Israeli defense officials, arming their old client now meant going behind the president's back. Jackel informed the South Africans that Libya had ordered fifty Mirage jets from Dassault and he urged South Africa to place a similar order so that the company could decline the Libyan request. He also openly inquired whether "South Africa would be prepared to acquire *Mirages* for re-export to Israel."[19] Even though the stridently anti-apartheid Golda Meir was in power in Jerusalem, the behind-the-scenes military contacts in Paris were escalating.

In June, South African foreign minister Hilgard Muller met Eban in Brussels to discuss the future of their countries' relations. Two years had passed since Eban's showdown with Shostak in the Knesset; by this time, Unna had arrived in Pretoria and the relationship was warming. Still, Eban was adamant that any evidence of Israel's ties with South Africa— beyond Unna's presence in the country—be kept under wraps lest they provoke a reaction against Israel at the U.N.[20] The Middle East conflict was now a mainstay of the OAU agenda, and Arab states, buoyed by newfound petroleum reserves, were attempting to lure African states to their side with oil and aid.

Meanwhile, Israel was desperately trying to hang on to its friends throughout black Africa and to prevent a larger anti-Israeli bloc from forming at the U.N. In 1971, in an effort to shore up support in Africa, Israel offered a trivial donation of 10,000 Israeli pounds (a paltry $2,850 at the time) to an anti-apartheid outfit known as the OAU's Fund for Assistance to the Peoples Struggling Against Colonialism and Racism. Israel insisted that the donation would cover only innocuous humanitarian supplies such as blankets and medicine.[21] South African leaders did not see it this way, however, expressing shock that Israel could send money to its enemies when they had just announced that the South African government would allow the Jewish community to transfer R8 million (then approximately $11 million) of aid to Israel over a period of three years.[22]

The South African press followed the government's lead, denouncing Israel for aiding and abetting terrorism. "The terrorists are not guiltless idealists. . . . They are murderers who are fully trained by Communist powers and equipped by Communist weapons," *Die Transvaler* fumed. "If they are provided with blankets, they are blankets which cover a terrorist at night. . . . If medicines are donated, they are medicines for someone who is responsible for destroying a police vehicle on the Zambezi border."[23] Somewhat less hysterically, *Die Vaderland* chastised Israel for opportunistically currying favor with black Africa and subsidizing the dark forces seeking to overthrow their government. Drawing parallels to the Middle East conflict, the paper editorialized: "But now Israel with its 'gesture' towards 'liberators' in Africa has abandoned the whole principle of its opposition towards 'liberation' in the Middle East . . . it has recognized the right of its Arab neighbor states, and all of the terrorist movements within them, to 'liberate' the territories conquered by Israel."[24]

South Africa's Jewish leaders were panic-stricken once again.[25] They insisted on condemning terrorism "wherever it occurs, by whomsoever perpetrated, or whoever supports it," and emphasized that "our Jewish boys are also among those who are confronting terrorism at the borders."[26] A delegation of Jewish leaders, headed by Isie Maisels—who ironically had defended Nelson Mandela and many left-wing Jews during the treason trial of 1958–61—went to Israel to meet with Golda Meir and protest the proposed donation. Conveniently, the OAU never replied to Israel's small offer and Eban eventually withdrew it, quelling the anger of South Africa's government and Jewish community. By late June, only three weeks after the story broke, this last bump on the road to smoother diplomatic relations had disappeared.

Harry Hurwitz, the editor of the *Jewish Herald*, a widely read newspaper in Jewish communities throughout the country, began calling for stronger ties between Israel and South Africa immediately after the OAU spat subsided. Hurwitz was a close friend of Israeli opposition leader Menachem Begin, and a powerful and influential voice in the South African Jewish community. Like many South African Jews of Lithuanian and Eastern European origin, Hurwitz was also a follower of the militant Revisionist school of Zionism, an ideology that would later form the basis for Menachem Begin's Likud Party.

· · ·

IN THE YEARS PRIOR TO Israel's independence, the Revisionist Zionist movement had gained widespread support among Eastern European Jews. The Revisionists rejected the purely diplomatic approach to Jewish statehood advocated by the mainstream World Zionist Organization and its chairman, Chaim Weizmann, a chemistry professor at the University of Manchester who had aided the British war effort by developing vitally important explosives for the Royal Navy in 1916.[27] During World War I, he had also befriended South Africa's prime minister, Jan Smuts, writing to him regularly, and transforming him into a zealous supporter of the Zionist cause while Smuts was serving as a key adviser to David Lloyd George in the British Imperial War Cabinet.[28] Weizmann relied on Smuts as a key source of influence in Whitehall's corridors of power, often using him as an intermediary to arrange meetings with Winston Churchill, Lord Balfour, and other key British officials in the 1920s.[29]

By contrast, the Revisionists were skeptical of the British government's commitment to a Jewish national home in Palestine and advocated a more aggressive form of Jewish nationalism, as well as a more ambitious territorial claim to a Greater Israel on both sides of the Jordan River—an area including what is today the kingdom of Jordan. They were led by a fiery Russian Jewish intellectual named Vladimir (Ze'ev) Jabotinsky, whose tirades against mainstream Zionism helped lead to Weizmann's ouster as head of the WZO in 1931.[30]

Jabotinsky was born into a middle-class Jewish family in the port city of Odessa in 1880. Apart from the poetry of Pushkin and Lermontov, most of which he had memorized before high school, Jabotinsky did not care much for academics and preferred to cut class. He was a budding writer, though, and as a teenager published a Russian translation of Edgar Allan Poe's "The Raven." Soon he was contributing regular dispatches from abroad in the pages of a major Odessa newspaper.[31]

While studying and reporting in Italy as a nineteen-year-old, he fell under the influence of Italian nationalist ideas, and in later years developed a critique of liberalism colored by debates among Italian Marxists, the rise of Mussolini, and the advent of fascism. It was a harsh view of society:

> Stupid is the person who believes in his neighbour, good and loving as the neighbour may be; stupid is the person who relies on justice. Justice exists only for those whose fists and stubbornness make it possible for them to realize it. . . . Do not believe anyone, be always on guard, carry your stick always with you—this is the only way of surviving in this wolfish battle of all against all.[32]

In this Hobbesian world, Jabotinsky believed that Jews needed military-style discipline and he enthusiastically supported the Revisionist youth movement Betar, which aimed to train young Jews in self-defense as a way to instill national pride and unity. Throughout Europe, Jews were routinely caricatured as effete intellectuals or money-grubbing capitalists, but never the strong and defiant soldiers that Jabotinsky envisioned defending the Jewish homeland he dreamed of.

Jabotinsky became a leading voice of Russian journalism and published prolifically in Yiddish, German, French, Italian, English, and Hebrew as well—often under the pen name "Altalena." He was openly secular, hostile to the Orthodox Jews of Eastern Europe (who were then largely suspicious of the Zionist project), and mocked biblical injunctions to love the stranger as "childish humanism." Jabotinsky argued that for Jews to fully realize their dream of building a nation, they would have to return to the land from which they had been uprooted and fight to make it a Jewish state. In his eyes, territory played a crucial role in "shaping the national genius."[33]

Like the Afrikaner ideologues of the 1930s, Jabotinsky was deeply influenced by nineteenth-century European nationalism and its notions of a unique *volk* with its own destiny. He believed that an inherent genetic code shared by a population determined the collective identity of nations and that these immutable traits accounted for the ongoing cultural cohesion of the Jewish nation during two millennia in exile.[34] In his 1913 essay "On Race," Jabotinsky argued that each racial community had its own respective psychology "which appears in one form or another, in every member of the community despite all their individual differences."[35] He believed that these distinctive, genetically determined psychologies necessitated that each people should have its own national home—a tall order for European Zionists who did not at the time enjoy the support of any of the great powers.

Jabotinsky applied his ideas about race directly to the Arabs in Palestine. He regarded Arab culture as the "complete antithesis to European civilization, which distinguishes itself by intellectual curiosity, free investigation, dynamism and a minimum of interference of religion in everyday life."[36] Though Jabotinsky saw Arabs as culturally backward and militarily inferior, he had no illusions about the nationalist ambitions of the Arab population in Palestine. He may have belittled the legitimacy of the Arabs' claim to the biblical land of Israel, but he regarded their attachment to the land as authentic, conceding that the Arabs felt "the same instinctive jealous love of Palestine as the old Aztecs felt for ancient Mexico and the Sioux for their rolling prairies."[37]

The clash of these two national projects led him to declare that a voluntary political compromise was impossible. Instead, Jabotinsky argued, overwhelming force would be necessary to bring about Jewish statehood.[38] "History has decreed that the realization of Zionism will be accompanied by fierce Arab opposition," and only Jewish statehood imposed by force and maintained by an "iron wall" of military power could stop the Arabs from derailing the Zionist project.[39] Jabotinsky mocked Weizmann and other Labor Zionists, whom he regarded as "peace-mongers" for believing the Arabs were fools or could be bribed out of their national home,[40] and he planned instead to establish a Jewish state with an Arab minority possessing some individual rights but no political power.

During the 1930s, Jabotinsky visited South Africa three times, raising significant amounts of money for his Revisionist movement among the immigrant Jews of Johannesburg and Cape Town, who enthusiastically supported his views. One of his closest associates was the South African–born Shmuel Katz, whom Jabotinsky later sent to represent the Revisionists in London. In 1937, Jabotinsky founded a newspaper entitled the *Eleventh Hour*, which soon became the most widely read Jewish paper in the country. It advocated a Jewish-majority state on both sides of the Jordan River and helped disseminate Revisionist ideas to a South African Jewish community that was already receptive to Jabotinsky's worldview.

After Israel's independence in 1948, the South African Jewish community became the largest per capita contributor to Israel in the world; Revisionists channeled separate funds to Begin's opposition Herut Party (the precursor to Likud), much to the chagrin of the mainstream Zionists in both countries. Indeed, the bulk of Herut's funding came from South Africa, and Katz was elected to the first Knesset on the Herut list. The Jewish communities of Johannesburg and Cape Town were such a crucial support base for the cash-strapped opposition party that Begin, like Jabotinsky before him, visited the country three times to fund-raise, in 1953, 1957, and 1971.[41] The *Eleventh Hour*, since renamed the *Jewish Herald*, remained a powerful force in the Jewish community throughout the 1960s and early 1970s with Begin's friend Harry Hurwitz as its editor.

Under Hurwitz's leadership, the *Herald* was unabashedly right-wing. Its logo featured a borderless map of Israel and Jordan, leaving little doubt of its readers' territorial ambitions. In September 1971, Hurwitz penned an article in its pages contending that South Africa and Israel faced common threats and shared fundamental interests. He called upon the Israeli government to "adopt a new attitude towards South Africa and to communicate it from the top right down the line to the lesser officials" and boldly proposed upgrading diplomatic ties and conducting cabinet-level exchanges.[42]

While well circulated in the South African Jewish community, the *Herald* had never been an influential force in shaping government policy. Yet this time, Hurwitz made sure he distributed his article widely. When he ran into a Middle East desk officer from the Foreign Ministry at a dinner party, Hurwitz thrust upon him a copy of his manifesto. Within a few weeks, the article was on Prime Minister Vorster's desk.[43] And when Begin visited South Africa two months later, in December 1971, to fundraise for his party, he met with Vorster and brought his friend Hurwitz along to discuss the need for closer relations between the two countries. The editor of an obscure community newspaper now had the ear of the South African prime minister.

Israel's strategic thinking—colored by Cold War politics and new threats to its security—changed dramatically in the early 1970s. The young state had become an occupying power, the Soviet stance toward Israel had hardened, and the old Labor Zionists who were born in Eastern Europe and immigrated to Palestine in the early 1900s were giving way to a younger generation with an entirely different worldview. Though Golda Meir was leading the country in the early 1970s, younger leaders like Shimon Peres, Moshe Dayan, and Yitzhak Rabin were becoming more and more influential and battling the older generation over who would inherit the leadership of the Labor Party.

Dayan and Rabin were sabras and hardened military men. Dayan, known for the trademark black eyepatch that he donned after losing an eye during World War II, commanded Israel's forces during the 1956

Suez invasion and became a national hero when he led Israel to victory in the Six-Day War, presiding over the conquest of Jerusalem's Old City. He fancied himself an expert on Arab culture and frequently spent weekends in the occupied territories he administered, plundering antiquities from Palestinian villages.[44] Rabin was also born in pre-Israel Palestine and was in many ways groomed for Labor Party leadership from birth; Golda Meir had known him since he was a baby. He went on to distinguish himself as a commander in the battle for Jerusalem during the 1948 War of Independence and became IDF chief of staff in 1964.[45]

Shimon Peres lacked the heroic battlefield record of his colleagues, but he counted Israel's founding father as his political mentor. Rising to prominence under the tutelage of Ben-Gurion, Peres became the ultimate technocrat, eschewing ideology and embracing science and technology to solve the country's problems. Acquiring the weapons needed to defend Israel's existence was his primary objective. When the Knesset was sharply divided over an arms deal with West Germany in 1963, Peres berated his colleagues for harping on the past: "Is Israel's enemy Germany or Egypt?" he fumed, insisting that the "past must not be forgotten, but neither must the future, which is the future of our existence."[46] Peres viewed global politics strictly in terms of national interest, and when strengthening the defense establishment meant going behind the backs of his Foreign Ministry colleagues, he didn't hesitate to circumvent them.[47]

Peres developed a bitter personal rivalry with Meir during her tenure as foreign minister, from 1956 to 1963, after effectively appointing himself the unofficial foreign minister to the military establishments of Western Europe, where he cut deals with Abel Thomas and other French government officials.[48] Meir was insulted by this undermining of her authority, especially coming as it did from a junior bureaucrat who was younger than her own children.[49]

By the early 1970s, with Israel's image as a socialist bastion tarnished by occupation and Arab states attempting to lure African countries to their side with promises of cheap oil, Meir's dream of a staunchly Zionist African continent was fading. Its disappearance suited the new guard well: Peres, Dayan, and Rabin saw Israel's security as paramount and they were willing to make moral compromises in order to ensure it. It was precisely this worldview that gave birth to the alliance with South Africa.

As diplomatic and economic ties between Israel and South Africa increased, a few hints of a burgeoning secret relationship began to seep out into the open. In April 1971, the veteran *New York Times* columnist and correspondent C. L. Sulzberger wrote of a "Strange Nonalliance" between Israel and South Africa. He noted that the two countries were collaborating more and more closely on strategic matters and that South Africa's economy had enjoyed a boom as a result of the post-1967 closure of the Suez Canal.

Sulzberger also marveled at the expressions of ideological and historical affinity voiced by South African leaders. Prime Minister Vorster told him, "We view Israel's position and problems with understanding and sympathy. Like us they have to deal with terrorist infiltration across the border; and like us they have enemies bent on their destruction."[50] Sulzberger concluded that the era of icy relations was over: "For some time Israel's policy of cultivating black African nations was resented. Now this has been forgotten in the belief that Israel's stand against Russia and Russian proxies at this continent's extreme north helps prepare a position for a similar stand, if need be, when the day for such comes to the extreme South."[51] South African radio went even further, asserting that "the Jordan Valley and the Zambezi Valley are alike frontiers today of the free world."[52]

As economic cooperation increased, the two countries set up a joint venture in steel manufacturing called Iskoor, owned by the Israeli company Koor Industries and the South African Steel Corporation.[53] South Africa also began to supply Israel with most of its coal and the rough stones needed for its growing diamond-cutting industry.[54]

Diamonds had first come to Israel by way of Antwerp. The Belgian city was the heart of the world diamond-cutting industry prior to World War II, and the trade was dominated by Orthodox Jews. As the Nazis overran Belgium and occupied the Netherlands, Jews fled to Palestine. By 1945, there were six thousand Belgian diamond cutters in Israel, mostly in the northern coastal town of Netanya. De Beers—a company owned by the South African Oppenheimer family—controlled the worldwide diamond trade and during the 1950s and 1960s it shipped millions of dollars' worth of midsized diamonds to Netanya for cutting and polishing.[55] By the early 1970s, the Israeli industry employed twenty thou-

sand workers and accounted for 40 percent of the country's nonagricul-
tural exports (a share that would soon drop with the expansion of the
arms industry).[56]

All of this trade led to a public debate over whether to upgrade diplomatic ties with South Africa to the full ambassadorial level. In April
1972, Israel Radio broadcast a "mock trial" in which Israel's policy of
low-level diplomatic ties with South Africa was in the dock. The radio
trial featured the fugitive anti-apartheid activist Arthur Goldreich as wit-
ness for the defense and pro–South African Knesset member Eliezer
Shostak as the prosecution's expert, arguing that the old policy should be
scrapped in favor of fully normalized relations.

Goldreich had become a prominent architect and academic in Israel,
but he had not forgotten the struggle in his homeland or his ANC comrades languishing in jail. In his spare time, Goldreich assisted the anti-
apartheid movement however he could. Now, for the first time in nearly
a decade, his services were needed in Israel as Jerusalem abandoned its
staunch opposition to apartheid and inched closer to Pretoria.

On the stand, Shostak insisted that if Israel could maintain ties with
the Soviet Union under Stalin, there was no reason it couldn't set aside
its moral discomfort and normalize relations with South Africa. Goldreich countered by denouncing the South African government's repression and urged the Israeli government to build closer ties with South
Africa's black majority instead.[57] In the end, the on-air jury delivered its
verdict in Shostak's favor.

The South Africans were elated at the outcome. Satisfied that it would
not face the embarrassment of mass anti-apartheid protests, Pretoria
opened an official mission in Tel Aviv one month later under the leadership of Charles Fincham, a finicky and proper anglophone diplomat who
seemed ill-prepared for the brusque informality of Israeli politics. Even
the Israeli press seemed pleased; the left-leaning *Haaretz* only lamented
the fact that relations were not fully normalized at the ambassadorial
level.[58] The only opposition came from a small group called the Committee Against Apartheid, led by Goldreich.[59]

As diplomatic officials cemented their relationship with Pretoria, Israel's
Africa policy was collapsing. In the spring of 1972, after years of close

relations with Israel and despite his participation in an IDF paratrooper course, Ugandan dictator Idi Amin abruptly shut the Israeli embassy and expelled all of his Israeli advisers—along with the country's large Indian population of eighty thousand later that year. The mercurial Amin promptly switched his allegiance to Libyan leader Muammar al-Gaddafi and the Soviet Union, sending the first warning signal of Israel's impending diplomatic downfall in Africa.

After Amin's abandonment, Israel opened a diplomatic mission to Botswana, Swaziland, and Lesotho, moving to align itself with states geographically close to South Africa and within Pretoria's economic orbit. Compared to other black African states, these neighboring countries seemed a safer bet; they were not as openly hostile toward the apartheid regime due to their economic dependence on South Africa, and therefore Israeli ties with them did not alienate Pretoria in the same way that relations with Nigeria or Ghana did. Still, dissent was brewing in Israel's defense establishment. General Zvi Zur told Fincham that Israeli engagement in black Africa was a "washout" and insisted that Israel was too small and beleaguered by its own problems to "play the role of philanthropist" in an effort to win votes at the U.N.[60] According to Zur, it was only a matter of time before other African states kicked the Israelis out as Amin had done in Uganda.

Fincham saw clearly how the army's disillusionment with Meir's Africa policy could eventually work to South Africa's advantage, but it happened sooner than he expected. On the morning of September 25, 1972, he paid a routine visit to officials in the Israeli Foreign Ministry. After engaging in the usual diplomatic niceties, Fincham reiterated his oft-repeated request that Israel stop voting against South Africa at the U.N. To his great surprise, the Israelis told him that "South Africa would find the Israeli voting pattern more acceptable this time" and read aloud a Foreign Ministry directive instructing Israel's U.N. ambassador to "indulge in a minimum of rhetoric on issues touching South Africa," and "not take the initiative" in denouncing Pretoria. Most crucially, the memo instructed the Israeli delegation to abstain from voting on resolutions seeking to punish South Africa with sanctions or suspension of its U.N. membership.[61] This decisive shift was confirmed three days later when Israel abstained from a vote to grant U.N. observer status to the ANC and other black liberation movements.[62]

The Israeli press picked up on the change, but was clamoring for an even more dramatic break with black African leaders.[63] The newspaper *Yediot Ahronot* chided the Foreign Ministry for forsaking "ties with South Africa in favor of ties with a collection of states that change their names as fast as their leaders" and sacrificed their Israeli friends on the altar of Arab financial aid.[64] The most damning critique came in the form of a *Haaretz* political cartoon depicting Idi Amin and other African leaders feasting on a stew of Israeli diplomats. The menu features "Ambassador Hot Pot" and "Chopped Consul." Abba Eban's head is shown floating in a pot as Idi Amin, with his Israeli-issued rifle strapped on the back of his chair, beckons for more African leaders at the door to join the feast. In the kitchen, Gaddafi stirs the pot, Saudi king Faisal serves a plate of crude oil, and Egyptian president Anwar Sadat washes the dishes. In the background, pictures of Golda Meir dancing with an African general and Eban walking arm in arm with another adorn the walls.

The cartoon, with its caricatures of cannibalistic African leaders, was so politically incorrect that even the South Africans decried its "sheer racialism" and compared it to "the anti-Semitic cartoons of the Nazi era."[65]

Haaretz, *January 12, 1973.* CREDIT: ZE'EV FARKASH

By the time the cartoon appeared in January 1973, Israel's situation in Africa was becoming dire. Chad, Niger, and Congo-Brazzaville had broken off relations and Libya began to pressure other OAU members to sever ties. Even so, most black African leaders continued to bristle at Arab efforts to dictate their foreign policy.[66] But eventually, in May 1973, Algerian president Houari Boumedienne, a liberation hero who commanded far more respect than Gaddafi, convinced the African leaders to take sides on the Israeli-Palestinian question. Boumedienne insisted that "Africa cannot adopt one attitude toward colonialism in Southern Africa . . . and a completely different one toward Zionist colonialism in North Africa."[67] The OAU passed a resolution denouncing Israel's ongoing occupation of the Sinai Peninsula as a "threat to the security of the continent."[68] It seemed that Israel's romance with Africa was finished.

Yet Foreign Minister Abba Eban was still trying to salvage it. In September 1973, he signed an aid and cooperation agreement with Upper Volta (now Burkina Faso) and made sure the press took notice.[69] Fincham wrote to Pretoria that Eban was "bending over backwards to polish Israel's image among the African states in order to avoid further defections." The same day that the Upper Volta delegation was visiting Israel, South African information minister Connie Mulder came to town for a quick meeting with Eban. Fincham, hypersensitive and obsessed with diplomatic protocol, complained that "one could not help comparing the red-carpet treatment accorded to an Upper Volta official with that given to Dr. Mulder, who was entertained to tea in the public lobby of a hotel." To add to the offense, "Eban . . . (contrary to his usual practice) was dressed only in an open-necked, short-sleeved shirt, for all the world as though the encounter was a chance affair."[70] The easily offended Fincham was unaware that Mulder was busy laying the groundwork for agreements that would be far more strategically valuable to Israel than the U.N. vote Upper Volta could offer.

One week later, Egypt and Syria attacked Israel on Yom Kippur, the holiest day of the Jewish calendar. Along the Suez Canal, the full force of the Egyptian army—hundreds of thousands of men, 2,000 tanks, 2,300 artillery guns, and over 500 planes—bore down on 436 Israeli soldiers and 177 tanks. Most IDF army reservists were at home or in synagogue and it would take twenty-four hours before all soldiers reached their units. By the evening of October 6, 30,000 Egyptian troops had moved across the Suez Canal. On the northern front, Syrian tanks poured across the 1967 cease-fire line into the Golan Heights.[71]

South African defense minister P. W. Botha immediately declared his solidarity with Israel "in its struggle against forces supported by communistic militarism" and promised to "find ways and means to prove our goodwill towards Israel."[72] Dozens of Jewish South Africans joined the war effort and eighteen of them fell in battle, including one of the IDF's most promising young officers, twenty-three-year-old Gideon Weiler.

On the first day of the war, Syrian forces pushed into the Golan Heights and reclaimed the town of Quneitra, which Israel had conquered in 1967. IDF forces were vastly outnumbered, often ten to one, but they fought tenaciously to stave off the Syrian advance until reinforcements arrived. On the night of October 8, after three Israeli tanks went missing, Weiler crossed enemy lines to find them. Syrian missiles slammed into the turret of his tank, killing him and two other men instantly.[73]

That night in Washington, Israeli ambassador Simcha Dinitz was desperate. He called Henry Kissinger at 1:45 A.M. on October 9, insisting that the United States send weapons to Israel. The secretary of state was perplexed; just twenty-four hours earlier Dinitz had seemed optimistic and was predicting a swift Israeli victory. Kissinger went back to sleep without making any commitments. At Prime Minister Meir's urging, Dinitz woke him again at 3:00 A.M., warning that Israel could face imminent defeat without emergency military aid from Washington. Kissinger scheduled an 8:20 A.M. meeting at the White House. There, Dinitz told him that forty-nine aircraft had been shot down and that the IDF had lost almost five hundred tanks, a staggering toll for only seventy-two hours of fighting.[74] Dinitz had another card to play that morning: a threat to deploy the most powerful weapon in Israel's arsenal.

The Israelis believed that preparing their nuclear weapons for deployment would force the Soviets to rein in Egypt and Syria; more importantly, they could use the weapons as leverage with the Americans. While the Soviets resupplied the Arab armies, and Israel faced mounting losses, the Nixon administration was still refusing to resupply Israel with urgently needed arms. While neither Kissinger nor Dinitz has ever revealed the exact details of the conversation, many experts believe that Israel signaled that its nuclear weapons were ready for use on the morning of October 9 and that, rather than risk nuclear war, the United States agreed to Israel's demands.[75]

The Nixon administration abruptly reversed course and agreed to resupply Israel the next day despite opposition from Pentagon officials, who believed Israel would eventually win the war and did not want to antagonize the Arabs. President Nixon had no patience for the Pentagon's stalling, however, and told Kissinger, "Goddamn it . . . tell them to send everything that can fly." The airlift of over twenty thousand tons of weaponry began on October 12; the first shipment arrived in Israel two days later.[76]

The lesson of the airlift was not lost on the South Africans, who were building their own atomic weapons and formulating a nuclear strategy throughout the early 1970s.[77] Without an overt declaration of its nuclear weapons capability, Israel's deterrence rested, as Israeli nuclear historian Avner Cohen has written, "on the presumption—to be encouraged by sporadic rumors and leaks—that it had a nuclear weapons capability and that, under certain conditions of extreme threat, it might be compelled to use it."[78] Indeed, according to Yuval Ne'eman—the Israeli nuclear physicist who had received the news that Washington knew of Israel's bomb from Edward Teller in 1968—Golda Meir prepared some of Israel's nuclear Jericho missiles for use in mid-October 1973.[79]

In the end, bolstered by the airlift, Israel did not need to resort to overtly flexing its nuclear muscle. Remarkably, by October 15, Israeli forces had already regrouped, crossed the Suez Canal, encircled the Egyptian Third Army, and were threatening to march on Cairo. Israel made impressive gains on the northern front as well, closing to within ten miles of Damascus. Egypt and Syria pushed for a cease-fire at the U.N. and Secretary of State Henry Kissinger flew to Moscow in the wee hours of the morning on October 20 to negotiate it. By the following evening, he and his Soviet counterparts, who were negotiating on behalf of Egypt and Syria, had finalized the terms.

Back in New York, just after midnight on October 22, the U.N. Security Council approved Resolution 338, requiring that all hostilities end within twelve hours. The Israelis, hoping to push ahead with their incredibly successful counteroffensive, reacted angrily and Kissinger did little to discourage them from fighting on. With its army besieged, starving, and thirsty, Egypt began to doubt Kissinger's sincerity as a peacemaker and sensed he was giving Israel a wink and a nod. Soviet premier Leonid Brezhnev publicly denounced Israel and vowed that a continued Israeli advance would have the "gravest consequences."

Kissinger and other leading officials in Washington took this threat and other alarming intelligence reports so seriously that they placed U.S. forces on nuclear alert for the first time since the Cuban Missile Crisis of 1962—without the consent of President Nixon, who, dejected and exhausted from the Watergate scandal, was fast asleep at the time of the alert.[80] Both superpowers backed down the next day after agreeing to a new U.N. resolution ending the war and establishing an emergency force in the Sinai Peninsula. The peace institutionalized a stalemate that would not be fully resolved until the Camp David Accords in 1979.

Israel may have fended off catastrophe, but its enemies had won the propaganda war. Egypt framed the Yom Kippur War as a Zionist invasion of the African continent, and twenty more African states severed ties with Israel during the fighting.[81] The reaction in the Israeli press was swift and furious. Shlomo Shamgar, writing in *Yediot Ahronot*, denounced the Africans for "spitting into the well from which they drank only yesterday" and insisted that "the time for smiling has now come to an end. All that remains is to be sorry for the enormous ditch that we have to dig for the Israel-Africa friendship—our illusion of the sixties when many of us thought the road to Damascus and Cairo winds through Timbuctoo."[82] Meanwhile, as journalists competed to give voice to Israel's sense of betrayal, South Africa resupplied Israel with spare parts for its damaged Mirage fleet.[83] An appreciative *Haaretz* editorial asserted, "No political fastidiousness can justify the difference between one who has been revealed a friend and one who has betrayed friendship . . . in our hour of fate." The editors urged the government to establish full diplomatic ties with South Africa as soon as possible.[84]

South Africa's Jewish press wasted no time in echoing the Israeli papers' calls for closer ties between the two countries. Hurwitz's *Herald* beamed, "One of the few pleasing by-products of the Yom Kippur War is a noticeable positive change in the attitude of Israel leaders, opinion makers and a wide section of the public towards South Africa."[85] The pro-Israeli American publication *World Jewish Review* lauded the new-found cooperation, which it saw as long overdue, likening Israel's honeymoon in Africa to an adolescent romance that had been replaced by something more "solid and secure."[86]

It was not a shotgun marriage. Ever since the Six-Day War, Israel's alliances throughout black Africa had been tenuous. Calls from the Israeli right to upgrade ties with the apartheid regime, Arab pressure on African leaders to abandon the Jewish state, and clamoring among Johannesburg Jews for closer links to Jerusalem—all this strained Israel's relationships throughout Africa. Even so, with the exception of Idi Amin, Israel's network in Africa did hold fast for six years. It wasn't until after the Yom Kippur War that the African strategy so carefully crafted by Golda Meir and Abba Eban was left in tatters. Military leaders' doubts about Africa's strategic value to Israel, the IDF's clandestine military cooperation with Pretoria that had originated in France, and a widespread feeling of betrayal in the press all contributed to the unraveling of Israel's Africa policy. Most important, the rising stars of Israel's Labor Party did not see Africa through Meir's moral prism, and they were perfectly comfortable aligning themselves with the apartheid regime if it enhanced Israel's national security. As an uneasy peace settled over the Middle East in November 1973, Israeli and South African defense officials quietly began to lay the foundations for a lucrative and far-reaching alliance.[87]

. . .

AS ISRAEL BEGAN the slow process of rebuilding, the South African nuclear engineer André Buys and his colleagues were busy putting the finishing touches on a gun-type nuclear fission device, in which a projectile of highly enriched uranium is fired into a larger mass of uranium, creating the critical mass necessary for a nuclear explosion. They successfully conducted a test using nonnuclear material in May 1974 and, later that year, the South African Atomic Energy Board told Vorster that it was able to build a full-scale nuclear explosive device for peaceful use.[88] Louw Alberts, one of the country's leading nuclear scientists at the AEB, leaked to the press what this really meant: South Africa had the ability to build the bomb.[89]

Warmer diplomatic ties between Israel and South Africa made the

U.N.'s Special Committee Against Apartheid suspicious that a major realignment was taking place on the African continent, but it remained largely in the dark about the details of military cooperation between the two countries. The committee began to collect evidence that Israel was helping South Africa circumvent European boycotts of its products, from fruit to textiles, by re-exporting South African goods under Israeli labels.[90] At the time, Abdul Minty, head of the Anti-Apartheid Movement in London, was particularly concerned about a joint Israeli–South African campaign to promote the sale of their orange juice in British supermarkets, which he regarded as "just one illustration of the growing links . . . that are contributing directly to the maintenance of apartheid and white domination in South Africa."[91] In the coming years, Minty and the Special Committee Against Apartheid would have much more than orange juice to worry about.

5

BROTHERS IN ARMS

A Military Alliance Is Born

Small nations do not have a foreign policy. They have defense policy.
—Moshe Dayan[1]

MAGNUS MALAN WAS GREETED by scenes of utter devastation when he arrived in Israel in late 1973.* On the northern border with Syria, South Africa's newly appointed army chief gazed out over battlefields littered with the charred remains of tanks.[2] Israel had fought back to win the Yom Kippur War, but at a devastating cost. Over 2,500 IDF soldiers were killed in the span of less than three weeks; for a nation of just over three million people, it was the equivalent of the United States losing 175,000 men.[3] Leading generals were forced to haul the bodies of their sons from trenches and interrupt news briefings to receive news of other fallen family members. Just a month after this bitter victory, Israel lost its founding father. David Ben-Gurion suffered a massive brain hemorrhage in mid-November and died two weeks later, on December 1.

Malan was hosted in Israel by General Yonah Efrat, an old pal from his days at the American Command and General Staff College in Leavenworth, Kansas—an elite military finishing school that had trained everyone from Dwight Eisenhower and George Patton to the leaders of countless Latin American military coups.[4] It was there that Malan learned the counterinsurgency techniques that helped shape his handling of the conflict in Southern Africa. He became close friends with Efrat and his wife during their time in Kansas and they stayed in touch after graduating in 1963. Efrat, who helped conquer the Old City of Jerusalem

* Magnus Malan is distantly related to former prime minister D. F. Malan.

in 1967, was a rising star in the Israeli army by the time Malan came to Israel. "Having Yonah Efrat there made entrée to the military and most of the generals very easy," he recalls.[5] As Malan began to lay the foundation for an Israeli–South African alliance, these contacts were crucial.

The Yom Kippur War left the Israeli economy in shambles, and the arms industry was quickly becoming its biggest export earner. Washington's refusal to resupply Israel in the opening days of the war convinced the Israelis that they could not rely on their American allies for military hardware, prompting a massive expansion of the domestic arms industry. The war had cost Israel an entire year's worth of its gross national product, yet the government still managed to increase military expenditures by 40 percent in 1974.[6]

Like the economy, the Israeli political establishment was in disarray. In the spring of 1974, a postwar commission of investigation lambasted the IDF chief of staff for not giving the army sufficient warning of an imminent attack, but it largely let Defense Minister Dayan off the hook and went so far as to praise Meir for her handling of the war. The public was outraged at the commission for absolving the country's leaders; protesters flooded the streets clamoring for Dayan and Meir to step down. Weary and unable to continue, Meir resigned on April 10, unleashing a decidedly undemocratic race for the premiership that would be left to the Labor Party's leadership to decide.[7] The presumed favorite was Finance Minister Pinchas Sapir, a longtime power broker within the party. But Sapir withdrew his name early on, telling Yitzhak Rabin he'd rather jump from the tenth floor of a building than serve as prime minister. The eloquent foreign minister, Abba Eban, wanted to run but was advised that he didn't have a chance, due to his lack of strong support within the Labor Party. That left the two young lions of Labor—Shimon Peres and Yitzhak Rabin—to battle each other for the prime minister's office. Their differences were more style than substance. Peres, the technocratic whiz kid, had the support of Dayan's old loyalists, while Rabin had proven himself a consummate battlefield leader and Washington dealmaker. Eventually, after a narrow 298–254 vote in the party's central committee, Rabin emerged as prime minister.[8] Internal party politics forced him to offer Peres the job of defense minister as a consolation prize, much to his chagrin. Rabin did not consider Peres up to the job because he lacked combat experience and later wrote that the appointment was "an error I would regret."[9]

With arms production booming, Peres took charge of rebuilding Israel's battered military. Though he had never risen above the rank of sergeant in the army, Peres had extensive defense policy experience and quickly earned the respect of the top brass—if not the prime minister's.[10]

Israel's nascent arms industry brought in much needed foreign currency, helped redress the country's severe trade imbalance, and provided work for countless engineers and scientists returning from overseas with advanced degrees.[11] It also forced factories to produce in excess of the IDF's own requirements. Higher volume meant lower costs, and it was only a matter of time before the arms industry had to find export markets to offset research and development costs and absorb its surplus supply.[12] Israel's defense contractors sought to fill every niche for its own armed forces and those of other countries—all without the help of foreign suppliers. Their goal was to prove Israel's military superiority to its Arab enemies despite the advanced Soviet technology nations such as Egypt and Syria possessed.[13]

Prior to the Yom Kippur War, the arms industry had seen only a modest increase in exports, but after the war, production increased and external sales skyrocketed.[14] Total exports for all Israeli arms producers would increase nearly fifteenfold from $70 million in 1973 to nearly $1 billion in 1981.[15] The government even began to push arms exports as the key to resolving Israel's economic woes, using expanded military budgets to stimulate the economy during recessions and election campaigns.[16] Selling weapons was not the only source of income for the defense industry; Israel also modernized the aging weapons systems of foreign armies and provided training for soldiers in countries ranging from Colombia and Sri Lanka to Mobutu's Zaire.[17]

As Israel's military-industrial complex grew, an increasingly influential cadre of IDF officers who moved from the battlefield to the boardroom began to lobby for the defense industry at every opportunity.[18] These included decorated generals like Moshe Dayan and other prominent defense officials such as Shimon Peres. This "security network" wielded enormous power at the upper levels of government and industry.[19] Israel's economy was plagued by inflation during the 1970s, and the defense sector was a rare bright spot: a highly educated workforce and sophisticated technological base allowed weapons makers and dealers to flourish.

Before long, this thriving industry would have an eager new customer. The precarious security situation of the apartheid regime was deteriorating, and Pretoria wanted all the arms it could get. To the Israeli Defense Ministry, South Africa seemed the ideal customer: a developing country with a defense-conscious, right-wing government that did not have close ties to the Arab-Muslim bloc.[20] It was a perfect match.

. . .

IN LATE FEBRUARY 1974, a small book titled *Portugal and the Future* was published in Lisbon. The author, General António de Spínola, was a renowned veteran of Portugal's colonial wars in Africa, and the impact of his book would be felt across two continents. Upon returning to Portugal, the general had tried in vain to convince his government to grant autonomy to the colonies. Spínola's book argued that Portugal's colonial wars—including those in Angola and Mozambique—could never be won. It was a message that stunned and excited his countrymen. When Portuguese dictator Marcello Caetano read the book cover to cover in the wee hours of the morning just before it hit newsstands, he knew his days were numbered. Two months later, Spínola launched a coup, deposed Caetano, and took power.[21]

The Portuguese soon began to formally withdraw from Angola, paving the way for its independence. Suddenly, South Africa was faced with two Soviet-supported regimes on its doorstep in Angola and Mozambique, with a dying white supremacist regime fading fast in neighboring Rhodesia. Pretoria had long relied on these colonial "buffer states" as a front-line defense against the rest of black Africa. Now they were gone, and the successor regimes were openly hostile toward the apartheid government. To add to the complications, an independence movement was brewing in Namibia (formerly known as South-West Africa). In 1971, the International Court of Justice had ruled that South Africa's presence in Namibia—a relic of the post–World War I League of Nations mandate granting South Africa rights to the former German colony—was illegitimate and that the territory should be administered by the U.N. As the Portuguese began to loosen their grip on Angola, the

South-West Africa People's Organization (SWAPO) established bases in southern Angola to fight for Namibian independence.

South African leaders began to view themselves as under siege. P. W. Botha—once Prime Minister D. F. Malan's youthful lieutenant— had risen through the ranks of the National Party in Pretoria to become a powerful political force in his own right. In 1966, Botha—also known as *Die Groot Krokodil* (the Big Crocodile) for his ruthlessness and stubbornness—became defense minister. Botha believed that South Africa's enemies were trying to foment a Marxist revolution in the region and overthrow the white regime in Pretoria.[22] In response to what Botha considered a "total onslaught," South African defense spending increased dramatically. Beginning in the early 1970s, the budget tripled to over R1 billion by 1975 ($1.35 billion in 1975 dollars).

While Botha obsessed over the communist threat across the border, his colleagues set about purging South Africa of its black citizens. Appropriating the rhetoric of decolonization, the Vorster administration began to establish "independent, self-governing" black homelands (also known as bantustans) on some of the nation's least desirable land in an attempt to fool the West into thinking Pretoria had granted independence to blacks. Information Minister Connie Mulder, who had been in Tel Aviv meeting with Abba Eban and other high-level officials as Israel's Africa policy collapsed, declared, "If our policy is taken to its full conclusion, there will not be one black man with South African citizenship. There will then no longer be a moral obligation on our Parliament to accommodate these people politically."[23] As the bantustans gained "independence" in the early 1970s, millions of black South Africans were forcibly relocated to these rural puppet states; Mulder and his spin doctors claimed it was self-determination and billed the policy "separate development."

As news of the inhumane apartheid legislation spread, South Africa's international isolation deepened. Pretoria's fledgling arms industry dreamed of becoming self-sufficient, but in the meantime the government was desperate to buy weapons from any willing seller.[24] Money was not an obstacle; in the late 1960s South Africa had enjoyed higher growth rates than most of the industrialized world (apart from Japan), seeing its gross national product increase 5 to 10 percent per year. The price of gold skyrocketed in the wake of the mid-1970s oil crisis, rising from under $100 per ounce in 1972 to over $800 in 1980.[25] Coal prices soared and uranium prices quintupled during the same period, and South Africa rode this mineral export boom. Flush with cash, Pretoria continued to buy arms from France and other European countries, but it was becoming clear that Israel was a more reliable supplier. Whereas in the past discussions of military matters had been held quietly by junior officials in Paris, the two countries were now ready for a more formal and far-reaching arrangement. The French back channel was no longer necessary and high-level talks between the Israeli and South African defense ministers soon began.[26]

In November 1974, Shimon Peres came to Pretoria to meet secretly with South African leaders. After the trip, he wrote to his hosts thanking them for helping to establish a "vitally important" link between the two governments. Peres—who routinely denounced apartheid in public—went on to stress that "this cooperation is based not only on common interests and on the determination to resist equally our enemies, but also on the unshakeable foundations of our common hatred of injustice and our refusal to submit to it." Peres predicted that "the new links which you have helped to forge between our two countries will develop into a close identity of aspirations and interests which will turn out to be of long-standing benefit to both our countries."[27] Over the next two decades, Peres's prediction would prove to be remarkably accurate.

He met South African defense minister P. W. Botha the following year in Switzerland, and it was there that the two ministers laid the foundation for an enduring military relationship.[28] They also signed the original ISSA (Israel–South Africa) agreement, according to Dieter Gerhardt, then a high-ranking South African naval officer, who saw the thick document when it was circulated for discussion throughout the South African military establishment.[29]

Gerhardt was born in South Africa to German parents and he grew up speaking their language at home and attending a German school. His father had Nazi sympathies and was interned during World War II along with militant Afrikaner nationalists. Dieter did not share his father's radical right-wing politics and, as he grew older, he started to rebel against his parents, the Church, and everything about his austere upbringing.[30] As a teenager, he attended a high school for navy cadets. Despite his liberal politics, Dieter did what was expected of him after graduation and joined the South African Navy.

Gerhardt recalls the original ISSA agreement that Peres and Botha produced as "a very detailed layout of how they were going to cooperate on a technical level" and how each country would store spare weapons and parts for the other. It also established procedures for keeping everyone outside the defense and intelligence establishment in the dark. Indeed, the Israeli–South African relationship was quickly becoming the exclusive domain of the defense ministries and heads of state. Beginning in 1974, the two governments began holding biannual gatherings for Defense Ministry and arms industry officials. Likewise, military intelligence officials convened annually, alternating between Tel Aviv and Pretoria, to discuss strategic cooperation.[31]

In January 1975, South Africa hosted visiting Israeli Air Force officers in Pretoria. The group, chaired by military intelligence chief Hein du Toit, addressed Soviet and Chinese influence in Africa, weapons sales to African and Arab states, Soviet and Arab naval movements in the Indian Ocean, and, most importantly, "Palestinian terrorist organizations and [their] cooperation with terrorist organizations that operate in Southern Africa."[32] Du Toit's staff also passed information to Israel about a ship bound for the Red Sea port of Aqaba with a cargo of ammunition, igniters, and gunpowder destined for the Jordanian army.[33] Israeli officials were more focused on financing for new weapons systems; they saw themselves as experts on war and did not seek advice from South Africans when it came to counterinsurgency and combat. "They were more interested in what we could supply them [with] than what we could teach them," du Toit recalls, reminiscing over a shot of whiskey in his suburban Pretoria home. More than anything, the Israelis wanted access to the massive—and largely untapped—export market that South Africa represented for its defense industry.

On March 31, 1975, leading Israeli and South African defense officials met again. This time, rather than exchanging intelligence, they came to do business, discussing the sale of tanks, missile boats, and the joint development of airplane engines. Most significantly, the Israeli delegation formally offered to sell South Africa some of the nuclear-capable

Jericho missiles in its arsenal—the same missiles that were readied for use during the Yom Kippur War.[34] South Africa's leaders yearned for a nuclear deterrent—which they believed would force the West to intervene on their behalf if Pretoria were ever seriously threatened—and the Israeli proposition put that goal within reach. Excited by the offer on the table, R. F. Armstrong, chief of staff of the South African Defence Force (SADF), wrote an enthusiastic memo analyzing the benefits of nuclear weapons for South Africa's defense strategy and sent it to his boss later that day.[35] Armstrong argued that purchasing the Jericho missiles would provide South Africa with a deterrent if Russia or China became more invested in the Southern African conflict. Armstrong attached maps of the Jericho's three-hundred-mile range and praised its accuracy. He concluded by recommending that South Africa purchase the weapons despite the high cost because, he believed, a nuclear capability would make the West take Pretoria seriously.[36]

Three days later, on April 3, 1975, Peres and Botha signed a security and secrecy agreement governing all aspects of the new defense relation-

(From left) South African propaganda chief Eschel Rhoodie, Israeli prime minister Yitzhak Rabin, South African intelligence head Hendrik van den Bergh, and Israeli defense minister Shimon Peres at the Prime Minister's Residence, Jerusalem, April 11, 1975.
CREDIT: DAVID RUBINGER

ship. The agreement, known by its abbreviation SECMENT, even provided for denial of its own existence, stating: "It is hereby expressly agreed that the very existence of this Agreement . . . shall be secret and shall not be disclosed by either party."[37] The SECMENT agreement would remain in force for an indefinite period and dictated that neither party could unilaterally renounce it.[38]

Israel's offer of nuclear missiles, code-named "Chalet," came up again two months later, on June 4, when Peres and Botha held a second meeting in Zurich.[39] Now the discussion turned to warheads. Minutes from the June meeting reveal that Botha expressed interest in buying the Jerichos if they came with "the correct payload," and that "Minister Peres said that the correct payload was available in three sizes."[40] Armstrong's exclusive focus on nuclear-armed Jerichos in his March 31 memorandum makes clear that Botha was talking about nuclear warheads when he asked for "the correct payload." Eventually Botha backed out of the deal—due to its high costs and the fact that planning for nuclear weapons in South Africa was only in its early stages—and the nuclear transfer never occurred.[41] The abortive deal in 1975 was only the beginning of Israeli–South African cooperation on nuclear missile technology, however: a decade later, the two countries would begin work on a secret testing range along South Africa's rugged Indian Ocean coast.

Nuclear missiles notwithstanding, the Israelis were extremely eager to sell anything and everything to Pretoria, including weapons from third parties. South Africa conveniently used Israel as an intermediary to buy arms from countries off limits to them because of embargoes.[42] This much was clear from a 1975 Israeli Defense Ministry letter informing the South Africans that one of their orders could not be filled because the item "is at present not available and we have instructed our Purchasing Missions abroad to scan every available source."[43]

South Africa was growing desperate, and increasingly Israel was the only country willing to help it. Having returned to Downing Street in 1975 after four years of Tory rule, British prime minister Harold Wilson abrogated the Simonstown Agreement, a naval treaty that had maintained close military ties between South Africa and the United Kingdom and allowed the British Royal Navy to use the strategically positioned Simonstown Base, which guards the waters surrounding the Cape of Good Hope. France continued to sell some weapons to South Africa but pres-

sure was increasing to abide by the voluntary 1963 U.N. arms embargo—
a measure that became mandatory in 1977. At Henry Kissinger's urging,
President Gerald Ford's administration was still helping Pretoria, but this
source, too, would soon dry up in the face of mounting anti-apartheid
pressure in Congress. Only Israel remained steadfast.

In addition to selling existing weapons, the Israelis were also intent on
convincing the South Africans to join them in developing new ones.
Israel possessed a great deal of scientific expertise and advanced technology, but South Africa had more money and Pretoria was an attractive
partner for financing such projects. The defense ministers discussed
South African purchases of new Israeli tanks at $810,000 per unit, but
Peres was much more concerned about securing South African investment in his ambitious projects to build a lightweight fighter aircraft
engine and a longer-range missile code-named "Burglar." Peres had initially asked South Africa to finance 25 percent of the aircraft project and
33 percent of the missile project. In the end, however, Botha declined the
latter, claiming "we have no aggressive intentions" and hence no need
for long-range missiles.[44] Turned down by the South Africans, Israel
resorted to its strategy of the periphery, initiating a joint missile project
with Iran, code-named "Flower," that would continue until the fall of the
Shah in 1979.[45]

The minutes of the third ISSA meeting—held in Pretoria on June 30,
1975—for the first time put a concrete price tag on the Israeli–South
African relationship. At this meeting, the two countries closed a deal for
two hundred tank engines with a total value of $84 million. In addition,
they negotiated a massive ammunition purchase from the arms manufacturer IMI, Israel Military Industries, totaling over $100 million.[46] These
deals alone accounted for the bulk of Israel's total arms exports in 1975.[47]

Little did the top brass know that each line of every one of these top
secret contracts was being scrutinized in Moscow. Unbeknownst to his
colleagues, Dieter Gerhardt was not just a commodore in the South
African Navy; he had been working as a spy for the Soviet Union's military intelligence wing, the GRU, since the 1960s.

By mid-1975, Angola was descending into chaos. An agreement signed
in the Portuguese town of Alvor in January had given the feuding libera-

tion movements only nine months to prepare for a democratic election. "During five hundred years of colonial domination, the Portuguese had done nothing to prepare [Angola] for self-determination," writes former U.S. State Department official Witney Schneidman. "It was now about to be granted independence essentially overnight."[48] The Portuguese were leaving in droves and full-scale civil war seemed inevitable.

The Soviet-backed Popular Movement for the Liberation of Angola (MPLA in Portuguese) was vying for power with other armed independence movements. Holden Roberto's National Front for the Liberation of Angola (FNLA) movement and Jonas Savimbi's National Union for the Total Independence of Angola (UNITA) were receiving funds and military advice from China, Romania, and neighboring Zaire and Zambia. Despite this aid, South African intelligence predicted an MPLA victory in the absence of Western or South African intervention, and soon Pretoria began supplying weapons to the FNLA and UNITA and preparing its own forces for action. The prospect of a Soviet-backed MPLA government in Angola terrified Pretoria and threatened to disrupt the Cold War balance of power. Both Vorster and Kissinger preferred the MPLA's rivals; even if they were receiving funds from Beijing and Bucharest, an FNLA or UNITA government would not expand the Soviet sphere of influence.

Winks and nods from Washington encouraged the anti-MPLA forces and prompted Vorster to approach U.S. president Gerald Ford for arms.[49] He was not disappointed. Between July and August 1975, the United States provided $25 million in covert aid to anti-MPLA forces in Angola. As the MPLA secured large swaths of territory at the expense of the northern FNLA and southern UNITA movements, South African Defence Force units crossed the border from South African–controlled territory into Angola and occupied two major dams that were part of a South African hydroelectric project.[50]

Faced with a growing threat from the north, the top brass in Pretoria dispatched Dieter Gerhardt and two other high-ranking officials to Israel. Their assignment was to learn as much as they could from the IDF's recent battlefield experience, with a focus on strategic planning and operations. Chief of Staff Armstrong, who had enthusiastically recommended purchasing Israeli nuclear missiles a few months earlier, saw Israel as "probably the only country that would be prepared to pass on" the information about contemporary Soviet weaponry that South Africa so desperately needed.[51] Given that the South Africans were preparing to invade Angola a few weeks later, they needed all the help they could get.

The full-scale invasion of Angola began in October 1975. The SADF attacked bases belonging to SWAPO—the Namibian independence movement—in southern Angola and pushed north with their UNITA allies. Meanwhile, CIA-funded FNLA and Zairean troops closed in on Luanda. Angola was quickly becoming a major Cold War battleground and the Soviet Union and its allies were not prepared to sit out the fight.[52]

On November 4, Fidel Castro dispatched Cuban troops to Southern Africa, beginning an intervention that would last more than a decade and send upward of forty thousand Cubans to Angola, dwarfing Castro's previous forays into African liberation wars in Algeria, Zaire, and elsewhere.[53] The Cubans were airlifted with the aid of both Soviet military aircraft and chartered planes from Aeroflot.[54] Without the Cuban presence, South Africa almost certainly would have prevailed; with Castro's troops on the ground, the war took an entirely different course.

Ford administration officials did not foresee the large-scale Cuban intervention, nor did they consider the fallout in Congress and the damage to the United States' image that an apparent alliance with apartheid South Africa would cause.[55] The Congress elected in the wake of the Watergate scandal was radically antiwar and intensely suspicious of foreign interventions and covert operations.[56] The fall of Saigon and America's humiliating withdrawal from Vietnam just a few months before was fresh in the minds of legislators, and the specter of another potential Vietnam in the jungles of Africa did not appeal to them.

Senator Dick Clark (D-Iowa), chairman of the Senate Foreign Relations Subcommittee on Africa, traveled to Angola in late 1975 and met with FNLA leader Holden Roberto, UNITA leader Jonas Savimbi, and MPLA leader Agostinho Neto. Clark returned to Washington and told CIA director William Colby that he thought covert aid to the Angolans was "a bad idea"; soon afterward, he proposed an amendment barring such funds.[57] In December 1975, the Senate voted overwhelmingly to discontinue covert aid to Angola.[58] President Ford fumed that members of Congress "had lost their guts," and by early 1976 the flow of American funds to the anticommunist forces in Angola had slowed to a trickle.[59]

Politically and economically isolated, South Africa withdrew from Angola after the Clark Amendment passed and concentrated its troops in northern Namibia.[60] They felt betrayed and abandoned and never forgave the Americans.[61] As P. W. Botha complained bitterly to Parliament: "They encouraged us to act and, when we had nearly reached the climax, we were ruthlessly left in the lurch."[62]

In 1975, Israel encountered a rough patch with its patrons in Washington as well. Following the Yom Kippur War, the United States had assumed the role France had played until 1967 and began supplying the Israelis with military aid on a large scale; much of it was quickly reinjected into the U.S. economy because the Israelis used it to buy American-made weaponry.[63] But Israel remained skittish about relying too heavily on the United States, and these fears proved to be well founded.

In early 1975, talks between Israel and Egypt came to a standstill over the question of further disengagement in the Sinai Peninsula, where Israeli troops had remained deployed after the Yom Kippur War as a buffer against future Egyptian attacks. Egyptian president Anwar Sadat argued that Israeli withdrawal was necessary to prove to his people that the 1973 war effort had been as much of a victory as his government had claimed. Despite Henry Kissinger's urgings, Israel did not budge.

President Ford became impatient with Israel's intransigence and declared in March that he would "reassess" American relations with Israel, claiming the United States "would not finance a state of deadlock that would damage its interests."[64] For a period of seven months, Washington halted economic aid and significantly reduced military aid to the Israelis.[65] Ford refused to sell them F-15 fighter jets and missiles and expressed fears that a new war in the region could lead to another damaging oil embargo, such as the one imposed by the Organization of the Petroleum Exporting Countries (OPEC) in 1973. The American move caused Rabin to reconsider his excessive reliance on Washington.[66] He resented Ford for signaling to Israel's enemies that the Jewish state was still dependent on the United States and could be forced to make concessions in order to obtain arms. Meanwhile, the Soviets were rearming Arab states with no similar strings attached.[67]

Dieter Gerhardt was busy spying on Israel in the fall of 1975, and he had a front-row seat to Israeli strategic planning during the reassessment crisis. Much of what Gerhardt saw and heard during his trip confirmed that the Israelis were hedging their bets to avoid relying exclusively on the United States for their security. Increasingly, Israel viewed South Africa as a crucial pillar of its defense strategy.

While in Israel, Gerhardt was hosted by General Abrasha Tamir, who told him that the country needed "another leg to stand on" if the United States ever left it out to dry again.[68] Israel was looking for a nation that "could invest enough in our projects so that they could be pursued independently," a role that South Africa was beginning to play, thanks to Shimon Peres's work in Pretoria.[69]

With Tamir, Gerhardt visited IMI; Israel Aircraft Industries' research and development division; the Defense Ministry's central computing division; and the Lakam scientific intelligence service. Gerhardt took careful notes and sent all of them on to his minders in Moscow. Only when he was captured years later and revealed all that he knew did the Israeli security establishment realize how many of its most sensitive military secrets had been passed to the enemy.[70]

By the end of September 1975, the crisis had passed. The U.S.-Israeli relationship was now sufficiently strong to survive this kind of diplomatic tiff, and thanks to pressure from Congress and Jewish organizations in Washington the flow of American arms to Israel resumed. In the meantime, Rabin's popularity had skyrocketed. Rather than caving in to American pressure, he had hardened his negotiating position and sought alternative allies.[71] Indeed, it was precisely during the months when the Ford administration was "reassessing" its relations with Israel that Shimon Peres was busy meeting with P. W. Botha and leading South African defense officials, negotiating deals that promised to infuse the struggling Israeli economy with nearly $200 million.[72] When Israel was briefly left out in the cold by the United States, South Africa had enthusiastically welcomed it as a partner.

The reassessment crisis drove home the lesson that selling arms, or withholding them, was increasingly becoming a crucial diplomatic tool for the United States. Writing in *Foreign Affairs*, the political scientist

Andrew Pierre noted that old displays of force such as formal alliances and foreign bases were on the way out. Instead, major powers were inclined "to shore up friendly states through the provision of arms."[73] Or, as Henry Kissinger later put it more bluntly in his memoirs, "contrary to what my colleagues at Harvard have been teaching for 10 years, history shows you get much more influence with military sales than with economic aid."[74] For Israel, arms sales were becoming a form of diplomacy as well.[75] Israel sold to unfriendly states, including post-revolutionary Iran, under the pretext that these arms sales would ensure good treatment of Jews.[76] The same argument was advanced to rationalize sales to South Africa, though the true motives were far less noble. Arms sales to Pretoria were really driven by the massive revenues they generated for the Israeli government's coffers.

. . .

AS DEFENSE COOPERATION between Israel and South Africa intensified, politicians in both countries began to come out of hiding. In 1976, Prime Ministers Vorster and Rabin decided that it was time to make a public show of friendship, even if they continued to conceal the underlying reasons for their bond.

Vorster had long doubted that Israel would ever invite him to visit because of his World War II allegiances. However, as relations warmed after the Yom Kippur War, Vorster decided to test the water. It would be the first visit by a South African head of state since D. F. Malan's pilgrimage to the Holy Land in 1953. And unlike most high-profile diplomatic initiatives, the South African Foreign Ministry had virtually nothing to do with it. Vorster authorized Hendrik van den Bergh, Information Minister Connie Mulder, and Mulder's deputy, Eschel Rhoodie, to bypass the Foreign Ministry and arrange a trip to Israel to meet with defense and intelligence officials.

Rhoodie was a master operator. Tall, handsome, cosmopolitan, and refined in his tastes, he could hold forth on the relative charms of the George V and Hôtel de Crillon in Paris, wowing his less cultivated South African colleagues with his sophistication and puzzling them with his quirky habit of shunning alcohol and meat—staples of any self-respecting Afrikaner male's diet. The son of a prison warden, Rhoodie went on to earn his doctorate from the University of Pretoria. After a brief stint as a star provincial rugby player, he pursued his true passion: selling South Africa to the world. Brash, confident, and quick to get things done, he was a hit with the Israelis.[77]

While the official diplomats advocated treading cautiously, Rhoodie and van den Bergh made a strong alliance with Israel their priority.[78] Rhoodie believed that "Israel and South Africa formed the two pillars supporting the Free World's strategic interest in Africa and the Middle East." He and van den Bergh firmly believed that both countries were surrounded by hostile, implacable enemies and sought to convince the rest of the world that if either government fell, the odds were good that black African countries and Arab states would gang up against the other, endangering vital oil supplies in the Middle East and strategically valuable mineral supplies in Southern Africa. They saw the partnership as a rare example of two isolated states joining hands and striking out on their own and concluded that an Israeli–South African alliance would therefore have "great historical significance." Although the clandestine military alliance was already well established, Rhoodie and van den Bergh wanted to deliver a diplomatic victory for the embattled Vorster regime—a task that would require staging a public display of affection for South Africa.[79]

Rhoodie laid the groundwork for Vorster's visit while Peres was in Pretoria in 1974 and continued on a series of subsequent visits to Israel.[80] Vorster's secretly planned trip was news to the South African ambassador in Tel Aviv, Charles Fincham, as well as Foreign Minister Hilgard Muller and his secretary, Brand Fourie.[81] Rhoodie's shadow foreign ministry had arranged everything behind their backs. Even Ambassador Unna had surprisingly little to do with the arrangements, although he did join Vorster on the trip.[82]

As we have seen, South African prime minister Vorster began his five-day state visit by touring the Yad Vashem Holocaust memorial on April 9, 1976.[83] The South African leader faced surprisingly little opposition while visiting Israel. Apart from a few mildly critical newspaper articles, Israelis seemed to collectively shrug their shoulders.[84] *The Jerusalem Post* even praised Vorster for "recharting his country's racial and foreign pol-

South African prime minister B. J. Vorster, left, at the Wailing Wall, April 1976.
CREDIT: RAHAMIM ISRAELI

icy" and being a rare breed of leader "who has not flinched from the political perils of re-educating his people in that direction."[85]

Arthur Goldreich was one of the few anti-Vorster protesters out in the streets. As the escaped fugitive plastered telephone poles with posters featuring Vorster's name alongside swastikas, he was confronted by passersby, including one elderly man who spat on his poster. At first he thought the man might be a disgruntled South African immigrant who supported apartheid, then he got a closer look at the vandal. "He had an Auschwitz number on his arm," Goldreich recalls, still shaken three decades later by the memory of the confrontation. The Holocaust survivor lashed out at Goldreich, telling him, "We will make agreements with the devil to save Jews from persecution and to secure the future of this state." He was left speechless as the old man walked away. "That was the climate of the time," Goldreich recalls with dismay.[86]

The old man's diatribe represented the views of the young, security-minded technocrats running the country as much as those of the older generation of fearful Holocaust survivors. There was an acute sense that Israel's existence was threatened and that most of the world didn't care—and that those who did had betrayed the Jewish state in its hour of need.

By the time Vorster set foot in Jerusalem, the idealism of Israel's early years had been replaced by hardened self-interest.

After his visit to Yad Vashem, the erstwhile Nazi sympathizer was treated to an opulent dinner hosted by Prime Minister Rabin, who toasted "the ideals shared by Israel and South Africa: the hopes for justice and peaceful coexistence" during the banquet at the Knesset.[87] A beaming Vorster told the press, "Relations between South Africa and Israel have never been better."[88] The visit gave South Africa a surge of confidence and helped relieve its feelings of growing isolation.

In the South African press, the visit was billed as an event "of profound importance" and "one of the most successful diplomatic coups in [Vorster's] ten years of office." Newspapers praised the prime minister for signing agreements with Israel and delivering "a triumph for his country."[89] For the Jewish community in South Africa, it was "manna from heaven," recalls Mervyn Smith, a longtime member of the Jewish Board of Deputies.[90]

The *Zionist Record*, a mainstream Jewish paper that was usually far less vitriolic than the Revisionist *Herald*, launched into a bitter diatribe against

(From left) Israeli defense minister Shimon Peres, South African prime minister B. J. Vorster, and Israeli prime minister Yitzhak Rabin, Jerusalem, April 1976. CREDIT: RAHAMIM ISRAELI

"the moral degeneration of the UN and its virtual conversion into a tool of communism, terrorism, and moral nihilism [that] have had their inevitable consequences." Tracing Israel's new fondness for South Africa to its betrayal by other African states, the *Record* praised Jerusalem's new diplomatic pragmatism.[91]

While this reflected the mainstream view within the South African Jewish community, a minority of left-wing Jews opposed the Vorster visit. "Here was the guy who was the ultimate monster in South Africa, who had rammed through all of these appalling laws and then become prime minister, was grinding people into the ground," recalled Benjamin Pogrund, then deputy editor of the liberal *Rand Daily Mail.* "And to see *him* at Yad Vashem as an honored guest, I just thought was beyond the pale."[92]

Much to the chagrin of Pogrund and other dissenters, leaders of the South African Jewish community invited Vorster to another banquet in his honor when he returned to South Africa. As news of the event spread, more opponents began to speak out.

Dennis Diamond was executive director of the Board of Deputies at the time of Vorster's trip to Israel. Diamond was a rarity in that he came not from Cape Town or Johannesburg but from rural Natal, spoke fluent Zulu, and published poetry in Afrikaans. He was also several decades younger than most members of the organization he would be leading. Diamond had risen to that prominent position at the age of twenty-eight with the encouragement of Mendel Kaplan, a steel magnate and prominent Jewish and Zionist leader sometimes referred to as the "King of the Jews" in South Africa.

Diamond, who now lives on a quiet, tree-lined street in Jerusalem, describes the Vorster visit as "a terrible and amazing thing." Looking back, he remains torn. "We thought it was very good that relations had improved between the two. We hoped that would lead to better things, we hoped that the relationship with Israel would challenge South Africa generally to change its social structure."[93] But such hopes were unrealistic in 1976. The Israeli moralism of the 1960s was a thing of the past: far from echoing Golda Meir's denunciations of apartheid, Prime Minister Rabin was now toasting the two countries' shared ideals and Peres was speaking of "their common hatred of injustice."

On May 10, as a group of angry Jewish university students protested outside, Cape Town's Heerengracht Hotel hosted a gala affair boasting a guest list that included the entire National Party cabinet. Inside the ornate, five-star hotel, Diamond recalls sitting beside colleagues and friends who opposed the banquet. Toward the end of the evening, board chairman David Mann—an old acquaintance of Vorster's from their days as lawyers at the Johannesburg bar—rose to give a speech with the prime minister sitting directly in front of him.

He began by lauding the state's tolerance and endorsing the government's policy of separate development. "South Africa has long affirmed and lived by the political philosophy of cultural pluralism. It has jealously guarded the right of each group of the population to preserve its own traditions and to maintain its own way of life," he affirmed. It was not until the very end that Mann confronted Vorster:

> I believe that there is a wide consensus today that attitudes and practices, the heritage of the past, bearing upon the relations between our various racial groups are no longer acceptable. . . . [We] must move away as quickly and effectively as is practicable from discrimination based on race or colour, and that we must accord to every man and woman respect, and human dignity and the opportunity to develop to their fullest potential.[94]

Diamond was pleased. "Of course there would be those who'd say it could've been more. I think it was perfectly pitched. . . . It was a speech correct for its time."[95] Mendel Kaplan, King of South Africa's Jews, agrees. "Who else stood up and said that?" he asks. "Not the leader of the Anglicans. Maybe we didn't do enough. But the Board of Deputies was not elected to go in the streets and lead a street movement."[96]

Others were not so placated. Dennis Davis, who is now a judge on Cape Town's High Court and a well-known television personality, remembers protesting outside the banquet that night. "It was hardly a rebuke," says Davis. "It was the minimum that could be done to show some sense of commitment to Jewish ethics," and to acknowledge the "controversy that was brewing both outside the hotel and generally that Vorster the Nazi had been invited." At the time, Davis was editor of the Jewish student newspaper, *Strike*, at the University of Cape Town. In its pages, he lashed out at the Jewish community's leaders: "Mr. Vorster is . . . leader of a political party whose policies, based so firmly on race, are the antithesis of the very body and soul of Jewish ethics," he wrote.

"We cannot surely honour and pay homage to the leading proponent of such policies even if he has pulled off a diplomatic coup with Israel."[97]

Davis saw Mann's speech as pathetic. The board had heralded Vorster as a hero and then lightly rapped him on the knuckles.[98] Board dissident Mervyn Smith was even more adamant: "Here he was standing before *Der Führer*; there were a hundred students or a thousand students saying apartheid is evil [outside]. . . . In Vorster's life it was a total nonevent," says Smith. "The crying shame was that the board hosted him."[99]

The Vorster visit may have been hailed as a public relations coup in South Africa, but its primary purpose remained largely obscured. The media in both countries stressed that the agreements signed were limited to trade, investment, and peaceful scientific and industrial cooperation.[100] Only the *Cape Times* hinted briefly at the true reason for the visit, reporting Vorster's stop at the headquarters of Israel Aircraft Industries, where he saw Kfir fighter jets on the assembly line.[101]

Indeed, much of Vorster's time in Israel was spent shopping for weapons. To facilitate this, Admiral Binyamin Telem—the commander of Israel's navy during the Yom Kippur War—joined Ambassador Unna in showing the South African prime minister around Israel. Due in part to the $100 million ammunition contract signed the previous year, Israel's defense industry now had excellent ties with South Africa and Vorster's visit helped seal a much bigger deal, totaling more than $700 million, Telem recalls.[102]

As Vorster casually visited Israeli arms manufacturers and journalists began to notice, pro-Israel organizations abroad sought to convince the public that nothing unseemly was happening. Moshe Decter of the American Jewish Congress insisted in a shrill *New York Times* column that "Israel's small arms trade" with Pretoria was "dwarfed into insignificance by the South African arms traffic of other countries," pointing fingers at France, Britain, and others. He decried the focus on Israel as evidence of "rank cynicism, rampant hypocrisy, and anti-Semitic prejudice."[103]

Soon after, in late 1976, Telem was sent to South Africa at the personal request of Defense Minister Shimon Peres. The navy was the only element of the IDF to emerge from the Yom Kippur War relatively unscathed, owing largely to the tremendous success of its Reshef missile boats, which, along with the ships smuggled out of Cherbourg, outperformed their Soviet-made counterparts.[104] As the commander of the navy and because one of the first major sales to Pretoria was the 450-ton Reshef attack craft, Telem was a natural choice for the job.[105] Peres even managed to convince Golda Meir, who had stubbornly resisted closer relations with South Africa for over a decade, that Telem's posting to Pretoria was necessary. Meir, no longer at the country's helm, was scarred by the Yom Kippur fiasco. "He went to Golda and she was not very happy with it," recalls Telem. "I think she finally gave in once she realized . . . we needed this relationship economically."[106]

. . .

TELEM HAD BEEN DISPATCHED to a country in flames. A few months before his arrival, black schoolchildren in the sprawling Johannesburg township of Soweto had organized a demonstration against mandatory instruction in Afrikaans—a language most of them did not understand and many of their teachers could not even speak. Early in the morning, thousands of students in school uniforms poured into the streets, converging at a high school in the Orlando section of the township. The security forces were caught off guard and released police dogs into the crowd, followed by tear gas and live ammunition. Students reacted by pelting police with stones and officers fired on them as they fled, gunning down dozens. A single image—showing a weeping man fleeing the police with the bloody, limp, uniformed body of twelve-year-old Hector Pieterson in his arms alongside the dead boy's screaming sister—was splashed across the front pages of newspapers worldwide and came to symbolize the brutality of the South African government. Urban unrest spread quickly, prompting further police violence throughout the country and the greatest outpouring of international outrage that Pretoria had ever seen. The riots lasted for months and the death toll exceeded five hundred, dwarfing the sixty-nine killed in the Sharpeville massacre of 1960.

As many Western countries began to formally distance themselves from the apartheid regime, Israel Shipyards signed a contract to build six Reshef missile boats for South Africa and a licensing agreement was concluded for the remainder to be built in Durban. It was a boon for both sides. "They were able to develop their own military industries by using our know-how and our expertise which we sold sometimes, I thought, too easily," says Telem. "But we did because we were very much in need of this relationship."[107]

Naval officers and engineers began streaming back and forth between Israel and South Africa and Rabin gave the relationship "the highest priority," insisting that it take place under the table in order to maintain deniability and prevent negative publicity. "Nothing was official," recalls Telem. He therefore performed the duties of a military attaché but on paper held the title "counselor," as his predecessor had, in order to avoid any attention and maintain the secrecy of the Defense Ministry's mission in Pretoria.[108]

At the Israeli embassy in Pretoria, Telem and Ambassador Unna got along well, maintaining an understanding to stay out of each other's business. Following the model Peres established during the 1950s in France, the Defense Ministry and its export office all but eclipsed career diplomats when it came to conducting foreign relations in South Africa, where arms sales were crucial.[109]

Israel was not only building and modernizing weapons; it was also offering formal advice to the South African military. In 1976, the Israeli Defense Ministry sent Colonel Amos Baram as a special adviser to the chief of the SADF. Baram viewed the situation as one of friendly cooperation and was happy to advise the South Africans. His attitude was, "We have a common interest—security problems. Not just borders, internal problems too." The challenge was not simply fighting communist troops in Angola, but helping South Africa maintain domestic security, according to Baram. "If you know how to defend yourself against an enemy outside the borders you know how to deal [with him] within your borders."

Baram's first recommendation was to extend the term of military service in South Africa to a compulsory two years. He also attempted to shift the SADF's doctrine away from the British system toward the Israeli one, incorporate a full year of training for new soldiers instead of three months, and to reform the staff command school.[110] During Baram's two years in South Africa, the period of compulsory service for white males—the only soldiers for whom conscription was required—did in fact increase to two years. More and more reservists were called up to serve under a new active-reserve duty requirement that lasted eight years, eventually leading to widespread protests against conscription.[111]

Baram and Telem were often invited to join the army chief, General

Constand Viljoen, on trips to the front lines. Viljoen, a serious, intelligent farmer-turned-soldier, was the archetypal military man. He was born into an aristocratic rural Afrikaner family whose lineage went back to the seventeenth century and he had risen quickly through the ranks to become chief of the army, and eventually head of the SADF. His identical twin brother, Braam Viljoen, had gone in the opposite direction, studying theology. When his moral opposition to apartheid alienated him from the Dutch Reformed Church, he had joined forces with the black political and religious leaders that his brother's men sought to silence and defeat. As Braam immersed himself in the liberation theology of the South African Council of Churches—considered a terrorist front by the government—his brother, Constand, was spearheading South Africa's invasion of Angola and managing its aftermath.[112]

In the wake of South Africa's failed intervention, General Viljoen was eager to learn all he could from the Israelis. "We flew with his official plane a lot to Angola," recalls Telem. "He used to take us along and ask our opinion on everything."[113] The two Israelis were also taken on a security-oriented helicopter tour of the Mozambican border and afterward treated to a stay, with their wives, in South Africa's premier safari spot—the Kruger National Park.[114]

Telem insists that he had no qualms about selling Israeli arms to South Africa, especially the Reshef boats, which he did not envision being used against South African blacks. But he was tremendously unsettled by the country's racism. When Telem discovered that the German embassy paid its black workers ten times more than the Israeli embassy, he was shocked by the disparity and demanded authorization from his superiors to pay the same wages as the Germans—a salary that would put black workers on par with the Jewish South African and Israeli employees at the office. His superiors at the Defense Ministry—generally immune to moral arguments when it came to arms sales—agreed with Telem about workers' rights, telling him that they refused to pay "apartheid wages." Telem was able to give his chauffeur such a massive raise that the driver began building himself a new house, but draconian apartheid laws that controlled blacks' movements and banned interracial relationships continued to grate on Telem's conscience.

Nevertheless, he continued his job, which required him to interact continuously with leading SADF and Armscor officials. "We had an excellent understanding on the professional side, I would not say the same on the political side," Telem recounts. "I had to go along with it, but the longer I stayed in South Africa, the more it became difficult for me to cooperate with them."[115]

The turning point came when the head of Armscor, Piet Marais, invited Telem and his wife to spend a long weekend at his farm in the countryside. Marais was a Boer to the bone. With a farmer's rough hands and reeking of tobacco, he spoke English with a harsh Afrikaans accent.[116] At his farm, this pipe-smoking proponent of white supremacy set out to convince Telem of apartheid's virtues. "He tried to persuade me that our way of trying to solve the Israeli problem [with] Palestinians is the best way and we should carry on with it even though we were an occupying, we still are, an occupying entity," says Telem. Marais attempted to persuade him that Israel "should further apartheid as [South Africans] do . . . in the name of the God of Israel." It was too much for Telem. Soon afterward, he asked to be transferred home.[117]

By contrast, Telem's good friend Colonel Baram had no such reservations. Baram never raised his voice against apartheid. "How could I? I was advising them on how to defend it," he says bluntly. Those who don't like it, says Baram, should "stay at home." The dramatically different perspectives of Telem and Baram, who remain friends to this day, are closely related to their domestic politics in Israel now. While Telem speaks regretfully of the ongoing occupation, Baram describes Israel's Arab citizens as "a cancer" and advocates gerrymandering electoral districts to prevent any Arab majorities capable of electing Arab members to the Knesset.[118]

Unlike Telem, Ambassador Unna did not let moral qualms stop him from carrying on with his work. When he returned as full ambassador in 1974, Unna was already acquainted with many South African politicians from his first stint in the country as consul-general. He and the South African intelligence chief, Hendrik van den Bergh, had become even closer in the wake of a hostage crisis in downtown Johannesburg.

On the morning of April 28, 1975, an employee of the Israeli consulate crept into the downtown Johannesburg building housing the consular offices and shot the mission's chief security officer. The shooter took the entire office staff hostage, claiming it was a security exercise. Initially, the South African authorities thought they were dealing with terrorists. They soon discovered that the consulate had been seized by a mentally unstable Jewish South African named David Protter, who had once served in the Israeli army and had been hired as a security guard despite warnings from high-level officials about his psychological problems. Protter and his younger brother used the consulate's formidable arsenal to fire at police and snipers through the windows, injuring more than forty people caught in the crossfire. It was Johannesburg's first full-scale hostage crisis, and crowds of onlookers camped out overnight with blankets and picnic baskets to watch the spectacle unfold. Van den Bergh took control of the scene, commandeering the phones of a nearby shopkeeper to keep an emergency line open for instructions from Prime Minister Rabin in Jerusalem.[119] Protter finally surrendered the next morning, descending in an elevator behind a human shield of hostages.[120]

The Fox Street crisis cemented Unna's friendship with van den Bergh and they began to see each other socially. At the time, Unna and his wife were living in the luxurious twin towers on the slope of Table Mountain in Cape Town—South Africa's legislative capital during parliamentary sessions. They enjoyed a panoramic vista from their balcony, overlooking the city, the harbor, and the steep face of the mountain.[121] Unna found van den Bergh surprisingly forthcoming with political gossip after he'd had a few drinks. And although his habit of leaning over the railing to enjoy the view while sipping vodka made Unna extremely nervous, van den Bergh's visits proved to be an invaluable asset for the Israeli embassy.

Yet ironically, despite his close friendship with the man many regarded as the power behind Vorster's throne, Unna was arguably the most outspoken critic of apartheid in the diplomatic community. Television had only reached South Africa in early 1976, and Unna was invited by the South African Broadcasting Corporation to be the first foreign guest interviewed live on screen. He conducted the interview in Afrikaans, explaining that Jews could not accept apartheid because it was humiliating and discriminatory. The next morning, Unna went to see Information Minister Connie Mulder, who congratulated him on his interview. Unna was shocked. He asked Mulder if he had not heard his criticism of apartheid. According to Unna's account, Mulder told him, " 'If the ambassador of Israel appears on our T.V. and speaks in our language, Afrikaans, he can be as critical as he likes, we love to hear him.' "[122]

This was not the only instance of Unna spitting in the face of his hosts. A few years later, he caused a stir by driving his diplomatic car into a black township during a police raid. "The Africans were being hunted like stray dogs, and the look in their faces as they were trying to hide was that of frightened and desperate fugitives," Unna later wrote in his unpublished autobiography.[123] He told the officer in charge that such raids were self-defeating because the "illegal Africans" found to be violating apartheid laws by living in the city without passes simply returned after being expelled to the bantustans. Later that day, he gave a lecture at Stellenbosch University, the Harvard of Afrikanerdom, and told an audience of prominent NP members that the township raid made him "sick"—an outburst that earned him praise from liberal English-language newspapers. Unna caused yet another uproar when he refused to attend a play about the life of Golda Meir because blacks were not allowed in the theater. The entire Pretoria diplomatic corps eventually joined him in boycotting it.[124]

Unna's criticism of apartheid and his closeness with the South African regime's leading figures presents an intriguing paradox. Unlike other Israelis who hypocritically paid lip service to the anti-apartheid movement, Unna followed through with concrete actions. While most diplomats resist the impulse to criticize a host nation's internal policies lest it damage relations, Unna took every opportunity to lambaste apartheid. Despite these outbursts, he was revered by the white minority government more than any other Israeli ambassador in history. Unna claims that "we could get away with anything . . . even our criticism was accepted because it came from friends." Proudly, he adds, "They regarded me personally as an architect of the good relations between Israel and South Africa."[125] This is not boasting; General Magnus Malan, who headed the SADF during Unna's tenure, agrees.

Sipping coffee in the basement of a shopping mall outside Pretoria, the retired general brightened at the mention of Unna: "The relations between South Africa and Israel, I give him the credit for it. He was very good, a hell of a bright chap." And Unna's denunciations of apartheid did not bother him. "He even was prepared to defend that on the SABC and I thought that was fantastic," Malan exclaims. "And he did it in

Afrikaans!"[126] The fact that Unna was not meeting with black political leaders made his personal crusade even less threatening.

Unna's trenchant moral criticisms were heartfelt and genuine but they did not reflect a change in state policy. Malan and other key South African leaders were savvy enough to realize that allowing Unna to criticize them served their interests so long as he didn't seek to undermine the alliance. Condoning and even encouraging Unna's televised outbursts against apartheid made South Africa seem more democratic and tolerant of dissent than it actually was, convinced Israelis of the dubious proposition that they could remain morally pure while selling arms to Pretoria, and permitted the alliance to proceed without a hitch. Only the straitlaced secretary of foreign affairs, Brand Fourie, protested Unna's boycott of the Golda Meir play, for which the ambassador refused to apologize.

While Unna abhorred apartheid, he remains unapologetic about his role in furthering ties between Israel and South Africa. He retired long ago and now lives with his wife and cats in a modest condominium in a small subdivision near Netanya built by South African immigrants to Israel. Many of his neighbors have South African ties. As he argues, "We were isolated and here was an important big country developing relations with Israel." Turning down a far-reaching partnership with clear economic benefits—especially when Israel had few other options—would have been anathema to the new foreign policy thinking emanating from Jerusalem in the mid-1970s. Unna maintains that the relationship was "important from a strategic point of view and from a commercial point of view and from a Jewish point of view." The latter, of course, was a less pressing concern. Unna admits, "We structured our whole relationship with South Africa through our trade and our defense relationship."[127]

Unna had learned a valuable lesson in a United Nations bathroom twenty years earlier: vicious criticism of a government on the public stage need not impede close personal relationships with its representatives behind the scenes. It was another instance of the Janus face Israel presented to the world.

The years that Telem, Baram, and Unna spent in South Africa helped to cement the Israeli–South African alliance and bring leading military figures into regular, close contact affording one another an insider's view of the security operations being carried out against Israel and South Africa's enemies.

South Africa's army chief, Constand Viljoen, visited Israel's occupied territories in the spring of 1977, marveling at the Israeli checkpoint system and the searches of Arabs conducted by soldiers at each road-block.[128] "The thoroughness with which Israel conducts this examination is astonishing. At the quickest, it takes individual Arabs that come through there about one and a half hours. When the traffic is heavy, it takes from four to five hours," he observed admiringly.[129] In addition to studying how Israel controlled the movement of Palestinians, the SADF was also interested in Israel's battlefield training methods and sent twenty-two members of the army to Israel to study the IDF's combat school with the goal of establishing a replica in South Africa.[130]

Business was thriving, too. The Armscor subsidiary Naschem sent three representatives to Israel Military Industries to study the manufacturing of bombs, while the South African Air Force flew a team to Israel to work on plans for a new, heavily fortified base.[131] Armscor and IMI signed two large contracts for bombs and ammunition and tested them together, paving the way for even closer cooperation between the two countries.[132]

That same month, the South African government entered into final negotiations for yet another massive ammunition contract with IMI, known as Project Decor. After a visit to Israel in late July 1977, Armscor officials reported that they had bargained the contract down from $450 million to $370 million—an amount fifteen times greater than the published International Monetary Fund figure that defenders of Israel used to downplay the extent of Israeli exports to South Africa (the IMF data excluded arms sales).[133] It was the biggest infusion of cash ever from South Africa and a major boost to the Israeli economy. During their visit, the Armscor representatives met Defense Ministry director-general Pinchas Zussman, a university professor turned weapons czar, who greatly impressed them. They reported proudly to Pretoria that "he views the contract as more than a transaction between IMI and Armscor; indeed, he views it as a transaction between two governments, with all that this entails."[134]

By now, the Ford administration, which had aided South Africa's adventure in Angola until Congress shut it down, was out of office. Jimmy Carter had been president for six months when Zussman and the South

Africans negotiated the ammunition contract and Washington's foreign policy had lurched to the left, placing a new emphasis on human rights and nonproliferation. It wasn't long before the White House began to show signs of a tougher stance toward both Israel and South Africa, canceling the sale of five-hundred-pound concussion bombs to Israel and publicly denouncing apartheid soon after Carter entered office. It was not an auspicious time for secret arms deals between international pariahs, and the situation became even more perilous in November 1977, when the U.N. passed a mandatory arms embargo against South Africa.[135]

Reacting to news of the embargo, Moshe Dayan, who had become Israel's foreign minister after his embarrassing fall from grace after the Yom Kippur War, misleadingly told Israeli Radio, "Firstly, whatever the Security Council decides, or has decided, Israel will act accordingly . . . we have no hidden under-the-table relations with the South African government." The South African ambassador in Tel Aviv worried that Dayan might actually honor his word, but privately hoped that Israel would go on "publicly professing to uphold the embargo and, at the same time . . . continuing for as long as possible, covertly, to disregard it."[136]

At Armscor there was no such uncertainty. South African defense officials knew the alliance they had forged was impressive and unique. While covert arms sales occurred in many places during the 1970s, contracts of this magnitude—negotiated at the ministerial level and approved at the highest levels of government at a time of intense international scrutiny—were exceptional. As Zussman had told them, "the size of the recent contract . . . had made a big impression on the whole cabinet."[137] Indeed, by signing it, Israel took a huge political risk and reaped an even greater economic windfall. Three years after Peres and Botha had initiated the alliance, it elevated the Israeli–South African relationship to a whole new level.

The captains of South Africa's arms industry were well aware that the nearly $400 million contract they had just signed would provide a major stimulus to Israel's sagging economy and help the country "to become more independent of the United States through the extension of their own production capacity."[138] As General Tamir had told the visiting spy Dieter Gerhardt back in 1975, Israel needed another leg to stand on. Professor Zussman had found one.

6

A COMMON LOT

Likud, Apartheid, and the Quest for Minority Survival

And it has further been taught: One should not sell [idolaters] either weapons or accessories of weapons, nor should one grind any weapon for them.

—Babylonian Talmud, Tractate Avodah Zarah, 15b

IN MAY 1977, Menachem Begin's Likud Party stunned the Israeli political establishment by deposing the Labor Party dynasty—dominated by Eastern European Ashkenazi Jews—that had ruled Israel since independence. Begin was from Eastern Europe, too, but much of his support came from the disillusioned masses of immigrant Jews from North Africa and the Arab world who were fed up with the Ashkenazi elite and resented being treated as second-class citizens. Likud took 33 percent of the overall vote and formed a right-wing coalition that excluded the Labor Party from the government for the first time in the nation's history. As opposition leader, Begin had for many years been a proponent of closer and more overt Israeli–South African ties.[1] By 1977, Pretoria had already become Israel's single largest customer for arms, and exports only increased after Begin took office.

Begin's government was more than happy to violate the U.N. embargo against South Africa. Just a week after the international ban on arms sales to Pretoria was approved, a South African army team arrived in Israel to shop for antitank weapons.[2] Begin's brand of neo-Revisionist Zionism emphasized military might, national survival, and the denial of political rights to the enemy. Likud's platform may have appealed to religious settlers, but the party's leaders had little patience for ancient Talmudic dictates forbidding arms sales to oppressive foreigners.

Likud ideology fit perfectly with the worldview of South Africa's white rulers, who saw force as the only method for holding on to power and steadfastly refused to grant equal rights to the black majority for fear that it would imperil their survival. As Begin expanded settlements and Arab resistance to the occupation intensified, similar views toward the Palestinians became popular.

Menachem Begin had staked his claim to leadership of the Zionist right four decades earlier at a 1938 convention in Warsaw. There, Begin confronted his mentor, Vladimir Jabotinsky, by openly calling for armed revolt against the British Mandate government, which had controlled Palestine since the end of World War I and heavily restricted the number of Jewish immigrants allowed to enter the territory. "We have had enough of renunciation," Begin declared to a raucous crowd, "we want to fight—to die or to win."[3] His speech called for replacing political Zionism with military Zionism—which would eventually be led by an armed underground, the Irgun Tzvai Leumi (National Military Organization).[4] Jabotinsky interrupted Begin numerous times during the speech and denounced the youthful anti-British rebellion, telling Begin and his young followers to " 'go ahead and commit suicide.' "[5] But Jabotinsky would soon depart from the Zionist political scene; with his death in 1940, Begin emerged as his more radical heir, moving beyond Revisionism to craft a more militant form of Zionism.

Some of Begin's peers were even more extreme. Abba Achimeir, one of Begin's right-wing contemporaries, was a self-declared fascist sympathizer and an admirer of the cult of personality surrounding Italian and German leaders. Achimeir opposed liberal democracy and defended politically motivated assassination.[6] His maximalist brand of Revisionist Zionism envisioned the Messiah arriving in the Promised Land not riding a donkey but driving a tank.[7]

When Jabotinsky had come to Palestine in 1928, Achimeir welcomed him with the declaration "I am not a democrat, and it is my firm conviction that the only kind of government is an active minority ruling a passive majority,"[8] a view fully in line with the thinking of Afrikaner nationalists in South Africa at the time. The unifying principle among Jabotinsky's more radical followers was a belief in the use of force and the glorification of violence as a means of national liberation.

By the time World War II broke out, a majority of right-wing Zionists, especially the maximalists, had abandoned Jabotinsky's teachings when it came to the question of resisting British rule in Palestine. Before his death Jabotinsky had written to the commander of the Irgun, stressing the need to cooperate with the British against Nazism, but the far right saw the situation differently. Avraham Stern and other Irgun leaders were planning to train fighters in Poland, smuggle Polish surplus arms into Palestine, and then invade it from the sea.

In May 1939, the British government imposed new limits on Jewish immigration to Palestine—permitting only ten thousand Jews per year, infuriating Stern and his anti-British followers. Contrary to the wishes of Jabotinsky and the Irgun's jailed commander, David Raziel, the Irgun began attacking both the British and the Arabs in June.[9] Stern's men dismissed Jabotinsky's and Raziel's cooperation with the Allies and argued that the British were morally equivalent to the Nazis. And thus the Zionist right split again.

Stern seceded from the Irgun in 1940 and created Lohamei Herut Yisrael (Fighters for the Freedom of Israel), known by the Hebrew acronym Lehi.[10] While several more moderate right-wingers joined the British army to fight Hitler, Stern proposed an agreement with Italy and met with Nazi officials in Beirut to discuss a pact that would enable them to attain the shared objective of forcing the British from Palestine. Stern went so far as to suggest that his plan would help the Nazis cleanse Germany of its Jews by establishing a nationalist, totalitarian Jewish state bound to the German Reich by a treaty. He despised anything that smacked of Zionist kowtowing to the West, especially to "perfidious Albion." For Stern and the men of Lehi, political alliances were strictly utilitarian; any allies were welcomed, no matter how unsavory.[11]

Lehi was also unabashedly racist toward Arabs. Their publications described Jews as a master race and Arabs as a slave race.[12] The members of Lehi thought Jabotinsky was foolish to assume the Arabs would submit to Jewish rule after a show of force. Stern's men considered this a dangerously utopian vision, and they advocated a mandatory expulsion of all Arabs in Palestine and Transjordan instead.[13]

In addition to courting Axis powers, Lehi carried out a series of terrorist attacks on the mandate government's representatives, killing dozens of British police officers and soldiers. The British retaliated with arrests, hangings, and targeted assassinations; they killed Stern in 1942, and with his death the terrorist torch was passed to younger leaders including future Israeli prime minister Yitzhak Shamir. Begin became the Irgun's commander in late 1943, and by February 1944, the Irgun had followed Lehi's lead and declared war against Great Britain. When an Irgun soldier was flogged by British troops, Begin wrote defiantly: "Zion is not exile . . . Jews are not Zulus. You will not whip Jews in their homeland."[14]

In November 1944, Lehi agents assassinated Lord Moyne, a close friend of British prime minister Winston Churchill.[15] For mainstream Zionist leaders, such as Chaim Weizmann and David Ben-Gurion, Moyne's death was a political disaster. As these two men struggled to win international support for a Jewish state and help the British defeat Hitler in Europe, their Revisionist-inspired colleagues were killing British troops in Palestine, an approach that risked turning key leaders, such as Churchill, against the Zionist project.

"If our dreams for Zionism are to end in the smoke of assassins' pistols, and our labours for its future to produce only a new set of gangsters worthy of Nazi Germany," Churchill declared upon hearing of his friend's death, "many like myself will have to reconsider the position we maintained so consistently and so long."[16] In the eyes of Ben-Gurion and Weizmann, the extremist right-wing groups were a political liability and a threat to Jewish statehood. And so, in late 1944, Ben-Gurion's forces, known as the Haganah, went after Lehi and the Irgun.[17]

The crackdown was known as the Hunting Season and it forced Irgun and Lehi leaders underground and into exile, and those who were captured to British prison camps in Eritrea. Even so, in 1946, the Irgun managed to carry out its most dramatic act yet by bombing the King David Hotel, home to British government offices at the time—killing ninety-one people and injuring nearly fifty more. The following year, the Irgun liberated its prisoners from the Acre prison, a crusader fortress so secure that not even Napoleon's armies had been able to breach its walls.[18]

Facing violent attacks from the Irgun and Lehi and mounting international sympathy for the Zionist movement, the British finally announced their intent to withdraw from Palestine in early 1947. In November of that year, the U.N. proposed a partition plan granting the Jews 56 percent of Mandate Palestine between the Jordan River and the Mediterranean Sea. Ben-Gurion and other Labor Zionist leaders accepted it, an act seen as high treason by the right. To Begin and his colleagues, who believed in a Greater Israel that included all of the kingdom of Jordan, acceptance of partition was the ultimate proof that the Labor Zionist leadership was selling out the true interests of the Jewish people.[19]

Ben-Gurion declared Israel's statehood on May 14, 1948. The Haganah became the Israel Defense Forces, the IDF, and within twenty-four hours of independence, it found itself facing five invading Arab armies. Yet even as war raged, tensions still remained between Ben-Gurion's IDF and the more militant members of Lehi and the Irgun.

On June 20, 1948, a ship laden with smuggled arms approached the shores of the newly independent state of Israel. The vessel bore Jabotinsky's old pen name, *Altalena*. Its cargo, loaded in France, was destined for the Irgun. As the ship approached Tel Aviv, Begin and his commanders were bickering with Ben-Gurion's newly established government about the destination of the weapons on board and the integration of Irgun soldiers into the newly formed IDF. The prime minister feared that independent armed groups not under his control could pose a threat to the stability of the newborn state. Eventually, on June 21, Ben-Gurion issued an ultimatum to the ship's commander, Eliahu Lankin, ordering him to surrender immediately.[20] Begin and Lankin did not respond in time, and when the crew began unloading the cargo of weapons on the evening of June 22, the IDF opened fire on the ship.[21] By nightfall, the *Altalena* was in flames. More than a dozen Irgun soldiers were killed and others, including Lankin, struggled to shore, dodging bullets amid the waves.[22]

Menachem Begin preserved this political rivalry as the leader of the opposition during the 1950s and 1960s. In addition to deep policy differences regarding Labor Zionism's socialist principles, Begin had an additional rhetorical weapon: the memory of the *Altalena* and the charge of fratricide. During these years of Labor Party dominance, historians generally dismissed Revisionist Zionism as an insignificant ideological blip. When Begin pulled off his shocking upset victory in the 1977 Israeli elections, Jabotinsky's ideas—and those of his more militant followers—suddenly became the cornerstone of the Israeli government's agenda.[23]

Begin carried forward Jabotinsky's worldview—which painted the outside world as hostile to Jews, glorified military might as an instrument of foreign policy, and advocated a Greater Israel—and transformed it into a right-wing political platform defined by hard-nosed realism in international relations and zealous encouragement of settlements in the West Bank and Gaza.[24]

With Begin at the helm, the Israeli–South African relationship intensified. He and his colleagues were not racists but, like their mentor, Jabotinsky, they were ethnic nationalists. They were willing to tolerate xenophobic and racist ideas—and even occasional anti-Semitism—if those ideas served broader nationalist aims that they admired.[25] This ethnonationalist ideology allowed Begin and other Likud leaders to stomach racist apartheid policies because these were part of a larger nationalist project designed to protect a minority group that believed its survival was threatened.

The rightward shift in public opinion that brought Begin to power in 1977 sidelined the Labor Zionist old guard and entrenched the security establishment's domination of foreign policy.[26] Although it was the Labor Party that launched the alliance with South Africa for material and strategic reasons in the early 1970s, the confluence of interests and similar ideologies pushed the two countries into a much more intimate relationship after 1977. Even Labor stalwarts like David Hacohen—a diplomat and high-ranking party official—were abandoning the legacy of Ben-Gurion and Meir and beginning to change their tune on South Africa after Begin came to power. Hacohen declared in *The Jerusalem Post* that granting equal rights to blacks "would mean the end of the white minority," and warned that sanctions and other "extremist propaganda aimed at toppling the Republic of South Africa" would lead to "a heap of ruins for both white and black."[27]

The primary South African proponent of closer ties between the two countries, Harry Hurwitz, moved to Jerusalem and became an adviser to his old friend Begin. Suddenly, a large number of influential South Africans had the ear of the Israeli prime minister.[28] And as military, scientific, and industrial cooperation between the two countries increased, Israel's once resolute opposition to apartheid faded further. The ideological prescription provided by Revisionist Zionism and Afrikaner nationalism was the same: use military force to ensure national survival.[29] And as Likud's more militant platform moved from the political wilderness into the mainstream in Israel, this shared worldview served as the ideological glue for the Israeli–South African alliance.

Starting in the late 1970s and throughout the 1980s, leading Israeli generals continued to make frequent trips to South Africa and became close friends with their counterparts in Pretoria, often sharing battle plans, weapon designs, and advice on "defeating terrorists." And as South Africa's nuclear weapons program moved forward in the face of international nonproliferation efforts, the Israeli model of deception and covert development was enticing.

. . .

WHILE ANDRÉ BUYS and his colleagues were busy building a nuclear explosive device in the mid-1970s, the South African Atomic Energy Board began searching for an underground test site where they could detonate it. They settled on a remote area in the Kalahari Desert that had strong underground rock formations. The Vastrap site, as it came to be known, was taken over by the SADF so that the movement of large numbers of civilian scientists did not arouse suspicion.[30] By August 1977, the preparations for an underground test were in full swing. The scientists planned to test a "cold" device without the enriched uranium core because Pelindaba's secret Y-Plant, also known as Valindaba, had not yet produced enough highly enriched uranium for a bomb. A full test of a real nuclear explosive was still at least a year off.[31] In anticipation of the underground test, the army set up trials for its new rocket artillery gun at the site in order to distract satellites and prevent them from detecting the deep boreholes they were digging at Vastrap.

Buys confesses that he had reservations about the test as he and his colleagues were building the explosive device. He argued with his superiors, warning them that South Africa would be accused of testing a weapon and possibly face punitive sanctions, or, in a worst-case scenario, an attack on its nuclear facilities by the Soviet Union. Buys claims that Pretoria was two years away from being ready to detonate a genuine nuclear bomb because an accident had delayed the development of weapons-grade uranium from Valindaba.[32] But the South Africans did not wait and, as Buys had feared, they were discovered.

On the afternoon of Saturday August 6, 1977, the acting head of the Soviet embassy arrived at a near empty White House with an urgent message for President Jimmy Carter. Like most of Washington in August, the president was away on vacation. His national security adviser, Zbigniew Brzezinski, was in Maine. William Hyland, the senior National Security Council official on duty, received Soviet premier Leonid Brezhnev's emissary, who told him that Soviet intelligence had detected preparations for a South African nuclear test in the Kalahari Desert and Moscow wanted Washington's help in stopping it. In Brezhnev's view, such a test "would have the most serious and far-reaching aftermaths for international peace and security."[33]

The test-firing of the SADF's new artillery had not hidden the telltale signs of a nuclear test site from the Soviet Cosmos 922 satellite, which passed over the area one month before Brezhnev's message to Carter. Soviet military intelligence (the GRU) then sent a second satellite in for a closer look at the Vastrap site on July 20. On August 2, the Russian satellite returned pictures revealing a cluster of small buildings, a tower, and cables running to a solid structure far from the other buildings—all textbook signs of an underground nuclear test.

The satellite's discovery was not accidental. Dieter Gerhardt had been transmitting South African and Western intelligence to Moscow for over a decade. In August 1977, he was stationed at SADF headquarters in Pretoria as a senior staff officer in the Directorate of Force Development. Gerhardt took a keen interest in South Africa's nuclear program, and when he learned that something related to the program was being built in the middle of the Kalahari, he went to visit. Gerhardt had been trained in various espionage techniques, including the use of miniature photography equipment and the developing of microscopic negatives.[34] He discreetly gathered what he needed at Vastrap and passed all of the photos and information to his handlers in Moscow.

On August 7, the day after the meeting at the White House, an unmarked plane belonging to the American military attaché's office in Pretoria flew low over the Kalahari and photographed the Vastrap site.[35] Within days, an American satellite was rerouted to do further reconnaissance.[36] U.S. analysts who saw the aerial photos claimed they were 90 to 100 percent sure that preparations were under way for an underground nuclear test.[37] After seeing the reconnaissance plane, the South Africans began to panic. Fearing imminent inspections, they packed and left the Vastrap site as fast as they could, taking all the important scientific testing and measurement equipment with them. The program's leading scientists later claimed that "never before or after have there been, during this program, such hectic nights . . . as during that week of August 1977."[38]

Brezhnev approached French, British, and German leaders in an effort to form a united diplomatic front against Pretoria. Carter joined him in urging the European powers to pressure Pretoria, and the French threatened to withdraw construction contracts for a civilian nuclear reactor near Cape Town they had sold to South Africa years earlier. By August 21, Carter had received Vorster's promise to halt test preparations.[39] The president called a news conference two days later and told the press, "No nuclear explosive test will be taken . . . now or in the future."[40] But the Russians were suspicious of South Africa's promises, and rightly so.[41] Just days after giving his word to Carter, Vorster issued confidential orders shutting down the Vastrap test site, ending the "peaceful nuclear explosives" program, and formally approving the clandestine construction of nuclear weapons.[42]

The Vastrap discovery was a turning point in South Africa's nuclear strategy. Faced with aggressive nonproliferation policies in Washington and constant scrutiny by Moscow, Vorster realized just how valuable nuclear weapons could be and decided to take the program underground. "For the first time the politicians became aware of the whole importance of this nuclear capability . . . that this has a lot of value in international politics [and] that you can actually use this hopefully to your advantage," says Buys.[43]

The only debate was between the nuclear scientists and the military officials, who disagreed on what sort of bomb to build. The Atomic Energy Board scientists were content with a crude, bulky, nuclear device; in the eyes of the SADF and Armscor, however, a nuclear deterrent was only credible if it could be miniaturized and delivered by a plane or a missile.[44] The military men won the debate. As a result, the nuclear project was placed under the aegis of Armscor, and Buys and his colleagues began building deliverable nuclear bombs.[45]

South Africa may have resented the United States after the 1975 debacle in Angola, but Pretoria still needed Washington—and Westminster—on its side. A pamphlet distributed by the South African embassy in London in an effort to convince Western governments that Pretoria was an essential strategic ally reminded its readers that South Africa produced 70 percent of the world's gold and half of its diamonds, held 25 percent of the noncommunist world's uranium reserves, and was the largest producer of chromium outside the Soviet Union.[46] Pretoria was also the world's leading platinum producer and a crucial supplier of iron alloys essential to the steel industry. Security experts warned that any disruption of mineral supplies from South Africa would have a "catastrophic" impact on American and European industry.[47] Governments took note as well. Chester Crocker, soon to become Washington's chief policymaker on Africa, wrote in 1980, "It is a fact—not opinion or propaganda—that South Africa is the Saudi Arabia of minerals."[48]

To prove its indispensability, South Africa did more than boast of its mineral supplies. NATO members made use of South Africa's signals surveillance facility at Silvermine, near Cape Town, in order to monitor shipping traffic in the South Atlantic and Indian oceans. In 1976, this access to Silvermine's data enabled the CIA to close its communications center on Diego Garcia Island in the Indian Ocean—a lonely tropical airstrip more recently used as a secret U.S. prison for the rendition of terrorism suspects.

South Africa had long maintained that its position along the Cape Route, around which much of the oil from the Middle East flows in tankers too large to pass through the Suez Canal, was of prime strategic value to the West.[49] In the mid-1970s, all of these arguments were central to the South African government's efforts to salvage its image in America and Europe. Realizing that the country's public relations operation was in dire straits, Information Minister Connie Mulder and his jet-setting deputy, Eschel Rhoodie—both of whom had been instrumental in setting up Vorster's 1976 visit to Israel—decided to spearhead a propaganda war. They spared no opportunity to repair South Africa's increasingly bad reputation.

Rhoodie had first taken an interest in propaganda as an up-and-coming diplomat on a foreign posting to the United States during the mid-1960s. In America, the suave and sociable Rhoodie sought contacts in high places and he soon befriended an aging ex-CIA agent. Rhoodie was new to government, but quickly became disgusted by the soft-sell approach of

South Africa's career diplomats and complained to his new American friend that Pretoria's propaganda effort would have to become more aggressive or the regime would not survive.[50]

The retired American spy urged Rhoodie to use government resources to secretly finance anti-apartheid groups and radical student movements and then infiltrate them. He was even more crass when it came to the media: "The only way to influence the media was to own it, or to own some of the senior people in it," Rhoodie later recalled.[51] The old agent and his CIA colleagues gave Rhoodie a copy of Paul Blackstock's *The Strategy of Subversion* and convinced him that the South African government had to sell a more favorable narrative to the U.S. media and American investors.[52] As Rhoodie told journalist Chris Day years later, "We could not hope to go through official channels, nor through diplomatic channels, to make any headway in the world." South Africa's official mouthpieces lacked any credibility overseas due to their endless parroting of the government line on the communist menace to South Africa and the necessity of segregation. The solution, said Rhoodie, was to "create new avenues, instruments, organizations and people who could speak on behalf of South Africa without being openly tied to us."[53] Pretoria's defenders would have to sell their product by stealth.

Beginning in 1973, just as the Israeli–South African alliance was taking shape, Rhoodie and Mulder went on a worldwide spending spree, buying magazines, newspapers, publishing houses, and film studios in an effort to counter widespread anti-apartheid press coverage with a rosy image of the country. They retained lobbyists in Washington, funded a right-wing political party in Norway, and financed political campaigns to unseat anti-apartheid Democrats in the United States—including Iowa senator Dick Clark, who had put an end to covert U.S. aid in Angola in 1976.[54] Most famously, they sought to purchase *The Washington Star* newspaper to influence opinion inside the Beltway and published the pro-government *Citizen* at home to counter the liberal *Rand Daily Mail.* Over the course of five years—from 1973 to 1978—Mulder and Rhoodie spent R85 million (then approximately $100 million) with the full support of South Africa's intelligence chief, Hendrik van den Bergh.

As the cosmopolitan Rhoodie milked his contacts across the globe for help with the propaganda campaign, Shimon Peres introduced him to a young Israeli businessman named Arnon Milchan, whose sensitive work on behalf of the Israeli government suggested he might be able to help South Africa as well. Sharing a penchant for globe-trotting, international intrigue, and high-stakes deals, they hit it off immediately and began meeting on the French Riviera to discuss ways of improving South Africa's image. Milchan held passports from Israel and Monaco and owned thirty companies in seventeen countries; his business interests ranged from chemical production to arms sales and movie deals. Through their meetings in Cannes, the two men became so friendly that Rhoodie even sold Milchan his condominium in the exclusive South African beach resort of Plettenberg Bay, adding to Milchan's list of properties across the globe. For Rhoodie, whose goal was to project a more favorable image of South Africa to the world, an ally in Hollywood was a godsend.

As a young man, Milchan had played center on the Israeli national soccer team but when his father fell ill, he left the field to take over the family fertilizer business, soon transforming it into a chemical industry giant. When the Shah of Iran decided to build a new airport, Milchan pulled together experts and submitted the winning bid within ten days despite having no prior experience in the field. Everything he touched, it seemed, turned to gold. After a stint as a professional gambler, Milchan went to Hollywood, where he bankrolled and produced a string of block-busters including *Brazil, The War of the Roses, JFK*, and *Pretty Woman* and socialized with the likes of Robert De Niro, Sydney Pollack, and Barbra Streisand.[55] With his modest office, Fruit of the Loom T-shirts, and self-deprecating demeanor one would not have guessed that Milchan was a billionaire, let alone one of Israel's largest arms dealers.

During the 1970s, using Peres and other high-level defense connections in Israel, Milchan funneled equipment from the United States to the Israeli missile program, including rocket fuel and nuclear triggers. All of the materials went from a front company called Milco to Milchan's companies in Tel Aviv. Scientific advisers to the U.S. Air Force accused Milchan and his American colleague, Milco founder Richard Kelly Smyth, of diverting sensitive nuclear materials, including uranium tetrafluoride and depleted uranium. When the scheme finally unraveled, the FBI indicted Smyth on thirty counts of perjury and illegally transferring restricted materials. Five days before his trial, Smyth disappeared; Milchan denied any wrongdoing.[56] In Hollywood, no one seemed to care. If anything, it added to his mystique.

Milchan has studiously downplayed his involvement in the Smyth affair and the South African propaganda effort. He admitted to working with Rhoodie in the late 1970s but claimed that seeing apartheid-era signs forbidding blacks, Asians, and dogs at a zoo so deeply offended his conscience that he never set foot in South Africa again. But there is a more likely explanation; in 1977, while Milchan was beginning to dabble in the film industry in London, he hired a young South African as his secretary. Her name was Shawn Slovo and her father, Joe—a Jewish radical, exiled leader of the South African Communist Party, and close associate of Nelson Mandela's—was one of the biggest targets on the South African government's hit list.[57] Milchan was keen on making a movie about the arms trade and Shawn Slovo introduced him to the British journalist Anthony Sampson, author of *The Arms Bazaar* and himself an anti-apartheid crusader, who had befriended Mandela before his imprisonment. Soon afterward, Milchan's feelings about South Africa began to sour. He was not alone. When white police opened fire on unarmed schoolchildren in Soweto on June 16, 1976, the world reacted in horror and much of Pretoria's carefully choreographed propaganda campaign went down the drain overnight.

Apartheid brutality was not the only cause of the propaganda campaign's demise, however; Mulder and Rhoodie's elaborate plans began to collapse under the weight of their own corruption and intrigue. They laundered government funds through Swiss bank accounts to avoid oversight by the Treasury, pilfered the Defense Ministry's special account to finance their propaganda efforts, and deviously manipulated coverage of the government in the English-language press. As details of their exploits leaked and the so-called Information Scandal broke, the auditor general launched an investigation and Benjamin Pogrund's newspaper, the liberal *Rand Daily Mail*, probed for clues while the Vorster administration scrambled to cover up.[58]

Rhoodie led journalists on a wild-goose chase around the world, leaking details of the government's covert influence peddling in distant cities ranging from Miami to Quito, where he was photographed in a Panama hat feeding llamas. Rhoodie's luck finally ran out on the French Riviera, however. He was arrested, held in a rank cell in the perfume capital, Grasse, and eventually extradited to South Africa, where he was sentenced to six years in prison before ultimately winning his case on appeal and moving to the United States.[59] The Information Scandal became South Africa's Watergate. As with Nixon, it would cost Vorster his job.

7

THE BACK CHANNEL

Nuclear Diplomacy and the Fall of Vorster

BY JULY 1978, the South African government was collapsing under the weight of the Information Scandal. As the fallout from Pretoria's propaganda war spread, a battle to succeed Vorster was raging within the National Party. Although Information Minister Connie Mulder and Defense Minister P. W. Botha were favored to win, the less experienced minister of mines, Stephanus (Fanie) Botha, fancied his chances as a candidate as well. In order to determine his level of support among the NP leadership, he arranged for the telephones of prominent party leaders to be tapped.[1] The targets of the eavesdropping included future president F. W. de Klerk as well as Foreign Minister Pik Botha—another contender for Vorster's job—who was implicated in a sex scandal as a result.*

But Fanie Botha's meddling was not limited to dirty campaign tricks. He was also a central figure in the development of South Africa's nuclear weapons program. As the succession battle intensified, some of the apartheid regime's most closely guarded secrets threatened to emerge—along with embarrassing and potentially career-ending revelations about Fanie Botha's personal finances and the contributions he had received from the Israeli intelligence services in exchange for nuclear favors.

Almost a decade earlier, in 1968, a year after Israel put the finishing touches on its first nuclear weapons, Dr. Ernst David Bergmann, one of the architects of the Israeli bomb, paid a public visit to South Africa. "Neither of us has neighbours to whom we can speak and to whom

---

* The three Bothas are not related.

we are going to be able to speak in the near future," Bergmann declared to an audience of prominent South Africans. "If we are in this position of isolation, perhaps it might be best for both countries to speak to each other," he added, urging Israeli and South African scientists to cooperate.[2]

Bergmann, the son of a rabbi, was born in Germany. He had written the definitive German-language textbook on organic chemistry, which still remained in use in 1939, when the Nazis had the Jewish author's name removed from the cover. Soon after Hitler came to power, he left for England, where he befriended WZO leader Chaim Weizmann—himself one of Britain's foremost chemistry experts. After independence, Ben-Gurion recruited Bergmann to put Israel's scientific research institutions at the disposal of the new state's defense establishment, much to the chagrin of Weizmann, who wished to keep academia insulated from the politics of defense research. Weizmann eventually fired Bergmann and on the same day, the prime minister hired him as a scientific adviser. Ben-Gurion and Bergmann also agreed on the necessity of a nuclear program; neither had any qualms about building the ultimate weapon.[3]

For the most part, Israel and South Africa conducted their military cooperation clandestinely through their defense ministries, but an informal and intimate network of scientists was an essential part of the alliance. After the initial agreement was signed by Shimon Peres and P. W. Botha in April 1975, the movement of leading scientists between the countries became much more fluid. There were reciprocal visits to secret facilities by scientists involved in each country's weapons program, recruitment of Israeli atomic scientists by South Africa's Atomic Energy Board, and exchanges of sensitive scientific intelligence.

As South Africa's military-industrial complex boomed, it brought the business world into a close relationship with the SADF. When Johannes Maree, the chief executive of mining and steel giant Barlow Rand, became the CEO of Armscor in 1979, mingling between business and government elites increased and the private sector became focused on satisfying the military's growing appetite.[4] The defense industry also penetrated academic research centers such as the University of Pretoria's Institute for Strategic Studies and the Rand Afrikaans University, whose faculty was recruited to produce research for military audiences and advise the government.[5] Most significant in the nexus of research and militarization was the Council for Scientific and Industrial Research (CSIR), an ostensibly academic research institute.[6]

In fact, South Africa had placed its premier scientific research facility at the service of the apartheid government with the aim of making the regime militarily strong enough to survive diplomatic pressure and the U.N. arms embargo, which most countries other than Israel were observing. As the U.S. Defense Intelligence Agency reported, CSIR and Armscor were helping the apartheid regime "withstand anticipated pressures to change its racial policies."[7] With such ambitious goals and so few allies, scientific exchanges with Israel became essential.

Armscor in the mid-1970s was "a kind of Winston Churchill toy shop," recalls former research and development director Hannes Steyn, referring to Britain's secretive World War II weapons development office. "[We] had to do everything ourselves."[8] This included casual forms of industrial espionage, such as gleaning secrets over beers and in dorm rooms as South African scientists attended conferences and foreign universities. "[Our] main task was reconnaissance, to find out what the other buggers are doing. You want to steal as much as you can with your eye . . . to glean what others are doing," says Steyn. "I had students going all over the world: Oxford, Stanford. . . . You sit in a bar and talk to guys. If you're a good physicist, they tell you. There's a network of top-class scientists and they talk to each other."[9]

The Israelis and South Africans were already talking. Louw Alberts, who served as director-general of the Ministry of Mineral and Energy Affairs after his time at the AEB, fondly recalls his own visit to Israel and the Israeli nuclear scientist Yuval Ne'eman's lectures at Pelindaba.[10] He still hangs a picture of Ne'eman on his living room wall. According to Alberts, these high-level exchanges were very common, though he claims the cooperation dealt only with the harmless field of nuclear isotope application for medical uses and food irradiation.[11]

But these scientific exchanges between Israelis and South Africans went beyond innocent civilian research.[12] In March 1975, Dr. C. V. Brink, the president of the CSIR, and Dr. W. A. Verbeek, an agriculture expert, went to Israel. In addition to many other facilities, they toured the Soreq Nuclear Research Center, Israel Aircraft Industries, Israel Military Industries' research and development center, as well as the military's central research laboratory. While his companion was studying plant genetics at the Weizmann Institute, Dr. Brink was holding more consequential meetings with scientists and engineers at the Ministry of Defense.[13]

Just a week before Prime Minister Vorster's historic trip to Israel in April 1976, a more secretive visit took place during which a team of South African military intelligence officials toured the offices of Israel's renowned Council for Scientific Liaison: a scientific espionage unit known by its Hebrew acronym, Lakam. It was Lakam that had master-minded Israel's 1968 operation to divert the *Scheersberg A*'s cargo of ura-nium to an Israeli naval vessel in the middle of the Mediterranean.[14] The South Africans were shown around by Lieutenant Colonel Dudu Benaya and viewed a variety of captured enemy military equipment, including Soviet T-62 and T-54 tanks, Egyptian artillery pieces, Chinese and North Korean guns, Katyusha rockets, and nuclear-capable FROG-7 missiles.[15]

As a result of the arms deals signed by Vorster and Israeli prime minister Yitzhak Rabin later that month, a formal exchange program was drawn up between the Israeli National Council for Research and Development and South Africa's Council for Scientific and Industrial Research.[16] Immediately after Vorster returned from Israel, many of these new scientific agreements began to go into effect. But more impor-tant than any new pacts signed by Vorster and Rabin was a much older agreement, a contract that was broken, consensually, in the interest of both nations.

· · ·

IN LATE JULY 1976, as South Africa's black townships convulsed with vio-lence, the minister of mines and labor, Fanie Botha, flew to Israel. Botha was mesmerized, as Vorster had been, by the biblical sites he recalled from his Sunday school education. Between high-level meetings, Botha recalls, "I wanted to see places from the Bible, wells from the Bible . . . some of them are still working today," he marveled. But Botha's hosts at the Israeli Ministry of Defense did not leave him much time for biblical or historical tourism. He arrived before dawn at Ben-Gurion Airport and was met by the former IDF chief of staff General Chaim Bar-Lev, the namesake of the infamous Bar-Lev Line that Egyptian forces breached on the first day of the Yom Kippur War. After allowing him a few hours of rest, Bar-Lev drove Botha to the Israeli Atomic Energy Commission for a meeting with its director, Uzi Eilam. From there, Botha was driven south to Yavne, where he had lunch at the Soreq Nuclear Research Center and visited the facility. After Soreq, Botha was whisked away to a meeting with Defense Minister Shimon Peres. In the following days, he dined at the homes of Bar-Lev and Eilam, visited a tank repair facility and an air force base, and met with senior managers at Israel Aircraft Industries. Botha was even granted a one-hour audience with Prime Minister Rabin—hardly the itinerary one would expect of a minor cabinet minister.[17] In the South African press, the visit was reported as an exploration of cooperative mining ventures and mineral production.[18]

In fact, it was a sensitive nuclear negotiation focused on the five-hundred-ton stockpile of South African uranium that had accumulated in Israel since shipments began in 1965. Israel had consumed the *Scheersberg A* cargo by this time and Dimona needed yellowcake to fuel the weapons program.[19] The five hundred tons of safeguarded South African uranium would be enough to fuel Dimona for the next five to ten years and produce enough reprocessed plutonium for dozens of nuclear bombs.[20]

Within months of starting the job in January 1976, Botha found himself at the center of one of the government's most secretive and delicate relationships. The previous year, Binyamin Blumberg, chief of Israel's Lakam, had approached intelligence chief van den Bergh with a request to buy another one hundred tons of yellowcake. Although Vorster approved the sale, Botha's predecessor in the Mining Ministry was reluctant to cut a deal with Israel on something as sensitive as uranium—a reticence that cost him his job and paved the way for Fanie Botha's rise.[21]

Botha, a political climber who had set his sights on the Defense Ministry, knew that a sensitive deal like this could make his career. Now, with a more amenable mining minister in office, Blumberg requested the yellowcake once again, and this time he also asked South Africa to lift the safeguards that had remained in effect since the bilateral agreement of 1965. Since the Atomic Energy Board had negotiated the original contract in 1965 and the Ministry of Mines oversaw the AEB, such a deal could not go through without Botha's approval.

Lifting bilateral safeguards meant that South Africa would no longer have a right to inspect the sealed drums of yellowcake, as it had in the past, nor would it be allowed to verify whether Israel was using the uranium for peaceful purposes. The Israelis could now use the South African raw material as they liked without any contractual obligations hanging over their heads. Botha did not dare second-guess Vorster and van den Bergh and, after returning from Israel, he went ahead and lifted the safeguards.[22]

Well into his eighties, Botha's memory of the deal is clear. He was told by his counterparts in Israel that the safeguarded yellowcake could be very useful to Israel in the nuclear field. "I didn't sell it to them, I didn't give it to them, but when I became minister they had it," says Botha. "But they couldn't use it unless South Africa lifted them [the safeguards]. So that's what I did." Botha is not apologetic about his decision to lift the safeguards, nor does he seem to mind that his actions contributed to nuclear proliferation and bolstered the growing arsenal of an undeclared nuclear power.[23]

Sitting in the modest living room of his retirement home, Fanie Botha is remarkably nonchalant about the whole affair. "We were good friends," he says, pointing to a locked glass cabinet where he keeps his most valuable possessions. In the cabinet is his ministerial desk plaque reading "Sy Edele [The Honorable] Min. S. P. Botha," flanked by the flag of the old South African regime and a small Israeli flag—a lasting testament to his service to Israel. On the top shelf is another, a silver-plated Hebrew Bible embossed with turquoise stones given to him as a gift by General Bar-Lev. "We worked together for some years," Botha recalls fondly. "It was easy for friends to cooperate in this field."[24]

But Botha did not execute the sensitive uranium deal alone. There was a middleman: a grade-school classmate of Botha who became a decorated air force officer during World War II and the Korean War and who had close ties to South African intelligence and the Israeli security establishment—Jan Blaauw.

Jan Blaauw was a war hero. He had joined the South African Air Force in 1939 and rose to the level of squadron commander by the age of twenty-one. At twenty-two, he was seconded to the Royal Air Force and sent to command a British base in Palestine, where he met Jewish soldiers for the first time. Blaauw returned to South Africa briefly but then joined the Berlin Airlift in 1948, flying coal into the divided city. During the Korean War, he led a South African squadron attached to the U.S. Air Force and received a Distinguished Flying Cross and a Silver Star for aiding the Americans. And as war raged in Southern Rhodesia during the mid-1960s, Blaauw served as a liaison between the SADF and the white Rhodesian regime's security services. It was then that he met General van den Bergh and the two quickly became friends.[25]

The top brass of the South African military all knew Blaauw well, and all agree that he was "a brilliant pilot"—even those who profess a strong dislike for the man. Many retired generals also remember him as a maverick and an individualist. General Jan van Loggerenberg, chief of the South African Air Force from 1988 to 1991, recalls Blaauw taking his friends for rides in Mirage fighter jets.[26] Air force veteran Pieter John Roos remembers him joyriding Cessna planes to a friend's farm, and having the air force fly in spare parts for his Land Rover. He also flaunted his wealth, keeping piles of banknotes in his safe and carrying tobacco bags filled with diamonds. The younger officers generally showed him great deference. "He was quite a legend in his time," says Roos.[27]

In the upper echelons of the SADF, however, Blaauw's reckless behavior made leaders bristle. General George Meiring, head of the SADF during the early 1990s, remembers Blaauw as "a bloke very loose with his tongue," and not someone to be trusted. And, says air force general Tienie Groenewald, he was "a chap who would do anything to make money," despite the fact that he had a great deal of it already. Blaauw was eventually considered for the position of air force chief but he was passed over due to a scandal involving drunkenness and reckless behavior by officers under his command that Groenewald helped to expose. General Magnus Malan shared Groenewald's disdain, citing Blaauw's habits of drinking and womanizing. Though he was a stellar fighter pilot, says Malan, "He wasn't the type of officer I wanted."[28]

Blaauw had retired honorably at the end of 1975 as a result of bad blood with Malan. He went to work for the West German firm Hydroma, which in the years prior to the 1977 mandatory U.N. arms embargo served as a front to supply British and American military equipment to South Africa. During his final years of military service, Blaauw had already set up the networks he would need during his busy retirement as an arms dealer. Through Leon Zimmerman, a South African Jew living in Israel, Blaauw had arranged for South Africa to supply Israel with spare parts for its Mirage fleet—similar to South Africa's own—which had been damaged during the Yom Kippur War.[29] Most important, Blaauw had made the acquaintance of Lakam chief Binyamin Blumberg—Israel's point man for sensitive nuclear deals.

Fanie Botha acknowledges that Blaauw was instrumental in setting up the 1976 visit to Israel and the deals that he struck there. "He had contacts with the Israelis," says Botha. "When I turned up in Israel I saw him walking about, I was amazed. When I had meetings, he was there," he recounts.[30] Blaauw was even present when Botha cut the deal with Blumberg to formally lift the safeguards on over five hundred tons of South African uranium in Israel and supply the Israelis with one hundred tons more.[31]

In return for the yellowcake and the lifted safeguards, South Africa received thirty grams of tritium, a radioactive substance that thermonuclear weapons require to increase their explosive power.[32] Thirty grams was enough to boost the yield of several atomic bombs.[33] The substance was delivered to South Africa in small installments over the course of a year between 1977 and 1978 as Vorster's scandal-tainted administration struggled to hold on to power and P. W. Botha, his archrival at the Defense Ministry, set his sights on the premiership.[34]

The atomic weapons South Africa was building at the time were crude Hiroshima-style devices—which derive their power from a fission reaction alone—but Armscor was also planning a new generation of more powerful thermonuclear weapons, which rely on both fission and fusion reactions. These next-generation designs included miniaturized warheads and implosion devices, for which tritium was a potentially useful ingredient.[35] The tritium was not the only quid pro quo, however.[36] There was a financial reward for Fanie Botha as well—money that he desperately needed in the midst of his campaign for the premiership.

In September 1978, Vorster finally stepped down, unleashing a four-way battle for his job pitting the figurehead of the propaganda war, Connie Mulder, against Defense Minister P. W. Botha; the new foreign minister,

Pik Botha; and Fanie Botha, who was then the Transvaal Province's NP leader. Mulder had the crucial endorsement of van den Bergh and was the favorite; Pik Botha was eliminated when he came third in the first round of balloting; and Fanie Botha dropped his candidacy for lack of money and a weak electoral base in the Cape Province. Mulder very nearly became prime minister despite his central role in the Information Scandal. Further revelations of Mulder's improprieties disillusioned crucial party leaders, however, and P. W. Botha took office as prime minister on September 28, 1978.[37]

The international intrigue surrounding the 1978 campaign would have remained under wraps had it not been for a closed-door trial years later in which Fanie Botha accused Blaauw of extortion. Blaauw claimed that his old classmate Botha had promised him compensation in return for his sensitive services on behalf of the country. Blaauw became enraged when Botha reneged on his supposed promise, threatening to expose state secrets and Botha's personal demons if he didn't get his reward. The trial revealed some of the apartheid regime's most closely guarded secrets.

Kenneth Prendini, one of Blaauw's defense lawyers during the trial, explains that the uranium-tritium revelations were merely the tip of the iceberg. The crux of the matter was Fanie Botha's precarious financial situation. In the midst of the 1978 political campaign, Botha owed the Volkskas bank R1.7 million (approximately $2 million at 1978 exchange rates) and was facing R200,000 ($230,000) in annual interest payments on his debt. Botha learned that Johannesburg's *Sunday Times* was preparing to publish an article on his impending bankruptcy—the kind of negative publicity that could ruin his political career.

Desperate, he reached out to prominent contacts in the mining industry for help in mid-1978. Botha requested that Harry Oppenheimer, chairman of the gold and diamond mining giants Anglo American and De Beers, exert his influence to kill the story. As the head of the largest and most powerful company in the country, Botha assumed Oppenheimer could convince the editor of the *Sunday Times*, Tertius Myburgh, to halt publication. Oppenheimer testified that he had relayed Botha's request to Myburgh and the article was killed.[38]

As Fanie Botha's bank account sank deeper into the red in 1978 and 1979, Blaauw—with the help of Botha's private secretary, Frances

Whelpton—was trying to obtain an overseas loan to shore up the embattled minister's finances. When this failed, the independently wealthy Blaauw fronted the money himself, totaling R420,000 (approximately $480,000 at 1978 exchange rates) over the course of three years from 1977 to 1980 (although the conniving Whelpton managed to siphon off a great deal of it).[39] Blaauw told the court that he had received payment of $1 million from the Israeli government for his mediation services in the uranium deals, making it easier for him to prop Botha up financially.

Even after Vorster's downfall and Fanie Botha's failed bid for the prime minister's office, the Israeli government had a vested interest in seeing Botha stay afloat because, as the trial record puts it, "the yellowcake transactions with which they were at that stage engaged had not yet fully materialised."[40] The presiding judge, Gerald Friedman, found that "the Israelis would, because of the co-operation between themselves and South Africa, have preferred Fanie Botha to hold that portfolio" until the deal was done.[41] There was also the possibility that Vorster would promote Fanie Botha to minister of defense. Thus, Blaauw's business partner in Israel, Leon Zimmerman, told him to "look after Fanie Botha."[42] Advocate Mike Hannon, who argued most of the case on Blaauw's behalf, is much more blunt in his interpretation of the evidence: "In order to keep a sympathetic guy to Israel in the position he was in, the Israeli government, through Jan Blaauw's good offices, agreed to keep [Fanie Botha] solvent so he didn't lose his portfolio."[43]

Fanie Botha was grateful to all those who helped him stay afloat financially, and as a gesture of gratitude for Oppenheimer's efforts to squelch press coverage of his financial woes and to thank Blaauw for propping him up, he invited the Anglo American Corporation and Blaauw's company, Ondombo Holdings, to apply for the rights to five new underwater diamond-mining zones in June 1979. Blaauw claimed that Fanie Botha led him to believe that two of the five concessions would be his.

This was no small favor. The mining areas offered to Blaauw and Oppenheimer were located off the western coast of South Africa adjacent to the South African–Namibian frontier, near a restricted zone of southern Namibia that already provided massive revenues for Anglo American and De Beers. Using a series of dams and a massive machine as long as a football field that created a ten-story mound to literally stem the tide, De Beers managed to gather an astonishing profusion of pure gem diamonds, a grade far superior to the rougher stones found in South African and Botswanan mines. The restricted zone was hemmed in by dunes hundreds of feet high, barbed wire, packs of guard dogs, and hovering helicopters searching for people or vessels that might make off with some of the millions of dollars' worth of diamonds recovered from the beach every day.[44]

De Beers chairman Ernest Oppenheimer had acquired the Namibian offshore diamond zone from German investors during World War I, when he established the Anglo American Corporation in order to manage diamond-rich areas owned by Germans. Fearful that they would lose their lucrative property if British-aligned South Africa took over the German colony of South-West Africa, the Germans exchanged their holdings for shares in Anglo American.

In the coming years, De Beers developed a stranglehold on the worldwide diamond supply by purchasing as many mines as possible and rigorously controlling supplies.[45] Now Blaauw was being offered a mining concession outside the control of the De Beers–led cartel that he could use to gather rough diamonds for sale back to the cartel or on the open market. Even in a worst-case scenario, it promised to yield massive profits.

During the trial, independent industry evaluators conservatively estimated the value of a single diamond-mining concession like those offered to Blaauw at R900 million ($400 million at the time of the appraisal) and predicted a potential value of over R3 billion ($1.3 billion).[46] For several years after he left the Ministry of Mines in 1979, Fanie Botha refused to confirm or deny whether he had formally granted Blaauw the diamond concessions. Finally, in 1983, under pressure from Blaauw, Botha denied ever making the promise. Blaauw was furious, and he threatened to go public with Botha's financial predicament and the details of the top secret uranium-tritium deal. Fearing for his political career, Botha retaliated by charging Blaauw with extortion and fraud and appointing state prosecutors to try him.[47] His plan backfired, however, when a 1983 *Sunday Express* article exposed his bankruptcy;[48] Botha resigned from government two days later, and when the case finally went to court in 1987, Blaauw was acquitted on all charges.

Although Fanie Botha's legal battle with Jan Blaauw occurred years after the yellowcake-tritium deal, it offers a rare window into the innermost workings of the Vorster administration and the secretive nuclear transactions between Israel and South Africa. Blaauw's ties to the highest levels of the South African intelligence community were crucial in allowing him to act as a shadow diplomat between Israel and South Africa during the 1970s, but his star fell with that of his patrons. The Department of Information's overseas propaganda war and the ensuing Information Scandal brought down Vorster's government in 1978; killed the political career of his preferred successor, Connie Mulder; ended the career of Hendrik van den Bergh; and installed in power Vorster's political nemesis: Defense Minister P. W. Botha. A massive overhaul of the South African intelligence establishment soon followed and Blaauw was never granted his concessions. He is now nearing ninety and lives on a farm in rural Namibia. The old war hero refuses to discuss any of his dealings with Israel. After several phone conversations and requests for a face-to-face interview, Blaauw refused to meet, claiming he feared for his life if he disclosed details of his nuclear deals with Israel.

. . .

AS DEFENSE MINISTER, P. W. Botha had deeply resented the seemingly limitless budget allocated to van den Bergh's Bureau of State Security and the simultaneous dwarfing of the military intelligence coffers.[49] When BOSS was created in 1969, the Defense Ministry's intelligence budget plunged from almost R800,000 to R39,000 while van den Bergh's ballooned to over R4 million and his allies in the Department of Information routinely raided the Defense Ministry's special account to subsidize their foreign escapades. The disdainful intelligence chief didn't think much of Botha's military intelligence wing and even attempted a bureaucratic takeover of its offices.[50] Botha successfully resisted that move but never forgot it, and when he came to power, he exacted revenge.

Virtually overnight, the balance of power between the intelligence agencies shifted.[51] BOSS was renamed the Department of National Security (DONS) and placed under the prime minister's direct control. Botha slashed its budget and reduced the van den Bergh empire to the role of a think tank and intelligence evaluation center while promoting his own protégés at the Defense Ministry.[52] The new prime minister's first intelligence briefing came from a uniformed general rather than from a civilian, and the Division of Military Intelligence soon rose to primacy.[53]

Botha and his generals believed that South Africa was a primary target in Moscow's crosshairs and faced a "total onslaught" both from within and from neighboring Marxist countries.[54] Magnus Malan, now the head of the SADF, called on all white South Africans to mobilize for "total war" because "survival concerns every citizen in South Africa directly and personally."[55]

As Malan warned of barbarians at the gate, Prime Minister Botha was busy overhauling the executive branch of the South African government, promoting key security advisers to the status of an inner cabinet.[56] He also devised a National Security Management System of astonishing depth involving representatives in 12 designated regions, 60 subregions and 450 mini-regions—giving him an ear on every corner.[57] Despite his staunch anticommunism, Botha's sprawling bureaucracy was uncannily similar to the Soviet system.[58] His Orwellian ideas about psychological warfare followed in the same vein.

Botha, like Malan, drew much of his rhetoric and intellectual inspiration from the work of the French general and military strategist André Beaufre, who had commanded French forces in Algeria and Indochina. Beaufre's writings on "total strategy" were part of the core curriculum at South Africa's West Point—the Joint Defence College.[59] He believed that when fighting an insurgency, military force had to be complemented by indirect psychological, economic, and diplomatic tools, and he encouraged reforms that undermined the grievances of antigovernment revolutionaries.[60]

In this spirit, Malan attempted to integrate nonwhite soldiers into the SADF,[61] and Botha sought to further the "independence" of black homelands while granting limited rights to Coloreds and Indians in the hope that such reforms would diminish the appeal of the ANC and other anti-apartheid groups. By "revising the trappings of apartheid without tampering with the essentials," Pretoria hoped to reduce anti-apartheid opposition at home and abroad.[62] In the end, however, South Africa's total strategy failed to live up to Beaufre's ideal. Pretoria's fundamental attachment to white minority rule precluded the sort of meaningful political reforms that could have actually undermined resistance movements.[63]

As Malan and Botha halfheartedly followed Beaufre's prescriptions for indirect warfare, the SADF found itself mired in a real war on the Angolan border. An elite unit known as Koevoet (Afrikaans for "Crowbar") staged counterinsurgency raids in northern Namibia while SADF troops continued to cross the border into Angola to target Namibian rebels operating from there. In 1978, the SADF dropped paratroopers deep inside Angola to attack a SWAPO base in Cassigna, killing several hundred soldiers and civilians. According to General Jannie Geldenhuys, who commanded the war in Namibia and Angola from 1977 to 1980, the raid, known as Operation Reindeer, was considered so daring and successful that top Israeli officials immediately flew to South Africa "to find out how the hell did we manage to do that operation."[64]

Even after the SADF's success in Angola, Botha remained deeply paranoid about Soviet encroachment. He declared in 1979 that "the military threat against the Republic of South Africa is intensifying at an alarming rate and the country is increasingly being thrown on its own resources to ensure survival."[65] The scientists at Armscor received orders to begin research on advanced weapons systems, including the sort of long-range, nuclear-capable missiles Israel had offered and South Africa had turned down in 1975.

Despite the rise of P. W. Botha's securocrats and a multimillion-dollar propaganda campaign to make South Africa more palatable to Western powers, the nation was becoming more isolated and more threatened. Although Washington wanted to curb Soviet and Cuban influence in Angola, U.S. officials simply did not share the siege mentality of the Botha government.[66] Lacking reliable military aid from the West, South Africa pushed forward in its quest for military self-sufficiency.

As the influence of the SADF grew in the political sphere, so, too, did the influence of Armscor in the economic sphere. Between 1970 and 1980, the South African defense budget increased more than fivefold. By 1983, it had topped R2.6 billion ($2.3 billion at the time)—5 percent of South Africa's gross national product.[67] Armscor became one of the country's three largest companies along with industrial giant Barlow Rand and the De Beers–Anglo American mining empire, employing an estimated 100,000 South Africans.[68]

Unlike Israel, which had large export markets for its arms industry, it was impractical for South Africa—a country with limited numbers of skilled workers and a small internal market for arms—to develop its own jets, missiles, and advanced weapons systems. To maintain their edge over neighbors armed with new Soviet weapons, the South Africans desperately needed Western technology.[69] More and more, they were turning to Israel to provide it.[70]

By 1979, South Africa had secured its position as Israel's single largest customer for arms, accounting for 35 percent of military exports from Israel and dwarfing other clients such as Argentina, Chile, Singapore, and Zaire.[71] When François Mitterrand's Socialist Party came to power in France in 1980, the few remaining postembargo arms sales from Pretoria's former patron evaporated. The French cutoff also forced the South Africans to turn to Israel for naval cooperation, given that its officers had previously learned French and traveled to France for submarine training.[72] Already a major source of arms, the Jewish state had now become a vital partner in combat training and the joint production of weapons.

Isolated and ostracized, "with only marginal and tenuous control over its own fate . . . and lacking dependable big-power support," South Africa was a textbook pariah state.[73] The pariahs of the Cold War era were not simply a group of stray stars in a constellation of superpowers, but a potentially destabilizing geopolitical force to be reckoned with. Nor were they simply pawns and proxies. The lack of consistent arms supplies led pariah states to chart their own course, and created a major incentive for them to acquire nuclear weapons in order to ward off any potential threats from the multiple enemies surrounding them. Turning to other outcasts to buy, sell, and jointly produce arms made economic and strategic sense.[74]

When the 1979 Islamic Revolution toppled the Shah of Iran, depriving Israel of its primary partner in missile development and leaving a gaping hole in Israel's strategy of the periphery, Israeli–South African military cooperation deepened, moving into yet another extremely sensitive area. The generals in Tel Aviv now turned to South Africa for help in developing and testing its arsenal of medium and long-range ballistic missiles—the preferred delivery system for nuclear weapons.

In March 1979, Israel conducted a highly secretive test, launching a missile three hundred miles westward over the Mediterranean. This new missile was a modernized version of the Jericho system Peres had offered to South Africa four years earlier, and the Israelis were keen to show off their new technology and confirm its reliability. In Israel, knowledge of the test was limited to cabinet officials, senior generals, and the engineers working on the missile. But as the new weapon was unveiled, the SADF's head of special operations, I. R. Gleeson, was at the testing range standing beside Israeli chief of staff Raful Eitan.[75]

Born in 1929, Eitan was the archetypal sabra. On the agricultural settlement of Tel Adashim, near Nazareth, security was paramount from an early age; Eitan's father taught him to fire a gun when he was seven and he joined the army at seventeen.[76] His hostility toward Arabs began early and his belief that Israel needed to assert its control over the land by force of arms, and by using collective punishment if necessary, defined his career.[77] After distinguishing himself during the Sinai campaign and the Six-Day War, he was credited with turning back the 1973 Syrian assault on the Golan Heights and was named IDF chief of staff in 1978.

Malan, then the head of the SADF, wrote personally to Eitan apologizing that he hadn't been able to attend the missile test himself and thanked Eitan for allowing his envoy to observe.[78] In his report to Malan, Gleeson noted that if the SADF were to acquire or build similar missiles they would only be worth the price if the warhead were extremely advanced "with a nuclear warhead as the ideal."[79] In the coming years, development of a longer-range missile to deliver such a warhead became a major joint project for Israel and South Africa.

In May 1979, a few months after the first test, Eitan wrote to Malan, inviting him to Israel to view a second missile launch. The Israelis also hoped to discuss the various IDF training courses in which SADF personnel could enlist.[80] Later that year, Malan traveled to Israel for the test, accompanied by Major Wouter Basson of the SADF's medical service. The official reason given for Basson's visit was an evaluation of equipment for military hospitals,[81] but Basson's research interests and subsequent assignments for the SADF strongly suggest that he was not only in Israel to look at the latest surgical equipment. During the 1980s, Basson would become better known as "Dr. Death," the head of South Africa's notorious biological and chemical weapons program. He traveled the globe, gathering as much information as he could about the development and use of these weapons. Basson's most twisted and ambitious goal was the creation of a "black bomb," which would kill only blacks while sparing whites. In preparation for this ill-fated project, he conducted extensive research on ethnic-specific genes, which he hoped to isolate and target with certain chemicals. In addition to stockpiling samples of anthrax, Ebola, and the plague, he became known for using captured enemy soldiers as experimental subjects and dumping their corpses out of planes over the Atlantic Ocean.[82]

In addition to Basson's sinister projects, research on other weapons of mass destruction was moving forward in Pretoria.

· · ·

DESPITE THE BOTCHED underground test at Vastrap in 1977 and Vorster's declaration to President Carter that South Africa was not pursuing nuclear weapons, Blaauw's execution of the tritium deal demonstrated that Pretoria was still aggressively seeking an advanced nuclear capability. And deepening diplomatic and economic isolation only made the apartheid regime want it more.

In 1976, Washington had cut off nuclear fuel exports for South Africa's SAFARI-1 research reactor. In addition, the United States canceled a 1974 agreement to provide nuclear fuel for the civilian power plant at Koeberg, forcing Pretoria to produce its own. To add insult to injury, South Africa was not reimbursed for payments it had already made to the United States. In 1977, the IAEA removed South Africa from its Board of Governors and gave its seat to Egypt, a move that infuriated Pretoria.[83] Then, in March 1978, the U.S. Congress passed the Nuclear Non-Proliferation Act, halting nuclear exports to countries that did not accept IAEA safeguards and inspections. South Africa found itself more alone than ever before.[84]

In 1978, Washington hoped to strong-arm Pretoria into signing the NPT—which the United States had signed ten years earlier—but the new law had the opposite effect; punitive measures and the cutoff of fuel supplies negated any influence the United States might have had over South Africa. Even Andrew Young, then President Carter's ambassador to the U.N. and a major critic of South Africa, argued, "If you break the relationship altogether there is no way to monitor."[85] While isolation can stop states from developing weapons, says former AEB director Waldo Stumpf, "a point may be reached where political leverage is lost and the isolation becomes counter-productive, pushing the would-be proliferator toward full proliferation."[86]

As would be the case with North Korea in the 1990s, punitive measures and isolation simply caused Pretoria to accelerate its covert nuclear and missile programs. The aborted test at Vastrap had proved to South Africa that a nuclear weapons capability—or even the appearance of one—earned it the attention, if not the respect, of the great powers, a discovery that government officials exploited as they crafted Pretoria's nuclear strategy.[87] In 1977, Niel Barnard, a future head of South African intelligence who had written his Ph.D. thesis on nuclear strategy, proclaimed that "the acquisition of nuclear weapons will not necessarily isolate South Africa any further."[88] Washington's decision to wield a big stick had backfired; instead of bowing to U.S. pressure, South Africa refused to sign the NPT, claiming it would be a sign of weakness to the Soviets.[89]

At the time, proliferation experts were warning that Israel, South Africa, and Taiwan—pariah states with already strong links in the conventional arms trade—had every incentive to forge a nuclear alliance.[90] After all, as political scientist Richard Betts argued, nuclear weapons gave pariah states leverage, "turning supplicants into blackmailers."[91] But just as South Africa moved toward completion of its first atomic weapon, another incident involving spy satellites and charges of a South African nuclear test threatened to throw a wrench into Pretoria's plans once again.

8

OVER THE EDGE

South Africa Joins the Nuclear Club

TEN MINUTES BEFORE SUNRISE on the morning of September 22, 1979, the American surveillance satellite VELA 6911 recorded an unusual double flash over the South Atlantic Ocean. The personnel monitoring VELA's transmissions at Patrick Air Force Base in Florida immediately noticed the signature pattern produced by nuclear explosions: a short blast of light followed by a nearly complete blackout and then a second longer flash.[1] VELA had detected forty-one previous nuclear explosions during its ten-year life span and had never been wrong.[2]

The air force base issued an alert in the wee hours of the morning on September 22. By evening, President Jimmy Carter had convened a meeting in the Situation Room of the White House with the secretary of state, the secretary of defense, his national security adviser, and intelligence representatives to discuss the possibility of a clandestine nuclear test. The most likely culprits were Israel and South Africa.

When reports that VELA had detected a nuclear flash reached South Africa on September 22, 1979, Buys and his Armscor colleagues were baffled. They had not been involved in any test preparations, nor had they heard anything from military colleagues. Most importantly, says Buys, "we were not ready."[3] Even though he maintains that a South African bomb did not cause the flash, Buys is convinced it was a nuclear test. The pattern and timing of the double flash signature is so unique, says Buys, that it could not have been anything else.[4]

Back in Washington, there was pandemonium. Assistant Secretary of State Hodding Carter III described the situation as "sheer panic" when news of the VELA incident reached Foggy Bottom. After all, the president "had draped himself in the flag of non-proliferation," according to journalist Seymour Hersh, and if he did not crack down on whoever had detonated the bomb, critics would accuse him of hypocrisy.[5] Making matters worse, Africa and nonproliferation were the least of the Carter administration's concerns in October 1979. That same month, the ailing Shah of Iran was admitted for medical treatment at an American hospital, setting off riots across Iran that culminated in the takeover of the American embassy in Tehran and a hostage crisis that would paralyze the Carter administration for well over a year.

Carter was gearing up for a reelection campaign in which he had hoped to showcase his success in orchestrating the Israeli-Egyptian Camp David agreement and the successful Strategic Arms Limitation Talks (SALT II) with the Soviets in June 1979, which limited the number of nuclear weapons launchers. The possibility that Israel or South Africa had tested a nuclear weapon threatened to derail his agenda and the bureaucracy struggled to bury the story.[6]

In Washington, many of the country's top scientists assembled to investigate the mysterious double flash, and the Carter administration commissioned dozens of studies from intelligence agencies and the military. Most of the initial reports concluded there had been a nuclear explosion. The CIA's December 1979 report to the National Security Council estimated the explosion had a yield of less than 3 kilotons, and that it was detonated in the atmosphere somewhere in the Southern Hemisphere.[7] The nuclear scientists at the Los Alamos National Laboratory concluded that no natural phenomenon could have caused both the intensity and duration of the VELA signature, which was unmistakably that of a nuclear explosion.[8]

Carter was not satisfied by these preliminary reports and in late 1979 he appointed an expert panel, led by the eminent MIT physicist Jack Ruina, to assess the data. Two visiting scientists from the Arecibo ionospheric laboratory in Puerto Rico, home to the world's largest radio telescope, came to Washington to brief the panel. The scientists had detected a ripple in the earth's atmosphere in the early morning hours of September 22 traveling on an unusual southeast to northwest trajectory. But the Ruina panel did not seem particularly interested in any evidence suggesting a nuclear test in the South Atlantic Ocean; it dismissed the Arecibo findings and moved on.[9]

The panel's members were far more intrigued by disparities between the VELA satellite's two sensors.[10] This led them to focus on two alternative explanations for the double flash: a meteorite striking the satellite or light reflected from a nearby object.[11] The meteoroid theory was dismissed in a June 1980 Defense Intelligence Agency report as having odds of less than 1 in 100 billion. This DIA report, which is still largely classified, was quoted in major newspapers on July 15 as evidence that what VELA detected was a nuclear test.[12] But Carter's panel was not convinced. In what was becoming an interbureaucratic publicity war between the White House and the intelligence agencies, presidential aides retaliated the same day by publicizing the detailed findings of the panel, with its questionable theories of a nonnuclear flash.[13]

Although Carter's panel couldn't find any radioactive debris in the atmosphere, the potential for political fallout from the VELA incident was apparent to the White House from day one. On October 22, 1979, exactly a month after the double flash—and before it became public knowledge—the State Department wrote to the National Security Council warning that a clandestine nuclear test would have a devastating impact on the administration's much touted nonproliferation policy. The diplomats at State were particularly worried about efforts to achieve peace settlements in Rhodesia and Namibia and recommended U.N. sanctions, strong-arming Pretoria into signing the NPT, or subjecting all its facilities to IAEA safeguards.[14]

By the first week of October, the State Department had realized that South Africa was probably not the guilty party; Israel was a more likely candidate. Suddenly, Washington let Pretoria be. Waldo Stumpf, who headed the South African Atomic Energy Board at the time, recalls that for two weeks after the mystery flash South Africa was subjected to intense diplomatic pressure "and then overnight, just like that, the pressure disappeared."[15] Still, the State Department foresaw a potential disaster if the VELA information became public: "We should stress the extreme sensitivity of the information and the perhaps irreparable harm that a leak would cause to U.S. interests, particularly to other African and non-proliferation initiatives." Only a few key members of Congress should be informed, a State Department official wrote, and in the event of a leak they were to argue that "no corroborating evidence has come to light."[16]

Much to their chagrin, the leak came three days later, on October 25, courtesy of ABC News journalist—and former U.N. ambassador—John

Scali, who had famously acted as an intermediary between Soviet officials and the Kennedy administration during the 1962 Cuban Missile
Crisis.[17] With a strong incentive to sweep VELA under the rug, the
White House responded just as State had advised: by denying there was
any evidence.[18]

In the summer of 1980, new information emerged, further calling into
question the Ruina panel's findings. The U.S. Naval Research Laboratory submitted a three-hundred-page report, detailing its efforts to find
corroborating data in the air, the sea, glaciers, plants, and even the
remains of slaughtered sheep. The NRL found that air force missions
flown in the days after September 22 could not have detected fallout
from a nuclear explosion because the radioactive debris would have been
caught in a passing storm. Only one pilot had flown through the storm's
trajectory and by the time he did so, heavy rain would have already
caused the radioactive particles to decay to levels too low for detection.[19]

Then, in November 1980, the NRL's head, a no-nonsense scientist
named Alan Berman, wrote to the White House after receiving a highly
unusual report from an eminent biophysicist. The University of Ten-
nessee's L. van Middlesworth had been studying the thyroid glands of
slaughtered sheep from across the world for twenty-five years. Because
sheep concentrate iodine in their thyroids, the glands can be measured
as an indicator of exposure to radioactivity. Van Middlesworth found
iodine-131, a fission by-product, in Australian sheep slaughtered in Mel-
bourne during October 1979. Never before or after had he detected this
radioactive material.[20]

To test the significance of the data, Berman mapped the footprint of
the fallout from the location of the suspected nuclear detonation in the
vicinity of the Prince Edward and Marion islands—"a splendid place to
go" for a clandestine nuclear test because of their shallow water and high
mountains for observation, according to Berman.[21] The map indicated
that the fallout from the test would have been carried by the prevailing
winds over southern Australia between September 26 and 27, showering
the sheep with radioactive rain. Berman also noted that weather stations
at the South Pole and in Chile had detected the highest incidences of
radioactive cesium and strontium in three years.[22] Despite this convincing evidence, the White House barely paid attention. Berman was so
angry that he leaked news of his team's findings to *Science* magazine,

complaining that the White House had issued the Ruina report before the Naval Research Laboratory was finished analyzing its data, and then had the nerve to dismiss it.[23] As the interagency bickering intensified, *The Washington Star* contacted Berman to ask why the White House was ignoring the NRL report and lying about the significance of its conclusions. Berman diplomatically explained the key findings to reporter John Fialka and told him, "I have no desire to get into a urinating contest with the White House."[24]

Meanwhile, however, Berman kept pressing his case. He wrote to White House senior adviser for technology and arms control John Marcum in December 1980 after analyzing hydroacoustic data—sound waves moving across the ocean—picked up by American listening stations in the vicinity of Ascension Island, which lies in the middle of the South Atlantic between the West African coast and Brazil.[25]

His letter explained that hydrophones near Ascension picked up a sound that was 25 decibels louder than typical background noise at 2:43 A.M., Greenwich Mean Time, approximately two hours after VELA had detected the flash.[26] Following the acoustic pattern established by an earlier French atomic test in the Pacific, Berman calculated that if these sound waves had traveled through the ocean from the presumed detonation point in the southern Indian Ocean and then bounced off the Antarctic ice shelf, it would have taken them one hour and fifty-one minutes to reach the listening station, producing an irregular noise at almost the exact time the hydrophones recorded the 25 decibel spike.[27] He offered to produce a broader study but told Marcum with barely disguised contempt that he doubted new data would "cause the Panel to come to a position that is significantly different from its present view."[28]

Berman was right to be skeptical. By the time Los Alamos issued a more detailed report in 1982, the Carter administration had left office and the event was largely forgotten. The nuclear science gurus in New Mexico had generated a model proving that VELA might even have detected a nuclear explosion of a clean device with no nuclear debris, possibly a neutron bomb. Few countries other than the United States and the Soviet Union would have possessed such advanced technology at the time, but Israel may have. *The New Yorker*'s Seymour Hersh has argued that Israel planned to test a low-yield nuclear artillery shell on a cloudy day, but that a break in the clouds allowed VELA to detect the flash.[29] By 2003, even Carter's CIA director, Stansfield Turner, was willing to weigh in—albeit cryptically—arguing that VELA detected "a man-made phenomenon."[30] Many of the country's leading scientists came to the same conclusion. Members of the U.S. Nuclear Intelligence Panel—which included Edward Teller—wrote a report that remains classified to this day. Nevertheless, they have openly called the conclusions of the Ruina panel a cover-up. Panel member Louis H. Roddis Jr., a prominent nuclear weapons scientist, claims, "There was a real effort on the part of the administration to downplay it. . . . Everybody in [Los Alamos] New Mexico was convinced that it was a test."[31] As Donald Kerr, the chairman of the panel, told Hersh: "We had no doubt it was a bomb."[32] And the only plausible perpetrator was Israel.

In the months following the mysterious double flash, CIA analysts argued that Israel had a strong incentive to conduct a secret nuclear test and South Africa would have likely "had enough confidence in Israeli security to consider conducting a joint test"—a highly unusual practice that only the United States and Britain had undertaken together in the past.[33] Unlike other countries that wished to stage nuclear tests, secrecy was essential if Israel was to maintain its opaque nuclear posture. "However," the CIA noted, Israel's ambiguous nuclear policy did not preclude "the possibility of a clandestine test conducted in a remote ocean area . . . a clandestine approach would have been virtually its only option."[34]

By the time the VELA event occurred in 1979, South Africa had learned from Israel that nuclear ambiguity could make the world take them seriously. Even though their first bomb was not yet armed and ready for testing, Defense Minister Malan knew how to use the mysterious double flash to his advantage. He explicitly told South Africa's ambassador in the United States not to deny that Pretoria had been involved. "We wanted the Russians to notice. . . . We didn't do it . . . but it suited us," recalls General Malan. "Remember one thing in this type of situation: bluffing. It's a hell of a good thing if you can use it to your advantage and I did," he says with a grin.[35]

But the CIA had called Malan's bluff. The analysts in Langley realized that it was unlikely that a South African test had caused the VELA flash because Pretoria was almost—but not quite—advanced enough to test its own weapon in late 1979. They recognized that South Africa had simply used Malan's public statement to hint that it might have already produced a working bomb—even though it hadn't.[36] The CIA predicted that Pretoria's program would "remain clandestine unless South Africa were to perceive a drastic deterioration of [its] security situation."[37] They were right. South Africa's nuclear strategy rested on three pillars: an Israeli-style ambiguity over the extent of their weapons program; an intent to reveal their nuclear capability only under dire circumstances and in order to obtain Western intervention; and finally, if the West did not intervene, a test to demonstrate their deterrent capability.[38]

Outside the CIA—and even within it—few people cared about Pretoria's budding arsenal. South Africa was not on the agency's nonproliferation A-list, according to Bob Campbell, a CIA veteran who was charged with trying to undermine Pretoria's nuclear program. While working for a domestic CIA station during the late 1970s, Campbell had targeted South African scientists studying abroad in the United States and lured one into defecting in exchange for U.S. citizenship. But by the early 1980s, halting South Africa's nuclear program was a secondary objective, and Israel's was accepted as a fait accompli. Both were far removed from more pressing proliferation concerns, such as India and Pakistan. After Carter left office, "There was a diplomatic reluctance to go up against either one of these countries," says Campbell. "They weren't interested in South African nukes anymore."[39] With Washington turning a blind eye and Israel lending a hand, South Africa's nuclear weapons program accelerated and its conventional capabilities grew stronger.

. . .

IN FEBRUARY 1980, while Israeli and South African intelligence czars met for their annual conference and exchanged information on enemy weapons and training, General David Ivry, the head of the Israeli Air Force, and his intelligence chief, Oded Erez, were off hunting wild animals.[40]

When air force general Tienie Groenewald picked up his Israeli visitors at Pretoria's Waterkloof Air Force Base, he found them reserved and withdrawn. "Ivry didn't want to talk," recalls Groenewald. Rather than turning to the serious business of aircraft upgrades, he decided to fly the taciturn Israelis straight to Kruger National Park, South Africa's biggest game-spotting destination. On the third day, desperate to get his guests to open up, Groenewald called the control tower to tell them they were going to shoot game. The Israelis sent their wives to a nearby chalet and set off into the bush with Groenewald.

"We landed on a farm not far from Hoedspruit and a friend picked us up," says Groenewald, paging through yellowed photographs of the Israelis in an old album. Groenewald gave the men rifles and within a few minutes Ivry had shot a zebra. "Erez and Ivry were very excited," he recalls. Groenewald had the zebra skin prepared for Ivry to take home and invited him to fly the Super Frelon helicopter back to base. "After that, he was another man," Groenewald recalls with great relish.[41] For his part, Ivry, still a man of few words, remembers it as "a professional visit" and claims that he was not involved in defense contracts as head of the IAF. He does recall, however, that the South Africans took him to Angola to see the front lines of their war against Cuba and the MPLA, a level of access rarely afforded to foreign visitors—unless they were Israelis.[42]

Things were heating up on the home front for South Africa as well. ANC guerrilla fighters were now regularly sabotaging railway lines and striking government offices. In June 1980, they successfully attacked a massive oil refinery in Sasolburg, causing R66 million (then $85 million) in damage. "The urban terrorist threat has become more real to us with a number of incidents in recent months," SADF chief Malan complained to Israeli chief of staff Raful Eitan.[43] As these internal threats to the apartheid regime mounted, it was Malan who took over the reins at the Defense Ministry.

Upon hearing of Malan's promotion, Yonah Efrat, the man who had helped give birth to the Israeli–South African alliance in 1973, scrawled a handwritten letter to his old friend Malan to congratulate him. "May the Mighty God be with you in all you do!!," he wrote in October 1980. "Remember, you have here a friend, and if I can be of any assistance to you, I can do it without formalities, and it always will be my pleasure."[44] The sense of a shared predicament had become so strong that Israeli and South African generals saw fighting the ANC and PLO as a joint mission—one that leaders in both countries pursued with great zeal and devotion.

While much of the governmental correspondence between Israel and South Africa during the 1970s and 1980s bears the formal tone of diplomatic business, the letters between military leaders are characterized by a remarkable sense of familiarity and friendship. They reveal the extent to which close personal relationships developed in the course of countless visits, during which they were afforded unfettered access to each other's military installations and close-up views of the front lines of their respective wars.

Yonah Efrat had retired from the military after serving as head of Israel's Central Command and became director of Israeli Petroleum Services.[45] Soon after becoming the new chief of the SADF, Constand Viljoen invited Efrat to South Africa and the following year Efrat returned the favor, hosting Viljoen and his wife in Israel.[46] He wrote to Malan praising Viljoen and reminded him in shaky English: "You know my deep friendship to you and my feelings towards South Africa, I hope the special relationship that you so carefully have build up will develop for the advantage of our both countries." Efrat assured Malan, "We know what is good for us, we can't depend on anybody but ourself, and we can do what is necessary, I truely believe it can be done better if we do it together. So let us hope and help each other."[47]

During the year 1980, two dozen South Africans attended a variety of courses in Israel on helicopter assault, air supply, antitank infantry, and intelligence, among other subjects.[48] Eitan told Malan, "We are only too pleased to have your men as our guests and to instruct them as an expression of the excellent relations between our armed forces."[49] The following year, just as he was planning one of the most daring military operations in Israeli history, Eitan came to South Africa with his entire family to spend time with the Viljoens.

Just before four in the afternoon on June 7, 1981, eight Israeli F-16s and six F-15s took off from Etzion Air Force Base, at the eastern edge of the Sinai Desert. Flying in a tight formation, the Israeli jets traversed the Red Sea, almost skimming the water, and flew below radar across the Saudi desert. As they crossed into Iraqi airspace and approached Baghdad, the F-15 escorts climbed steeply to create an umbrella and the F-16s unloaded their bombs on Osirak, the Iraqi nuclear reactor, which Israel considered a direct threat to its existence. Emerging from the glare of the setting sun, the Israeli jets evaded Iraqi antiaircraft fire; fifteen of sixteen bombs hit their target, destroying the reactor and killing ten Iraqi soldiers and one French scientist. They returned to Israel without a scratch.[50]

Three days after Israel's surprise attack on Iraq, Eitan wrote to Malan triumphantly: "Well, we did the deed with iron determination not to allow these crazy Arabs to possess nuclear weapons." Eitan expected an international outcry but felt it was worth it, melodramatically telling his friend, "We are not perturbed by all the 'righteous souls' that all the crocodiles in South African rivers could not provide with enough tears to wipe out their hypocrisy. . . . I am certain that you understand us very well."[51] Malan praised the attack and encouraged Eitan to disregard U.N. criticism, referring to the organization as "the international platform and propaganda machine of South Africa's enemies." He closed by telling his Israeli colleague, "It is comforting to know that South Africa does not stand alone in facing criticism from the international community. Our respective countries will have to withstand this in all its many manifestations."[52] Reams of such letters sent back and forth between leading generals recount battles fought and the number of terrorists killed by the SADF and IDF.[53]

The generals were not simply sharing intelligence and battlefield pointers but acting as advocates for each other on the international stage. Later that year, Israeli defense minister Ariel Sharon visited South Africa and publicly urged the West to rearm Pretoria in its fight against Cuban and Angolan communist forces—a comment that made the pages of *The New York Times.*[54] Malan replied, thanking Sharon for his "grave concern over the Soviet expansionism in Southern Africa and that you are prepared to speak up about this."[55]

When Viljoen traveled to Israel with his wife, Risti, in July 1981, Eitan showed him video footage of the Osirak operation that he had until then shared only with the Pentagon.[56] Just as Viljoen had invited visiting Israeli officers to join him on helicopter flights to Angola, Eitan returned the favor by allowing South African officials unfettered access to highly classified information on Osirak and Israel's new missile systems. So impressed was Eitan by the South African officers he met that he told Viljoen he preferred to make Israeli instruction available to the SADF over and above any other military force in the world.[57]

The South African general was entertained by Prime Minister Menachem Begin, Chief of Staff Raful Eitan, Dieter Gerhardt's old host, Abrasha Tamir, as well as familiar faces like Amos Baram and air force head David Ivry, all of whom had recently been in South Africa.[58] Ivry urged Viljoen to step up cooperation between the two militaries even further, pressing him to update the South African Air Force's fighter jets with new Israeli weapons systems rather than relying on what he deemed "a 1968 model."[59] The South Africans took his advice, setting the stage for one of the most lucrative arms deals yet between the two countries.

· · ·

ON JUNE 3, 1982, Israel's ambassador to the United Kingdom was shot in the head as he got into his car outside London's Dorchester Hotel. Miraculously, he survived. But the assassination attempt by the Abu Nidal terrorist organization gave Israel a casus belli. Israel and the PLO had been exchanging fire for months in southern Lebanon, and the growing entrenchment of the PLO in Beirut worried the Begin government. The organization had reconstituted itself in Lebanon after being expelled from Jordan in the early 1970s and now the Israeli army, led by Ariel Sharon, intended to destroy it. The next day, Israeli fighter jets strafed Shiite villages across southern Lebanon and the Palestinian refugee camps surrounding Beirut. On June 6, ground forces pushed twenty-five miles north into Lebanon while Katyusha rockets rained down on northern Israel in retaliation. Christian Lebanese forces—the South Lebanese Army and Bashir Gemayel's Phalangist movement— joined the Israeli assault. Sharon even attempted to send Israeli troops into West Beirut.

Hirsh Goodman, a South African–born defense correspondent for *The Jerusalem Post*, remembers senior military commanders thinking Sharon had gone mad. "His arrogance was monumental, his brazenness beyond belief," wrote Goodman, who routinely left his home in Jerusalem at 3:00 A.M. to drive north to the border, where he rubbed mud on his Israeli license plates and drove fast to avoid snipers.[60] This time, Begin stopped Sharon in his tracks and restricted him to laying siege to the city while the air force pounded West Beirut from above.

Finally, in late August, the PLO leadership left Lebanon as part of a U.S.-brokered agreement that allowed them to set up a safe haven in Tunisia. The war appeared to be over. Then, on September 14, Phalange leader Bashir Gemayel, upon whom Sharon had placed all his hopes for the future of Lebanon, was killed by a massive car bomb. Israeli troops moved into West Beirut the next day and, on September 16, surrounded the Sabra and Shatila refugee camps as Phalangist soldiers entered them, seeking to avenge their leader's death.

Thomas Friedman, on his first foreign assignment for *The New York Times*, was among the journalists who entered the camps after the killings. He and his colleagues were confronted with piles of decomposed corpses and the stench of death. "Entire families had been slain as they sat at the dinner table. Others were found dead in their nightclothes," Friedman wrote in the first of a series of articles that would win him a Pulitzer Prize. "Some people were found with their throats slit. Others had been mutilated with some kind of heavy blade, perhaps axes," he wrote, as if still in shock.[61] Robert Fisk of London's *Independent* was even more graphic: "There were babies . . . already in a stage of decomposition—tossed into rubbish heaps alongside discarded US army ration tins, Israeli army equipment and empty bottles of whiskey," he wrote in his book *Pity the Nation*.[62]

In Israel, 400,000 demonstrators—close to 10 percent of the country's population—took to the streets in protest, forcing the government to convene a commission of inquiry two weeks after the massacre. Although Sharon eventually resigned in disgrace after the commission found him responsible for failing to prevent the Sabra and Shatila massacres, Israel would remain mired in Lebanon for nearly two decades fighting the Iranian-funded Shia militia Hezbollah, which inherited the PLO's mission of expelling the Zionist invaders after Arafat's men departed.

It was in the midst of the IDF's Lebanese invasion that Constand Viljoen returned to Israel, and he was promptly flown north to the front lines deep inside Lebanese territory. His was the first foreign group allowed to visit the war zone, before even the United States. Viljoen marveled at the IDF's operational planning, calling it a "masterwork," and

detailed the various Israeli divisions and their roles in the invasion in a
report prepared for Malan.[63]

After hearing the news of Sharon's resignation, Malan wrote sympa-
thetically, "I have learned with regret of the circumstances under which
you vacated the Defense portfolio." Without a hint of disapproval, he
thanked Sharon for "the friendly and understanding way in which you
have conducted matters of mutual interest between ourselves and our
respective Defense Forces."[64]

As the top brass of the two countries grew more intimate, South Africa's
covert defense mission in Israel—a group of SADF and Armscor employees overseeing joint Israeli–South African projects—began to panic
about security. The early 1980s were the heyday of military cooperation
between Israel and South Africa, but it was becoming a much riskier
enterprise. The U.N. had imposed an oil embargo against South Africa
in 1980 and Israel remained the only major violator of the arms embargo.

The years from 1981 to 1983 also marked the height of the academic
divestment campaign on campuses throughout the United States. Thousands of leftist students across the country pressured university adminis-
trators to remove South African investments from their portfolios,
making the abolition of apartheid the focus of campus political activism
in much the same way civil rights and Vietnam had been in the 1960s and
1970s. A nineteen-year-old Barack Obama gave his first political speech
in February 1981, urging the trustees of Occidental College in Los
Angeles to divest from South Africa.[65]

As the movement gained popularity and calls for sanctions on Capitol
Hill became louder, more and more U.S. universities ended their South
African investments. It was a particularly sensitive time and Israel espe-
cially feared any leaks about its involvement with the apartheid regime.
The close ties between South African and Israeli military officials could
be kept a secret for only so long.

In 1981, there were twenty South African students attending the
American School in Tel Aviv; all but four of them were the sons and
daughters of South African defense officials working clandestinely in
Israel. While the students were given cover stories about their parents'
occupations, teachers and other parents at the school were becoming suspicious about the unusually large South African contingent, and Armscor

officials were afraid that their covert mission in Israel—and the extent of the military ties between the two countries—might be exposed.[66]

While the press was aware of cooperation between the two countries, the existence of a sizable South African defense mission in Tel Aviv was not public knowledge. When two long-serving members of the mission departed, the South African embassy begged for replacements without school-age children so they would not have to invent another set of cover stories. The SADF mission cabled headquarters complaining that it was hard to keep such stories intact while learning Hebrew in an *ulpan* (language school) because it was difficult for children to conceal their parents' true identity in a classroom setting. South Africa's naval attaché was pretending to be an underwater researcher but had no idea who the prominent Israeli oceanographers were; his predecessor, posing as a computer engineer, was caught off guard when asked to help a friend's son with math problems, which he could not solve.[67]

As Armscor representatives in Israel fretted about blowing their cover, their colleagues in Pretoria were beginning work on more advanced nuclear delivery systems. The growing Cuban presence in Angola and the increasingly advanced Russian weapons in their arsenal meant that the apartheid regime could no longer rely exclusively on airplanes as the sole means of delivering nuclear weapons. As three veterans of the nuclear program have admitted, "The decision was accordingly taken to develop medium range ballistic missiles as a second element of South Africa's nuclear armoury."[68] In addition to TV-guided glide bombs to be dropped from aircraft, the government instructed the Armscor scientists to build a nuclear warhead for the new missiles.

Israeli and South African scientists were also beginning to travel back and forth between the two countries more frequently. In 1980, the Atomic Energy Board sought to recruit Israelis to work at the Pelindaba reactor, luring scientists to South Africa, where wages were significantly higher. SASOL, the energy giant, followed the AEB's example and placed ads in Israeli papers for chemical engineers and technicians offering superior salaries as well as moving expenses and annual leave.[69] These scientific exchanges worried both governments, lest they become public and lend credence to the anti-apartheid movement's oft-repeated claim that South Africa and Israel were cooperating in the construction of nuclear weapons.

Maintaining secrecy became a much bigger problem in May 1984, when James Adams of London's *Sunday Times* published a book on the Israeli–South African relationship entitled *The Unnatural Alliance*. Using unclassified sources and a variety of anonymous informants, Adams made far-reaching assertions about military cooperation between the two countries. The covert mission in Tel Aviv read Adams closely and wrote to military intelligence headquarters in Pretoria, warning that his work was partially true and could cause problems. An officer marked up the book in different colors based on the truth or falsity of allegations, classified it as secret, and sent it to Pretoria via diplomatic pouch. The greatest danger, he cautioned, was that the book could "serve as the chief source of reference for propagandists" seeking to tarnish either South Africa's or Israel's image.[70]

The revelations in Adams's book and the press attention it received did little to slow the thriving arms trade between the two countries, however. In addition to precision-guided missiles built by IAI, the Israeli and South African governments were also discussing a potential deal for riot prevention equipment to use against black protesters in the townships.[71] Having seen in the press that the IDF chief of staff was inspecting new antiriot equipment "being used against demonstrators in the West Bank," Eddie Webb, the head of the defense mission in Tel Aviv, asked the Israeli Defense Ministry "to arrange for me to see this new equipment."[72] In January 1984, the IDF took Webb on a tour of the West Bank to see the military headquarters and to observe the workings of the occupying military government. A few months later, the SADF requested Israeli training courses in antiterrorism techniques.[73]

The annual Israeli–South African intelligence conference was held at IDF headquarters in Tel Aviv in 1984. The two governments exchanged information on the Soviet military presence in North Africa, Libyan pilots in Lesotho, Cuban activities in Mozambique and São Tomé, Chinese military aid to Tanzania, Algeria's air force cooperation with Madagascar, Soviet contacts with the PLO leadership, and the more mundane matter of Russian fishing activities.[74] Now, with 25,000 Cuban troops in Angola and more on their way, there was no end to the war in sight. P. W. Botha and Magnus Malan's theory of "total onslaught" was beginning to sound more credible.

As the Cuban presence grew during the early 1980s, South Africa entered Angola several more times and SWAPO continued its cross-border raids to attack SADF positions in Namibia. By this time, South Africa's air force was becoming obsolete. The last aircraft from France had come in the early 1970s; British prime minister Harold Wilson had canceled all orders placed in the United Kingdom in the mid-1970s; and the United States, which had enforced the embargo on South Africa earlier than others, forbade the export of aircraft engines. "We couldn't buy any damn aircraft," says Hannes Steyn, Armscor's R&D director in the 1980s.[75] Israel therefore became a vital source for the South African Air Force, and it was heavily involved in Pretoria's quest to maintain air supremacy in Angola, modernizing the aging Mirage III fleet that Pretoria had acquired from France in the 1960s. "Israel was probably our only avenue in the 1980s," admits Jan van Loggerenberg, the head of the air force from 1988 to 1991.[76] As David Ivry had warned Viljoen back in 1979, no country could defeat the latest Soviet technology with "1968 models," and so they began two major projects—code-named Brahman and Gate—to update the Mirage fleet, giving birth to what came to be known as the Cheetah jet.[77] It was a massive investment for South Africa and a huge boon for the Israeli defense industry.

Plans were also in the works to build a new South African Air Force headquarters, hardened to withstand attack. Pieter John Roos traveled to Israel under a pseudonym to discuss the project with Defense Ministry officials in April 1984.[78] "The Israeli government knew exactly what was going on," says Roos, but in order to avoid ruffling feathers in Washington, "we traveled under false passports," he recalls. Many Israelis subsequently moved to South Africa to work on this and other air force projects.[79] Israel also supplied Pretoria with remote-piloted drone aircraft and two Boeing 707s, which were used for air-to-air refueling and extended the range of South Africa's strike capability dramatically.[80]

By August 1984, two Cheetah prototypes were sent to Israel for upgrades of their weapons systems and avionics—the electronics, communication, and navigation capabilities of the aircraft—based on systems used in Israel's Kfir fighter jets.[81] As the updated Cheetahs rolled off the IAI assembly line, the South African Air Force began placing orders for spare parts and requesting training sorties in Israel for South African pilots.[82]

When the first two Cheetah prototypes returned to Pretoria, the South African company Atlas Aircraft disingenuously presented them to the press and the public as homegrown designs. But their origin was obvious to informed observers. The United States' Defense Intelligence Agency observed that the "Cheetah is an upgraded version of the French Mirage III," without explicitly pointing to Israel as the contractor.[83]

Although it had grasped Pretoria's defense strategy, the CIA was still in the dark regarding the precise details of South Africa's nuclear cooperation with Israel. As late as 1983, analysts wrote: "Other than the sale of 10 tons of nominally safeguarded uranium to Israel in 1963, we have little confirmed information." However, they acknowledged that it was probably happening. Given that Israel had technical expertise and South Africa had natural resources, it was clear that "each side could contribute to the nuclear weapons program of the other."[84]

. . .

DURING THE EARLY 1980S, the scientists and engineers in charge of the South African nuclear weapons program were based at a facility on the outskirts of Pretoria known as Kentron Circle. The plant was located adjacent to a vehicle testing track about ten miles away from the reactor at Pelindaba. South Africa produced its first Hiroshima-style nuclear weapon in April 1982.[85] In addition to these gun-type fission bombs, Kentron's engineers studied implosion technology and thermonuclear fusion devices, which rely on tritium and deuterium.[86] For high-tech weapons like these, the sensitive cargo Jan Blaauw acquired from Israel would be essential.[87]

Late in 1984, the South African chief of staff for intelligence wrote to SADF chief Constand Viljoen, requesting his approval for a top secret visit to Israel regarding cooperation on building and testing missiles. The visitor was Armscor's head of international acquisitions and research, B. C. de Bruyn. The subject line of the letter was telling; it revealed that de Bruyn's visit was part of Project Kerktoring (Church Tower), one of the code names given to the South African nuclear program since its inception.[88]

De Bruyn traveled to Israel with the security manager of the Overberg Test Range—a military installation located along South Africa's rugged shoreline near Cape Agulhas, the continent's southernmost point. The sleepy neighboring town of Arniston was best known for whale watching, secluded beaches, and its spectacular natural beauty. Overberg, facing thousands of miles of open sea, was the perfect location to launch a missile.

Test-firing long-range missiles without flying them over enemy territory was not a luxury Israel had; South Africa, on the other hand, had the space, money, and good scientific infrastructure necessary. Most important, co-production and joint testing helped offset research and development costs for Israel. The centerpiece of the joint Israeli–South African effort was modernizing the Israeli Jericho 2 missile, an intermediate-range ballistic missile capable of carrying a nuclear warhead more than nine hundred miles—much farther than Israel had been able to launch its missiles over the Mediterranean during the 1979 tests South African observers had attended.[89]

In Tel Aviv, de Bruyn and his colleague focused on security operations. They wanted to make sure information security was tight when Israelis moved to South Africa to work at the missile testing range. The top secret memo to Viljoen laid out de Bruyn's mission in Israel: "He must evaluate the credibility of existing cover stories and the ability of the new families to live up to them," and also get to know all those involved.[90]

In 1985, the year after de Bruyn's visit to Israel, Prime Minister P. W. Botha was forced to slash the country's military budget for fear of impending international sanctions. Although he dealt a blow to some of the nuclear program's most advanced projects by halting research on plutonium and tritium production, he allowed research on implosion technology and boosted thermonuclear warheads to continue.[91] Consequently, the Overberg Test Range and the missiles being tested there were not affected. Quietly, as many as seventy-five Israelis—who were far more advanced in the field of rocketry than their South African counterparts—came to South Africa during the 1980s to work on the missile program while more than two hundred South Africans went to Israel.[92]

Security at Overberg was tight. Although the CIA was aware that the two countries were working together, the analysts in Langley did not know the full extent of Israeli–South African military and nuclear cooperation in the mid-1980s—and de Bruyn intended to keep them in the dark.[93] For the next five years, the formidable propaganda machine both states had created to downplay and deny their ties would help Overberg remain shrouded from public view, giving South Africa and Israel the breathing—and testing—room they needed to develop a nuclear missile.

9

MASTERS OF SPIN

Propaganda, Denial, and the Concealment of the Alliance

In theory, you will give equal rights to all. . . . In practice, it's another matter. But make the world believe you are sincere. You have to be hypocritical to survive.

—*Yediot Ahronot* editor Aharon Shamir to
South African Foreign Ministry official J. J. Becker[1]

SOUTH AFRICA FOUND ITSELF with an image problem in Israel, of all places, in the early 1980s. Six years in opposition and the massive protests against the Lebanon War after the Sabra and Shatila massacres had energized the Israeli left. Unlike the tame response to the Vorster visit in 1976, critics of apartheid were beginning to speak out against the alliance and clash with the conservative legislators and military officials who sought even closer ties.

In April 1983, Israeli journalist Yoav Karni stumbled across an article in the Labor Party newspaper, *Davar,* announcing that the A. D. Gordon School—named for a socialist Zionist pioneer—had "adopted" the South African embassy as part of an Education Ministry initiative designed to bring local schools and the Tel Aviv diplomatic community closer.[2] *Davar* likened the partnership with South Africa's embassy to "a poor joke," given the left-wing values of the school's namesake. An eighth-grade student went further, writing a militant article in the student newspaper denouncing his school's adoption of the embassy. Karni one-upped the teenager by appearing at the grand finale of the event dressed in a white colonial suit and stepping, uninvited, to the microphone, where he recited the popular anti-apartheid poem "The Child Who Was Shot Dead by Soldiers at Nyanga" in both Hebrew and English. The principal called the police.[3]

Karni defended his actions as "an elementary act of protest" and insisted that "only a madman, a clown or a misanthrope could request the auspices of the South African embassy for children's week and crown it with slogans of human brotherhood." The event became a national news story. Liberal Knesset members declared the school's principal unfit to serve;[4] radio shows condemned Karni's outburst; and a sympathetic far-left newspaper noted that "A. D. Gordon would certainly have turned over in his grave this week had he known what was done in the school named after him."[5] When the Labor Party—still in opposition—took an official position and condemned the Gordon School for adopting the South African embassy, the principal responded with great chutzpah, writing publicly to Labor Party chairman Shimon Peres and telling him, "[We] would be pleased to hear from you and from other members of your party about our ties with South Africa over the years, your visit and the visits of others there. I am sure that our pupils will find that very useful."[6] Peres did not reply.

As the Gordon School event threatened to become a diplomatic incident, the mayor of Tel Aviv wrote a letter to South African ambassador David du Buisson, apologizing for Karni's "unspeakably outrageous behaviour" and promised to protest to the reporter's boss at *Yediot Ahronot*.[7] The former South African ambassador to Israel Stuart Franklin wrote to friends in Tel Aviv telling them, "Yoav Karni is really going out of his way to endeavor to embarrass South Africa and to harm Israel South Africa relations." Franklin reached out to prominent South African Jews, appealed to the country's chief rabbi, and, along with the head of the South African Zionist Federation, established a committee to counter anti–South African press in Israel.[8]

This marked the beginning of a modest effort by Pretoria to buy influence in the Israeli media by providing all-expenses-paid trips to journalists visiting South Africa. Yet such blatant boosterism was doomed to fail in a country where anti-apartheid sentiment was slowly spreading beyond lefty journalism circles.

South Africa may have scored a diplomatic coup when Vorster was invited to Israel in 1976 but that did not provide Pretoria with the international legitimacy it craved. After the Information Scandal, the South African government had been forced to retreat on the PR front and give up its ambitious program of buying influence and airbrushing its image in the West. Preserving South Africa's image as a bastion of Western civilization and a bulwark against communism remained vital, however, and Pretoria still faced the daunting challenge of selling the world's most unpopular product: apartheid.

Israel may have had many enemies and a formidable propaganda machine arrayed against it in the 1980s, but its legitimacy was never questioned by key Western powers in the way South Africa's was. Being identified as an ally of the apartheid regime was deeply damaging to the Jewish state's reputation. Now, with anti-apartheid groups increasingly pointing to Israel as the lead violator of embargoes and boycotts against South Africa, downplaying trade ties with Pretoria became a priority for the Israeli government and Jewish organizations throughout the world—regardless of the facts.

Given the constant attacks both countries faced at the United Nations, secrecy about the extent of their ties was paramount. And where secrecy was impossible, spin became essential. Indeed, the relationship would never have survived had it not been for the cover provided by propagandists, who managed to deny ties, downplay trade, and sugarcoat the data that could not be hidden. Government spokesmen in the two countries went to great lengths to paint a picture of low-level, inconsequential relations while concealing the true extent of economic ties and military cooperation. Disguise and denial became the norm.

· · ·

BY THE EARLY 1980S, sharp divisions were emerging within the Israeli government. Certain right-wing parliamentarians and retired military officials became enthusiastically involved as investors in South Africa's black homelands (bantustans) of Ciskei and Bophuthatswana, whose "independence" was recognized only by Pretoria. These bantustans were the pinnacle of the apartheid government's separate development policy, and were meant to be its crowning achievement. By creating "independent" black states arranged along tribal and linguistic lines in far removed locations, the apartheid intelligentsia had hoped to externalize its race problem. If officials in Pretoria relocated large numbers of urban blacks to places like Bophuthatswana and Ciskei, so the logic went, they could strip blacks of South African citizenship and drastically reduce the black population in South Africa proper, thereby neutralizing criticism of white minority rule as well as demands for black political enfranchisement.

Much to Pretoria's chagrin, the United Nations did not recognize the bantustans, and no other U.N. member states formally acknowledged their existence. But Israel came remarkably close to granting the bantustans de facto recognition by allowing massive investment by private citizens, opening offices for their trade representatives, and welcoming visits from leaders the rest of the world deemed illegitimate.

Lucas Mangope, Bophuthatswana's "president," visited Israel for the first time in 1981. Mangope was widely considered a puppet and a joke in South Africa; but in Israel, he was taken seriously and met with luminaries such as General Moshe Dayan.[9] When Mangope visited again on a trade mission in 1983, Shabtai Kalmanovitz, a Russian immigrant to Israel who proclaimed himself Bophuthatswana's "ambassador" to Israel, chauffeured Mangope's wife around Tel Aviv in a black Mercedes flying Bophuthatswana's flag.[10] By May 1985, Bophuthatswana's "embassy" in Tel Aviv, located prominently beside the British embassy along the seafront, was flying its flag proudly, despite the objections of the Israeli Foreign Ministry, which did not recognize it as a country.[11] Relations with the smaller bantustan of Ciskei were similarly cozy. Ciskei's "president," Lennox Sebe, visited Israel frequently and established a trade office in Tel Aviv operated by two Israelis with connections to the radical right-wing Gush Emunim settlers' movement. Fittingly, the Ciskeian capital, Bisho, signed a sister-city agreement with the West Bank settlement town of Ariel. Sebe even went so far as to claim that Israel had granted official recognition to Ciskei, which the Foreign Ministry immediately denied.[12]

From the beginning, Israeli diplomats were uncomfortable with private Israeli investment in the bantustans. David Kimche, a former high-ranking Mossad official who had helped mastermind Israel's Africa strategy in the 1960s—and played a key role in the American Iran-contra scandal of the 1980s—was the most skeptical. In 1980, Kimche had become director-general of the Foreign Ministry and was an early advocate of changing policy toward South Africa. Kimche supported the idea of beginning a political dialogue with black South African leaders at a time when relations with the apartheid government were strongest. At the same time, he tried to prevent Israeli involvement in the bantu-stans.[13] Kimche told reporters he regretted that "some Israeli citi-zens . . . for purely pecuniary reasons, have connected themselves with these homelands," and worried that it would damage his ministry's efforts to rekindle ties with the black African states that had severed them a decade earlier, a pet project that Kimche pursued for strategic rather than sentimental reasons.[14]

But many other Israelis were more interested in the financial opportu-nities presented by the bantustans. Colonel Efraim Poran, an influential former military adviser to Prime Minister Begin, served as a security adviser to the Ciskei government;[15] other Israelis started textile factories or went into construction.[16]

These relationships soon soured, however. Ciskeian military officers taking lessons from Israelis described the lectures on security as useless because the instructors spoke lousy English; Israeli-built hospitals with broken panels and cracked joints were cited for inferior construction work; and the owner of an Israeli flight school where Ciskeian pilots were training was indicted by a U.S. court for trying to smuggle Ameri-can helicopters into the bantustan. Sebe eventually declared that the West Bank settlers acting as his trade representatives in Israel no longer spoke for Ciskei and he suspended all economic ties in late 1985 as cor-ruption investigations began.[17]

The Israeli Foreign Ministry's opposition to ties with these bantustans stemmed from simple diplomatic logic rather than a moral crusade against apartheid, but it marked the beginning of a major rift between the defense establishment and the diplomatic corps that would grow wider in the coming years. The diplomats hoped to spare Israel the embarrassment of being seen doing business in pseudo-states shunned by the rest of the world; meanwhile, the Defense Ministry wanted to forge even closer ties with the government in Pretoria.

It was not only left-wing journalists and diplomats who frowned upon Israel's relationship with South Africa. In June 1983, Bank Hapoalim—Israel's largest bank—withdrew its sponsorship of an Israeli–South Afri-can Chamber of Commerce event under pressure from left-wing Knesset members.[18] One of those ministers announced she would submit a par-liamentary question to Prime Minister Shamir regarding Israeli arms sales to South Africa, despite the Foreign Ministry's insistence that Israel was honoring the U.N. arms embargo.[19] It was not only a matter of political grandstanding and moral disapproval; like Kimche, many on the left worried that relations with the apartheid regime would tarnish Israel's image throughout the world at a time when South Africa evoked near universal condemnation.

The same year, Naomi Chazan, a Hebrew University professor who later became a member of the Knesset for the left-wing Meretz Party, published an article in the journal *African Affairs* entitled "The Fallacies of Pragmatism." The crux of her argument was that "Israel has become embroiled in an unequal relationship with ambiguous returns," having given a great deal to South Africa while receiving nothing but a growing chorus of international opprobrium in exchange.[20] For Chazan, like most Israelis outside the security establishment, it was easy to argue that Israel was getting the short end of the stick. But there was a blind spot in her analysis: the crucial role the arms industry played in Israel's economy. As Chazan may have discovered later, after she joined the Knesset, South Africa's massive export market for Israeli weapons made the returns on the relationship anything but ambiguous.

The chorus of anti-apartheid voices in Israel grew louder in March 1985, when, twenty-one years after Arthur Goldreich's arrival, another South African Jewish political prisoner, Denis Goldberg, was released and came to Israel. Goldberg had been a defendant alongside Nelson Mandela in the 1963 Rivonia trial and was one of the most prominent ANC political prisoners. A kibbutznik named Herut Lapid—on a personal crusade to free Jewish prisoners across the world—decided to take up Goldberg's case after meeting the prisoner's daughter on a kibbutz. Lapid "went to England and found every influential Jew in the Tory government and he badgered them" to exert pressure on South African leaders, says Goldberg of his savior. He was so annoyingly persistent that Goldberg's own wife, living in London, "shrank with embarrassment." But, in the end, Lapid's efforts succeeded.[21]

As part of the deal Lapid negotiated, Goldberg was required to renounce violence as a condition for his release, something that no other ANC prisoners were willing to do at the time. He struggled with the decision, knowing that he might be shunned by the ANC leadership in exile for making such a concession. "I was tired of being a symbol . . . I wanted to be active," says Goldberg, who figured that younger ANC militants could carry forward the armed struggle more effectively than he could.[22] In the end, the ANC leadership supported his choice. By the time he was freed from prison, Goldberg had served twenty-two years in Pretoria, far away from Mandela and his other black and Indian comrades, most of whom were detained on Robben Island—South Africa's Alcatraz—off the coast of Cape Town. After his release, Goldberg was flown straight to Tel Aviv.

Goldberg arrived in Israel amid a media frenzy. He granted interviews to journalists from all over the world, who had not had the chance to speak with a major South African political prisoner since Arthur Goldreich and Harold Wolpe escaped in 1963. Goldberg made it his goal to convince Israel to sever its close ties to the apartheid government. "Through its relations with South Africa, Israel aids in the government's oppression," he told the *Chicago Tribune*'s Jonathan Broder. "I believe it is not in Israel's long-term interest to ally itself with oppression. The Jews, who have experienced centuries of oppression, have a moral duty not to ally themselves with the South African regime,"[23] he told his hosts, urging them to "stop killing black South Africans" by selling arms to the white regime.[24]

Given that the details and extent of the alliance were still well-kept secrets, many did not believe Goldberg's claims of extensive military cooperation. Still, the initial public response to him was quite positive—until Goldberg was quoted in the magazine *Koteret Rashit* expressing sympathy for the plight of Palestinians and defending terrorism as a political tactic. "Terrorism must be effective. The question is not a moral one," Goldberg was quoted as saying. "It is very possible that innocent people will get killed, but that is the price."[25] The Israeli right immediately lashed out at him, urging the authorities to expel him from the country. Right-wing parliamentarian Ge'ula Cohen called him a terrorist on the Knesset floor and insisted that the Law of Return—permitting any Jew to claim Israeli citizenship—should not apply to him. "This is a woman who put bombs in wells in Arab marketplaces," Goldberg says, laughing, referring to Cohen's days in the Lehi underground movement prior to Israel's independence.[26]

The SADF mission in Tel Aviv relished the backlash against Goldberg; they saw Cohen's outburst in the Knesset as "a golden chance" to show the public that the ANC and PLO were one and the same and to enlist the Israeli public's support for the South African government.[27] Suddenly a pariah, Goldberg left Israel a few weeks later and moved to London, where he began working at the ANC office and keeping a lower profile than he had in Israel.[28]

While Karni, Chazan, and Goldberg spoke out, other Israelis reacted by enthusiastically defending ties with South Africa.[29] The same year that Goldberg was released, Professor Moshe Sharon moved to Johannesburg to become director-general of the South African Zionist Federation. Sharon had been an Arab affairs adviser to Menachem Begin and to IDF forces during the invasion of Lebanon. Upon arrival in South Africa, he immediately offered his services to the South African Foreign Ministry, telling them "the SAZF would do all in its power to blunt anti–South African agitation." Sharon quickly absorbed the paranoia of his white South African neighbors. When his pistol was stolen from his Johannesburg home just before his domestic servant left to return to the Transkei bantustan, Sharon reported the incident to authorities, noting with alarm that the maid's husband was "connected to the ANC." South African government officials were pleased that Sharon had "plainly put the SAZF in the service of our department."[30] When it came to repairing Pretoria's image in Israel, Sharon seemed a powerful ally.

Meanwhile, back in Israel, a new organization called Soviet Jews for South Africa surfaced under the leadership of Avigdor Eskin, a recent immigrant from Russia. Eskin wrote to South African president P. W. Botha, telling him, "All of us are former Soviet citizens, and we are troubled in the light of defeatist tendencies of the West today." Eskin went on to assure Botha: "We pray that you will maintain enough strength to resist the growing pressure being exerted by liberal Western politicians. Moreover, we hope that the bloody leader of terrorism, Nelson Mandela, will never be released."[31] As an anticommunist Soviet Jew, Eskin knew exactly which buttons to push—an indication that he might make an effective mouthpiece for Pretoria.

South African government officials saw promise in Eskin because Jewish organizations had paraded him around the United States five years earlier with great success. Fresh from the Soviet Union, the twenty-one-year-old Eskin had spoken at prominent venues such as the Simon

Wiesenthal Center and was interviewed by the *Detroit Free Press*. As an articulate young Russian refugee he proved successful as a fund-raiser for the cause of Soviet Jewish resettlement in Israel and diplomats in Pretoria believed they could refashion him as a pro–South African lobbyist in powerful American Jewish circles. When Eskin led a pro–South African demonstration back home in July 1986, the Foreign Ministry in Pretoria brimmed with enthusiasm at reports that dozens of right-wing Israelis had demonstrated in favor of South Africa in front of foreign TV cameras.[32] They requested copies of the videotape and forwarded it to SABC News.

· · ·

AS THE SANCTIONS MOVEMENT gathered steam in 1985, the South African government found itself buckling under the weight of international criticism. Having abandoned the covert influence peddling and subversion of the Rhoodie era for a softer approach internationally, officials in Pretoria were desperate for Israeli advice on public relations.

Throughout the mid-1980s, J. J. Becker, the chief director of foreign affairs, held a series of discussions with visiting Israelis about media strategy and the common lot of Israel and South Africa. When Aharon Shamir, the editor of *Yediot Ahronot*'s weekend magazine, came to Becker's office in October 1985, it was as if Eschel Rhoodie had returned from exile.

The prim and proper Becker explained to his guest that South Africa was moving away from apartheid, dutifully citing P. W. Botha's constitutional reforms permitting Coloreds and Indians to vote for their own chamber of Parliament. He lamented the fact that, "despite our efforts to do so, the international onslaught against South Africa not only continues but has increased in its scope." Becker seemed shocked at what the Israeli editor had to say in response.

Shamir, a former Irgun member, had no time for protocol and pleasantries. He told Becker bluntly: "You are faced with a hypocritical world. . . . The trend is to sound liberal. To be liberal is to be nice. It is a nice thing to give political rights to all the subjects of a country. Yet what we see in so many places in this world are governments giving those rights and then suppressing them."[33] Becker protested that granting full political equality would "lead to a Soviet-orientated black dictatorship."

Shamir, with a knack for political spin, asked, "Why do you not seem to be giving those rights by not really giving them?"

Becker was perplexed and asked how. "Take Israel," said Shamir "I am ready to give the Arabs equal rights but not now, not today. But we can say that after ten or twenty years, once we have allowed the Arabs to try out their rights, they might be ready for full and equal political rights with the Jews in Israel." The old Irgun fighter went on to suggest: "Give the blacks the vote very slowly. See how it works. Bit by bit. Explain your course of action, stress that it has never been done before. If you see that your bit by bit approach is not working, change it. But make the world believe you are sincere. You have to be hypocritical to survive." Citing his homeland as an example, Shamir insisted: "Look at Israel, it survives, and yet it is only a pinpoint in a sea of over 100 million Arabs. . . . Let the world see or think that there is agreement between Black and White."[34] Becker admitted, sheepishly, "You see, we are too honest, we perhaps do not know how to be hypocritical, we do not know how to mislead." Shamir explained, "That is because you are too far away from the West geographically. So you have not been able to study how hypocrisy is managed. But you have to try."[35]

A few months later, Likud Party Knesset member Ariel Weinstein and his wife visited the Foreign Ministry. Once again, Becker was lectured on how to sell South Africa to the world. "You must sell South Africa by yourselves and through your own people," said Weinstein. "Look what we did with the Arabs," he continued, referring to Israeli PR efforts. "We sent our Arabs abroad to sell our political product." By doing this, Weinstein explained, "we create the impression for the visitors that Arabs and Druzes are very much part of our society. You now have Coloureds and Indians in your parliament. Use them. Send them abroad to sell your product," he urged.[36]

When Becker complained that apartheid was quickly becoming a domestic political issue in the United States, Weinstein lectured him that "you need not always rely on the Congress. Build up your contacts with the Pentagon if Congress proves too difficult."[37] Weinstein's wife added that, as an Israeli, she found disenfranchisement based on skin color unacceptable. However, she added, "we nevertheless give less rights to our Arabs than the Israeli Jewish population enjoys . . . we have to take some measures to protect ourselves. . . . So you should explain that what you do is necessary to your own security." As if he'd had an epiphany,

Becker replied, "So you can discriminate for security reasons and that is acceptable?"[38]

Unfortunately for the South Africans, they had never managed to make this argument as effectively and successfully as the Israelis had, nor had they started making it as early. Israeli treatment of Palestinians had long since transformed Israel from a victim into an oppressor in the eyes of leftist organizations throughout the world. But for many Western governments, supporting Israel still offered the possibility of "continuous exorcism from fascism."[39] South Africa had no such moral claim, and supporting a white settler state did not help assuage Europe's guilty conscience; if anything, apartheid reminded European leaders of the ugly legacy of colonialism that they thought they had put behind them when African nations gained independence in the 1960s and 1970s.

With powerful countries challenging its right to rule, the South African government became defensive and spent most of its money on damage control. The Cold War argument—that Pretoria's resources and shipping lanes made it a strategic ally against communism—still held currency with the administration of Ronald Reagan in Washington and Margaret Thatcher's Tory government in London, but it was losing its value.[40]

According to former U.S. assistant secretary of state Herman Cohen, who served under President George H. W. Bush, it was "a very good campaign . . . the Reagan Republicans bought into it." But, by 1986, he says, the anti-apartheid movement had simply become too strong.[41] And to make matters worse, Becker's efforts to cultivate a positive image of South Africa overseas did not enjoy the unlimited financial resources of the Rhoodie era. In a 1986 telegram, Becker noted that only R200,000 was available for "image building items," a far cry from the tens of millions at Rhoodie's disposal a decade earlier and at a time when U.N. attacks on both countries were becoming more aggressive.[42]

Israel had been singled out by the U.N. as early as 1975, when the General Assembly passed a resolution equating Zionism with racism. South Africa had also been a favorite target of the General Assembly over the years, and the news that the two pariah nations were working together was a dream come true for their critics.

When the Special Committee Against Apartheid—which was dominated by Eastern bloc nations—convened its 1983 conference in Vienna to discuss "the alliance between Israel and South Africa," the Israeli embassy in Austria denounced it as "another anti-Israel propaganda orgy." The preconference polemic went on to characterize the material distributed at the "Vienna farce" as "concocted charges of cooperation between Israel and South Africa in the development of nuclear weapons . . . [and] conventional arms."[43] Of course, the Israelis were wrong on this count, but given the Defense Ministry's habit of keeping the Foreign Ministry in the dark, the diplomats at the Vienna embassy might have actually believed their own propaganda.[44]

The South African ambassador in Vienna later reported with great satisfaction that only twenty countries attended the conference and that the meeting was so insignificant that it had to be moved to a smaller venue after the first session.[45] Still, it received some attention. The Canadian broadcaster CBC devoted a Sunday morning radio program to the Vienna conference, charting the history of the Israeli–South African relationship, including Vorster's visit to Jerusalem in 1976, and citing international security experts on South African purchases of Israeli military hardware. Most interestingly, listeners from Toronto to Vancouver were treated to an unusual moment of honesty when the president of the Israel–South Africa Chamber of Commerce, Maurice Medalowitz, offered a rare admission of some of the true motives driving the relationship: "We have a budget to balance. Our exports are very important and it is a tremendous pity that we in Israel have to depend so largely on a defense capability," he said. "When it comes to choosing our friends, we haven't got too many friends that we can afford to antagonize. We need as many exports as possible."[46]

Israel made its comeback effort at the U.N. a few years later. It was not ultimately successful, but the attempt was far more convincing than previous responses to criticism of its ties with South Africa. Benjamin Netanyahu, then a rising star in the Likud Party, gave a powerful speech to the General Assembly in November 1986. Lacking any strong anti-apartheid role models from his own party, he quoted Shimon Peres—a moral beacon in his rhetoric, if not his actions—telling the Assembly: "For the Jewish people, apartheid is the ultimate abomination. It is an expression of the cruelest inhumanity. Israel will do everything possible to eliminate this odious system."[47] Netanyahu further stressed that "Israel believes that apartheid is not reformable and that it must be abolished if greater suffering is to be averted."[48] He then accused the Special Committee Against Apartheid of omission and distortion. Netanyahu mocked the committee for "proceeding to single out Israel without the slightest hesitation" while letting other countries off the hook. He argued forcefully that "the Arab oil producers provide the umbilical cord that nourishes the Apartheid regime." Furthermore, Netanyahu insisted, "they do so in direct violation of the 1979 United Nations oil embargo on oil shipments to South Africa, to which they themselves are signatories. And they have the audacity to single out Israel for 'special' trade links with South Africa!"[49]

While his speech was riddled with falsehoods and denials of Israel's military and trade ties with South Africa, Netanyahu was absolutely right that Arab and Iranian oil was flowing to the apartheid regime. The Amsterdam-based Shipping Research Bureau reported that 671 of the 845 documented tankers supplying oil to South Africa between January 1979 and December 1993 originated from ports in the Persian Gulf region. Many of these ships flew European flags and their cargoes were often owned by middlemen operating on behalf of the South African government, most notably the notorious tax evader Marc Rich, who was controversially pardoned—for other crimes—by U.S. president Bill Clinton just hours before he left office. The crude oil pumped into those tankers and delivered to South Africa came primarily from Saudi Arabia, the United Arab Emirates, and Iran.[50]

Saudi Arabia, the largest supplier, denied all of the Israeli accusations and referred to the Shipping Research Bureau reports as " 'unauthenticated' rumours and allegations."[51] But it is clear from a leaked advocate general's report in South Africa that Saudi oil flowed freely to South Africa throughout the early 1980s. Premiums of $2.00 to $4.50 per barrel on top of the listed price went to middlemen like Rich as well as oil traders in the producer countries, making violation of the embargo too lucrative to resist. South Africa's Muslim organizations were upset about the Arab countries' role in fueling the apartheid regime, but found that no one except the PLO had time for their grievances. And even the PLO did not protest the oil sales, because doing so would have jeopardized its own funding sources in the Gulf states.[52]

Although Netanyahu was correct on the issue of Arab and Iranian oil supplies, he went on to argue that allegations of special ties between Israel and South Africa were "flat nonsense" given that "independent IMF figures" (which excluded diamonds, uranium, and arms) revealed the trade to be a minuscule $100 million annually (when it was actually closer to five to ten times that amount, depending on the year). He denounced Israel's critics as "those who wish not only to defame Israel but also to deflect attention from their own furtive and enormously profitable trade with Pretoria." Netanyahu concluded with a rhetorical flourish, telling the Assembly, "The battle against Apartheid has reached an historic junction. It can either surge forward on a straight path to the total abolition of this hateful system. Or it can sink into the mud of falsehood and vindictiveness."[53]

The ANC had exposed itself to charges of double standards by failing to point fingers at its professed Arab allies when they circumvented oil sanctions. Anti-apartheid activists refrained from targeting Arab oil suppliers, they claim, because it would have allowed other sanctions violators to "use [Arab states] as a scapegoat in order to absolve themselves."[54] This is precisely what the Israelis did anyway by bringing the shipping data to the attention of the General Assembly while downplaying and denying their own involvement with South Africa.

What Netanyahu conveniently neglected to mention was that the oil deals between Saudi Arabia and South Africa were not negotiated at the ministerial level, approved by the cabinet, or seen as financially vital to the Saudi kingdom's economy. Moreover, because they were carried out by profiteering middlemen, South Africa's oil deals with Saudi Arabia did not require the same degree of trust, high-level coordination, or ongoing government-to-government cooperation necessary in its arms deals with Israel. Netanyahu's sudden rage at Arab violations of the oil embargo was also remarkably hypocritical, given that Israel had remained absent from the 1980 U.N. oil embargo vote in deference to their South African friends.[55] But he managed that hypocrisy exceedingly well.

. . .

JEWISH ORGANIZATIONS around the world jumped to the defense of Israel and downplayed its relationship with South Africa. Many began to publish their own pamphlets on the topic in the mid-1980s. B'nai B'rith International (the parent organization of the Anti-Defamation League) published a pamphlet entitled *Jews, Zionism and South Africa* and distributed it on American university campuses in 1985. The thin red-and-black booklet accused Arab states of selling oil to South Africa in much the same way as the Israeli delegation had at the U.N. and Moshe Decter's *New York Times* column had after Vorster's visit to Israel in 1976. The argument that "they are doing it too" was not particularly persuasive but by downplaying the true extent of the alliance it managed to convince many Jews that even if Israel's hands were not entirely clean, its critics' were dirtier.

The pamphlet clearly laid out the challenge facing left-wing Zionists: "Pro-Israel college students involved with the anti-apartheid movement have been placed on the defensive regarding Israel–South African relations. . . . Our objective is to strengthen the anti-apartheid movement by removing extraneous and intellectually dishonest issues."[56] Its author, a Boston University student named Yosef Abramowitz, was a zealous anti-apartheid activist whom the university's president threatened to expel for hanging a "divest" banner from his dormitory window.[57] Abramowitz wanted to prevent Israel's reputation from being tainted by association with the apartheid regime he reviled.

As was the case with other left-wing Jews who loved Israel but hated apartheid, Abramowitz's idealized image of the Jewish state blinded him to the reality on the ground and the pamphlet he wrote sought to disprove reports of an intimate Israeli–South African alliance. It argued that the strategy to discredit Israel through South Africa was "a two-pronged attack," involving the exposure of trade ties and the perpetuation of "the Zionism-equals-racism lie."[58]

Abramowitz had a sophisticated understanding of the propaganda forces lining up against Israel and was correct in his assertion that various anti-Israel groups were joining forces with the anti-apartheid movement in order to target Israel. However, he accepted the Israeli counterpropaganda uncritically. The Abramowitz pamphlet took the incomplete International Monetary Fund statistics at face value, arguing that Israel accounted for less than one percent of South Africa's total trade.[59] In fact it was approximately ten times that amount, and a 1984 report in the British journal *Intelligence Digest* ventured so far as to say, "It is probable that South Africa is Israel's largest trading partner," citing the diamond industry, arms, electronics, and steel and coal supplies.[60] While this assertion may have been a slight overstatement, there is no doubt that South Africa was one of Israel's primary trading partners after the United States, surpassing Germany and the United Kingdom as a market for Israeli exports throughout the 1980s.[61]

Furthermore, the Abramowitz pamphlet regurgitated the propaganda emanating from South Africa that painted leaders of the Jewish community in a glowing light. He praised South African Jews as "more progressive than the society around them" and lauded the 1985 Board of Deputies resolution proclaiming that the organization "rejects apartheid." But by 1985, this was a meaningless pronouncement, given that Botha's government itself claimed that it was doing away with apartheid. Even South African Zionist Federation head Marcus Arkin acknowledged that the board had "done nothing more daring than if it had affirmed its faith in motherhood."[62] Contrary to Abramowitz's imagined community of progressive Jews fighting apartheid, the voices of Jewish student activists opposed to apartheid were being silenced by their elders.[63]

Later that year, the American Jewish Committee issued a publication similar to Abramowitz's pamphlet. The study, titled *Israel and South Africa*, provided a useful historical overview of Israel's Africa policy prior to 1973 but argued, baselessly, that "Israel's continued involvement with Black African nations, nevertheless, continues to outweigh its relations with South Africa," citing the same incomplete IMF trade statistics and recycling arguments used ten years earlier by Decter. The AJC did admit to certain Israeli arms sales, but defended them inaccurately as limited efforts "helping South Africa protect shipping lanes that are vital to Western interests" and as being of "no use to the apartheid regime in carrying out repressive measures against its Black population"—a claim put to rest by Israel's 1983 demonstration of West Bank antiriot equipment for prospective South African buyers, not to mention the numerous multibillion-dollar ammunition and aircraft deals inked between 1975 and 1986.[64] The AJC insisted that the sole purpose of discussing Israeli–South African ties was "delegitimizing the State of Israel" and that "South African Blacks, the victims of apartheid, deserve better." [65] Even the mayor of New York, Ed Koch, entered the fray, downplaying

Israeli ties with South Africa using many of the AJC's arguments in front of two hundred angry political science students at York College in Queens.[66]

In Jewish publications across the Atlantic, the defense of Israel was far more blunt. Echoing the paranoid fantasies of white South Africans, the Paris-based magazine *France-Israel Information* declared that in South Africa "universal suffrage means the destruction of the white community if not its extermination."[67] The pro-Israel publication likened the anti-apartheid movement to the Islamic fundamentalist campaign waged against the Shah in Iran and warned that a pro-Soviet government would emerge in Pretoria if apartheid crumbled.

Despite their spirited defenders, Israel and South Africa were not yet willing to reveal the full extent of their ties and they made every effort to keep evidence of their military relations under wraps. When a Reuters reporter identified a group of South African soldiers and an SADF officer touring the West Bank with IDF troops, he called the South African embassy in Tel Aviv, which reflexively denied it. Israeli army officials were upset about the discovery and "immediately arranged for the military press censor to suppress any reports which might be written about the SADF officer's visit."[68] But the IDF military censor's power only reached as far as Israel's borders and could not stop leaks from causing havoc when they appeared in the foreign press. Stories like these were especially incendiary in the United States, where Israeli–South African cooperation was driving a wedge between two of the Democratic Party's core constituencies, who had long seen themselves as allies.

10

LOSING THE LEFT

*Israel, Apartheid, and the Splintering of the
Civil Rights Coalition*

IN EARLY 1968, just months before his death, the Reverend Martin Luther King Jr. declared to a Harvard University audience: "When people criticize Zionists, they mean Jews. You're talking anti-Semitism." At the time, Israel was still a popular left-wing cause in the United States and relations between blacks and Jews were at their pinnacle. The civil rights coalition of the 1960s had a distinguished Jewish pedigree: Rabbi Emil Hirsch had helped found the NAACP, and Joel Spingarn, a Columbia professor involved in the civil rights movement, became its president in 1914. During the 1930s, the Chicago businessman Julius Rosenwald bankrolled the expansion of black education in the South in the face of opposition from the Klan, and in the 1960s the renowned rabbi and philosopher Abraham Joshua Heschel had marched arm in arm with King in Selma. When Thurgood Marshall became the first black justice on the Supreme Court in 1967, the Jewish attorney Jack Greenberg replaced him as head of the NAACP's Legal Defense Fund.[1]

Indeed, the American left that today almost uniformly denounces Israel was once one of its greatest proponents. In the 1930s, black Americans saw Hitler as another white-robed Klansman and spoke out forcefully against Nazism. The Baltimore-based newspaper *Afro-American* declared in 1933, "Germany is doing to its Jewish people what the South does to the negro," under the headline "Adolph Hitler, K.K.K."[2] During the early 1940s, the civil rights leader Adam Clayton Powell Jr. raised $150,000 for the Irgun, which he proudly described as "an underground terrorist organization in Palestine."[3] And Freda Kirchwey, the editor of the quintessential left-wing magazine *The Nation*, was instrumental in lobbying the Truman administration to recognize a Jewish state in Palestine.

Kirchwey was a scion of the New York liberal intelligentsia; her father served as dean of Columbia Law School and, after becoming editor of *The Nation* in 1933, she used her magazine to promote the New Deal and the antifascist struggle in Spain. As the debate over the future of Palestine reached its climax in 1947, Kirchwey and her colleagues prepared influential briefing papers backing Jewish statehood and distributed thousands of copies to U.N. delegations, members of Congress, State Department officials, and leading media personalities. They rejected calls for a binational state and aggressively promoted partition as the only solution. Relying on leaks from the State Department, *The Nation* revealed the Palestinian leader Grand Mufti Haj Amin al-Husseini's wartime ties to the Nazis, embarrassing several Arab representatives at the U.N. Kirchwey's report found its way to President Harry Truman's desk and Zionist leaders credited her in no small measure with influencing his decision to recognize Israel on May 14, 1948.[4]

The left's honeymoon with Israel would last for over two decades, but by 1967 the bliss was fading. Even as Arab countries, the Soviet Union, and many left-wing groups in the United States and Europe began to cast Israel as an occupying imperial power in the wake of the Six-Day War, King and other black American leaders—as well as many of Israel's friends in Africa—continued to stand by the Jewish state. Soon after King's assassination, however, the powerful black-Jewish coalition that formed the foundation of the 1960s civil rights movement began to fray.

As we have seen, the Six-Day War had a profound impact on Jews around the world, demonstrating both Israel's extreme vulnerability and its tremendous military power. Many American Jews who hadn't paid much attention to Israel since the campaign for independence—preferring to donate their money and time to the civil rights movement—began to see Israel in a new light.[5]

The same was true for Arab-Americans. Growing up in Mobile, Alabama, James Zogby didn't even think of himself as an Arab. "In 1967, I had no sense of Arab nationalism. I just knew my daddy came from there and we were Christian," says Zogby, head of the Arab American Institute and a long-standing advocate of the Palestinian cause in Washington. He hung out with the Jewish kids in school. "We were close friends because we weren't WASPs," quips Zogby, and there was no sense of an adversarial relationship. "I didn't think anything of the Middle East; they didn't think anything of it," says Zogby. But all of that changed after the Six-Day War. "Sixty-seven awakened something in them, and something in us and created a divergent sense of identity. That began to eat away at some of the solidarity we felt before." The realignment that took place in the late 1960s and early 1970s, coupled with the rise of militant black nationalism, spurred the emergence of other identity-based causes, including his own.

Zogby soon found himself debating old Jewish friends who insisted that Zionism was a national liberation movement.[6] Arabs began to argue that Israel was "not the bastion of national liberation" Jews made it out to be. Rather, the New Left argued, Israel supported regimes that trampled national liberation movements, such as apartheid South Africa. Israel was no longer seen as an underdog, and as the American left began to identify Palestinians as victims, Israel's star fell.[7]

Harvard's Seymour Martin Lipset pronounced Israel's romance with the left finished in 1969. "The considerable support which the intellectual left once gave to Israel is gone," he wrote. "And it is not likely to be revived."[8] This realignment, predicted Lipset, "may well make life difficult for those who seek to remain both socialist and Zionist." And it did. The French author Michael Feher saw 1967 as the moment when "Jews lost their place in the anti-Western front that was imagined by black power and the Black Panthers," leaving them in the awkward position of appearing among the ranks of the oppressors.[9]

Prominent Jewish liberals who remained committed to Zionism and the civil rights movement were becoming increasingly disillusioned with this sort of anti-Israel rhetoric on the left. Martin Peretz, who would in 1974 purchase and take over *The New Republic* magazine, was a leading voice in the civil rights and antiwar movements of the 1960s. He and his wife, Anne Peretz, donated huge sums of money to left-wing organizations and convened meetings for activists at their Cape Cod vacation home.[10] The Peretzes even bankrolled the 1967 "New Politics" convention in Chicago, which sought to bring together antiwar and civil rights leaders, build a multiracial progressive coalition, and influence the future direction of the Democratic Party.

Soon after leftists from across the country converged in the Windy

City, the New Politics gathering descended into chaos.[11] As *The New Yorker*'s Renata Adler reported, the convention was "a travesty of radical politics at work." Martin Luther King Jr. gave an address and was heckled by black radicals as the meeting fragmented into a multitude of factions. A group declaring itself the "Black Caucus" denounced Israel's victory in "the imperialistic Zionist war" of 1967, and demanded the formation of "white civilizing committees" to deal with "the beastlike character" of "all white communities."[12] Peretz walked out. Black moderates such as future U.N. ambassador Andrew Young followed him to the door.[13]

The New Left was splintering as established organizations like Students for a Democratic Society (SDS) produced offshoots that were more violent and less democratic. As Paul Berman put it, "The 1970s became the golden age of the microparties. There were Maoist sects . . . Trotskyist sects. . . . And beyond the guerillas, the outlaws, the Leninists, the democratic socialists, the levelheaded organizers, the academics, and the weekly scribblers, the vast majority of people who had once felt a loyalty to the world that had come out of SDS and its fraternal organizations simply slipped away."[14] And as any semblance of left-wing unity faded, the era of identity politics began. The personal had become political; now, belonging to an oppressed group was enough to establish one's radical credentials. A Manichaean mind-set began to settle in over the American left and in this world of good and evil, Israel was seen as an enemy.

Amid the ruins of the civil rights coalition, the gulf between blacks and Jews grew larger. The black American freedom struggle exemplified by Martin Luther King, Bayard Rustin, and A. Philip Randolph—leaders who insisted that the United States live up to its liberal ideals and extend those ideals to African-Americans—was giving way to a more radical anti-imperialist ideology. Rather than pointing to the hypocrisy and unfulfilled promises of American liberalism, it was much easier for radical black organizations to support "a worldwide revolution by the colonized and nonwhite populations against the European and white imperialists." As the war in Vietnam intensified and the optimism of the civil rights era faded, disenchanted American leftists sought solidarity with anticolonial movements abroad. With Israel recast in the role of colonial occupier, it became an easy target. King's old heroes were replaced by new ones; "Instead of Gandhi, there was Nasser," writes Berman.[15]

The Student Nonviolent Coordinating Committee, SNCC, a leading civil rights group, began to publish anti-Israel leaflets, and its leader, Stokely Carmichael, declared on prime-time television, "We have begun to see the evils of Zionism, and we will fight to wipe it out wherever it exists, be it in the Ghetto of the United States or in the Middle East." The *Black Panther* newspaper was more explicit: "We're gonna burn their towns and that ain't all/We're gonna piss upon the Wailing Wall."[16]

The fallout from the Yom Kippur War of 1973 made the situation worse, as did the severance of diplomatic ties between Israel and most African countries. American blacks grew resentful and angry when Israel moved closer to South Africa during the 1970s and 1980s and reports of Israeli arms sales to the apartheid regime surfaced just as the worldwide anti-apartheid movement was gaining momentum. Even if the full extent of the alliance was not publicly known, Israel's relationship with South Africa was seen as a sinister embrace and Jewish efforts to defend these ties were taken as a slap in the face by black leaders committed to ending apartheid.

Black supporters of Israel, like Rustin, were lonely voices in the early 1970s. Rustin attempted to defend the Jewish state in his 1974 essay "American Negroes and Israel," pointing to Israel's work in Africa during the 1960s and attacking the Black Panthers and others who "equated black support for Israel with subservience to Jewish interests."[17] He denounced the simplicity of the radical left's arguments, reminding them that the Third World they so admired was full of brutal, dictatorial regimes.[18]

The Panthers weren't listening. They continued to praise Israel's enemies and condemn the Jewish state as "genocidal." Militant black groups began to identify with the PLO and black radicals came to speak to Arab-American graduate student groups on campuses across the country, denouncing Israel and South Africa as settler-colonial states that denied basic political rights to indigenous populations.[19]

While the radicals may have been right on that count, there was a certain irony to their reflexive acceptance of the Arab cause, given the history of Arab slave trading in Africa.[20] Rustin reminded the radicals that half a million people lived in enforced bondage in Saudi Arabia and that "[modern slavery] has undergone a steady increase during the past twenty-five years, a period which coincides with the era of growing wealth for the oil sheikhdoms of the Persian Gulf." And, seeking to explode "the myth of Arab-African brotherhood," Rustin cited the northern Sudanese Arabs' campaign of terror against black Christians in the country's south. But unlike France's radical Jewish leftists—who had supported the PLO for years but were shocked out of their ideological stupor and adopted a less strident position after the murder of Israeli athletes at the 1972 Munich Olympics—the Panthers and other black militants were not convinced by Rustin's diatribes against the Arab slave trade and the Sudanese government, and they refused to temper their anti-Israel rhetoric.[21]

As the 1970s wore on, the old Jewish left was becoming uncomfortable with the anti-Israel tenor of many black leaders. Intellectuals such as Norman Podhoretz, Irving Kristol, and Nathan Glazer feared black militancy and began to denounce it in the pages of *Commentary* magazine. Martin Peretz did not move as far to the right, but his magazine, *The New Republic*, became a staunch defender of Israel and a searing critic of the Palestinian movement and the black American leaders who associated with it.[22]

When *Newsweek* reported in 1979 that U.N. ambassador Andrew Young had met with the Palestinian representative to the United Nations for fifteen minutes, the White House forced him to resign, pleasing Jews and angering black Americans. Blacks believed that Jewish pressure on President Carter had led to Young's resignation. Young denied that Jewish groups had played any role, but it didn't matter: his meteoric rise to the upper echelons of government made him a hero to many black Americans and his fall was seen as an insult. One week after his resignation, moderate black leaders from organizations such as the NAACP convened in protest. The group issued a statement arguing, "Jews must show more sensitivity and be prepared for more consultation before taking positions contrary to the best interests of the black community."[23] The statement singled out Israel's ties with South Africa as reprehensible and condemned the relationship.

Black Americans were becoming Israel's most prominent domestic critics. It was leaders like Jesse Jackson, rather than Arab organizations, who gained the most attention for questioning U.S. policy toward the

Middle East and encouraging diplomatic contact with the PLO.[24] In late September 1979, just one month after Young stepped down, a group of black leaders traveled to the Middle East.[25] The same week that the Carter administration was struggling to contain the political fallout from the nuclear test detected in the South Atlantic, Jackson openly embraced PLO leader Yasser Arafat for all the world to see. In a speech to the Palestine Human Rights Campaign, he declared that "the no-talk policy toward the PLO is ridiculous."[26] Walter Fauntroy, the D.C. delegate in the House of Representatives and a founding member of the Congressional Black Caucus, went on the trip as well. He echoed Jackson's views, arguing that "the PLO is not the one-dimensional 'terrorist organization' we have been led to believe that it is . . . far from being the 'bloodthirsty killer' and 'wild-eyed terrorist' the Western press has made of him, Mr. Arafat appears reasonable and open to dialogue." Fauntroy went on to criticize Israel for using U.S. arms to bomb civilians in Lebanon. He angrily recounted seeing "unmistakable evidence of the use of American weapons on non-military targets" and returned home with pieces of shrapnel and bomb parts he had fished from the rubble of destroyed Lebanese villages.[27]

Despite these deepening divisions, many American Jews still eagerly brandished their liberal credentials by opposing apartheid. Liberal congregations joined activist church groups in opposing apartheid and Jewish students gravitated to pro-divestment organizations on campuses across the country. This put them at odds with their fellow Jews in South Africa, who lobbied them to tone down the anti–South African rhetoric lest the growing din of anti-apartheid activism hurt the government in Pretoria and damage the Jewish community's own interests.

In 1983, the South African Jewish Board of Deputies opposed a resolution adopted by B'nai B'rith International. Noting that "coercion and eviction of blacks . . . have revealed the ugly face of apartheid for what it is," it called on American firms doing business in South Africa to "assure equal treatment and equal pay" for blacks and for "the granting of freedom, justice and equal rights."[28]

It was a tame document, but the South Africans were outraged. Board leaders cabled their counterparts in the United States, complaining that they were "deeply shocked and greatly angered due to the entirely unsatisfactory language" used in the B'nai B'rith resolution. The angry telegram went on to argue that the "choice of language displays a lack of sensitivity and ineptitude which defies description." The board's chairman stressed that Jewish interests in South Africa were tied to those of the white community and instructed American Jews to stop speaking out on South Africa, lest it endanger his community.[29]

Diana Aviv, a South African who had emigrated to the United States in 1975 and risen to become the head of the National Council of Jewish Women, recalls the tension. "The South African Jewish community urged us not to take a position. But we saw it as a matter of conscience," she says. A group of prominent American Jews accompanied Aviv on a trip to South Africa, during which they attended a "series of very unpleasant meetings" with South Africans who scolded the Americans for dabbling in their business—and jeopardizing their positions of privilege—by supporting sanctions and divestment. To Aviv and the American visitors, it seemed that South African Jewish leaders were driven purely by fear.[30]

Even as American Jewish leaders stood up to the reactionary demands of their brethren in South Africa, they found themselves feuding more frequently with blacks and the political left back home. Black leaders like Louis Farrakhan may have been politically marginal but their anti-Semitic rants were symbolically powerful and provoked a visceral fear among American Jews. The advent of Farrakhan's anti-Semitic black nationalism further fragmented the old civil rights coalition at the core of the Democratic Party. This clash came into sharp relief as plans for a twentieth anniversary of Martin Luther King's March on Washington took shape.

. . .

IN 1982, AT THE tender age of twenty-two, Donna Brazile—later to become Al Gore's campaign manager during the 2000 election—was put in charge of organizing the anniversary march by Walter Fauntroy. Fresh from college at Louisiana State University, she was given a basement office in Washington to coordinate the massive event. Immediately, the sort of identity politics that had fractured the old civil rights coalition came into play, creating a rift in the steering committee for the march. When Brazile drafted a "Call to the Nation," Jewish groups objected to language critical of U.S. arms exports to the Middle East—and Israel, specifically—and they threatened to pull out of the march.[31] They also opposed granting a seat to Arab-American senator James Abourezk (D–South Dakota) on the organizing committee, claiming Arabs had not been a presence in the civil rights movement, a charge Arab American Institute president James Zogby resented. "We weren't visible as an organized group," Zogby concedes. But, recalling his cousins' business in Jim Crow Alabama, he adds, "In Mobile there was only one place a black man could go to buy a suit and that was Zoghby's department store."[32]

Certain Jewish organizations threatened not to march if the Arabs did, too. Washington, D.C., rabbi David Saperstein was an exception, believing it was vital to maintain a Jewish presence in the liberal coalition to prevent it from being dominated by the Israel-bashing far left. Not participating in the anniversary march, he argued, would symbolize Jewish withdrawal from the movement.[33] In the end, the two sides papered over their differences and the event gave Jesse Jackson a major political push as chanting marchers urged him to run for president. But the already strained relationship between blacks and Jews was becoming more fraught.

Brazile soon began working for the Jackson presidential campaign, which was having trouble finding Jewish supporters. Peretz's *New Republic* did not help the cause. During the 1984 presidential campaign, the magazine parodied Jackson's oratory with lines like "We don't want free grub, we want in the power hub" and "From having no fun to Air Force One." Many blacks saw it as racist. But soon Jews would level the same charge at Jackson. In February 1984, Jackson uttered a single word that would doom his campaign: he referred to New York as "Hymietown" while talking to reporters.[34] After weeks of denials, Jackson finally admitted to the quote. His friendship with Louis Farrakhan, whose bow-tied Nation of Islam bodyguards were protecting Jackson on the campaign trail, made the situation even worse. Although Jackson had managed to garner a substantial number of white votes, including some from liberal Jews, his slip destroyed any hope of rekindling the old civil rights alliance and instead poisoned the relationship between blacks and Jews for years to come.[35]

Walter Mondale eventually defeated Jackson and won the 1984 Democratic presidential nomination, but the damage to the old civil rights alliance had been done. And further feuds loomed on the horizon— pitting blacks who vehemently condemned Israel's relationship with South Africa against Jews who opposed apartheid but denied or down- played the Israeli connection. In the House of Representatives, Michigan Democrat Howard Wolpe, a Jew, and his African-American colleague Mickey Leland (D-Texas) worked tirelessly to keep the Israeli–South African issue from further poisoning black-Jewish relations. Wolpe and Leland even saw the potential for common ground: realizing that both blacks and Jews disliked the apartheid government in Pretoria, they moved to make sanctions against South Africa a unifying cause.

· · ·

BY THE MID-1980S, televised evidence of the apartheid regime's brutality was streaming into European and American living rooms on a daily basis. Prime Minister P. W. Botha imposed a state of emergency in July 1985, granting his government sweeping powers that effectively placed South Africa under martial law. Within a matter of months, his security forces had killed hundreds of protesters and detained seven thousand more. This violent crackdown focused the world's attention on South Africa and fueled a massive expansion of the global anti-apartheid movement. France recalled its ambassador, several European countries took punitive measures against Pretoria, and Chase Manhattan Bank refused to renew $400 million worth of loans to the apartheid regime.[36] Even the U.S. government began contemplating sanctions with teeth.

By the fall of 1985, the plight of blacks in Soweto had become a main- stream political issue in Washington. The anti-apartheid movement had succeeded in bringing a variety of groups together—churches, civil rights organizations, student activists—around the issue of South Africa and the sanctions debate in the United States was in full swing. At the same time, the Reagan administration's preferred policy of constructive engagement with Pretoria—which envisioned talking to South Africa's leaders rather than isolating them by imposing tough sanctions—was under attack.[37]

On September 5, President Reagan, Vice President George Bush, and CIA director William Casey convened for a National Security Council meeting on South Africa. National Security Adviser Robert McFarlane told them that the situation there had deteriorated, citing "unprecedented violence, reflected daily on U.S. television screens." Two weeks earlier, South African president Botha had given his infamous "Rubicon" speech, refusing to make concessions to the West or to his domestic opponents. McFarlane wrote, "Botha's poor presentation of reform and what the government was prepared to offer has undercut even moderate blacks."[38]

Reagan charged the NSC with deciding whether to veto an upcoming sanctions bill and risk a congressional override; sign it and alienate Britain and Germany, both of which opposed sanctions; or preempt it by issuing an executive order containing the mild sanctions already included in the constructive engagement plan.[39] McFarlane and his superiors were well aware that any policy perceived as soft on Pretoria would face strong bipartisan resistance in Congress. Hoping to avoid a humiliating showdown with Capitol Hill, Reagan issued an order imposing some moderate sanctions against South Africa, including the banning of exports to apartheid-enforcing branches of the government in Pretoria, and forbidding the import of armaments and gold Krugerrand coins. But anti-apartheid activists weren't satisfied and they rallied for even stronger measures against South Africa. This time, Israel was their target.

As the sanctions debate caught the attention of Beltway pundits, Israel's role as one of South Africa's major trading partners and arms suppliers finally came under the spotlight. Critics wishing to indict Israel for collaboration with the apartheid regime faced off publicly against spin doctors defending the Jewish state. In March 1986, PBS television invited Zogby, Rabbi Saperstein, Howard University political scientist Ronald Walters, and Maurice Roumani, an Israeli visiting professor, to address the issue in a live debate.

Zogby began the show by suggesting that Israel and South Africa had a natural affinity, infuriating Israel's supporters. "I think it's a natural relationship between two governments who view themselves as being in similar predicaments, and therefore needing to confront the enemies around them," said Zogby. He largely evaded the question of Arab oil supplies to South Africa, eventually conceding that it should be investigated. His evasiveness on the oil issue aside, Zogby was correct to point out that the Israeli relationship was unique because "there is in fact a state-to-state relationship and the trade takes place on that level." The Arab oil supplies were funneled through a shadowy world of middlemen—rather than being approved at the ministerial level—an arrangement that required far less trust and no shared strategic interests.

Rabbi Saperstein, known for his left-wing activism and opposition to apartheid, claimed Israeli involvement with South Africa was negligible in comparison to that of other countries, citing the incomplete IMF figures that excluded arms and diamonds. Roumani mentioned Israel's many U.N. votes against apartheid and its agreement, on paper, to support the U.N. arms embargo.[40] Saperstein denied all of the allegations about arms sales and turned his attention to France, which he incorrectly accused of being South Africa's primary arms supplier at the time. He admitted that there may have been sales during the years of Likud rule, from 1977 to 1984, but insisted, inaccurately, that "everyone in Israel opposes apartheid. Since Peres took over [as prime minister] . . . there have been no new arms sales."[41]

In fact, some of the biggest contracts and cooperative ventures went into effect on Peres's watch, from 1984 to 1986, including a nuclear missile project in South Africa and the updating of South Africa's fighter jets in Israel. Certainly, defense ties had accelerated under Begin's rule from 1977 to 1983 and ideological affinities had brought military leaders closer together, but Shimon Peres did nothing as prime minister to slow them down. While publicly denouncing apartheid, he simply maintained the alliance that he himself had initiated a decade earlier as defense minister. Writing in *The New York Times*, Thomas Friedman estimated that the two countries did $400 to $800 million of business in the arms sector in 1986, mostly under Peres's administration.[42] Then, in October 1986, in accordance with the principles of a National Unity government, Peres stepped down and was replaced by Likud's Yitzhak Shamir, who had even fewer qualms about selling to South Africa and was less prone to public criticism of apartheid.

Of course, because of the secretive relationship between the two countries, and the propaganda and counterpropaganda spread by both Israel and South Africa, it was difficult for members of Congress—or the general public—to know the extent of the alliance. However, with the benefit of hindsight and the more comprehensive data on the arms trade that is currently available, it is now possible to evaluate the various claims and counterclaims made during these media wars.

The actual amount of arms exports to South Africa exceeded even Zogby's most extreme estimates and was more than ten times the amount cited by Israel before the General Assembly and by her pamphleteering defenders.[43] According to correspondence between the Armscor mission in Tel Aviv and SADF chief Constand Viljoen, the aircraft updates undertaken in the mid-1980s alone cost "approximately $2 billion," making Friedman's 1986 estimate appear on the low side.[44] Taking into account declassified South African arms acquisition data (which excludes very lucrative cooperative ventures and shared financing arrangements that are difficult to appraise), Israel's average annual exports to South Africa between 1974 and 1993 amounted to approximately $600 million per year, placing South Africa in the company of the United Kingdom and Germany as Israel's second or third largest trading partner after the United States.[45] At the time, these damning statistics were not public knowledge, although critics of the alliance such as Zogby hinted at them. As details leaked and the Jewish state came under fire from Zogby and others, Peres and the coterie of left-leaning intellectuals surrounding him did all they could to project an image of Israeli solidarity with the oppressed even as their government remained in bed with the oppressors.

. . .

PROGRESSIVE DIPLOMATS in the Israeli Foreign Ministry wanted to reach out to black South Africans, but they did not want to be accused of talking to terrorists. In 1985, no one was prepared to meet openly with the ANC and other banned anti-apartheid groups—not even leftists seeking to end the alliance. Instead, they had to approach key leaders quietly and out of the public eye.

The Israeli left's overtures to the South African opposition began when Archbishop Desmond Tutu, the purple-robed icon of nonviolent resistance to apartheid, visited Los Angeles in late 1984. Tom Hayden and his wife, Jane Fonda, invited Tutu to join them for dinner. Hayden was a hero of the 1960s New Left; he had founded SDS, drafted the organization's famous Port Huron Statement, and gone on to become an antiwar activist and a progressive California state legislator. Fonda was a renowned actress who became infamous for posing alongside communist troops in Hanoi at the height of the Vietnam War, earning herself the ire of the Nixon White House and the nickname "Hanoi Jane." Despite their otherwise stellar radical-left credentials, Hayden and Fonda were regarded as pro-Israel, having visited during the 1982 Lebanon War and defended the Israeli invasion.[46]

Over dinner, Tutu attacked Israel's support for the apartheid government and the Haydens' other guests immediately became defensive. They subscribed to the conventional wisdom of the day, which held that Israel's trade with South Africa was insignificant and virtually nonexistent when it came to arms. Tutu's hostility toward Israel convinced Hayden that Israel needed help improving its image. Soon after the party, he contacted the Center for Policy Options, a small think tank in Los Angeles staffed by UCLA professor Steven Spiegel, Anti-Defamation League honorary chairman Maxwell Greenberg, and Osias Goren, a prominent member of the 1984 Reagan campaign staff. These Zionist heavyweights went to bat for Hayden in Israel, convincing high-ranking Labor leaders and government officials that something had to be done to counter growing anti-Israel sentiment among South African blacks.[47]

Hayden's goals coincided nicely with those of Yossi Beilin, a bookish young political scientist who had risen through the Labor Party ranks as a loyal assistant to Peres.[48] Beilin was a dove when it came to the Palestinian issue and he was a moralist when it came to South Africa. Having assumed the influential post of cabinet secretary during Peres's premiership, he now had the power to do something about South Africa, even if his boss was skeptical. Beilin was joined by Shimshon Zelniker, an academic Africa specialist turned Peres adviser who was vehemently opposed to the alliance that his boss, Peres, had helped to conceive. He believed that by allying itself with the apartheid regime, Israel had allowed its foreign policy to become infected with "short-term utilitarian values" and "a vulgar understanding of diplomacy."[49]

Zelniker was put in charge of recruiting black South Africans for leadership training programs in Israel and he arranged seminars for the visitors at the Afro-Asian Institute, a branch of Israel's massive public sector trade union, the Histadrut. Over the years, the Afro-Asian Institute had trained students from a variety of developing countries in an effort to build support for Israel in the Third World, and Zelniker wanted to do the same with black South Africans. When Zelniker flew to South Africa to initiate ties with black leaders and invite them to Israel, he saw his mission as nothing less than the redemption of Israel's name.[50]

At their first meeting, Tutu and his colleagues berated Zelniker, attacked Israel's domestic policies, and criticized its government for collaborating with the apartheid regime. After a lengthy debate, Tutu accepted the idea of sending black leaders to Jerusalem for leadership training at the Afro-Asian Institute on the condition that the Israeli government would have nothing to do with it.

Zelniker's program worried South African government officials and Pretoria attempted to influence its direction.[51] Miffed that they were excluded from selecting "acceptable" black candidates, the South African intelligence services focused on Zelniker and his colleagues instead, examining their files closely before agreeing to grant them visas.[52] Military intelligence officials in Pretoria even warned that the Histadrut, which managed the institute, was critical of apartheid, and its strong tradition of labor activism might have a "negative influence on the trade union activities in the RSA [Republic of South Africa]."[53]

Since welcoming Goldreich as a political refugee in 1963, Israel had never openly reached out to South African opposition leaders and it had certainly never engaged black leaders who were banned, imprisoned, or operating underground. All of a sudden, Israel seemed to be doing just that.

Pretoria's concern was not that Israel was beginning to play both sides of the street, which was predictable, but that its government might eventually take the side of the ANC and other left-wing groups that advocated the overthrow of the apartheid regime.[54] In lieu of meeting with these radical democrats, the South African government encouraged Israelis to sit down with the Zulu nationalist Mangosuthu Buthelezi, a more conservative leader known for staging rallies surrounded by shield- and spear-wielding men in traditional Zulu warrior garb. Buthelezi enjoyed cautious support from the white establishment, which viewed him as a reliable, anticommunist figure who subscribed to their theory of separate development because it served his ambitions for a separate Zulu homeland.

Israelis who harbored more conservative views toward South Africa

saw him as a legitimate alternative to the ANC, too. American congressman Howard Wolpe—one of the architects of anti–South African sanctions in the House of Representatives—visited Jerusalem as the new
Israeli policy was taking shape. The Israeli diplomats who invited him
did not share Beilin's and Zelniker's views and Wolpe recalls an exhaust-
ing day of meetings with so-called Africa experts. At the end of the day,
his hosts announced that they had invited a "major liberation fighter"
from South Africa. Wolpe asked who it was, and the Israelis told him
Buthelezi was coming. Incredulous, Wolpe asked if they were joking. He
was floored by the cluelessness of the Israeli diplomats, who actually
believed Buthelezi represented the mainstream black anti-apartheid leadership in South Africa. Before he even landed in Washington, Wolpe's
office had received calls condemning his "rude" behavior. "They were
genuinely surprised I didn't joyously embrace that," Wolpe recalls with a
chuckle.[55]

Back from Israel, Buthelezi began aggressively pandering to South
African Jews in the hope that they, too, would accept him as one of the
"good black leaders." He came home brimming with enthusiasm about
the Jewish state and its government, telling an audience of Johannesburg
Jewish leaders that "Israel itself is a miracle of human tenacity and
achievement and I am deeply inspired." He went on to assure them that
"we do not want to rob whites of our country."[56] Seeking an alternative
to the ANC, which they viewed as a band of communist terrorists, the
Jewish leadership seized the opportunity to cultivate ties with Buthelezi.

In the United States, the Zelniker initiative was a major public relations coup for Israel. Jewish organizations such as the Anti-Defamation
League were worried about growing anti-Israel sentiment among anti-
apartheid activists and they knew that news of Zelniker's program could
help blunt the message of Israel's critics. It was a golden opportunity to
flood the American press with positive stories on Israel that would over-
shadow the troublesome allegations of military collaboration coming
from the anti-apartheid movement.

The amount of coverage devoted to Zelniker's training program for
black South Africans was unusual for an obscure event in a foreign country involving only twenty people, but it made the front page of the *Los*

Angeles Times and was prominently featured in *The Dallas Morning News*, *The Washington Post*, and the *Chicago Tribune.*[57] Revealingly, an unnamed Israeli source told the *Morning News*, "We really want to help. We don't just want to use them for propaganda purposes."[58] Satisfied with the flurry of positive press, the ADL's director of international affairs sent out a memo urging staff to circulate the articles widely "to provide an updated picture of Israeli–South African relations."[59]

This rosy picture left out the controversy that erupted at an Afro-Asian Institute press conference just before the visiting South Africans left Israel. An Israeli reporter from *Maariv* asked Lekgau Mathabathe, the head of Soweto's Committee of Ten—a civil rights organization linking younger activists with veteran community leaders—whether blacks in Soweto resented Israel. Shocked by what seemed a question with an obvious answer, Mathabathe told the audience that no black person in their right mind could believe that "a friend of the South African government can be a friend of the Blacks."[60] This comment made its way into the *Los Angeles Times;* the remainder of the quote did not.[61] Mathabathe continued: "Israel also supplies arms to South Africa and South Africa uses those arms for killing people and even children of three years old. You don't expect any black person to be happy with that type of thing."[62] To the Afro-Asian Institute staff and the assembled journalists, Mathabathe's inflammatory comments about Israeli arms killing black children sounded like a paranoid anti-Israel screed, but he was not so far off base.

Mathabathe didn't know it, but just two months before his outburst at the institute, the annual Israeli–South African intelligence conference had been held outside Pretoria. In addition to game spotting at Kruger National Park, the agenda included a discussion of the development and use of chemical and biological weapons.[63] South African military intelligence files clearly reveal that the SADF was willing and ready to use these weapons. Outside the country, they would only be used as a last resort in situations "critical to the country's security." But the SADF was also willing to wage chemical and biological warfare against its own citizens. A report entitled *Waging Biological and Chemical War* stated: "Within RSA Borders: If a situation arises that is considered life-endangering for the RSA, chemical weapons in any category can be utilised in order to obtain a decisive advantage for RSA forces."[64]

Even if Israel's arms sales to South Africa did not include chemical and biological weapons, Israeli intelligence officials were well aware of the apartheid government's willingness to use these weapons of mass destruction if South Africa's oppressed black majority ever threatened the white regime's survival.

. . .

BY 1986, the Peres administration was openly pursuing diplomatic ties with the many African states that had cut Israel off in 1973. In late August, Peres flew to Cameroon to meet with President Paul Biya, bringing former Mossad man David Kimche with him. The visit occurred the day after an eruption of deadly gas from beneath a volcanic lake had decimated villages in rural northwestern Cameroon, leaving cattle and human corpses littering the roads. Along with Peres and Kimche, a team of seventeen Israeli doctors came to treat survivors—days before French or American aid teams arrived.[65]

It was the first visit of an Israeli prime minister to an African country since the 1960s and Pretoria was nervous. The night before he and Peres departed for Yaoundé, Kimche appeared on Israeli TV. When a news anchor asked him, "What's in it for us?" the old spy asked the nationwide audience: "Do you really want to see Israel . . . with close ties with South Africa's racist, tyrannical regime?"[66] Playing both sides, in South Africa and beyond, was now official government policy.

On the plane to Cameroon, Peres openly criticized South Africa; on the ground, he told Biya, "A Jew who accepts apartheid ceases to be a Jew. A Jew and racism do not go together."[67] The Israelis received an adoring welcome in Yaoundé as dancers clad in colorful robes bearing Biya's image surrounded Peres on the airport tarmac.[68] The *Cameroon Tribune* printed its headline, "Mr. Peres, Welcome to Cameroon," in upside-down Hebrew characters—an error the Israelis didn't seem to mind. After Peres's welcoming at the airport, his motorcade made its way into the city past crowds that local police compared to the throngs that had welcomed Pope John Paul II a year earlier.[69]

Flanked by Cameroonian soldiers wearing IDF-issue uniforms and carrying Israeli Galil rifles, the two heads of state issued a joint statement declaring that both nations would "do everything to dismantle this odious system of apartheid in order that a free multiracial and democratic order is established in South Africa which gives everyone equal chances of access to happiness and dignity."[70]

Just twelve years earlier, after initiating a series of arms deals in Pretoria, the same man had told his South African hosts that their alliance was based on "unshakeable foundations of our common hatred of injustice and our refusal to submit to it."[71] Peres's righteous pronouncements in Cameroon may have made Israelis feel better about themselves, but his sanctimony did not impress U.S. senators, who voted overwhelmingly a few days later to support U.S. sanctions against South Africa—and to punish Israel if it chose to violate them.

11

FORKED TONGUES

Domestic Debate and Diplomatic Schizophrenia

> Unfortunately governments . . . talk with many tongues, forked tongues.
>
> —South African community leader Lekgau Mathabathe,
> on a 1986 visit to Israel[1]

IN THE SUMMER OF 1986, as the sanctions movement gathered steam on Capitol Hill, a vicious debate was raging in the Knesset. Chase Manhattan Bank had already called in its loans to South Africa, sending the rand into free fall, and the European Community's foreign ministers and the British Commonwealth had joined Scandinavian states in pushing for sanctions against Pretoria. Among the states defining themselves as industrialized Western democracies, Israel seemed the odd one out.

The left was up in arms and insisted that Israel had a unique moral and historical responsibility to help put an end to apartheid. Victor Shemtov of the United Workers Party (Mapam) sought to shame his fellow lawmakers by reminding them that "twenty-two million people live in their country without basic democratic rights," and demanded to know, "Where does the State of Israel, the state of the Jewish people who paid the price of the Holocaust, stand in this struggle?" Shemtov lambasted government ministers who urged gradual action for dragging their feet and insisted that Israel must lead the world's opposition to racism. Otherwise, he told his colleagues, "The validity of our moral standing in the fight against the revival of racism and the revival of anti-Semitism throughout the world will be eroded."[2]

During the mid-1980s, Israel's alliance with South Africa remained strong, but the Israeli government was deeply divided over the future of its ties with the apartheid regime. The premiership revolved from Labor's Shimon Peres (1984–86) to Likud's Yitzhak Shamir (1986–88) and their fractured government struggled to put forward a coherent policy toward Pretoria.[3] Angry left-wing parliamentarians and anti-apartheid officials in the Foreign Ministry clashed with members of the security establishment over South Africa. The left believed that the apartheid regime's days were numbered, while the top brass and their political allies insisted that white rule was there to stay. The result was a complete policy breakdown.

Knesset member Yossi Sarid—still an icon of the Israeli left today—accused his colleagues of invoking morality when Jews were wronged but turning a blind eye when it concerned the suffering of others. Mordechai Virshouvski of the centrist Shinui Party went even further, denouncing apartheid as an extension of Nazism. He told the Knesset, "I ask myself, as a man living in the twentieth century, as part of a people almost entirely destroyed because of the racism employed against us . . . can I sit and keep quiet or should I take action expressing my protest with all the capacity a state can give?" Virshouvski urged the government to down-grade diplomatic relations to the lowest possible level.[4]

The Israeli right was not moved by all this moral outrage, and several right-wing Knesset members openly praised the apartheid government. Likud's Michael Eitan lauded the "far-reaching changes" he claimed had been implemented since 1976 and suggested that the government sought to "introduce change through tolerance, through patience towards grad-ual reforms."[5] These kind words for the Botha regime at the height of the state of emergency provoked more outrage from the left. Eitan was not fazed, however, drawing heckles as he denounced the ANC as a party "advocating change through terror, violence, bloodshed and the aboli-tion of one evil by substituting another infinitely greater."[6] Further to the right, Meir Kahane, better known for his calls to expel all Palestini-ans from the West Bank, joined Eitan in attacking South Africa's demo-cratic opposition. He predicted that the end of apartheid would lead to an autocratic ANC regime and therefore opposed any change in Israeli policy.[7]

In practice, the position of key Labor leaders on South Africa was not so different. When left-wing parliamentarian Chaim Ramon confronted Prime Minister Peres on the Knesset floor on October 11, 1986, demanding to know why Israel wasn't taking a tougher stance toward the apartheid regime, Peres responded with his customary sanctimony, telling lawmakers that "Israel repudiates any expression of racism on whatever level," while avoiding any mention of the ongoing arms sales.[8] For Ramon, maintaining the status quo was unacceptable, and he reacted to Peres's equivocation by lecturing the prime minister: "We are a state which was built by remnants of the results of a racist regime. We must be more sensitive than anyone on this subject."[9] Matityahu Peled, another leftist parliamentarian, saw Israel's failure to act as pathetic, arguing that, "more and more, relations between the Israel and South African governments are being regarded as a sign of Israel's disgrace by millions throughout the world."[10] He urged Israel to cease defense exports immediately, but it would be almost a year before Peled had his wish.

. . .

ISRAEL WAS A RELUCTANT latecomer to the community of nations taking action against South Africa. When Yossi Beilin first proposed sanctions against South Africa, his chances of success did not look good. "I was against the whole world," recalls Beilin. Only his friends supported him, and even they did it as a favor.[11]

By the time of the Knesset sanctions debates, Beilin had ascended to the post of Foreign Ministry director-general, a position that allowed him to propose resolutions in cabinet meetings. But his boss, outgoing prime minister turned foreign minister Shimon Peres, was adamantly opposed to any changes in the South Africa policy he had himself crafted more than a decade earlier. "It was Shimon Peres's intention to prove to me that this idea of taking sanctions against South Africa was a crazy idea," Beilin recounts. Peres called a meeting with Beilin and the head of the Mossad, Nahum Admoni. As Beilin recalls it, the spy chief told them that the white minority government in South Africa was strong and would not give up power anytime soon because doing so would be tantamount to suicide. Intelligence and defense officials claimed that the apartheid regime had another twenty or thirty years before it collapsed. Moreover, they argued, Israel would turn one of its few friends into an enemy in the process and pay an enormous price.[12] Beilin persisted on moral grounds and challenged their prognosis of long-lasting white rule. Still, he faced powerful opponents in his own party and on the right.[13]

The divisions were not only a matter of abstract political debate. During these years, the Israeli embassy in Pretoria was divided by a wall, through which not even the ambassador himself dared pass. The barrier separated the staff of the Foreign Ministry from those working at the Defense Ministry mission, and the two sides carried out diametrically opposed policies. This diplomatic schizophrenia continued throughout the mid-1980s; ongoing defense contracts were honored while left-leaning diplomats attempted to build bridges to highly skeptical and intensely suspicious black leaders in the townships. As Ambassador David Ariel, who served in Pretoria from 1985 to 1987, put it bluntly, "I was the ambassador of Israel in South Africa and I wasn't the only one. We were two. One was the official one who did protocol. I did that. And then there was another one . . . in their mission behind the wall."[14]

The Defense Ministry, led at the time by Labor heavyweight Yitzhak Rabin, was dead-set against Beilin's proposal. "Rabin was up in arms," recalls Beilin. "He said publicly that such a bureaucratchik cannot take decisions for the decision makers." The defense minister was simultaneously pulling rank and balking at Beilin's policies; he was both deeply annoyed that a junior colleague was attempting to derail a lucrative security relationship he had helped build and fundamentally opposed to forsaking a reliable customer and ally. Meanwhile, the trade unions warned Beilin that thousands of workers in the defense industry would lose their jobs, causing him to fear for his own political future.[15]

Rabin eventually decided to go public with his opposition to sanctions, even if it meant admitting to lawmakers just how vital an ally South Africa was. For Rabin, the core issue was economics. He reported that the defense industry had accounted for $1.5 billion of exports in the year 1986 and chided the Knesset for putting jobs at risk. "A change in the security export policy will mean the firing of tens of thousands of workers," Rabin threatened. "I hereby inform you that they will not find an alternative opportunity."[16]

The centrality of the arms industry to the nation's economy was not news to members of the Israeli security establishment or to their customers in Pretoria, who were well aware that at least 20 percent of Israel's industrial export revenue had come from South Africa in the previous year.[17] But it was a revelation to many left-wing Israelis and American Jews such as the Hebrew University professor Naomi Chazan and the campus activist Yosef Abramowitz, who had opposed apartheid while criticizing the alliance with South Africa as useless or downplaying its extent. As Thomas Friedman wrote in a groundbreaking four-thousand-word *New York Times* story that was buried in the paper's business section in December 1986, "The idea that the Jewish state should be so dependent on weapons sales for its economic or diplomatic survival is profoundly troubling to some people here, clashing with both their self-image and their vision of the Zionist utopia." Confirming Rabin's fears, he noted, "Existing contracts that carried the Israeli manufacturers to 1985–86 are now expiring and there is little new work to replace them."[18]

Rabin's prophecy of economic doom had largely convinced the Israeli press.[19] In *Maariv*, Gabriel Shtrasman lamented Washington's leverage over Jerusalem, declaring that "[we have] enslaved ourselves to the American treasury."[20] Veteran *Haaretz* journalist Akiva Eldar wrote an article titled "In Favor of Hypocrisy," arguing that "Israel is not a superpower and therefore one should not expect her to be a leader in a battle against South Africa,"[21] and his *Haaretz* colleague Yoel Markus insisted that nitpicking over customers' internal affairs could backfire because so many nations regarded Israel as immoral, too.[22] Others simply boiled it down to a conflict between the youthful idealism of Beilin's clique and the harsh realism of Rabin and the Likud hawks.[23]

But Beilin and his colleagues were not starry-eyed idealists. While they believed morality had a place in foreign policy, they insisted at the same time that there was a strong strategic argument for sanctions: apartheid was crumbling and Israel was on the wrong side. In late 1986, Beilin tapped Alon Liel, a Turkey expert, to be his assistant at the Foreign Ministry, where Liel's primary task was convincing the defense establishment that apartheid was a dying beast. If the security network accepted this projection, so the logic went, they would cut ties with South Africa out of fear that an ANC government would share sensitive Israeli aircraft and missile technology with Libya and Iran or sell it to Israel's enemies. "They had the image of Nelson Mandela that the whites created in their minds," recalls Liel, and they genuinely believed "that if Nelson Mandela came to power he would be a friend of Gaddafi and Khomeini and Castro."[24] Beilin and Liel realized that this fear of proliferation could be used as an argument to halt defense cooperation; they also strove to prove that there were alternative markets for Israeli arms to offset the massive export revenue losses that sanctions against South

Africa would produce.[25] Beilin also held an even more important trump card: he warned that due to an obscure provision in the congressional Anti-Apartheid Act, Israel would pay a much more serious price if it failed to comply with American sanctions against South Africa.

. . .

IN THE SUMMER OF 1986, as anti-apartheid legislation was making the rounds in the U.S. Senate, a paragraph that would have far-reaching consequences for Israel had crept into the bill. The amendment, known as Section 508, called on the U.S. government to issue a report on countries violating the arms embargo against South Africa. Convinced that the bill would never pass, the Israeli government did not take it seriously.

Section 508 had initially appeared when Senators Charles "Mac" Mathias (R-Maryland) and Daniel Evans (R-Washington) added it to the anti-apartheid bill in the summer of 1986. Other Republicans twice tried to strike the provision and eventually they succeeded.[26] But then, during a markup of the bill on August 1, 1986, Senator John Kerry (D-Massachusetts) managed to reintroduce Section 508. The paragraph now called for the president to document any arms sales to South Africa and "add the option of terminating U.S. military assistance to countries violating the embargo." It also mandated a presidential report on violators within 180 days, "with a view to terminating United States military assistance to those countries."[27]

It was not just American threats that were working to Beilin's advantage. Behind the scenes, AIPAC, the American Israel Public Affairs Committee, the most powerful Jewish organization in Washington, was also pressuring Israel to act. Leading AIPAC officials were convinced that Israel was tarnishing its image among American lawmakers by maintaining ties with South Africa when the mood in Washington was downright hostile toward Pretoria. Mindful of Section 508, a visiting AIPAC delegation urged the Israeli government to adopt a "more discreet and low profile" in South Africa to reduce its risk of exposure in the forthcoming congressional report on violators of the South African embargo.[28]

Israel's friends in Washington knew how invested in the alliance both Labor and Likud leaders were and how difficult it would be to pry Israel away from South Africa. AIPAC's chief lobbyist at the time, Douglas

Bloomfield, remembers clashing with the Israeli government and some of his organization's biggest donors over the South Africa issue. "Some big contributors to AIPAC were outraged," recalls Bloomfield. They were shocked that liberal Democrats, whom they had perceived as Israel's allies, were taking what they considered to be an "overtly anti-Israel step." These donors worried that Section 508 could hurt Israel financially. Their attitude was that ostracized, isolated states must take what they can get, and they knew the relationship with South Africa was economically and strategically beneficial for Israel. Furthermore, the fact that the ANC publicly declared Castro, Gaddafi, and Arafat among its greatest allies "was not exactly heartwarming," says Bloomfield.

But he and other Beltway insiders saw the bigger strategic picture. In their eyes, the ongoing and increasingly publicized relationship with South Africa "was going to undermine Israel's stature on the Hill" among some of the Jewish state's staunchest supporters, who were also committed to the anti-apartheid cause. If the United States did not pressure Israel to cease arms sales to South Africa, Bloomfield and his colleagues believed, attempts by anti-Israel groups to paint the Jewish state as an ally of the racist South African regime would sway the American public. "You couldn't put in a provision saying that it's bad for everyone to do business with South Africa, except Israel," insists Bloomfield. [29]

Despite AIPAC's pressure, the Israeli government still refused to take Section 508 seriously. "I met with Shamir on three occasions and told him this legislation is coming . . . and it's being led by some of our best friends," recalls Bloomfield. Shamir, then foreign minister, listened politely as Bloomfield warned that the United States might cut off military aid if Israel failed to distance itself from South Africa and then proceeded to ignore everything Bloomfield had said. [30]

In the upper echelons of the Israeli government, there was a widely held belief that AIPAC and other Jewish organizations, as well as pro-Israel members of Congress, would protect Israel and that Section 508, like other bumps in the road, would soon disappear. AIPAC's lobbyists saw plainly that Israel was shooting itself in the foot, but it would take a few months before this dawned on the leaders in Jerusalem.

President Reagan vetoed the sanctions bill on September 26, 1986, and reiterated his commitment to constructive engagement and the use of "quiet diplomacy" to bring change in South Africa. [31] The Israelis felt vindicated.[32] But the bipartisan appeal of the anti-apartheid movement was growing too strong; Congress immediately overrode Reagan's veto with overwhelming majorities of 78–21 in the Senate and 313–83 in the House. When the Comprehensive Anti-Apartheid Act became law a week later, on October 6, it was a rude awakening for Israel. "That's when the Israeli government came to its senses," recalls Bloomfield. Shamir, who replaced Peres as prime minister on October 20, personally apologized to him. Pinning the blame on Reagan, Shamir told Bloomfield, "Your president told me I didn't have to listen to you." Now, with Section 508 on the books, he did.[33]

. . .

SECTION 508 WAS IMMEDIATELY seen as a "sting" directed at the Jewish state, and calls for Israel to ignore it began at once. Commentators doubted that Israel would ever apply sanctions against South Africa. After all, as *The Jerusalem Post* observed, "the word 'sanctions' had an unpleasant ring in Israel. It would take a lot for Israel to support the use of a weapon which it has rejected unconditionally in the past."[34] Moreover, Shamir and Defense Minister Yitzhak Rabin had always been dead-set against sanctions of any kind.[35]

But the passage of the Comprehensive Anti-Apartheid Act forced Rabin to reconsider the Defense Ministry's approach to South Africa, and it helped Beilin and Liel make their case. "[With] Rabin, we knew we could not go through the moral arguments, we had to go through the realpolitik," recalls Liel, and the threat of a U.S. cutoff was just what they needed. A *Washington Post* article by two leading Israeli journalists noted that, "without U.S. military aid, valued at $1.3 billion this year, Israel could soon be defenseless, destitute or both."[36] Due to his past as ambassador in Washington, Rabin was very sensitive to perceptions of Israel on Capitol Hill and he therefore took the threat of losing U.S. military assistance extremely seriously. If staying in bed with Pretoria meant jeopardizing aid from Washington, Rabin was ready to end the affair, at least in the public eye.[37]

Ultimately, says Beilin, it was Prime Minister Yitzhak Shamir who pushed the sanctions resolution through. "I went to Shamir. He surprised me by saying that he understands what I'm trying to do and that he'll help me," recalls Beilin. Shamir was embarrassed by his miscalculation and, after apologizing to AIPAC for putting too much faith in Reagan, he now had no choice but to impose sanctions of his own.

Having converted the prime minister and defense minister to his cause, Beilin was confident he could prevail—and he did. Beilin's sanctions package passed in a narrow cabinet vote on March 18, 1987, just before the U.S. congressional report on sanctions violations was released. The Israeli resolution mandated that the government "refrain from new undertakings, between Israel and South Africa, in the realm of defense" and established a working group to consider further sanctions "in line with the policy in practice in the Free World."[38]

The unclassified version of the congressional report was released two weeks later on April 1. It named several European countries as occasional violators, but the focus was on Israel.[39] Despite the "efforts at concealment made by both importers and exporters," the congressional investigators stated confidently that "Israel appears to have sold military systems and sub-systems and provided technical assistance on a regular basis." The report also warned that the U.S. government would view "new agreements relating to the manufacture and maintenance of arms, ammunition, and military equipment (as well as extensions or renewals of preexisting agreements upon their termination)" as falling under the mandatory ban.[40] Most damningly, the report's authors concluded, "We believe that the Israeli government was fully aware of most or all of the trade."[41] The secret of Israel's alliance with South Africa that had for years leaked out in bits and pieces was now finally out in the open, and this time the revelation came from a source that was difficult for Israel and its allies in Washington to dismiss or ignore.

In the wake of Israel's sanctions resolution, former defense minister Moshe Arens immediately took to the airwaves, insisting to listeners that South Africa had been a trusted and reliable friend to Israel over the years while all of black Africa distanced itself and denounced Zionism as racism. He called for Israel to honor existing contracts with South Africa and criticized Washington for forcing Israel to impose sanctions.[42]

Eliahu Lankin, the man who had commanded the ill-fated Irgun ship *Altalena* in 1948, was an even stronger critic of the cabinet decision. In

1981, Lankin's close friend Menachem Begin had appointed him ambassador to South Africa. Lankin's wife, Doris, had gone to school in the Orange Free State, South Africa's Afrikaner heartland, and she remained friendly with several apartheid government officials she had known as a child.[43]

Soon after returning from his stint in South Africa in 1985, Lankin granted an interview to *Haaretz*. When a reporter asked the veteran freedom fighter why he did not sympathize with the black South African struggle for independence, he replied: "There is a fundamental difference between a Jewish-Israeli patriot's ideology and the blacks' struggle. It is true we have fought for Israel's independence; the Blacks are fighting for their rights. So far we are both equal. But we were fighting a foreign colonialist government which did not have any rights to [this] land." By contrast, South African blacks, Lankin argued—having completely absorbed the Afrikaner nationalists' sense of their entitlement to govern—were fighting Afrikaners who held an equal claim to the land "by virtue of history and [who] have become an objective and political reality."[44] Ironically, Lankin's logic did not extend to the "objective and political reality" of the Arabs living in pre-1948 Palestine.

Lankin also lambasted the U.S. Congress for seeking "to impose their political stand on other countries using the weapon of economic support as a means of blackmail." He complained that other occasional violators of the 1977 U.N. embargo, such as France, Taiwan, Italy, and West Germany, could afford to "thumb their noses" at the U.S. law because they did not depend on American aid. "The only really vulnerable 'transgressor' is Israel, which unfortunately is dependent on American economic support, and will have no alternative but to refrain from renewing certain contracts with South Africa," wrote Lankin. "This will rebound to Israel's serious disadvantage."[45]

Other right-wing Israeli politicians echoed Lankin's views on apartheid. Although Raful Eitan and Ariel Sharon often disagreed about military matters—Eitan once accused Sharon of needlessly sending men to their deaths and "chronically exceeding his orders"—the two shared many of the same views when it came to denying political rights to Palestinians in the occupied territories and they applied these ideas to the treatment of blacks in South Africa.[46] So deep was their sympathy for South Africa and their identification with its leaders that both generals were willing to go public with their support. Sharon routinely urged the West to sell South Africa arms; Eitan went even further, declaring to a Tel Aviv University audience that blacks in South Africa were not oppressed. The problem, according to Eitan, was that blacks "want to gain control over the white minority just like the Arabs here want to gain control over us. And we, too, like the white minority in South Africa, must act to prevent them from taking us over."[47] It was not surprising that leading right-wing figures such as Lankin, Eitan, and Sharon so easily absorbed the antidemocratic rhetoric of the white South African government. After all, the militant Zionist ideology that had shaped their worldview denied political rights to national minorities and its more radical proponents openly eschewed democratic principles.

Eitan had remained close friends with both Magnus Malan and Constand Viljoen after he stepped down as IDF chief of staff in 1983 and was convinced that a black revolution in South Africa could lead to a global confrontation. Soon after leaving the military, he went into politics as a representative of the far-right Tehiya and Tzomet parties.[48] From his Knesset desk, Eitan wrote to the South African ambassador in Tel Aviv, instructing him to warn European leaders that "it is a communist hand guiding the activities" in South Africa and that the apartheid government would "fight for its existence" rather than be "a willing sacrifice for the satisfaction of hypocrites."[49] In 1987, the war in Namibia and Angola was still far from over and Cold War thinking colored the interpretations of military men like Eitan and many of his old colleagues in the Defense Ministry. A superficial sanctions resolution may have been on the books, but beneath the surface things were much the same.

The imposition of sanctions in 1987 did not sever Israel's ties with South Africa. On the contrary, members of the security establishment in both parties sought to preserve the relationship—and derive as much export revenue as they could from it. This exacerbated the ongoing feud between Israeli defense officials and the Beilin clique at the Foreign Ministry and paved the way for dysfunctional policymaking in Pretoria.

David Ivry, the former air force chief who had so happily hunted zebras in South Africa in 1980, was director-general of the Defense Ministry at the time of the Israeli sanctions debate and is now an executive at

Boeing in Tel Aviv. From his stylish office overlooking the Mediterranean and the Defense Ministry complex he once presided over, Ivry
scoffs at Beilin's version of events. He belittles Beilin's and Liel's policy
contributions and claims that they were shut out of the decision-making
process on South Africa.

As Ivry tells it, policy shifts in Washington were far more important
than Beilin's push for sanctions. In fact, he claims, the reduction in
defense cooperation was already proceeding slowly when the Beilin proposal came before the cabinet.[50] "At the beginning, we had the blessing
of the U.S., not an official blessing," Ivry recounts, but then, in the late
1980s, "the U.S. tried to force us to stop." Ivry and other members of the
security establishment, such as Defense Minister Rabin, began contact-
ing their anxious South African counterparts and "talked with them very
frankly"; Beilin and Liel were not involved, for fear that the two of them
would leak to the press what was happening. "We couldn't tell Beilin,"
says Ivry. "We didn't trust him." While generals and defense industry
officials were angry about Section 508, they had little choice but to heed
the will of a superpower ally when the Anti-Apartheid Act became law.
"To respond to our national security needs, we had to respond to U.S.
requests," says Ivry.[51]

Meanwhile, in Pretoria, Israel's embassy was putting forth one policy
while its defense mission was advancing another from the opposite side
of the wall. As one side managed ongoing arms contracts and cooperation with the South African security services, Shlomo Gur, a young,
bespectacled member of the Beilin clique in the Foreign Ministry, was
working the street trying to improve relations with black South African
leaders by expanding the connections forged through the Zelniker program. Riding on the coattails of positive media reports about Israeli
sanctions, he attempted to make official governmental contacts with the
black community.

Gur's goal was to bring trade unionists and members of the United
Democratic Front, a loose-knit anti-apartheid coalition, to Israel for
leadership training and public health and agricultural courses. Although
the participants appreciated the opportunity to travel and learn, the program was more valuable as a tool to convince black South Africans that
Israel was not the enemy. Many blacks believed his overtures were plot-
ted by Pretoria, but eventually, by forging personal relationships, Gur

managed to convince them that not everyone in the Israeli government supported apartheid.

The same level of trust did not exist between Gur and his colleagues. Some of the defense officials "were very opposed to what I was doing and tried to narrow my ability to operate," says Gur. While their kids played together after school, the Israelis on opposite sides of the wall were promoting radically different policies and seeking to undermine each other.[52]

Israeli ambassador David Ariel faced an anxious crowd at the April 1987 Board of Deputies congress in Johannesburg. Ariel had always opposed apartheid and was pleased with the cabinet decision to impose sanctions. But now he had to explain it to an audience of angry South African Jews, many of whom had an economic stake in strong trade ties with Israel and coveted Jewish organizations' exemptions from Pretoria's strict foreign exchange controls when sending money to Israel.[53] Despite the ongoing military cooperation, the South African government and many Jews remained nervous that Israel might impose even harsher sanctions.[54]

"As long as the Arabs continue to receive massive and sophisticated armaments from the Soviet Union, Israel will have to depend upon the U.S. for its defense," Ariel told the scions of Johannesburg Jewry. The audience did not appreciate hearing that their economic well-being was not the Israeli government's paramount concern, and they immediately mobilized to reverse the new Israeli policy.[55]

A special interministerial committee led by Beilin had agreed to consider amendments to the sanctions package prior to the September implementation deadline and the board's leadership jumped at the opportunity. In a formal letter to Beilin's committee, they argued that the effect of lessened ties on the South African Jewish community would "be most demoralising" and pleaded for "the special relationships to endure."[56]

There was face-to-face lobbying, too. As Beilin recalls, Mendel Kaplan, the widely recognized spokesman for South Africa's Jews who was then also chairman of Israel's powerful Jewish Agency, "screamed and shouted," accusing the Israeli government of endangering South African Jewry.[57] Kaplan was outraged when he heard that South Africans could no longer participate in Israel's pan-diaspora Maccabi Games, and he threatened to cut off financial donations to Israel in retaliation.[58]

As usual, South African Jewish leaders also invoked the specter of anti-Semitism as a reason to support the apartheid government. If Jews vocally supported Israeli sanctions, so the argument went, Pretoria would once again bar donations to Israel and perhaps even target the community as National Party leaders had during the 1930s and 1940s.

This was a red herring, of course, seeing as how high-ranking government officials had assured Jewish community leaders that nothing of the sort would happen. South Africa's former ambassador to Israel David du Buisson hosted board leaders at the Union Buildings in Pretoria in late April 1987, urging them to lobby the Israeli government while promising them that the Jewish community had nothing to fear if their lobbying failed and Israel imposed harsher measures.[59] Nevertheless, community leaders opposed to sanctions continued to raise the phantom threat of a state-sponsored backlash against Jews. The old student activist Dennis Davis, by then a law professor at the University of Cape Town, mocked their logic, challenging board leaders to explain exactly how Israeli weapons sales helped promote the interests of the South African Jewish community.[60] Faulty as its logic was, the board was repeating a familiar trope.

The claim that arms sales helped beleaguered Jewish communities was a favorite excuse among Israeli officials seeking to rationalize military ties with South Africa and other unsavory regimes. They used it in the case of Iran in the 1980s, when covert Israeli arms sales may have prompted Iran to grant exit visas to some Jews.[61] And they used the same rationale, even less convincingly, to justify arms sales to the military junta in Argentina on the grounds that Jewish opponents of the government would be spared the fate of the *desaparecidos*. In South Africa, however, the argument had no merit because Jews—as a community—faced no danger from the state in the 1970s and 1980s.[62] It simply diverted attention from the commercial and ideological motives underlying the alliance. Much to the chagrin of Israeli officials and South African Jewish leaders, American policymakers did not fall for it.

When the April 1987 congressional report formally acknowledged Israeli military cooperation with South Africa, American Jewish organizations were forced to stop denying the relationship and defend Israel's more pressing interest: ongoing military aid from Washington. Pro-Israel organizations such as AIPAC clearly saw the prospect of losing U.S. aid as a greater threat to the Jewish state than cutting ties with

South Africa.[63] As the self-appointed guardians of Israel's interests in Washington, they told Prime Minister Shamir to make sure Israel's measures against South Africa were just as strong as those taken in the United States and Western Europe.[64]

Their pressure paid off on September 16, 1987, when the Israeli cabinet formally unveiled a comprehensive sanctions package that went far beyond the initial resolution adopted in March. The new policy dictated no new investments in South Africa, no new agreements in the area of science, no visits to South Africa by Israeli civil servants, no promotion of tourism to South Africa, a freeze on the import quota of South African iron and steel, and the prevention of Israel becoming a way station that assisted South Africa in circumventing sanctions.[65]

The one thing the new law did not touch was existing arms contracts.

Although Jerusalem's sanctions package received in-depth coverage in Israeli and American papers, in practice it amounted to little more than a cosmetic gesture. Ultimately, the sanctions had hardly any impact on the flourishing trade between the two countries, especially in the defense sector, where multibillion-dollar contracts signed before 1987 remained in effect. An August 1987 South African government memo reported smugly that top Israeli officials had promised Pretoria that the new sanctions would merely amount to "window dressing," because suspending trade with South Africa "would first and foremost injure Israel." In fact, Rabin himself had already assured the South Africans that the changes would be "mainly symbolic" and would be announced publicly to "lessen the negative effects of contact with the RSA," which was damaging Israel's image.[66]

Johannesburg's business leaders also continued to behave as if nothing had changed. According to a letter from the South African Inventions Development Corporation, a civilian-military establishment housed on the grounds of the Council for Scientific and Industrial Research, Israeli officials had promised the firm that trade sanctions "would have no effect on the functioning of the SA/Israel Industrial R & D Programme."[67] Reg Donner, chairman of Anglo American's Research and Development Division, wrote to the Foreign Ministry regarding cooperation with Israeli institutions. He insisted that "it is of the utmost importance for us to carry on fostering these friendly relationships on a low profile basis to the mutual benefit of both countries. . . . I will most certainly continue to promote [them] . . . even against the fiercest pressures by the U.S.A. or others."[68]

Getting money out of the country was also a prime concern for South African business leaders in the mid-1980s as sanctions began to take effect.[69] In order to circumvent the trade embargo, they used the hardest currency available to them: diamonds. According to Chaim Even-Zohar, a leading historian of the diamond industry, during these years virtually all polished diamonds from South Africa were channeled through Israel with the aid of South Africa's two-tiered currency system of financial and commercial rand. Designed to stanch capital flight, the financial rand was worth 40 percent less than the commercial rand. Foreign investors seeking to expatriate their profits were forced to liquidate any assets at the lower financial-rand exchange rate, thereby creating an incentive for them to keep their money in South Africa. The financial rand also encouraged new foreign investment by allowing noncitizens to make purchases and capital investments at the more favorable exchange rate. This turned the country into "a rough diamond nirvana" in the late 1980s because Israeli companies were able to buy rough diamonds at the massively discounted financial-rand rate and then earn windfall profits by selling the finished product abroad. As Even-Zohar notes, "Many of the South African polishing companies were transferred into foreign, mostly Israeli, hands in order to utilize the financial rand benefits."[70]

Military elites, the South African Jewish community, and leading businessmen were all determined to maintain the alliance—sanctions be damned.

. . .

AS U.S. SANCTIONS STARTED to sting South Africa in 1988 and Shlomo Gur worked tirelessly to build bridges to South Africa's future black leaders, Eliahu Lankin was still defending white rule as forcefully as ever.

After publicly fighting Israeli sanctions legislation throughout 1987, Lankin declared in the Israeli journal *Nativ:* "The real problem in South Africa today is not apartheid. . . . The problem is that the spokesmen of the black majority are openly demanding that rule over the country pass into their hands." To the old Irgun commander, this was unacceptable. Just like the apartheid government's leaders, Lankin believed that genuine democracy would spell the annihilation of white South Africans. "What the ANC is demanding today is nothing less than 'one man, one vote.' . . . If the whites were to agree to this in present circumstances, they would be committing suicide, not only politically but physically as well." He criticized the United States for adding fuel and legitimacy to the anti-apartheid movement and denounced Washington's pressure on Israel to stop arms sales to South Africa.[71]

Lankin did have some fellow believers in Washington; a June 1988 *National Review* article argued that the Israeli–South African alliance was a boon to Israel's economy and a "natural marriage of interests" that only bothered "the fringe Israeli left." One of the authors went so far as pitching a book proposal to the South African Foreign Ministry with chapters on the necessity of strong Israeli–South African ties for Israel's security and how "world Jewry must choose between what is good for the Jews and what is good for liberals." While much of the rest of the world was calling for negotiated transition to black majority rule in 1988, Lankin still clung tenaciously to the idea that embattled minorities deserved to rule. "If there is to be any prospect of avoiding the much-prophesied carnage and destruction," he wrote, "the first step must be to discard the doctrinaire conceptions of theoretical democracy—one man, one vote."[72]

Pleased by Lankin's rousing defense of apartheid and fearful that Yossi Beilin was an omen of things to come if Labor returned to power, Pretoria aligned itself with the Likud Party as the 1988 Israeli elections approached. In July, four months before the election, officials from the prime minister on down assured South Africa's ambassador in Tel Aviv that no further steps would be taken against Pretoria. The minister of science and development blamed the sanctions on "young leftists" in the Foreign Ministry and claimed that his ministry would ignore them;[73] Mordechai Gur, who had preceded Eitan as IDF chief of staff, explained that Peres made anti–South Africa comments simply "because it makes things easier for him in the international community";[74] and the South African newspaperman turned Likud adviser, Harry Hurwitz, promised the new ambassador that his boss, Shamir, remained committed to South Africa.[75] Despite his pro-sanctions assurances to AIPAC in Washington, the old Lehi guerrilla was still playing a double game.

In October, a month before the election, South African foreign minister Pik Botha wrote to Defense Minister Magnus Malan about the need to keep Likud in power in order to protect Pretoria's interests.[76] South African businessmen and leaders in the Jewish community were watching closely; they, too, feared further sanctions if Labor returned to power. With the Likud Party facing financial difficulties in the final weeks of the campaign, South African Zionist Federation leader Julius Weinstein encouraged the Finance Ministry to allow an exceptional transfer of funds—R500,000 ($200,000 at the time)—to the Likud election committee. This sizable donation came from none other than Reg Donner, Anglo American's enthusiastic violator of sanctions, and Bertie Lubner of the Israel–South Africa Chamber of Commerce, which had been one of the first organizations to promote closer ties between the two countries in the early 1970s.[77]

The Foreign Ministry enthusiastically supported the idea. "A Likud victory would improve Israeli–South African relations and perhaps roll back sanctions," Deputy Foreign Minister Kobus Meiring predicted, whereas he feared a Labor win might bring even harsher ones.[78] In the end, the finance minister rejected Weinstein's application to transfer such a large sum to an Israeli political party—despite the Foreign Ministry's attempts to reverse it—and Likud won the election anyway.

South Africa's decision to tie its fortunes to the Israeli right was a natural move, given the harsh anti-apartheid rhetoric emanating from the Labor benches and other left-wing parties in the Knesset. It was not necessary, however: South African diplomats fundamentally misunderstood the political dynamics at play in Israel and the stark contrast between the righteous public face Israel was displaying to the world and the darker reality underneath.

They had failed to grasp the lesson that Israeli visitors had taught them three years before: that managing hypocrisy was an art. Peres's denunciations of South African policy—"a Jew who accepts apartheid ceases to be a Jew"—were merely diplomatic doublespeak.[79] Veteran Labor Party leaders, despite their willing participation in the alliance, felt the need to speak out publicly against apartheid in order to pay homage to the moralism of their ideological forebears, such as Ben-Gurion and Meir. Likud heavyweights such as Ariel Sharon and Raful Eitan felt no such duty and were perfectly willing to express open sympathy for the Afrikaner government.

Kobus Meiring, the South African official who had pleaded with the

Finance Ministry to allow the transfer of funds to Likud, finally grasped this a few months later when a young *Jerusalem Post* reporter named Wolf Blitzer asked him about Israel's complicated relationship with South Africa. "I always get the impression that there is a big difference in what is said from the stage . . . and what is really happening between our two countries," Meiring told the future CNN anchor.[80]

. . .

AS APARTHEID CRUMBLED in South Africa, the proceeds from old arms contracts continued to fill the Israeli treasury. Making sure that no one exposed these ongoing military ties was a task that fell to Israel's allies abroad.

The Anti-Defamation League is known in the United States and across the world as the premier opponent of anti-Semitism. It was founded in 1913 and later led the fight against Nazi sympathizers and neo-Nazis while defending the rights of other minorities targeted by white supremacist groups. But it had a darker side. During the 1940s, the ADL targeted suspected communists, shared its files with the House Un-American Activities Committee, and provided information to FBI investigators.[81]

The ADL moved even further to the right during the Reagan years. Under the leadership of Irwin Suall—who was raised in Brooklyn, schooled at Oxford, and spent his early career working for unions and the Socialist Party—the ADL created a formidable "fact-finding" department that not only collected information on targeted organizations but also infiltrated those groups with informers in order to glean more information and potentially undermine them.

As a young man, Suall had moved in left-wing circles and counted James Baldwin among his drinking buddies. Once, when a Greenwich Village bartender refused to serve the gay black writer, Suall joined Baldwin outside in the snow, picketing the bar.[82] But by the 1980s, Suall's allegiances had shifted away from the protest politics of the left and he took to identifying himself as a "repentant Trotskyist," devoting his energies to fighting anti-Semitic groups of all political stripes.

By the early 1980s, Suall had come to believe that neo-Nazis and skinheads were no longer a major menace to American Jews or the state

of Israel; instead, he believed that the greatest threat to Israel ema-
nated from the Soviet Union and the American left. As a result, Suall's
fact-finding department shifted its focus from white supremacists and
Aryan nationalists to every imaginable left-leaning organization in the
country—from pro-Nicaraguan Sandinista groups to the anti-apartheid
movement.[83] Suall's ace fact finder was a man named Roy Bullock.

As a child growing up in the Midwest, Bullock was enthralled by Herbert Philbrick's tale of Cold War espionage, *I Led Three Lives*. He had
always wanted to be a spy and in the 1950s he traveled to Moscow,
attempted to infiltrate a socialist youth movement convention, and
began to work as an unpaid informant for the FBI. As a closeted gay man
in the 1950s, it was the perfect way to conceal his identity while fighting
the Reds.[84] San Francisco proved to be a more hospitable environment,
and Bullock soon began working for the ADL there. His first assignment
was monitoring right-wing hate groups. Due to the unusual nature and
questionable legality of his work, Bullock was never officially kept on the
ADL payroll; instead, he was paid circuitously through a Los Angeles
law firm for over thirty years.[85]

As the anti-apartheid campaign turned its attention to Israel's links
with South Africa, the ADL entered the propaganda fray, publicly
attacking Nelson Mandela's ANC with arguments that mirrored those of
the hard-line security officials in Pretoria. In May 1986, ADL national
director Nathan Perlmutter co-authored an article arguing, "We must
distinguish between those who will work for a humane, democratic, pro-
Western South Africa and those who are totalitarian, anti-humane, anti-
democratic, anti-Israel and anti-American. It is in this context that the
African National Congress . . . merits a close, unsentimental look."[86]

The ADL also became involved in the Israeli–South African propaganda war in a more covert manner, dispatching Bullock to attend the
meetings of U.S.-based anti-apartheid groups, collect their publications,
and take down the license plate numbers of leaders' cars—including visitors such as Archbishop Desmond Tutu and South African Communist
Party leader Chris Hani.

Bullock collaborated with Tom Gerard of the San Francisco Police
Department in order to gather information on the targeted groups.
Sharing a taste for espionage, Bullock and Gerard, who had worked for
the CIA in Central America before joining the SFPD, hit it off instantly

when they met in 1985. Soon afterward, they began supplying each other with information. Within six months, Gerard was giving Bullock access to computerized criminal histories, vehicle and driver's license information, and other data only available to police officers.[87] Gerard also gave Bullock information on the owners of various PO boxes, and photographs of demonstrators.

Years later, police seized Bullock's computer and raided ADL offices in Los Angeles and San Francisco to gather evidence for a lawsuit against the organization brought by anti-apartheid activists and a variety of other left-wing groups. They found files on thousands of people, the majority of them illegally obtained through Gerard, who had by then fled to the Philippines. San Francisco district attorney Arlo Smith released reams of documents to the public, the FBI began an investigation, and anti-apartheid activists and the Arab-American Anti-Discrimination Committee sued the ADL in 1993. In a settlement, the ADL agreed to pay the plaintiffs' legal fees and to cease collecting law enforcement files.

But Bullock was not only working for the ADL. During the late 1980s, he had begun to perform the same services for the South African government.

Bullock claims he first met with a South African intelligence agent in 1987 or 1988.[88] It all began when he saw a newspaper listing advertising that Willis Carto, a known anti-Semite, would be holding an investment seminar in Las Vegas and that the South African consul-general from Los Angeles would be speaking there. Bullock and Gerard decided to warn the consul that "the South African government's reputation is none too good as it is and associating with a known anti-Semite will do you no good."[89] The consul-general canceled the engagement and thanked Gerard and Bullock. It wasn't long before Bullock was approached by South African spies.

Six months after issuing the warning to the South African consulate, Gerard called Bullock to tell him a South African intelligence officer was in town and wanted to meet. The two went together and met with an agent named Humphries in a hotel room. Humphries had graying hair, a reddened face, and a thick jowl; he spoke with a slight but noticeable South African accent. The agent wanted information on anti-apartheid activities in the United States, and Bullock knew that helping him would be easy.[90] As Bullock later confessed in a deposition, the ADL "was interested in certain anti-apartheid groups . . . [that] shared a far left agenda," including the ANC.[91] He believed that the ANC's interests were fundamentally opposed to Israel's and, like his employer, he considered it a terrorist organization. Bullock later admitted to the FBI that funneling information to South African intelligence agents provided him with a supplementary income while presenting him with no additional work. After all, he was already monitoring the same anti-apartheid activists for the ADL.[92]

In 1989, Humphries left the country and was replaced by another agent. Despite the personnel change, Bullock's work as a South African spy continued. Pretoria's new man in San Francisco presented himself as Louie. He was much younger than Humphries, clean-shaven, well dressed, and had a strong, unmistakably Afrikaans accent. He was also deeply paranoid and refused to leave his hotel. Despite Bullock's many attempts to lure him out for a meal, Louie would insist on meeting in his hotel room and turning the radio's volume up to drown out their conversations each time they met.

Nevertheless, Bullock—who claimed he personally opposed apartheid—was put at ease by Louie, whom he described as "more liberal" and of the opinion "that blacks must eventually share power with whites in South Africa." Louie was adamant, however, that the ANC could not be part of any new government because they were "terrorists," a sentiment very much in line with Bullock's own views.[93] Bullock met Louie six or seven times between 1989 and 1991.[94] During this period, the ADL fact finder sent reports two to three times per month to a PO box in New York City,[95] describing anti-apartheid meetings and rallies he attended as an informer, including an event focusing on the movie industry's role in the anti-apartheid movement at the Hollywood Hotel.[96]

For South African spies in California, this was no laughing matter. The meeting at the Hollywood Hotel took place in the wake of *Lethal Weapon 2*'s blockbuster success: it was the number one R-rated movie of 1989, grossing over $220 million worldwide and dealing a body blow to South African public diplomacy efforts in the United States and across the globe. The film featured a multiracial LAPD duo, played by Mel Gibson and Danny Glover, battling a nefarious group of South Africans smuggling drugs and Krugerrands through the Los Angeles consulate under the cover of diplomatic immunity.

Although it is better remembered for exploding toilets and steamy sex scenes, *Lethal Weapon 2* had an unabashedly political agenda and provided theatergoers with equal parts shoot-'em-up drama and righteous anti-apartheid rage. The Nazi-like villains spoke in pitch-perfect Afrikaans accents, their consular seal resembled that of the Third Reich, and they repeatedly referred to Danny Glover's character—and other black Americans—as "kaffir" (the South African equivalent of "nigger") while indiscriminately killing anyone who got in their way.

The South African government and its operatives had hoped to stem the tide of negative publicity by infiltrating the film industry, but Hollywood's crusade continued, eclipsing Pretoria's counterpropaganda efforts. What had begun with the trenchantly anti-apartheid *Cry Freedom* in 1987—featuring Denzel Washington in his first starring role as the black consciousness leader Steve Biko—culminated in 1992, when a repentant Arnon Milchan produced *The Power of One*, a World War II–era tale of interracial friendship triumphing over racism in South Africa. In exchange for attending events such as the Hollywood Hotel meeting, infiltrating other anti–South African groups in California, and monitoring the leaders of left-wing organizations that supported the anti-apartheid movement, Bullock received over $15,000 in payments from his handlers over the course of four years.[97] At one point, as if following the *Lethal Weapon* script, they even offered to pay Bullock in Krugerrands.[98]

Bullock and Gerard made every effort to keep their intelligence bartering activities quiet, for fear that the FBI would discover they were selling information to the South Africans.[99] But the work was drying up and soon there would be little left to do on behalf of South African intelligence. In February 1990, Nelson Mandela was released from prison and embarked on a worldwide speaking tour; as change appeared on the horizon in South Africa, the Bay Area anti-apartheid movement slowly evaporated.

Some conservative South African Jews and skeptical Americans made a last-ditch effort to derail Mandela's visit to the United States, but they were warded off behind the scenes by Michigan congressman Howard Wolpe and the liberal South African Jewish activist Diana Aviv.[100] Aviv vividly remembers an eleventh-hour threat to prevent Mandela's visit, when a New York rabbi vowed to protest against Mandela because the South African had uttered kind words about Yasser Arafat and Muammar Gaddafi. Realizing that such a public protest "would be disastrous for Black-Jewish relations," Aviv cold-called the national coordinator of Mandela's U.S. tour from her apartment in New York. She implored him to convince Mandela to meet with ADL president Abe Foxman and other Jewish leaders before his trip to New York in order to defuse any possible Jewish protests against the ANC leader. A meeting was arranged in Geneva during which Mandela assured several prominent American Jews that he recognized Israel's right to exist.[101] Foxman, the head of an organization that had until then denounced the ANC as totalitarian and a threat to Israel, emerged from the discussions so pleased with Mandela's stance on Israel that he proclaimed the ANC leader "a great hero of freedom" in a letter to *The New York Times* two weeks later.[102]

Having assuaged the fears of Jewish leaders, Mandela's U.S. tour during the summer of 1990 turned out to be a remarkable success, drawing sold-out crowds and culminating in an address to Congress. (The only kink was a small protest by Miami Cubans upset about Mandela's friendship with Fidel Castro.) Given the heroic image he commanded in the American press, South Africa's intelligence operatives realized that demonizing the ANC in the United States was quickly becoming a lost cause. When Bullock showed up late to his final rendezvous with Louie, the South African handler was angry and acting jittery. He gave Bullock the final payment and thanked him, telling him "it just isn't worth it," and then walked off.[103]

The anti-apartheid movement had won the propaganda war in the United States. But in Israel, where ties with the South African government ran much deeper and severing them was much more costly, neither side found it easy to simply walk away.

12

THE END OF THE AFFAIR

*South Africa's Transition to Democracy
and the Demise of the Alliance*

IN MAY 1989, DEEP INSIDE Cheyenne Mountain on the outskirts of Colorado Springs, analysts at the North American Aerospace Defense Command (NORAD) were busy monitoring Russian missile and rocket tests. Accustomed to routine Soviet reconnaissance missions, the air force intelligence officers didn't think twice as they watched a rocket launch a satellite into orbit from the Arctic capital of Arkhangelsk. But within seventy-two hours, the Soviet satellite abruptly shifted course, dropped its altitude and zoomed in on a stretch of sea at the southern tip of Africa. The Russians knew something that the Americans didn't, and CIA satellites soon followed. On July 5, the U.S. surveillance satellite passing over the Indian Ocean detected a plume of smoke off the South African coast near Arniston. It appeared to be the exhaust trail of a missile, and the wake was identical to that produced by the Israeli Jericho 2. The match set off alarms in Washington.[1]

By imposing sanctions two years earlier, Israel had successfully distanced itself from South Africa in the eyes of the media. The smoking gun off the coast of South Africa threatened all this; it confirmed that Israel was still cooperating with Pretoria two years after pledging to halt military ties. Israel was suddenly charged with violating its own sanctions, and this time the accusation came not only from the press and the anti-apartheid movement, but from the White House.

South Africa's quest for long-range missiles had begun in the early 1980s as Pretoria was facing tens of thousands of Cuban troops in Angola. By 1987, the Angolan conflict had turned into the largest confrontation on African soil since World War II. Lacking a long-range missile capability,

South Africa's leaders had for years relied on their ground troops and the air force to gain the upper hand. As the fighting intensified, they scrambled to put the finishing touches on the nuclear-capable missiles being built with Israeli help in Arniston.

During the month of September 1987, South African ground troops inflicted massive casualties on both Cuban and Angolan forces in battles along the Lomba River in southern Angola, but they had no such luck in the skies. With only a few of the Israeli-updated Cheetah jets ready for battle, the SADF was losing its edge in the air as Soviet MiG-23 and MiG-27 planes entered the fray and the Angolans and Cubans built new bases and airfields.[2] By the end of the year, Cuban troops and their SWAPO allies from Namibia had achieved a decisive advantage over South Africa in southern Angola.[3] Six months after the Lomba River victory, the SADF fought an intense monthlong battle near the town of Cuito Cuanavale in an effort to clear the eastern bank of the Cuito River. The battle was indecisive, but the Cubans claimed victory. Then, on June 26, 1988, Castro's forces launched a surprise attack on the SADF, leading to further rejoicing in Havana.

Aware that it desperately needed to strengthen its air force, South Africa sent a team a month later to learn airspace control techniques from the Israelis. By this time, Israeli engineers had finished modernizing almost half of the Cheetah aircraft South Africa had sent to Israel for upgrades.[4] Yet another group of South Africans visited to shop for laser-guided weapons.[5] Most important, the two governments began to discuss cooperation on a next-generation South African aircraft after Israel canceled plans to build its own homegrown fighter jet, the Lavi.

Israel had decided to develop the Lavi in the mid-1970s, but the project soon began to consume billions of dollars, strain the Israeli economy, and unsettle the defense industry.[6] When it was canceled in 1987, it was a boon for the South African aircraft industry. At the Pentagon, Defense Intelligence Agency analysts reported that high-paying jobs in South Africa were being offered to former Lavi project employees. The salaries offered were close to $80,000 per year payable into any bank account in the world—a tempting package at the time for laid-off Israeli engineers.[7] This expanded military cooperation and sharing of expertise did not go over well in Washington, where U.S. assistant secretary of state Chester Crocker was painstakingly negotiating the withdrawal of all Cuban and

South African troops from Angola and independence for Namibia. In this new military landscape, American diplomats saw no compelling reason for South Africa's ongoing defense ties with Israel.

With Section 508 on the books, U.S. policymakers were speaking openly and disapprovingly about Israeli cooperation with South Africa—a topic that had long been shrouded in secrecy. Having recently signed the Missile Technology Control Regime, the MTCR, along with several other Western nations, the United States was getting serious about stopping missile proliferation.[8] In early 1989, U.S. ambassador Thomas Pickering complained to Shamir about Israel's ongoing aid to the South African missile program and warned him that President Bush was not happy about it. The scientists Israel had sent to South Africa in 1984 had been closely vetted, given cover stories, and committed to secrecy when they reached the Overberg missile testing range in Arniston. With Washington breathing down their necks, keeping their work secret became even harder.

Then, on July 5, 1989, hovering satellites observed another missile fly five hundred miles out to sea from Overberg.[9] The DIA immediately noted that a short-range ballistic missile had been launched and that "Israel's connection to the project has been rumored since the mid-1980s."[10] CIA analysts went into more detail, warning that "the possibility of a direct transfer of missile components from Tel Aviv to Pretoria" was likely.[11]

Israel responded to these accusations cryptically, declaring, "The defense establishment strictly abides by the inner cabinet decision of March 18, 1987, whereby no new contracts will be signed between Israel and South Africa in the defense realm."[12] This was meaningless, of course, because the missile cooperation at Arniston dated back to 1984 and was therefore part of an existing contract.

The South Africans claimed that the new missile, known as the RSA-3, was simply a satellite launch vehicle—an innocuous part of their "space program." But it was well known to all in the field that the same delivery system that launches a satellite into space could also be used for a nuclear-tipped ballistic missile. American intelligence agencies were well aware of South Africa's nuclear capability, and the possibility of a viable long-range delivery system worried them. In the CIA's opinion, "the program would not make sense unless the missile was intended to carry a nuclear warhead."[13] The recent U.S.-brokered negotiations between South Africa and Cuba had put peace in Angola and independence for Namibia within reach. To Bush, an old CIA hand himself, it seemed that Pretoria needed nuclear-tipped missiles less than ever and he demanded that the cooperation cease.[14]

Despite Bush's scolding, Israel's schizophrenic foreign policy toward South Africa continued, with Liel and Gur building a relationship with black opposition leaders while the defense mission sold weapons to their oppressors. Then, in 1989, the situation became even messier. A new Likud ambassador, Zvi Gov-Ari, was sent to South Africa, where he rekindled close ties with the National Party government—a link that had been weak since the end of Eliahu Lankin's tenure in 1985. Gov-Ari was a Likud Party loyalist who rejected Liel and Gur's strategy of courting black opposition leaders. In addition to cozying up to the NP leadership, Gov-Ari strengthened Israel's ties with Mangosuthu Buthelezi and other bantustan leaders whom the ANC and anti-apartheid legislators in the West saw as puppets.

Carrying out Israel's self-contradictory policy was both a political and logistical mess. "When Shlomo Gur went to Johannesburg to meet the ANC, I drove down to [KwaZulu's capital] Ulundi to meet Buthelezi," recalls Gov-Ari. "I saw my mission as trying to understand every side, even right-wingers."[15] To this day, he cherishes an award he received from F. W. de Klerk's government and keeps it prominently displayed in his office. But while Gov-Ari was reaching out to the right, de Klerk had already seen the writing on the wall; the South African president released several high-profile political prisoners in 1989 and began holding secret negotiations with Mandela.

The Israeli defense establishment, which had for so long banked on the survival of white minority rule, had to accept that a new era was dawning. Even Shlomo Brom, the Israeli defense attaché in Pretoria, could see that apartheid was eroding around him. Brom also found the Israeli government's policy bizarre from his vantage point on the other side of the embassy barrier from 1988 to 1990. "We didn't have one embassy in South Africa, we had three," he exclaims. The first was the ambassador's turf and focused on maintaining cordial ties with the NP government; the second was run by Gur and focused on developing a relationship with the black opposition; the third was Brom's defense mission. "I thought it would be better if we had one policy and one embassy," says Brom with a shrug.[16] But he kept his views to himself and continued to maintain relations with the South African military establishment. The crumbling of apartheid was not the only factor hastening the demise of the Israeli–South African alliance; larger geopolitical forces were quickly making it militarily and economically irrelevant.

. . .

THE END OF THE COLD WAR dramatically altered the political and strategic landscape of Southern Africa. Cuban troops were already withdrawing from Angola when F. W. de Klerk replaced P. W. Botha as president in August 1989. The Berlin Wall fell three months later and de Klerk soon embarked on a radically different course that led to the release of Nelson Mandela in early 1990. With the Soviet and Cuban threat gone, South Africa could no longer appeal for Western support by invoking anticommunist arguments, nor could it rationalize repression of the democratic opposition by cloaking apartheid in Cold War rhetoric.

In Washington, old Africa hands were trying to help facilitate a negotiated transition. Former senator Dick Clark, who was run out of office with Eschel Rhoodie's slush fund back in 1978,[17] began to hold separate Aspen Institute–sponsored seminars for black and white South African leaders and American members of Congress.[18]

In Pretoria, the Israeli government went to great lengths to improve its image after Mandela's release. Veteran left-wing critics of apartheid were appointed to key posts, including Alon Liel, who became ambassador in 1992 and worked hard to redefine Israeli–South African relations for the postapartheid era. Even so, the legacy of the 1970s and 1980s left Mandela with a sour taste.

A year before South Africa's first democratic elections, Elazar Granot of Israel's far-left Mapam Party addressed the delegates of the Socialist International—a global gathering of Social Democratic leaders attended by many European heads of state. Granot lavished praise on Mandela, comparing him to Moses and arguing that South Africa's president-in-waiting was even greater than Moses for he had actually reached the

Promised Land. But Mandela did not succumb to his flattery. As Granot recalls it, the first words from South Africa's icon of forgiveness and reconciliation were: "The people of South Africa will never forget the support of the state of Israel to the apartheid regime."[19]

When Liel arrived in Pretoria as ambassador in 1992 he faced an uphill battle against the sort of lingering resentment Mandela's comment betrayed. The fact that the previous ambassador, Zvi Gov-Ari, was seen as a friend of the apartheid government did not make it any easier. But despite bitter memories, the ANC leadership seemed surprisingly willing to forget the past if Jerusalem simply agreed to take steps toward ending the occupation and allowing the establishment of an independent Palestinian state. Israel's peace initiatives in the early 1990s, such as lifting a ban on direct talks with the PLO and establishing the land-for-peace formula in the 1993 Oslo Accords, pleased Mandela and helped improve Liel's standing in ANC circles immensely.[20]

Liel was dealing almost exclusively with black leaders, much to the chagrin of the de Klerk government, which didn't appreciate being sidelined and wanted to hold on to some influence in the new South Africa. As a result, Liel was not aware of some of the ongoing arms deals between his military colleagues and the de Klerk government.

Malcolm Ferguson, South Africa's ambassador to Israel at the time, was stunned to learn that Israel's South Africa policy was not only self-contradictory but that the diplomats and defense officials at the Israeli embassy had no idea what their colleagues were doing. A key adviser to Prime Minister Rabin had told Ferguson that the Foreign Ministry was deliberately kept in the dark about the nature of military relations between the two countries for fear that its liberal employees would leak information to the media.

When Ferguson finally met Liel, he was shocked to discover how little the Israeli ambassador actually knew about the alliance. "It is obvious to me that Liel knows absolutely nothing about the nature or extent of security cooperation between the two countries," he wrote in a cable to Pretoria. Ferguson could not resist telling Liel that he had been deceived for years because military leaders had feared a leak. Liel did not dispute this, and explained that military leaders resented him and Beilin for trying to shut down defense cooperation by imposing sanctions.[21] He admitted that he hadn't ever set foot in the defense mission on the other side of his wall. It was as if Liel did not want the moral purity of his and Beilin's 1987 anti-apartheid crusade to be marred by the crude reality of ongoing military cooperation six years later.

"I believe in morals in diplomacy," Beilin told Israeli television in 1993. "Today, everybody knows that if we did not impose sanctions against South Africa in 1987, we could not even look into the eyes of the new government that will be elected there in April next year."[22] Certainly, sanctions may have improved Israel's diplomatic relations with the ANC, but the harsh reality was that Israel's interests had once again trumped its morals.

In Tel Aviv, Ferguson kept tabs on all ongoing arms deals and maintained close contact with Ivry, who told him his door at the Defense Ministry was always open.[23] Just months before South Africa's first democratic election, there were still sizable active arms contracts to the tune of R6 billion (then almost $2 billion) over the coming four years. "Until advised to the contrary," Ferguson wrote to Pretoria, "I shall continue to regard it as one of the overriding priorities of this mission to protect this investment."[24]

The political landscape in Pretoria was changing, but the formidable arsenal that South Africa had constructed with Israel's help remained a major concern for the U.S. government in the early 1990s. Despite the ANC's commitment to the principles of nonproliferation, certain U.S. and British officials, as well as some Israelis, feared that sensitive nuclear technology might fall into the hands of ANC allies, such as Castro and Gaddafi, who were hostile to the West.

South Africa knew that it would never be welcomed back into the international community with a covert nuclear weapons program and in 1990, under pressure from Washington and London, de Klerk ordered the dismantlement of all existing nuclear warheads and the destruction of all proliferation-sensitive records associated with the program.[25] By signing the Nuclear Non-Proliferation Treaty, Pretoria could in one fell swoop shed its pariah status and gain a seat at the table in major international organizations dealing with nuclear energy and proliferation, such as the Nuclear Suppliers Group and the International Atomic Energy

Agency.[26] In 1991, South Africa admitted IAEA inspectors and became a signatory to the NPT. That same year, Israel agreed to abide by the terms of the Missile Technology Control Regime.

Official pronouncements aside, defense industry leaders in both countries wanted to hold on. The South Africans fought tenaciously to retain their missile technology for launching satellites until Washington imposed sanctions against Armscor. And the Israelis did not cave in on missile cooperation until Washington threatened to restrict import licenses for American weapons and bar Israeli firms from competing for U.S. defense contracts.[27]

Defending the South African missile program would be one of the first tasks for South Africa's new ambassador to the United States. In a signal of Pretoria's move away from hard-line apartheid policy and toward democratization, de Klerk appointed Harry Schwarz as ambassador to Washington in 1991, the first time a non-NP member had been named to such a senior post. Schwarz had arrived in South Africa as a child refugee from Nazi Germany in 1934, served in the South African Air Force during World War II, and became a leading opposition member of Parliament. He was an outspoken critic of apartheid as well as a staunch anticommunist, lending him hawkish credentials that earned him the respect of certain NP members. He represented a new beginning in South African diplomacy.

Upon arriving at Dulles Airport, Schwarz refused to be driven in the embassy's white limousine, an oddity among Washington's diplomatic fleet, which is dominated by sleek black Town Cars. For subsequent embassy engagements, Schwarz again turned down the limousine and opted for a nondescript blue Ford sedan instead. His Chilean driver later told him that this breach of protocol was the subject of intense discussion among the capital's diplomatic chauffeurs. "The drivers said there must be a change in the embassy because the white racist car has gone," recalls Schwarz.[28] Despite his decision to abandon the limousine, Schwarz still represented a National Party government and worked diligently to protect its interests. In 1991, he made a last-ditch effort to defend South Africa's missile program as a space launch platform vital to the nation's economy.[29] Washington doubted the commercial viability of such a program and feared that there was too great an incentive to use the same technology to build and export missiles.

Under heavy pressure from the United States, South Africa's satellite launch capability was eventually put to an end. With hindsight, Princeton Lyman, the U.S. ambassador to Pretoria at the time, admits that South Africa may have been able to compete in the satellite launch industry, but the prospect of proliferation was his overriding concern. In 1994, Washington paid Pretoria approximately $500,000 toward the destruction of the equipment and signed an agreement marking the end of the program and paving the way for South Africa's accession to the Missile Technology Control Regime.[30] It was a paltry sum in the eyes of those who had built and tested the missiles.

Those scientists remain bitter to this day about U.S. pressure to end the missile program. Three of the architects of the nuclear and missile programs claim that "South Africa sacrificed (on the altar of morality and acceptability to the international community) its leading edge defense technology, and its leading position as one of the world's important exporters of weapons systems," not to mention fifteen thousand job opportunities—creating a security threat in its own right.[31] On the eve of South Africa's transition to democracy, a group of disgruntled nuclear weapons engineers even threatened to go public with the details of cooperation with Israel if they were not given better severance packages by the government.[32]

It was not until March 1993, after all Pretoria's nuclear bombs had been dismantled, that President F. W. de Klerk went public and announced to Parliament that South Africa had in fact possessed nuclear weapons. De Klerk's announcement marked a watershed: it was the world's first case of voluntary disarmament, and his speech to Parliament produced a wave of skepticism. Indeed, there are a number of conspiracy theories regarding the end of the South African nuclear and missile program, represented most thoroughly by *The Mini-Nuke Conspiracy*, a 1995 book co-authored by Steve McQuillan and Peter Hounam, the British journalist who first published photographic evidence of Israel's nuclear program in London's *Sunday Times* in 1986. Their book suggests that South Africa's nuclear expertise and capacity was far too advanced to have only completed seven bombs by 1989, the number officially claimed by South Africa and the IAEA. They base their evidence on a variety of anonymous interviews with former Armscor officials who claim that over twenty bombs were produced as well as more than one hundred nuclear artillery shells. The absence of these weapons is attributed either to stockpiling by right-wing Afrikaners or transfer to Israel for storage.[33]

These claims are not outlandish, given South Africa's well-established research into thermonuclear and implosion devices. However, they assume that these programs were carried through to the production stage and that advanced nuclear weapons were actually built and deployed in the late 1980s.[34] These allegations are severely undermined by the IAEA's restricted 1993 report—based on 150 inspections of nuclear facilities over a two-year period. The IAEA found no such weapons and confirmed that South Africa's declared highly enriched uranium production totals were plausible based on their inspection of the facilities.[35] Indeed, former Atomic Energy Board head Waldo Stumpf is so doubtful that he has publicly challenged the authors of the *Mini-Nuke Conspiracy* to present their findings to the IAEA for examination and verification.[36]

Nevertheless, many questions do remain about the truthfulness of South Africa's nuclear declarations, though they center more on the issue of cooperation with Israel than a hidden nuclear stockpile. De Klerk declared in his March 1993 speech to Parliament, "At no time did South Africa acquire nuclear weapons technology or materials from another country, nor has it provided any to any other country, or co-operated with another country in this regard."[37] De Klerk has explained the tritium from Israel as an acquisition for commercial use; even if it was never used, this is an unconvincing excuse, given that the South African government was planning and researching thermonuclear weapons at the time.[38] Furthermore, de Klerk offered no explanation in his speech for the uranium supplied to Israel during the 1960s and 1970s or Fanie Botha's decision to lift the safeguards on that stockpile, a matter he was no doubt aware of, given that he succeeded Botha as minister of mines in 1979 and testified at Jan Blaauw's trial in 1988. By carefully choosing his terminology, de Klerk artfully sidestepped the truth in his 1993 address to Parliament and in so doing prevented the full exposure of three decades of Israeli–South African nuclear cooperation.[39] Even after Pretoria's program had been shut down, the secret—or part of it—had to be kept.

. . .

ON THE EVE of South Africa's transition to democracy, a variety of cooperative ventures were still moving forward despite the Israeli sanctions, which forbade new contracts.[40] The largest was Project Tunny, an agreement with Israel Aircraft Industries to further update South Africa's Cheetah fleet with advanced avionics.[41] The South African Air Force had sent thirty-eight Cheetah C aircraft to Israel for weapons system updates and they were scheduled to become operational in 1995.[42] Despite this R700 million ($220 million) contract, the number of South Africans in Israel was dwindling. Rather than the large teams of officers that had once frequented Israel, the biggest group of South African military personnel arriving in Israel in 1993 was the twelve-man boxing team of the Far North Command, including three blacks.[43]

Back in South Africa, the situation was growing tense. A spate of attacks on blacks by a mysterious "Third Force"—made up of former and current government security operatives seeking to derail the transition—outraged Mandela, leading him to believe that the apartheid regime had organized covert government death squads.[44] Then in April, the young and wildly popular South African Communist Party leader Chris Hani was shot dead in his driveway by white right-wingers. Hani had been widely seen as a potential heir to Mandela and his assassination left the country teetering on the brink of chaos. Mandela appealed to outraged black South Africans for calm and they heeded his call, but the white right remained angry for reasons of its own.

The bitter-enders of the Afrikaner right felt betrayed by de Klerk, and they lashed out at him for what they regarded as spineless capitulation. Fed up with de Klerk's compromises, General Constand Viljoen returned to politics in 1993, joining a group of fellow retired generals, including Tienie Groenewald, who called de Klerk "the biggest traitor in South African history." Together they established the Afrikaner Volksfront, a new Afrikaner nationalist organization, whose goal was to create a sovereign Boer state within the new South Africa—"an Israel for the Afrikaner," as Viljoen put it.[45]

On May 7, 1993, a panoply of white supremacist and Afrikaner nationalist groups convened in the town of Potchefstroom, south of Johannesburg. The white right was there in all of its splendor, from the Afrikaner

Volksfront to the Afrikaner Resistance Movement, AWB, a militant group led by the appropriately named gray-bearded firebrand, Eugene Terreblanche. AWB members sported brownshirt-style uniforms emblazoned with a three-armed swastika. A splinter extremist organization called the White Wolves and even a local branch of the KKK showed up. The crowd gave Viljoen a hero's welcome as he ascended the podium. "Every Afrikaner must be ready. Every farm, every school is a target. . . . A bloody conflict which will require sacrifices is inevitable, but we will gladly sacrifice because our cause is just," the old general intoned. "You lead, we will follow," the crowd bellowed in response.[46]

The following month, Viljoen, Groenewald, and their colleagues applied for a demonstration permit in the Johannesburg suburb of Kempton Park, where they intended to protest the power-sharing talks between Mandela and de Klerk by showing their disapproval in numbers. The Volksfront leaders assured the police that the five thousand expected demonstrators would not be armed. They were wrong; Terreblanche's militants arrived with a formidable arsenal.

On June 25, 1993, the SADF's chief of staff, Pierre Steyn, flew back from Israel—where he and his Israeli counterparts were holding their final intelligence conference—just in time to see Terreblanche's men drive a Viper armored car into the building where constitutional negotiations were being held next to Johannesburg's airport.[47] After shattering the glass facade of the conference center, the white extremists took over the building, ransacking it while shouting racial epithets at the negotiators.[48]

Constand Viljoen and his liberal twin brother, Braam, had not spoken about politics for decades, but after the Viper incident, Braam sensed that the country was on the brink of civil war and that his brother was the only man with the power to stop it. He pleaded with Constand to speak with Mandela in person. Constand conferred with his fellow Volksfront leaders and a few days later agreed to let his activist brother use high-level ANC connections to set up a meeting. On August 12, 1993, the Viljoen brothers, Groenewald, and two other key Volksfront leaders rang Mandela's doorbell in the upscale Johannesburg neighborhood of Houghton. Haunted by the schoolbook tale of Afrikaner peacemakers who met with the Zulu king Dingaan in 1838 only to be slaughtered after signing a peace agreement, the Volksfront men were wary of Mandela. But even they could not resist his political charms.[49]

The ever-gracious Mandela served his guests tea, launched into a lengthy monologue about his admiration for the Afrikaner people and their traditions, and shocked Viljoen by addressing him in the general's own native tongue, Afrikaans. Mandela paid the assembled generals the ultimate compliment by conceding, "Militarily we cannot fight you; we cannot win." But, the great conciliator warned them bluntly, "If, however, you do go to war, you assuredly will not win either . . . we are too many, you cannot kill us all."[50] Viljoen agreed that a civil war was no solution; instead he and his colleagues demanded a *volkstaat*—their own patch of land to create the "Afrikaner Israel" they dreamed of. Mandela was too savvy a politician to deny their request outright and wise enough to know that as negotiations moved forward and he further assured Afrikaners that they were safe in a multiracial South Africa, demands for self-determination would evaporate.

In March 1994, one month before the election and despite the growing rapport between Mandela and Viljoen, things nearly fell apart. The government had warned bantustan leaders that their territories would automatically be incorporated into the new South Africa—by force if necessary. Bophuthatswana's president, Lucas Mangope, the puppet head of state who relished flying his flag alongside the Union Jack on Embassy Row in Tel Aviv, had no intention of giving up without a fight. Viljoen's Volksfront, after all, was willing to stand between Mangope and the SADF, who had been ordered by de Klerk to force Bophuthatswana's integration.

On March 10, civil unrest spread across the bantustan and Afrikaner nationalists sent out a call to arms. Once again, as in Kempton Park, Terreblanche's Afrikaner Resistance Movement lost control. White men in pickup trucks rolled through the streets randomly firing on black men, women, and children, their leaders having urged them to go on a "kaffir shooting picnic." After angry black crowds began pelting the white men with stones, a Bophuthatswanan police officer stepped in and methodically shot three of Terreblanche's men in the head. The iconic photos of the bearded Boer extremists lying in pools of their own blood flashed across South African television screens, shocking blacks and whites alike. Their deaths marked the end of the right's march to war.

. . .

IT WAS NOW CLEAR to the decision makers in Jerusalem who had once believed the National Party had twenty years to live that apartheid was dead. Likewise, the Israeli right's flirtation with the bantustan leaders—but not the bantustan concept as a model for eventual Palestinian statehood—was a thing of the past.[51] The Israeli government's new priority was making sure that South Africa remained a customer rather than becoming an enemy.

As the April 1994 elections approached, ANC leaders negotiated with Viljoen, promising to hold a referendum on the question of an Afrikaner *volkstaat*, while fending off the menace of Buthelezi's Zulu nationalist followers, who were threatening to boycott the elections and create a state of their own. "We could have stopped the elections from taking place . . . we had the means, we had the arms, we had the tactics, and we had the will," says Viljoen.[52]

Despite all this, Viljoen reversed course after the debacle in Bophuthatswana. He was denounced as a Judas by those further to his right, but he had made up his mind. Twenty minutes before the election filing deadline he submitted paperwork for a new political party, the Freedom Front, and opted to pursue his dream of an Afrikaner *volkstaat* via the ballot box.[53] He was elected to Parliament in April 1994 and served for seven years. In 2001, after popular interest in an Afrikaner state had long since faded—as Mandela had predicted it would—Viljoen retired and returned to his rural farm three hundred miles east of Johannesburg.

As South Africa's domestic drama unfolded prior to the 1994 elections, South African officials continued to milk the Israelis for everything they could get before the handover of power. At this stage, any cooperation had to be kept hidden from the Americans.[54] When an Armscor official visited Israel to discuss a joint project to build guided missiles in 1993, he was instructed to remain silent outside the Israeli subcontractor's office "because there was a party of Americans in an adjoining part of the block where we were."[55] Technically, the axe of Section 508 still loomed over Israel's head, making defense officials extremely touchy about their ongoing cooperation with South Africa after the 1987 sanctions and the discovery of the missile test in 1989.[56]

Other South African arms deals bothered the Americans as well. A federal grand jury in Philadelphia indicted seven South Africans and several Armscor subsidiaries for violating the arms embargo by smuggling weapons components out of the United States.[57] Washington was also irritated by Pretoria's blatant disregard of U.N. sanctions in the world's trouble spots—from the Balkans to the Persian Gulf—where South Africa was selling arms.[58] This was not surprising behavior coming from a country that had for years depended on the evasion of sanctions for its survival. In the wake of the 1991 Gulf War against Saddam Hussein, Washington was particularly concerned about Armscor sales to Iraq, Iran, and Libya. So were the Israelis, who took arms transfers to their enemies extremely seriously.

Gerald Bull, a Canadian engineer who developed advanced weaponry at a research facility straddling the Vermont-Quebec border, worried Israel the most. Bull had once been seen as a great friend of the Jewish state, designing weapons that were vital to the defense of Israel and, later, South Africa. Bull's long-range artillery gun, the G5, proved itself in Israel during the Yom Kippur War, and Pretoria wanted the "supergun" to extend its artillery capability—a major priority after the Angolan debacle of 1975. In 1977, the G5 and its shells were smuggled from the U.S.-Canadian border to South Africa via Antigua in an elaborate operation involving Armscor, the CIA, Israel, and Taiwan that eventually led to Justice Department and Senate investigations in the United States and a brief prison term for Bull.[59]

Then, in the late 1980s, Bull attempted to sell the supergun to Saddam Hussein, alarming Israel. The new version of the G5, known as Project Babylon, was a long-range artillery gun capable of launching projectiles into orbit. Bull was found murdered outside his home in Brussels, where he had moved after leaving prison, just before he completed work on Project Babylon in March 1990. Both Israel and Iran had reason to fear an Iraqi supergun, but neither the assailant nor any evidence linking the murder to the Mossad or Iranian intelligence has ever been found.[60]

As with Bull, Israel was paranoid about betrayal by its old friends in Pretoria and when an Armscor representative went to Syria in 1994 without official permission from the South African government, Israeli intelligence tracked his every move. Prime Minister Rabin was so upset that he lodged an official protest, claiming Pretoria had violated the

Israeli–South African agreement to notify each other of any transactions involving their respective enemies.[61]

The real significance of this diplomatic confrontation was not South Africa's betrayal of old agreements with Israel, however, but its foreshadowing of South African realignment. The new South Africa no longer saw a need for a wartime arsenal and Israel was forced to replace its most important customer with new clients such as China and India.[62] Likewise, the demise of NP rule in South Africa and the Labor Party's return to power in Israel in 1992 removed the ideological glue that had helped hold the relationship together. Lacking strategic incentives and the shared bond of minority survivalism, Mandela looked elsewhere for allies.

Rather than turning to Israel, the ANC government fostered friendly diplomatic ties with those who had supported its struggle, namely Gaddafi's Libya, Castro's Cuba, and the PLO. And although it faced no external threats after 1994, Pretoria turned to European arms manufacturers for a slew of new weapons systems, shunning its old Israeli suppliers.[63] By the mid-1990s, the economic interests that gave birth to the alliance and the ideological affinities that sustained two decades of lucrative and intimate cooperation had ebbed away.

The alliance was over, yet extricating themselves from such an intimate relationship remained a challenge for officials in Jerusalem and Pretoria. As power passed into Mandela's hands, he asked many senior Afrikaner officers in the SADF to stay on as a gesture of reconciliation. And Israel, hoping to preserve at least some residual commercial ties and prevent its technology from passing into its enemy hands, kept a close eye on the transition. Fears of proliferation were warranted but somewhat overblown. As Israeli officials soon discovered, the pragmatic realists managing Mandela's transition—future presidents Thabo Mbeki and Jacob Zuma—were open to behind-the-scenes contact with Israeli intelligence agencies; they viewed Israel as competent and experienced in matters of state building and were happy to seek advice. Even so, the two countries quickly drifted apart as new strategic priorities and diplomatic partnerships took precedence.

Within months of South Africa's first-ever democratic election in April 1994, the aircraft project closed down; by August the last South African military families living in Israel had moved home. Israel was no longer South Africa's preferred ally, nor could Tel Aviv depend on Pretoria to generate revenue for the defense industry and stimulate Israel's economy as it once had. As Israel found alternative export markets and the new South Africa realigned itself politically with many of Israel's foes, the alliance that had once been so vital to apartheid South Africa's defense and Israel's economy simply disappeared.

. . .

WHEN ALON LIEL LEFT South Africa after the democratic transition in 1994, he was replaced by an even more overtly left-wing ambassador: Elazar Granot. As leader of Mapam and an honorary president of the Socialist International, Granot had long been an outspoken member of the Knesset, demonstrating against apartheid every year and advocating peace with the Palestinians long before the Oslo process began. All of this gave Granot a level of credibility with the ANC that no former Israeli ambassador had ever enjoyed.

The ambassador for the state of Palestine—which Israel did not recognize—soon became Granot's best friend in Pretoria.[64] They debated each other on television and saw each other socially on a regular basis. Following her husband's lead in disregarding established diplomatic protocol, Granot's wife introduced herself to the Libyan ambassador by asking him "how can such a nice person like you come from a country led by Gaddafi?" This sent the Libyan into fits of laughter and marked the beginning of a close friendship. South Africa's Deputy Foreign Minister Aziz Pahad, a Muslim well known for his criticism of Israel, was a regular guest at the Granots' Passover Seders.[65]

Amid the euphoria of South Africa's democratic transition and thanks to Israel's improved post-Oslo image, Granot was able to make connections that Liel had never managed. His friendships with Arab ambassadors opened many diplomatic doors for Israel and nowhere else in the world did Israeli officials mingle so freely with Arab diplomats. The Foreign Ministry in Jerusalem bristled at Granot's unorthodox diplomatic style, however, and tried to bar him from attending conferences where Palestine was officially recognized as a state.

When Granot first arrived in Pretoria, the wall dividing the diplomatic and military sections of the Israeli embassy remained, but the balance of power was shifting. Defense Ministry director-general David Ivry came to South Africa in 1994 and the two men had a frank discussion. Granot told Ivry that whereas in the past the political relationship between the two countries had depended on strong security ties, any limited defense ties with the new South African government would now depend on a friendly diplomatic relationship. Ivry understood that the era of multibillion-dollar defense contracts was over and Israel's arms industry would have to look elsewhere for export markets. The notorious wall was removed from the embassy and the defense mission's staff began to attend the ambassador's weekly meetings.

Surprisingly, these days even Ivry is willing to talk honestly about Israel's close ties with South Africa. He bluntly admits, "We didn't obey the boycott," adding that Israel's assistance was vital for South Africa. "We were giving them a lot of capability. South Africa couldn't get it from anyplace," Ivry insists.[66] The data supports his argument. Based on the most conservative reading of trade figures, excluding joint ventures, the total military trade between the two countries amounted to more than $10 billion over the course of twenty years.[67]

With the military relationship finished, Israel's focus in Pretoria reverted to the more banal matter of relations with the country's Jewish community. Unfortunately for Granot, South African Jewish leaders, who resented his secular ways and his chumminess with Arab ambassadors, didn't like him much. After November 4, 1995, when a right-wing extremist assassinated Israeli prime minister Yitzhak Rabin in a crowded Tel Aviv square, Granot's relationship with them deteriorated further.

Mainstream Orthodox rabbis in Johannesburg had criticized Rabin's pursuit of the Oslo peace process in their sermons for weeks before the assassination, while right-wing extremists in Israel—including Rabin's killer—took the argument a step further, claiming it was their duty to stop the prime minister from handing over land to the Palestinians. Immediately after news of the shooting reached Granot, the embassy put out a condolence book. The first signature in the book was from the Palestinian ambassador, followed by those of seven Arab envoys. The rabbis whose sermons Granot regarded as tantamount to incitement were initially silent.[68]

Within seven months of the assassination, Granot would be gone. When Prime Minister Benjamin Netanyahu came to power for the first time in June 1996, Granot left South Africa in protest before the Likud government could appoint a replacement. Once again, Israel's relationship with the South African government seesawed as Netanyahu's new envoy, skeptical of the Oslo process and rapprochement with the Arab world, undid much of Granot's work building bridges with Arab diplomats that had so impressed the ANC. Though later Likud ambassadors such as the South African–raised Tova Herzl went to great lengths to mend the relationship between Jerusalem and Pretoria, it has never been the same. The history of Israeli–South African ties since Granot's departure has been one of civil but cool relations.[69]

These days, Granot has more time to reflect. He is over eighty and drives around his kibbutz in the Negev Desert on a golf cart his doctor prescribed due to a heart condition. Looking back, Granot says he fully understands the Israeli policy that he protested so vehemently during the 1970s and 1980s. It is a surprising admission coming from an icon of the Israeli far left. While he does not approve of the military cooperation, Granot claims that it was of vital importance to Israel. His knowledge is grounded in the four years he served on the Knesset's Defense Committee from 1984 to 1988, during which he had nearly unfettered access to sensitive military documents and participated in high-level discussions of Israel's defense doctrine.

Toward the end of our six-hour conversation, after a leisurely lunch at the kibbutz's communal cafeteria, Granot sits me down in his small living room. Reclining on his sofa and gazing out the window at the late afternoon sun, he confesses, "I haven't told you what I know, and I wouldn't . . . until there is peace in the Middle East." But for a moment he lets down his guard.

"I had to take into consideration that maybe Rabin and Peres were able to go to the Oslo agreements because they believed that Israel was strong enough to defend itself," says Granot, uncomfortably. "It wasn't the Americans and it wasn't the French and it wasn't the English. Most of the work that was done—I'm talking about the new kinds of weapons—was done in South Africa."[70]

EPILOGUE

WHEN FORMER PRESIDENT JIMMY CARTER dared to title his 2007 book *Palestine: Peace Not Apartheid*, American Jewish organizations were up in arms before the first copy appeared in bookstores. The anti-Zionist left has used the term "apartheid" for years to describe Israeli treatment of Palestinians in the hope that the boycotts and divestment pioneered by the anti-apartheid movement in the 1980s would be revived and applied to Israel. Carter's book—a memoir of presidential peacemaking that devoted only five pages to Israeli–South African comparisons—outraged so many Jews precisely because it lent credibility to an analogy that was until then seen by most as the propaganda of a radical fringe.

This book does not seek to draw a comparison between contemporary Israel and the old South Africa but, rather, to document the development and the demise of an extensive and lucrative military alliance. Yet Carter's book has brought what was once a marginal debate among campus activists into the international spotlight, emboldening many of Israel's critics to point to the history of Israeli–South African military cooperation as evidence of the two countries' shared racist colonial roots and claim that there is "a moral and political congruence" between their systems of government.[1]

To argue that all Israeli leaders after 1967 supported apartheid South Africa's rulers due to natural ideological affinities between Zionism and Afrikaner nationalism is misleading. After all, it was a small—albeit powerful and influential—minority of leading right-wing generals and politicians, such as Raful Eitan, Eliahu Lankin, and Ariel Sharon, who openly admired the apartheid regime, defended its political program, and identified with its leaders. Many left-wing Israelis vehemently opposed the alliance both in rhetoric and practice—with the notable exception of the ever sanctimonious Shimon Peres. Yet rather than honestly confronting the complexity of Israel's relationship with apartheid South Africa or countering the apartheid analogy with evidence of the genuine differences between the two systems, Israel's defenders have resorted to vitriol and recycled propaganda.

The knee-jerk reaction to Carter's book, which began prior to its publication, resembled Jewish organizations' reflexive denial of the Israeli–South African alliance during the 1970s and 1980s. Lacking a firm knowledge of South African history and uninterested in the legacy of the two-decade Israeli–South African alliance, those attacking Carter seemed to have little time for substantive historical debates about the strengths and weaknesses of the apartheid analogy.

The Anti-Defamation League issued talking points to fuming Israel supporters across the country, noting that, "by using the term 'apartheid,' Carter insinuates a comparison between the racist South African government and Israel. . . . The South African apartheid regime was a minority imposing inhumane restrictions on a majority based on racial qualifications." This came from an organization that had defended P. W. Botha's so-called reforms at the height of the 1986 state of emergency while denouncing Nelson Mandela's ANC as "totalitarian, anti-humane, anti-democratic, anti-Israel and anti-American."[2]

Harvard Law professor and ubiquitous defender of Israel Alan Dershowitz jumped on the anti-Carter bandwagon, noting that "his use of the loaded word 'apartheid,' suggesting an analogy to the hated policies of South Africa, is especially outrageous."[3] Dershowitz further condemned Carter for bias against Israelis and lamented the fact that the former president, who had done so much good through his foundation, the Carter Center, had now chosen to attack Israel. By January, more than a dozen Jewish advisers on the Carter Center's board resigned in protest of the book—all because of that one word: apartheid.

Ironically, just one year later the Israeli prime minister himself deployed the dreaded South African comparison. En route to Israel after the November 2007 Annapolis peace conference, Ehud Olmert observed that if Israel failed to negotiate a two-state solution, the nation would "face a South African–style struggle for equal voting rights, and as soon as that happens, the state of Israel is finished."[4]

Moreover, the reaction in the Israeli press, where some commentators were openly supportive of Carter, was far more nuanced and thoughtful. Former minister of education Shulamit Aloni contributed an article in *Yediot Ahronot* entitled "Yes, There Is Apartheid in Israel." She wrote: "The U.S. Jewish establishment's onslaught on former President Jimmy Carter is based on him daring to tell the truth which is known to all: through its army, the government of Israel practices a brutal form of apartheid in the territory it occupies." Aloni went on to denounce the Jewish-only access roads in the West Bank as worse than anything in the old South Africa. "Jimmy Carter does not need me to defend his reputation that has been sullied by Israelophile community officials," she insisted. "The trouble is that their love of Israel distorts their judgment and blinds them from seeing what's in front of them. Israel is an occupying power that for 40 years has been oppressing an indigenous people, which is entitled to a sovereign and independent existence while living in peace with us."[5]

This Israeli refusal to succumb to the knee-jerk reactions so common in the American press was plain to see in a column by Shmuel Rosner, then the Washington correspondent for *Haaretz*. While Rosner was no fan of Carter's book, he admitted: "Arguing about apartheid is pointless. There is enough material evidence to prove that apartheid exists in the occupied territories in one form or another."[6]

Missing this point entirely, Michael Kinsley confidently declared in *The Washington Post*, "It's not apartheid." He asserted that "no one has yet thought to accuse Israel of creating a phony country in finally acquiescing to the creation of a Palestinian state. Palestine is no Bantustan."[7] But that is precisely the charge leveled by many of Israel's critics. It is the core of Carter's critique and the basis for persistent Palestinian complaints about the 1993 Oslo Accords (which created noncontiguous statelets and autonomous Palestinian zones) and George W. Bush's 2002 road map (which has allowed a twenty-five-foot wall to encircle several Palestinian towns).[8]

After all, apartheid was not simply racism, segregation, and colonial land theft. It was an extraordinarily intricate system designed to control the movement and labor of blacks and strip them of South African citizenship by removing them to bantustans where they would be granted nominal but meaningless independence. The South African bantustans comprised swaths of scattered land allotted by the government and maintained by leaders held on a tight leash by Pretoria. The state routinely bulldozed black neighborhoods to make room for whites, and the result of these "forced removals" was the growth of destitute urban townships far from the city centers. The police, through a regime of pass laws and "influx control," restricted the movement of blacks wishing to enter "white areas." If they lacked the proper permit, blacks were sent back to the bantustans.

There are ominously similar developments in today's Israel. Not only are there "Israeli-only" access roads crisscrossing the West Bank, but in January 2007 it became illegal for Israelis driving there to transport Palestinians in their vehicles without a permit. Identification requirements that resemble modern-day pass laws prevent West Bank Palestinians from praying at the holy Dome of the Rock on Jerusalem's Temple Mount and armed Israeli police turn away Arabs lacking a Jerusalem ID card at the gates to the Old City. The twenty-mile journey from Ramallah to Jerusalem can take a whole day due to lines at checkpoints. Forced removals on the scale of those perpetrated in Cape Town's District Six or Johannesburg's Sophiatown during the apartheid years have not occurred, but dozens of Palestinian homes are bulldozed each year in accordance with Jerusalem municipal codes that have designated certain areas of the city for the construction of "Jewish neighborhoods." These demolitions in East Jerusalem, and hundreds of others throughout the West Bank, are routinely documented by Israeli organizations such as B'Tselem, the Israeli Committee Against Housing Demolitions, and Rabbis for Human Rights.

Other Palestinians are made homeless on a regular basis due to the collective punishment meted out to family members of terrorism suspects. The result is a literally circumscribed existence for Palestinians, whether cordoned off from their fields and neighbors by the "separation barrier," forbidden from entering Jerusalem by pass laws, or restricted in their movements by segregated roads that cut up their prospective state into a series of discontiguous enclaves. Seen on a map, they bear a striking resemblance to the old Bophuthatswana or KwaZulu bantustans in South Africa—a model that Ariel Sharon touted as an ideal solution to the dilemma of Palestinian statehood in a 2003 conversation with former Italian prime minister Massimo D'Alema.[9]

Nevertheless, despite these many parallels, the apartheid analogy is an

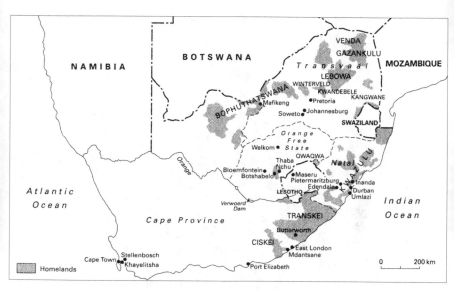

Homelands in Apartheid-era South Africa.
CREDIT: WILLIAM BEINART, *TWENTIETH-CENTURY SOUTH AFRICA*,
OXFORD UNIVERSITY PRESS, 2001

imperfect one. Unlike white South Africa and many other colonial regimes, Zionists never banned miscegenation or kept the people they had conquered as servants in their homes.[10] Nor did they rely on others to build the Jewish state they dreamed of.

Even before 1948, as Hannah Arendt marveled in *The Origins of Totalitarianism*, South Africa was a society premised on white laziness and the exploitation of cheap black labor.[11] Apartheid allowed a minority white population to live in ostentatious luxury with swimming pools, servants, and gardeners amid millions of blacks in abject poverty. Dispossession was not enough to maintain control; servitude was required as well.

The fight to maintain white supremacy was thus also a fight to preserve a lifestyle that depended on a high degree of inequality. Ultimately, apartheid crumbled because white South Africans were not willing to make their own beds or cook their own dinner: the oppressors were so dependent on the oppressed that the separate but unequal society they had created could not function without blacks. With such absolute dependency on black domestic and industrial labor, keeping the disen-

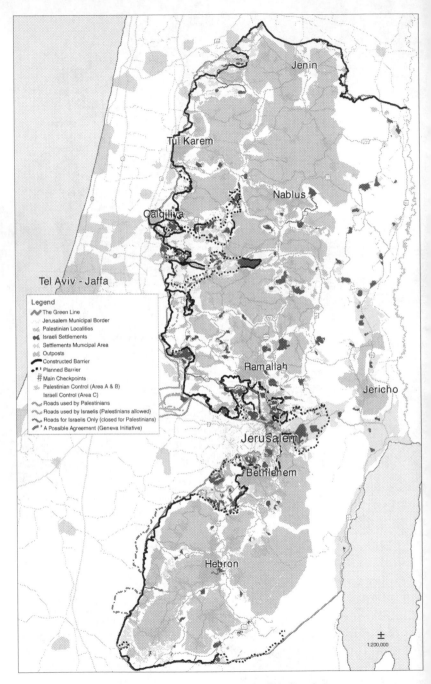

Legend

- The Green Line
- Jerusalem Municipal Border
- Palestinian Localities
- Israeli Settlements
- Settlements Municipal Area
- Outposts
- Constructed Barrier
- Planned Barrier
- Main Checkpoints
- Palestinian Control (Area A & B)
- Israeli Control (Area C)
- Roads used by Palestinians
- Roads used by Israelis (Palestinians allowed)
- Roads for Israelis Only (closed for Palestinians)
- A Possible Agreement (Geneva Initiative)

Jenin

Tul Karem

Nablus

Qalqiliya

Tel Aviv - Jaffa

Ramallah

Jericho

Jerusalem

Bethlehem

Hebron

1:200,000

*West Bank, including separation barrier, Israeli settlements,
and areas under Palestinian control.*

CREDIT: AMERICANS FOR PEACE NOW, JUNE 2009

franchised masses cooped up in faraway bantustans became economically and politically untenable. Either whites would have to survive without their black domestic servants and factory workers or live alongside them as equals.

By contrast, modern Israel was built by industrious Jewish settlers rather than through the systematic exploitation of Arab workers. Even if one dismisses the Zionist myth that Jews made the desert bloom, there is no doubt that Zionists of all stripes emphasized the use of Jewish labor. If anything, this ethos of self-reliance deprived Palestinians of jobs. As University of Massachusetts professor Leila Farsakh has argued: "South African apartheid wanted the land and the people, albeit with segregation; the Israeli leadership tried to take the land without the people"—an increasingly difficult proposition as Israel built sprawling settlements in the middle of major Palestinian population centers in the 1970s.[12] By the 1980s, a modernized Israel basking in its nouveau riche status did begin to import some Palestinian laborers to do its dirty work, but never relied on them to the extent that South Africa depended on black workers. And today, after two intifadas and with checkpoints everywhere, the people cleaning the gutters in Tel Aviv and shoveling shit on kibbutzim are much more likely to be Asian and African guest workers than Palestinians.

Finally, the aspirations and tactics of the South African and Palestinian liberation movements have always been fundamentally different. Whereas the PLO gradually came to accept the idea of a two-state solution by the early 1990s, the ANC never sought its own state devoid of white citizens and always called instead for a unitary, democratic, multiracial South Africa. Mandela and other ANC leaders explicitly rejected the apartheid regime's efforts to partition the country into ethnically defined bantustans in the 1970s and they never supported General Viljoen's proposal to create an Afrikaner homeland during the transition years. Moreover, although it waged an armed struggle and killed a number of civilians, the ANC's armed wing, unlike the PLO, focused on sabotaging military and government installations and explicitly avoided targeting civilians—a policy that earned it greater credibility in the international community.[13]

The apartheid analogy may be inexact today, but it won't be forever. The Palestinian population is expanding faster than the Jewish one and Israel's days of declaring itself both a Jewish state and a democratic one are numbered. As Prime Minister Olmert himself acknowledged in

November 2007, Israel will soon face a choice between an apartheid-style social order in which a Jewish minority rules over several million disenfranchised Palestinians in the West Bank or a two-state solution in which those Palestinians live independently outside Israeli control.

It was precisely this dilemma that prompted Olmert and former prime minister Ariel Sharon to break with Likud Party orthodoxy and promote disengagement from Gaza in 2005. Often referred to as "the demographic threat" by Israelis, this impending population parity—and the specter of an Arab majority—is seen as a mortal danger to the cornerstone of Zionism: a Jewish majority in a Jewish state.

With Palestinians nearing an absolute majority, calls for a binational state are becoming more popular. As former Israeli foreign minister Shlomo Ben-Ami has warned, this sort of binational state, with a Jewish minority, would create "a situation resembling the old South Africa, with two classes of citizens possessing vastly different political and civil rights. . . . [It] would not lend itself to a peaceful South African–style solution, because Israel, with its superior might, would never concede power to a Palestinian majority as white South Africans eventually did to the black majority in 1994."[14]

By ignoring Ben-Ami's warning and failing to heed the lessons of South Africa's demise, Israel risks remaking itself in the image of the old apartheid state. Pretoria's efforts in the mid-1970s to airbrush its image abroad ended in scandal; today, Israel's glitzy tourism promotion and marketing of its high-tech industry have in many ways been undermined by an overwhelmingly bad reputation generated by the use of devastating force against seemingly powerless civilians, most recently during the Gaza offensive of January 2009. And despite Olmert's disarmingly honest admission in 2007 that Israel risks facing a twenty-first-century anti-apartheid struggle, his successor, Benjamin Netanyahu, is clinging to a status quo that is demographically and geopolitically untenable.

· · ·

IN 1961, ANGERED BY Golda Meir's denunciations of his regime, the father of apartheid, South African prime minister Hendrik Verwoerd, declared to the U.N. General Assembly, "[Israelis] took Israel from the Arabs after they had lived there for a thousand years. In that I agree with them.

Israel, like South Africa, is an apartheid state."[15] While Verwoerd's comparison may not apply yet, given that a minority is not yet governing over a majority, it is hitting closer to home every day. Indeed, Israel is now facing the same propaganda onslaught and questioning of its legitimacy that South Africa faced two decades ago. Seeking to tar Israel with the same brush as the old South Africa, activists in the United States and Europe are adopting precisely the same demands as the anti-apartheid movement of the 1980s: divestment, academic boycotts, and economic sanctions.

In order to extricate itself from the current public relations nightmare, Israel desperately needs to reinvent its foreign policy. An abandonment of the Revisionist-inspired foreign policy that has defined Israel's international relations for much of the last three decades would dramatically improve its international standing. For years, Israel risked its good name to maintain a lucrative relationship with apartheid South Africa's leaders—with whom many Likud heavyweights identified politically and ideologically. Only when realpolitik of a higher order intervened, in the form of the 1987 American threat to cut military aid to Israel, did the Jewish state begin to retreat slowly from its military alliance with South Africa. Israel's gradual distancing was also the result of pressure from the left and from American Jewish organizations like AIPAC. Pro-Israel lobbyists in Washington knew apartheid's days were numbered and understood that maintaining a military alliance with Pretoria when a bipartisan majority in the U.S. Congress was pushing for sanctions would damage Israel's standing among some of its most enthusiastic supporters on Capitol Hill.

Likewise, today, Israel would do well to heed the criticisms of friends who disapprove of its excesses. Dismantling West Bank settlements, swapping land for those that remain, creating a viable Palestinian state, and negotiating with Lebanon and Syria would enhance Israel's image throughout the developing world and in the eyes of the old left that once supported it. For Israel, there is also much to glean from South Africa's leaders. Just as right-wing Israelis learned a great deal about apartheid from their National Party friends during the heyday of their covert military alliance, so, too, can the Israeli peace camp learn from the South Africans who guided their country through a negotiated transition.

The South African model cannot be imported wholesale, of course: it sought unification and inclusion while the two-state solution is premised on mutual exclusion and separation. But there are still lessons South Africans can teach Israelis and Palestinians when it comes to abandoning violence as a solution, appreciating the fears and political vulnerabilities of one's enemies, and crafting a mutually acceptable solution.

On the eve of the Gaza disengagement in August 2005, the Jewish population between the Jordan River and the Mediterranean dropped to below 50 percent for the first time since Israel became a state in 1948. As orange-clad settlers flooded Tel Aviv's streets to protest Ariel Sharon's decision to withdraw, *Haaretz* noted, "Following the upcoming disengagement, the proportion of Jews in territories under Israeli control will jump to 56.8 percent," giving Israel some breathing room.[16] But due to a much higher birthrate among Palestinians and the declining numbers of immigrants arriving in Israel, it will be scarcely more than a decade before the Arab population in Israel and the occupied territories exceeds the Jewish population.

Meanwhile, Israel's founding generation is disappearing. The old Holocaust survivors and their children, who saw Jewish survival in the shadow of genocide as Israel's raison d'être, are dying off. A new generation of cosmopolitan, tech-savvy Israelis is taking their place, with a vision of Israel as a modern, prosperous, industrialized state integrated into the global economy. They have known nothing but war, occupation, and international opprobrium and want desperately for Israel to be accepted as a "normal" country in the international community. The status quo of militarism, expanded settlements, and a refusal to offer Palestinians basic democratic rights is prolonging the conflict. If Israel does not move soon to dismantle West Bank settlements on a large scale and create a viable Palestinian state, it is only a matter of time before the demographic balance shifts and places Jews in a minority within the territories they control.

When that time comes, the charges leveled by Carter and others will begin to stick and, as Olmert feared, Jews will find themselves as a minority governing over a largely disenfranchised majority—a situation that will inevitably lead to a struggle for equal rights that garners worldwide sympathy. Worse still, Israel will be incontrovertibly branded with the apartheid label that it has fought tenaciously for decades to avoid.

Acknowledgments

First and foremost, I am grateful to the Rhodes Trust and the Harry S. Truman Foundation for providing me with the funding to study at Oxford and conduct the costly research necessary for my doctoral dissertation, which formed the basis for this book. I thank my thesis supervisor, William Beinart, for giving me insightful criticism along the way and prodding me when I was procrastinating in England rather than immersing myself in foreign archives. Others at St. Antony's College, such as Emanuele Ottolenghi and David Anderson, challenged my ideas and helped me formulate my research questions; Binyamin Neuberger provided me with a number of key contacts in Israel who were instrumental in kick-starting my research there; and Avi Shlaim and Shula Marks pushed me to go further after graduation.

This book would not have been possible without the many friends, colleagues, teachers, and relatives who housed me, fed me, and helped me find documents and meet sources. In Tel Aviv, my cousins Avron, Ofira, Shachaf, and Torr Polakow welcomed me into their home for several months during an extremely difficult time. They made my multiple visits to Israel comfortable and fun. In Jerusalem, I greatly appreciated the hospitality of my friends Dan Smokler, Beth Videlock, and Joseph Berman. I am forever indebted to Arnona Weiler for teaching me the basics of Hebrew more quickly and skillfully than any university or *ulpan* could have, while also serving as my mother in Israel and using her contacts to help me get interviews with reluctant sources. I would also like to thank Arik Bachar, Oren Barak, Ronen Bergman, Avner Cohen, Naomi Chazan, Tova Herzl, Tamar Golan, Yossi Melman, Benjamin Pogrund, Gideon Shimoni, Gary Sussman, and the late Harry Hurwitz for their help and advice in the course of my research, even if some of them may not agree with my conclusions.

My ability to penetrate the network of retired military and intelligence officials in South Africa was made infinitely easier by Peter Liberman and James Sanders, who not only provided me with countless sources but also gave me helpful suggestions and criticism along the way. I am also indebted to the late Tom Masland of *Newsweek* magazine, who connected me with a number of important sources before his tragic death.

Access to the South African archives would not have been as easy without the help of Norman Levy and Vuyo Zambodla, as well as the numerous archivists who aided me as I rummaged through box after box of documents. In particular, I would like to thank Neels Muller of the South African Department of Foreign Affairs and Naomi Musiker of the Johannesburg Jewish Board of Deputies. Although it came down to the wire, Steve de Agrela, Colonel Piet de Waal, and Sergeant Major Blaauw at the South African National Defence Archive sent me the documents I needed by sea, by air, and even by diplomatic pouch. Des Williams, Mike Hannon, and Judge Gerald Friedman assisted with background information regarding the top secret trial of Jan Blaauw; and Meshack Teffo, Neo Dichabe, Jan Mollendyk, and Carl Hafele at Armscor were also very helpful in providing quantitative data on South African arms purchases from Israel.

I am grateful to my uncle and aunt, Everard and Lilian Polakow, my cousin David Peimer, and Bev Tarpey for inviting me to stay with them in Johannesburg and making me feel at home in a stressful city, as well as Suzanne Goldberg and Richard van der Westhuizen, who rented me a nice apartment in Melville. My cousin Linda and her husband, Zed Ratzemore, always hosted me in London as I came and went from the United Kingdom, making all the traveling much easier.

Dozens of others helped me forge connections and find documents: I particularly appreciate the help of Glenn Frankel, Milton Shain, Claudia Braude, Stan Bergman, Max Coleman, Amy Davidson, Chris Saunders, Yotam Feldman, David Lelyveld, Henry Jeffries, Evelyn Groenink, Verne Harris, Rolf Sorensen, Sello Hatang, Piers Pigou, Kate Allan, Nicholas Badenhorst, Helmoed Roemer-Heitman, Amanda Mattingly, Jeffrey Richelson, Ronald Roberts, and Nikhil Bramdaw, as well as Erika Gibson and Waldimar Pelser of *Beeld*. Sy Hersh, Bob Campbell, Michael Oren, Marty Peretz, and the late Ze'ev Schiff also led me to key sources and provided useful background information. Herschel Nachlis was an excellent last-minute research assistant when I needed documents from the Library of Congress, and Asaf Sheratzky helped me with research on Knesset debates and Israeli newspaper coverage of South Africa. Doug Bloomfield and Tom Dine's recollections of AIPAC's role in the 1986–87 Israeli sanctions debate were extremely helpful in filling in the gaps in a story that has until now never been fully reported.

I am particularly indebted to Justice Edwin Cameron, Ambassador Malcolm Ferguson, Martin Welz, and Emil van der Merwe for the contacts they provided. While I cannot thank all of the people I interviewed, André Buys, Dieter Gerhardt, and General Jannie Geldenhuys were particularly helpful on numerous occasions after we first met. I thank Jeffrey Blankfort for allowing me to view his private papers in San Francisco and the many people whose feedback strengthened my work, especially Chester Crocker, Alex Gourevitch, Frank Pabian, Helen Purkitt, and Colin Shindler.

My parents, Valerie Polakow and Leonard Suransky, by virtue of their origins, are responsible for planting the seed for my interest in this topic and they have both been meticulous readers of countless drafts along the way. My late stepfather, Jerome Weiser, always took a keen interest in my research while I was at Oxford, despite his failing health. My brother, Shael, and his late wife, Brie, put up with my being a hermit in New York, as did my sisters, Sarafina and Sonya, and my stepmother, Carolina, during my visits to Holland. My friend David Plunkett gave me a roof and a desk with a view of the Rockies in Taos, New Mexico, when I needed to get out of the city and write.

I am grateful to my friends Alaka Holla, Malhar Nabar, Nadia Abu-Zahra, Giuliana Chamedes, Tracy Carson, Kim Chakanetsa, Ana Finel Honigman, Eusebius McKaiser, Nomi Stone, Kareem Saleh, Julie Taylor, Sam Charap, Negar Azimi, Aaron Jakes, Sean Jacobs, Sune Haugbølle, Michael Ellsberg, Alex Kellogg, Michael Horowitz, Rebecca Perry, Heidi Rosbe, Adam Lelyveld, Vipin Narang, Noa Schonmann, Jonathan Shainin, Meline Toumani, Graeme Wood, Meghann Curtis, Eric Tucker, and the late Michael Bhatia.

Kathryn Lewis, Alane Mason, Stephanie Hanson, Amelia Lester, Nydia Parries, Michael Shnayerson, and Bridget Wagner all offered excellent advice about the world of publishing. Ton Beekman, Sheena Chestnut, Mauro De Lorenzo, Sameen Gauhar, Michelle Goldberg, Swati Mylavarapu, Clayton Nall, Alix Rule, Reihan Salam, Madiha Tahir, and Andrew Woods gave me helpful feedback and suggestions. I am particularly indebted to Vanessa Mobley; this book would not be what it is without her expert editing and meticulous commentary.

I would like to thank Jim Hoge and Gideon Rose at *Foreign Affairs* and my colleagues Stéphanie Giry, Dan Kurtz-Phelan, Basharat Peer, Ann Tappert, Lorenz Skeeter, Ib Ohlsson, Joshua Yaffa, Rosemary Hartman, Katie Allawala, and especially David Feith and Stuart Reid, who read key chapters. At the Council on Foreign Relations, I also benefited from the insights of Peter Beinart, Michelle Gavin, Michael Levi, Frank Procida, and Gary Samore and the help of Michelle Baute and the CFR library staff. It is an ideal environment in which to write a book, discuss ideas, and get feedback from experts in various fields.

My editor at Pantheon, Andrew Miller, worked with me to turn an overly academic manuscript into what I hope is a more engaging narrative. He was patient while we went through draft after draft, his assistants Sara Sherbill and Andrew Carlson also provided valuable feedback, and Michiko Clark, Josefine Kals, Nicholas Latimer, and Erinn Hartman were excellent publicists (and photographers). Finally, I thank my agent, Larry Weissman, and his wife, Sascha Alper, who saw this book's potential from the very beginning, at a time when others thought it was too narrow and obscure.

Notes

ABBREVIATIONS OF ARCHIVAL SOURCES

AFD Armscor Financial Data, Pretoria

APC Author's Private Collection (from sources who wish to remain anonymous)

CIA Central Intelligence Agency Online Archive (www.cia.gov)

DFA South African Department of Foreign Affairs, Union Buildings, Pretoria

JBOD Jewish Board of Deputies, Johannesburg

JBP Jeffrey Blankfort Papers, San Francisco

NSA National Security Archive, Washington, D.C.

SAHA South African History Archive, University of the Witwatersrand, Johannesburg

SANA South African National Archives, Pretoria

SANDF South African National Defence Forces Military Intelligence Archive, Pretoria

USNA U.S. National Archives, Washington, D.C.

PROLOGUE

1. David Landau, "Vorster Denies Arms Deal; Tours Sharm Base with OC Navy," *Jerusalem Post*, April 11, 1976.

2. Patrick Furlong, *Between Crown and Swastika: The Impact of the Radical Right on the Afrikaner Nationalist Movement in the Fascist Era* (Johannesburg: Witwatersrand University Press, 1991), 246.

3. DFA, "Note on Israeli Attitude Towards South African Issues . . ." August 1963, 1/8/3, vol. 2.

4. Seymour Martin Lipset, " 'The Socialism of Fools': The Left, the Jews, and Israel," in *The New Left and the Jews*, ed. Mordecai S. Chertoff (New York: Pitman, 1971).

5. Derek J. Penslar, *Israel in History: The Jewish State in Comparative Perspective* (New York: Routledge, 2007), 91. As Derek Penslar, a meticulous and fair historian of Zionism, argues: "The Zionist movement as a whole was shot through with Orientalist conceptions of Arab degeneracy and primitiveness." In the early 1900s, the World Zionist Organization behaved as if it were a colonizing state. As Penslar writes, "It overtly emulated European practices by establishing a colonial bank . . . and supporting capitalist joint-stock companies that, like their counterparts in the service of European imperialism, were hoped to yield, eventually, a profit to their shareholders. The instrumental rationality, bureaucratic

procedure, and expectation of sustained profit that characterize modern colonialism (and distinguish it from mere conquest) were all present in the early Zionist project." See pp. 90–111 for an in-depth discussion of Zionism's triple heritage as a colonial, anticolonial, and postcolonial ideology.

6. Gershom Gorenberg, *The Accidental Empire: Israel and the Birth of the Settlements, 1967–1977* (New York: Times Books, 2006), 10, 39.

7. South Africa had good relations with other pariahs, such as Taiwan and Chile; leaders in Pretoria shared an ideological commitment to anticommunism with their counterparts in Taipei and Santiago. However, these ties never matched the extent of the Israeli–South African alliance.

8. See, for example, Benjamin Joseph, *Besieged Bedfellows: Israel and the Land of Apartheid* (Westport, CT: Greenwood, 1988); Naomi Chazan, "The Fallacies of Pragmatism: Israeli Foreign Policy Toward South Africa," *African Affairs* 82, no. 327 (1983): 169–99; James Adams, *The Unnatural Alliance* (London: Quartet, 1984); Benjamin Beit-Hallahmi, *The Israeli Connection: Who Israel Arms and Why* (New York: Pantheon, 1987).

9. Both of my parents were born in South Africa and most of my extended family still resides there.

10. While valuable, these interviews are in many cases burdened by the imperfect memories and self-serving accounts of individuals who are now over eighty years old. I have therefore sought wherever possible to corroborate oral accounts with documentary evidence.

11. I do not contend that ideology drove the alliance or that it trumped the material interests that gave birth to the relationship. Rather, I maintain that classical realist theory alone cannot account for the extensive, intimate relationship between Israel and South Africa. As Max Weber argued, "Not ideas, but material and ideal interests, directly govern men's conduct. Yet very frequently the 'world images' that have been created by 'ideas' have, like switchmen, determined the tracks along which action has been pushed by the dynamic of interest." See Max Weber, *From Max Weber: Essays in Sociology*, eds. Hans Heinrich Gerth and C. Wright Mills (New York: Oxford University Press, 1958), 280.

12. Heribert Adam and Hermann Giliomee, *Ethnic Power Mobilized: Can South Africa Change?* (New Haven: Yale University Press, 1979), 141–42.

1 THE REICH THAT WASN'T

1. Arthur Goldreich, interview by author, Herzliya, December 16, 2004; Gideon Shimoni, *Jews and Zionism: The South African Experience, 1910–1967* (Cape Town: Oxford University Press, 1980), 200. Four thousand were trained by the Jewish Ex-Serviceman's League and 646 actually went to Israel to fight in the IDF's Mahal section (Foreign Volunteers).

2. Ibid., 366.

3. Donald H. Akenson, *God's Peoples: Covenant and Land in South Africa, Israel and Ulster* (Ithaca: Cornell University Press, 1992), 73; André du Toit, "No Chosen People: The Myth of the Calvinist Origins of Afrikaner Nationalism and Racial Ideology," *American Historical Review* 88, no. 4 (1983): 927; Leonard M. Thompson, *The Political Mythology of Apartheid* (New Haven: Yale University Press, 1985), 71, 144.

4. Adam and Giliomee, 113.

5. Allister Sparks, *The Mind of South Africa: The Story of the Rise and Fall of Apartheid* (London: Mandarin, 1991), 176–77.

6. Ibid., 150–51.

7. T. Dunbar Moodie, *The Rise of Afrikanerdom: Power, Apartheid, and the Afrikaner Civil Religion* (Berkeley: University of California Press, 1975), 180.

8. Thompson, 185–86.

9. Furlong, 81.

10. Ibid., 80.

11. Johann Gottfried von Herder, "Reflections on the Philosophy of the History of Mankind," in Omar Dahbour and Micheline Ishay, eds., *The Nationalism Reader* (Atlantic Highlands, NJ: Humanities Books, 1995), 48–57.

12. Saul Dubow, *Scientific Racism in Modern South Africa* (Cambridge: Cambridge University Press, 1995), 261 and n43. For a discussion of the contrasts between Herder and Fichte, see Elie Kedourie, *Nationalism*, 4th ed. (Oxford: Blackwell, 1993), 46–48; Arash Abizadeh, "Was Fichte an Ethnic Nationalist?: On Cultural Nationalism and Its Double," *History of Political Thought* 26, no. 2 (2005): 334–59.

13. Shimoni, *Jews and Zionism*, 118, 366.

14. Dan O'Meara, *Volkskapitalisme: Class, Capital and Ideology in the Development of Afrikaner Nationalism, 1934–1948* (Cambridge: Cambridge University Press, 1983).

15. Charles Bloomberg, *Christian-Nationalism and the Rise of the Afrikaner Broederbond in South Africa, 1918–48* (Basingstoke: Macmillan, 1990), 138.

16. H. F. Verwoerd, "Die Joodse vraagstuk besien vanuit die Nasionale standpunt: 'n Moontlike oplossing," *Die Transvaler*, October 1, 1937.

17. Bloomberg, 148–49.

18. Furlong, 51.

19. Ibid., 53.

20. Ibid., 68.

21. Sparks, 153.

22. Ibid., 172–73. Hertzog's embattled moderate followers reorganized themselves as the Afrikaner Party.

23. Mark Suzman, *Ethnic Nationalism and State Power: The Rise of Irish Nationalism, Afrikaner Nationalism and Zionism* (Basingstoke: Macmillan, 1999), 11.

24. Furlong, 139.

25. Ibid., 141–42.

26. Ibid., 145–47.

27. Ibid., 206–7.

28. Dan O'Meara, *Forty Lost Years: The Apartheid State and the Politics of the National Party, 1948–1994* (Athens: Ohio University Press, 1996), 22–23, 34–35. Malan did not win a majority, but his Nationalist coalition won more seats due to the disproportionate electoral weight of the rural vote.

29. Benjamin Pogrund, interview by author, Jerusalem, December 12, 2004. Louw served in various portfolios in the 1950s and became foreign minister in the early 1960s. By this time, however, he had tempered his anti-Semitism along with the rest of his party.

30. Harry Schwarz, interview by author, Johannesburg, March 18, 2005.

31. Gideon Shimoni, *Community and Conscience: The Jews in Apartheid South Africa* (Hanover, NH: University Press of New England, 2003), 24–25.

32. Shimoni, *Jews and Zionism*, 211–12.

33. Steven Friedman, "Judaism, Apartheid and the Sojourner Myth," *Jewish Affairs* (Autumn 1997): 61. Jews had, of course, enjoyed racial privilege in preapartheid South Africa. Still, the fear that they would be targeted by Nazi-sympathizing Afrikaners was very real in 1948.

34. Shimoni, *Jews and Zionism*, 213–14; Shimoni, *Community and Conscience*, 26.

35. Benjamin Pogrund, interview by author.

36. As David Kimche, soon to become a high-ranking Mossad official, wrote in his Ph.D. dissertation: "Africa and Asia were the obvious targets of Arab political activity against Israel." And, as the academic turned spy recognized all too well, "this necessitated some form of counter-action." David Kimche, *Israel and Africa* (accessed December 10, 2004); at http://www.african-geopolitics.org/show.aspx ?ArticleId=3097.

2   A LIGHT UNTO THE NATIONS

1. Golda Meir, *My Life* (New York: Putnam, 1975), 321.

2. Avi Shlaim, *The Iron Wall: Israel and the Arab World* (London: Penguin, 2001), 120–22. According to Shlaim, there was a fleeting chance for peace in 1954 that Israel's second prime minister, Moshe Sharrett, failed to seize.

3. See ibid., 110–29; Michael Oren, *Six Days of War: June 1967 and the Making of the Modern Middle East* (London: Penguin, 2003), 9. The Egyptian death toll is disputed. Shlaim says there were thirty-seven, Oren fifty-one.

4. See David Kimche, *The Afro-Asian Movement: Ideology and Foreign Policy of the Third World* (Jerusalem: Israel Universities Press, 1973).

5. Shlaim, 113; Oren, 9.

6. Michael M. Laskier, "Israel and Algeria Amid French Colonialism and the Arab-Israeli Conflict, 1954–1978," *Israel Studies* 6, no. 2 (2001): 1–32; Shimon Peres, *Battling for Peace: Memoirs* (London: Weidenfeld & Nicolson, 1995), 117.

7. Eliahu Lankin, *To Win the Promised Land* (Walnut Creek, CA: Benmir, 1992), 222–56.

8. Michael I. Karpin, *The Bomb in the Basement: How Israel Went Nuclear and What That Means for the World* (New York: Simon & Schuster, 2006), 12–13.

9. The village, Wiszniewo, is in present-day Belarus.

10. Peres, 27.

11. Mapai is a Hebrew acronym for the Israel Workers Party.

12. Michael T. Brecher, *The Foreign Policy System of Israel: Setting, Images, Process* (Oxford: Oxford University Press, 1972), 405.

13. Karpin, 59–60. Prior to October 1958, the French head of government was known as *president du Conseil des ministres*, commonly referred to as the "prime minister" in English. The French did not begin using the term *premier ministre* until the advent of the Fifth Republic. I use the term "prime minister" to refer to French heads of government before 1958.

14. Ibid., 61–69.

15. Ibid., 71.

16. David Owen, *In Sickness and in Power: Illnesses in Heads of Government During the Last 100 Years* (Westport, CT: Praeger, 2008), 118–31.

17. Karpin, 86. While a 10 megawatt reactor can be suitable for civilian use, Israel's purpose in obtaining a reactor was always to acquire a military nuclear capability.

18. Ibid., 87.

19. Ibid., 89.

20. Meir, 321–23.

21. Ibid., 326–27.

22. Ibid., 318.

23. Shlaim, 192–99.

24. Raful Eitan, *A Soldier's Story* (New York: S.P.I., 1992), 139–49, 183–203.

25. Joel Peters, *Israel and Africa: The Problematic Friendship* (London: British Academic Press, 1992), 15–16.

26. A sabra is a Jew born in Israel.

27. Kimche, "Israel and Africa," 4. These training programs also paid dividends in 1976 when old contacts in Kenyan intelligence proved instrumental in facilitating refueling during Israel's famed raid on the Entebbe Airport to liberate hostages from a hijacked plane.

28. Olusola Ojo, *Africa and Israel: Relations in Perspective* (Boulder: Westview, 1988), 14.

29. Philip H. Frankel, *An Ordinary Atrocity: Sharpeville and Its Massacre* (Johannesburg: Witwatersrand University Press, 2001), 116–17. Frankel argues that the actual death toll was likely higher than the official figure of sixty-nine.

30. "The Sharpeville Massacre," *Time*, April 4, 1960.

31. Aleck Goldberg, interview by author, Johannesburg, March 7, 2005.

32. Shimoni, *Community and Conscience*, 7. Benjamin Pogrund recalls that his assistant editor Lewis Sowden (also Jewish) was in attendance at the U.N. that day and yelled "liar" from the public gallery during Louw's speech; Benjamin Pogrund, interview by author.

33. Apart from the Netherlands, which voted in favor of censure as well.

34. Shimoni, *Community and Conscience*, 47.

35. Brecher, 145, 234–35.

36. Ibid., 234.

37. On November 2, 1961, Prime Minister Verwoerd's top aide wrote a letter filled with veiled threats to a prominent Jewish Cape Town city councillor. "The attitude taken up by Israel in the United Nations Assembly is a tragedy for Jewry in South Africa," the aide wrote. More threateningly, he added, "The fact that during the last Election so many Jews had favoured the Progressive Party and so few the National Party, did not pass unnoticed." The letter caused a scandal when it leaked to the press. The Afrikaans press echoed the letter's tone and criticized Israel for betraying South Africa's friendship, while the English press attacked the letter as a blatant tactic to hold Jews hostage for Israeli foreign policy decisions over which they exerted no control. Eventually, Verwoerd defused the situation by declaring that he did not want to see anti-Semitism return to the South African political landscape. See JBOD "Letter from Prime Minister Verwoerd's Private Secretary J. Fred Barnard to Mr. A.S.A. East," November 2, 1961, A.S.A. East Biography Box; Shimoni, *Community and Conscience*, 50; JBOD, "Gustav Saron to Mr. Wiener," March 29, 1962, Public Relations Files, 1960–1970.

38. Shimoni, *Community and Conscience*, 51; Shimoni, *Jews and Zionism*, 316–18.

39. Yitzhak D. Unna, "As I Remember It," unpublished manuscript, 101. Unna describes the embassy purchase as "an offset arrangement with the S.A. Zionist

Federation, so that the I.U.A. funds, which had accumulated in blocked accounts in South Africa, were used to purchase the residence in Pretoria."

40. Meir, 336.

41. DFA, "Note on Israeli Attitude Towards South African Issues . . . ," August 1963, 1/8/3, vol. 2.

42. Brecher, 145.

43. Glenn Frankel, *Rivonia's Children: Three Families and the Cost of Conscience in White South Africa* (New York: Continuum, 1999), 80.

44. Ibid., 85.

45. Ibid., 84–85.

46. Nelson Mandela, *Long Walk to Freedom* (Boston: Little, Brown, 1994), 245; Chris McGreal, "Worlds Apart," *Guardian*, February 6, 2006.

47. Glenn Frankel, *Rivonia's Children*, 82.

48. Mandela, 243; McGreal, "Worlds Apart."

49. Glenn Frankel, *Rivonia's Children*, 188–89.

50. The Rivonia defendants were represented by a team that included Jewish lawyers such as Harry Schwarz and Arthur Chaskalson. According to Gideon Shimoni, Yutar was motivated "by a passionate desire to offset the negative image of Jewish disloyalty to South Africa" when he prosecuted Mandela and his Jewish comrades. See Shimoni, *Community and Conscience*, 66, 266–67; Frankel, 8–9, 335–37; Hirsh Goodman, *Let Me Create a Paradise, God Said to Himself* (New York: PublicAffairs, 2005), 44.

51. His name was George Clay and he was South African by birth.

52. See the riveting and more detailed account of the escape in Frankel, 129–44. Wolpe settled in London, and Goldreich moved to Israel in 1964.

53. Arthur Goldreich, interview by author.

54. JBOD, "Memo from Mr. Saron to Honorary Officers . . . ," September 3, 1963, Public Relations Files, 1960–1970; JBOD, "Memo from the General Secretary Johannesburg to Provincial Secretaries," September 4, 1963, Public Relations Files, 1960–1970.

55. Mordechai Kreinin, *Israel and Africa: A Study in Technical Cooperation* (New York: Praeger, 1964), 177.

56. Robert S. Jaster, *South Africa's Narrowing Security Options* (London: International Institute for Strategic Studies, 1980), 14.

57. DFA, "French Politico-Economic Investment in South Africa," April 30, 1964, 1/8/3, vol. 2.

58. Ibid., 3.

59. DFA, "Pinay-Rugina Project," March 16, 1964, 1/8/3, vol. 2.

60. DFA, "French Politico-Economic Investment in South Africa," 7. Schmittlein was seen as such an angel in Pretoria that he managed to convince the government to make an exception to Verwoerd's ban on the transfer of funds from South African Jews to Israel, a law that had remained in effect after Ben-Gurion's and Meir's anti–South African polemics at the U.N. In 1963, he approached the South African government on behalf of the Revisionist Zionist movement about lifting the ban on transfers in order to send R240,000 to Israel in order build a memorial to Ze'ev Jabotinsky, the father of Revisionist Zionism. Given the popular and active Revisionist movement, South Africa was a major funding source for this expensive project. But Schmittlein was repeatedly turned down. Finally,

in 1966, the Foreign Affairs Ministry recommended reversing course and allowing the funds for the Jabotinsky memorial to be transferred to Israel so as to avoid upsetting the French. "In these days of continuing and ever mounting pressure against South Africa internationally," the secretary wrote, South Africa should "make every effort to preserve and if possible strengthen these links of friendship with the one Great Power which might yet be willing to exercise a Security Council veto in our favor when others would leave us in the lurch." See DFA, "South African Contribution to the Jabotinsky Memorial," February 25, 1966, 1/8/3, vol. 2.

61. DFA, "Moontlike Verbreking van Diplomatieke Betrekkinge Met Israel," October 12, 1963, 1/8/3, vol. 2.
62. DFA, "Verhoudings Tussen Die Republiek en Israel," 1963, 1/8/3, vol. 2.
63. Ibid.

3   THE ATOMIC BOND

1. Thomas Borstelmann, *Apartheid's Reluctant Uncle: The United States and Southern Africa in the Early Cold War* (Oxford: Oxford University Press, 1993), 43–45.
2. Ibid., 46.
3. Ibid., 91.
4. Ibid., 96.
5. Ibid., 164.
6. Frank V. Pabian, "South Africa's Nuclear Weapon Program: Lessons for U.S. Nonproliferation Policy," *Nonproliferation Review* 3, no. 1 (1995): 2.
7. Karpin, 86.
8. Ibid., 52, 81.
9. For background on the fall of the Bourgès-Maunoury government, see Matthew Connelly, *A Diplomatic Revolution: Algeria's Fight for Independence and the Origins of the Post–Cold War Era* (New York: Oxford University Press, 2002), 147–48.
10. Karpin, 90.
11. Ibid., 91. The true capacity could have been two to three times greater; see Avner Cohen, *Israel and the Bomb* (New York: Columbia University Press, 1998), 59.
12. SANA, "Verkoop van Uraan aan Israel," July 7, 1960, BLO 353, PS17/109/12, vol. 2.
13. Even after the NPT entered into force, Israel and South Africa did not sign it and would therefore not have been subject to IAEA safeguards for a transaction of this sort at a later date.
14. SANA, "Sale of Uranium to Israel," July 19, 1960, BLO 353, PS17/109/12, vol. 2.
15. Seymour Hersh, *The Samson Option: Israel's Nuclear Arsenal and American Foreign Policy* (New York: Random House, 1991), 156.
16. SANA, "Ooreenkoms tussen die Regerings van Israel en Suid-Afrika (Uraan)," February 1, 1965, URU vol. 4835, Ref. 134, 37–38.
17. SANA, "Draft Agreement Between the Government of the Republic of South Africa and the Government of Israel on the Application of Safeguards to Source Material . . . ," February 1, 1965, URU vol. 4835, Ref. 134, 39–44.
18. Ibid., 42.
19. J. P. Hugo, interview by author, Pretoria, March 1, 2006.

20. For details, see Robert S. Norris et al., "Israeli Nuclear Forces 2002," *Bulletin of the Atomic Scientists* 58, no. 5 (2002): 73–75.

21. Cohen, *Israel and the Bomb*, 175–94; Karpin, 343. The progenitor of this concept was the nuclear physicist Shalhevet Freier. He urged discipline and modesty upon the country's nuclear inner circle in order to ensure that Israel's ambiguous capability deterred enemies, gave Israel confidence, and made it seem responsible to Western governments.

22. Cohen, *Israel and the Bomb*, 231.

23. Karpin, 125.

24. Peres, 132. Peres makes only an oblique reference here, calling nuclear power "a necessary option for a country bereft of natural resources and beset by danger."

25. Cohen, *Israel and the Bomb*, 149–51, 284–85; Yair Evron, *Israel's Nuclear Dilemma* (Ithaca: Cornell University Press, 1994), 5. See also Eitan, 381.

26. Oren, 70–71.

27. Ibid., 170–71.

28. Ibid., 176.

29. Ojo, 52.

30. Lipset, 128.

31. Ibid., 119.

32. Ojo, 47. South Africa's intelligence service, BOSS, believed Africa's souring relationship with Israel was a direct result of the closure and argued that later OAU resolutions were intended to pressure Israel to make peace with Egypt and hence reopen the canal.

33. Ibid., 118.

34. Ibid., 117–18.

35. Brecher, 244.

36. Cohen, *Israel and the Bomb*, 284–85. See also Shai Feldman, *Israeli Nuclear Deterrence: A Strategy for the 1980s* (New York: Columbia University Press, 1982).

37. Cohen, *Israel and the Bomb*, 175–94. Meir did tell Nixon the truth when they met in September 1969.

38. Ibid., 103–8.

39. Karpin, 187.

40. Ibid., 228–29.

41. Ibid., 243–46.

42. Ibid., 246–57. Israel could not pretend Dimona was simply for power or research, but it hoped to convince the United States that it was operating the reactor for peaceful purposes while retaining the option of eventually producing weapons-grade materials.

43. Cohen, *Israel and the Bomb*, 180–87.

44. The failure of American intelligence agencies to discern what was really happening at Dimona led to the unlikely scapegoating of Shapiro, who owned NUMEC, a nuclear fuel facility near Pittsburgh. A devout Jew and ardent Zionist, Shapiro frequently visited Israel and did business there and therefore seemed an obvious suspect. When two hundred pounds of his plant's highly enriched uranium went unaccounted for in the late 1960s, he became the target of FBI investigations. In fact, as the Nuclear Regulatory Commission later found, Shapiro had done no wrong: the missing enriched uranium was later recovered from the ducts, tubes, vents, and concrete floors of the NUMEC plant. See

Hersh, 253–57. Even Henry Kissinger believed the FBI's theory and cited it in a 1969 memo to President Nixon. See David Stout, "Nixon Papers Recall Concerns on Israel's Weapons," *New York Times*, October 28, 2007.

45. Cohen, "Crossing the Threshold: The Untold Nuclear Dimension of the 1967 Arab-Israeli War and Its Contemporary Lessons," *Arms Control Today* 37, no. 5 (2007): 12–16.

46. Isabella Ginor and Gideon Remez, *Foxbats over Dimona: The Soviets' Nuclear Gamble in the Six-Day War* (New Haven: Yale University Press, 2007), 121–37.

47. Karpin, 287–90.

48. Ibid., 289–93.

49. Peres, 133. Here Peres discusses Israel's need to acquire uranium from foreign sources.

50. Pierre Péan, *Les Deux Bombes: Ou Comment La Guerre du Golfe A Commencé le 18 Novembre 1975* (Paris: Fayard, 1991); "Uranium: The Israeli Connection," *Time*, May 30, 1977.

51. Cohen, "Nuclear Arms in Crisis Under Secrecy: Israel and the Lessons of the 1967 and 1973 Wars," in Peter R. Lavoy, Scott D. Sagan, and James J. Wirtz, eds., *Planning the Unthinkable: How New Powers Will Use Nuclear, Biological, and Chemical Weapons* (Ithaca: Cornell University Press, 2000), 104–24. For a discussion of nuclear strategy and the Yom Kippur War, see Scott D. Sagan, "Lessons of the Yom Kippur Alert," *Foreign Policy* 36 (Autumn 1979): 160–77; Barry Blechman and Douglas Hart, "The Political Utility of Nuclear Weapons: The 1973 Middle East Crisis," *International Security* 7, no. 1 (Summer 1982): 132–56; Michael I. Handel, "The Yom Kippur War and the Inevitability of Surprise," *International Studies Quarterly* 21, no. 3 (September 1977): 461–502; T. V. Paul, "Nuclear Taboo and War Initiation in Regional Conflicts," *Journal of Conflict Resolution* 39, no. 4 (December 1995): 696–717.

52. André Buys as quoted in Peter Liberman, "The Rise and Fall of the South African Bomb," *International Security* 26, no. 2 (2001): 62. Israelis were eager to influence South Africans with their strategic ideas.

53. APC, "I.A.E.A.: The Agency's Verification Activities in South Africa: Report by the Director General," September 8, 1993, GOV/2684, 93–03174, 5.

54. Liberman, "The Rise and Fall of the South African Bomb," 50n12; "Out of (South) Africa: Pretoria's Nuclear Weapons Experience," United States Air Force Institute for National Security Studies Occasional Paper #27, August 1999; Helen E. Purkitt and Stephen F. Burgess, *South Africa's Weapons of Mass Destruction* (Bloomington: Indiana University Press, 2005), 41n63.

55. Liberman, "The Rise and Fall of the South African Bomb," 50–51.

4 THE RISE OF REALPOLITIK

1. Paul Berman, *A Tale of Two Utopias: The Political Journey of the Generation of 1968* (New York: W. W. Norton, 1996), 30–32, 123.

2. DFA, "M. Denan to Brigadier Clifton," March 4, 1968, 1/8/3, vol. 2; DFA, "Aanbod van Samewerking: Israeli Militere Nywerhede," March 7, 1968, 1/8/3, vol. 2.

3. DFA, "The Israel–South Africa League, Interpellation No. 5776," November 27, 1968, 1/8/3, vol. 2a.

4. Abba Eban, *Abba Eban: An Autobiography* (New York: Random House, 1977); Eric Silver, "Abba Eban: Brilliant and Eloquent Israeli Statesman," *The Independent*, November 20, 2002; John Calder, "Abba Eban: Israeli Foreign Minister Who Put His Country on the Map but Was Later Confined to the Wilderness," *The Guardian*, November 18, 2002.

5. DFA, "The Israel–South Africa League, Interpellation No. 5776," November 27, 1968, 1/8/3, vol. 2a.

6. Unna, 1.

7. Ibid., 10.

8. Ibid., 27.

9. Ibid., 35.

10. Ibid., 48–49.

11. Ibid., 80–82.

12. Ibid., 103.

13. See Warren Bass, *Support Any Friend: Kennedy's Middle East and the Making of the U.S.-Israel Alliance* (New York: Oxford University Press, 2003).

14. Ian Black and Benny Morris, *Israel's Secret Wars: A History of Israel's Intelligence Services* (New York: Grove, 1991), 234–35.

15. Ibid.

16. Abraham Rabinovich, *The Boats of Cherbourg* (New York: Seaver, 1988), 118.

17. Ibid., 126–35.

18. Black and Morris, 235.

19. DFA, "Supply of Mirages to Israel," January 16, 1970, 1/8/5, vol. 2.

20. DFA, "Minutes of the Meeting Between Dr. Hilgard Muller and Mr. Abba Eban," June 30, 1970, 1/8/3, vol. 3.

21. DFA, "Israeli Contribution to the Organisation of African Unity," June 4, 1971, 1/8/3, vol. 2a.

22. DFA, "Letter to Mnr. Viljoen," June 3, 1971, 1/8/3, vol. 2a. This and all subsequent rand-dollar exchange rates were calculated using data from the South African Reserve Bank available at: http://www.resbank.co.za/economics/histdownload/histdownload.htm.

23. "Help to Murderers" (translated), *Die Transvaler*, June 7, 1971.

24. "An Odious Decision" (translated), *Die Vaderland*, June 4, 1971.

25. The South African Jewish community, too, was up in arms. An outraged Jewish lawyer wrote an open letter to Prime Minister Vorster, beseeching him: "Please do me and those other like-minded Jewish South Africans a favour. Ask that two-faced, double-dealing, lying Israeli Consul, Mr. Unna, to get out of our country. . . . My grandfather would turn in his grave to hear of Israel's treachery." DFA, "Ronald Meltz to Prime Minister Vorster," June 7, 1971, 1/8/3, vol. 3; Paul Hofmann, "Israel's Offer to Aid Blacks Irks South Africa," *New York Times*, July 5, 1971.

26. JBOD, "Some of the Phone Calls Received," June 4, 1971, Public Relations Files, 1970–1980.

27. Howard M. Sachar, *A History of Israel* (New York: Alfred A. Knopf, 1976), 97–99.

28. Margaret MacMillan, *Paris 1919: Six Months That Changed the World* (New York: Random House, 2001), 44.

29. SANA, "Chaim Weizmann to Jan Smuts," July 17, 1921, Smuts Correspondence Files. Jabotinsky never rejected the diplomatic path, but his more extreme followers had little faith in Britain.

30. Jabotinsky did not succeed Weizmann in the end, but his attacks helped to precipitate Weizmann's downfall. Nahum Sokolov, another Labor Zionist, became the WZO's leader.

31. Joseph B. Schechtman, *Rebel and Statesman: The Vladimir Jabotinsky Story* (New York: Thomas Yoseloff, 1956), 25–48; Michael Stanislawski, *Zionism and the Fin de Siècle: Cosmopolitanism and Nationalism from Nordau to Jabotinsky* (Berkeley: University of California Press, 2001).

32. Shlomo Avineri, *The Making of Modern Zionism: The Intellectual Origins of the Jewish State* (London: Weidenfeld & Nicolson, 1981), 164. Jabotinsky did not move as far to the right as some of his Marxist mentors, who became fascists, and he was critical of Mussolini during the 1920s.

33. Yaacov Shavit, *Jabotinsky and the Revisionist Movement, 1925–1948* (London: Frank Cass, 1988), 111–12. See also Mordechai Sarig, ed., *The Political and Social Philosophy of Ze'ev Jabotinsky: Selected Writings* (London: Vallentine Mitchell, 1999).

34. Shavit, 114.

35. Avineri, 166–67. As Gideon Shimoni reminds us, one must be careful to read these lines within their historical context and the prevalent understanding of the word "race" at the time, which did not necessarily denote skin color. Gideon Shimoni, *The Zionist Ideology* (Hanover, NH: University Press of New England, 1995), 240, 389n9.

36. Shavit, 245–46.

37. Colin Shindler, *Israel, Likud and the Zionist Dream: Power, Politics and Ideology from Begin to Netanyahu* (London: I. B. Tauris, 1995), 13.

38. Shlaim, 13–14. According to Jabotinsky, a political agreement would only be possible later, after Arabs were convinced they could not breach the "iron wall."

39. Shavit, 254.

40. Shindler, 12–13.

41. Shimoni, *Jews and Zionism*, 245.

42. Harry Hurwitz, "Time for a Closer S.A.-Israel Accord," *Jewish Herald*, September 14, 1971.

43. Harry Hurwitz, interview by author (#1), Jerusalem, December 20, 2004. Hurwitz's memory for dates and details was imperfect. He wrote many articles of this sort but this particular one was found in the South African Foreign Ministry archive and explicitly calls for upgrading relations and therefore is most likely the article he is referring to, though he said 1974, not 1971. He died in October 2008.

44. Gorenberg, *The Accidental Empire*, 161–62.

45. Ibid., 272–74.

46. Brecher, 340.

47. Ibid., 340–41.

48. Ibid., 220, 325.

49. Ibid., 311, for a discussion of Meir's realism. See also Shlaim, 283–89. Peres also acknowledges the tension that existed between him and Meir and her disapproval of his missions to France. See Peres, 113–16.

50. C. L. Sulzberger, "Strange Nonalliance," *New York Times*, April 30, 1971.

51. Ibid.

52. DFA, "S.A.-Israeli Relations (S.A.B.C. Radio Transcript)," March 16, 1972, 1/8/3, vol. 3.

53. "The Israeli Connection," *The Economist*, November 5, 1977, 90.

54. "Israel Seeks Diamond Trade Lead," *Christian Science Monitor*, January 6, 1971.
55. Stefan Kanfer, *The Last Empire: De Beers, Diamonds, and the World* (New York: Farrar, Straus & Giroux, 1993), 331–32.
56. Ibid., 316. In the early 1970s, Israel was challenging Belgium for dominance in the diamond cutting business and began to enter the market for larger stones. De Beers was not pleased with the decline of Antwerp and cut supplies to Israel by 20 percent. But the Israelis reacted by going it alone. With generous low-interest bank loans, Israelis accumulated diamond reserves on the open market, especially from Liberia, and threatened to undermine De Beers's control of the world diamond trade. At a time of high inflation and economic crisis in Israel, the growing diamond reserves of the banks provided a measure of "hard currency" stability. The Israelis now had the ability to flood the world market with their reserves at any moment and drive prices down. De Beers declared war. The De Beers–controlled international diamond cartel retaliated by barring many dealers who had done business with Israel from future allocations—or "sights"—and by imposing an artificial price increase of 40 percent and a simultaneous threat to withdraw it at any moment. Banks in Israel panicked as the value of their reserves suddenly became volatile and unpredictable. The banks ceased their generous lending to diamond traders and a massive sell-off began, driving many Israeli dealers into bankruptcy by 1980. It took the industry five years to recover to pre-1980 levels. Despite Israeli challenges to the cartel, a large proportion of uncut stones arriving in Israel in the 1980s still came from the De Beers–controlled Central Selling Organization in London. But because the stones distributed in London came from sources all over the world, it is impossible to quantify what percentage originated in South Africa or to calculate the precise value of Israel's imports from South Africa. See Kanfer, 333–34; Edward Jay Epstein, *The Death of the Diamond* (London: Sphere, 1983), 158–62; "The Israel Diamond Industry: Facts and Figures 1988," Table 1, Israel Diamond Institute, Tel Aviv; "The Israel Diamond Industry: Facts and Figures 1994," Table 2, Israel Diamond Institute, Tel Aviv; Chaim Even-Zohar, interview by author, Washington, D.C., October 18, 2007.
57. DFA, "South Africa on Trial (Transcript of Israel Radio Broadcast)," April 1972, 1/8/3, vol. 3.
58. DFA, "First Reactions to the Establishment of a South African Consulate-General in Israel," May 2, 1972, 1/8/3, vol. 3.
59. DFA, "The Committee Against Apartheid," August 23, 1972, 1/8/3, vol. 3.
60. DFA, "Opening of Israeli Diplomatic Mission to Botswana, Swaziland and Lesotho," September 13, 1972, 1/8/6, vol. 1.
61. DFA, "Israel's Vote in the United Nations," September 25, 1972, 1/8/3, vol. 3.
62. DFA, "Israeli Voting in the United Nations," September 28, 1972, 1/8/3, vol. 3.
63. DFA, Shaul Ben-Haim, "Policy in Africa Readjusted" (translated), *Maariv*, November 19, 1972.
64. DFA, "The South African Lesson" (translated), *Yediot Ahronot*, January 15, 1973.
65. DFA, "Israeli Policy in Africa," January 17, 1973, 1/8/5, vol. 2.
66. For example, black African leaders killed a Libyan motion to boycott the OAU summit in Ethiopia.
67. Peters, 34–35.
68. DFA, "Crisis in Israel's Africa Policy," June 26, 1973, 1/8/6, vol. 2.

69. DFA, "Israel: Tendense en/of gebeure wat 'n nadelige invloed op die Republiek mag he," 1972, 1/8/3, vol. 3.

70. DFA, "Israel's Africa Policy," September 26, 1973, 1/8/6, vol. 2.

71. Sachar, 755–60.

72. DFA, "P. W. Botha Speech on Yom Kippur War," October 13, 1973, 1/8/3, vol. 5.

73. Desmond Blow, *Take Now Thy Son: The Yom Kippur War, South Africa's Involvement* (Cape Town: Howard Timmins, 1974), 38–43.

74. Henry Kissinger, *Years of Upheaval* (Boston: Little, Brown, 1982), 491–93. See also Walter J. Boyne, *The Yom Kippur War and the Airlift That Saved Israel* (New York: Thomas Dunne, 2003).

75. Cohen, "Nuclear Arms in Crisis Under Secrecy," 111–121. There are several explanations for what happened. One theory holds that Dayan ordered the Israeli Air Force to load nuclear bombs onto fighter planes and fit nuclear warheads to Jericho missiles, but that Meir feared Soviet detection and instructed Dayan to remove them. Former U.S. defense secretary James Schlesinger and former CIA director William Colby lend credence to another, more plausible, explanation: that Israel signaled that it might use nuclear weapons if Washington did not act. They have argued that an Israeli suggestion of nuclear readiness on October 9 prompted the U.S. airlift. More recently, W. Seth Carus of the Center for Counterproliferation Research at the National Defense University has suggested, based on statements by the late Israeli nuclear physicist Yuval Ne'eman, that, having observed Soviet Scud missiles that they feared were nuclear-armed, the IDF reasoned that a counterdeployment of nuclear-capable Jerichos would get the Russians' attention and send a strong message to Sadat. See W. S. Carus, "Israeli Ballistic Missile Developments," Unclassified Working Papers, Appendix III, Commission to Assess the Ballistic Missile Threat to the United States, at http://fas.org/irp/threat/missile/rumsfeld/pt2_carus2.htm. See also Karpin, 324; Hersh, 227–30; Amos Perlmutter, Michael Handel, and Uri Bar-Joseph, *Two Minutes over Baghdad*, 2nd ed. (London: Frank Cass, 2003), 30. For a broader discussion of nuclear strategy and the Yom Kippur War, see Sagan, 160–77; Blechman and Hart, 132–56; Handel, "The Yom Kippur War and the Inevitability of Surprise," 461–502; Paul, 696–717.

76. Boyne, 67–68, 119.

77. For a thoughtful discussion of strategic emulation and South Africa's incentives for mimicking Israel's nuclear posture, see Peter Liberman, "Israel and the South African Bomb," *Nonproliferation Review* 11, no. 2 (Summer 2004): 19–20.

78. Cohen, *Israel and the Bomb*, 238.

79. Carus, "Israeli Ballistic Missile Developments," Appendix III. Ne'eman used the phrase "decided to deploy."

80. Sagan, 163–69.

81. Ojo, 50.

82. DFA, Shlomo Shamgar, "Over the Grave of an African Elephant" (translated), *Yediot Ahronot*, October 19, 1973.

83. Supreme Court of South Africa (Cape of Good Hope), *The State v. Johann Philip Derk Blaauw*, September 9, 1988, 20.

84. "Editorial," *Haaretz*, November 14, 1973.

85. Harry Hurwitz, "New Phase in S.A.-Israel Relations," *Jewish Herald*, February 19, 1974.

86. Lucretia McCalmont Marmon, "Israel and South Africa: The Odd Couple," *Times of Israel and World Jewish Review,* 1974.

87. In the upper echelons of the South African diplomatic community, there was a growing fear that closer ties with Israel would alienate the Arab states and Iran, upon whom South Africa depended for oil. The secretary of foreign affairs, Brand Fourie, telegraphed Fincham warning that Pretoria's support for Israel during the war meant that South Africa was "widely regarded as one of Israel's very few reliable friends, a contention which is already giving impetus to an oil boycott against us." See DFA, "Krisis in Israel se Afrika Beleid," July 4, 1973, 1/8/6, vol. 2; DFA, "Telegram: S.A. Consul-General, Tehran to Secretary for Foreign Affairs, Pretoria," July 9, 1974, 1/8/3, vol. 5.

88. David Albright, "South Africa and the Affordable Bomb," *Bulletin of the Atomic Scientists* 50, no. 4 (1994): 41; Mitchell Reiss, *Bridled Ambition: Why Countries Constrain Their Nuclear Capabilities* (Washington, D.C.: Woodrow Wilson Center Press, 1995), 8; APC, "I.A.E.A.: The Agency's Verification Activities in South Africa: Report by the Director General," September 8, 1993, GOV/2684, 93–03174, 5.

89. Jeffrey T. Richelson, *Spying on the Bomb: American Nuclear Intelligence from Nazi Germany to Iran and North Korea* (New York: W. W. Norton, 2006), 266; Louw Alberts, interview by author, Pretoria, February 27, 2006.

90. DFA, "Recent Developments in the Relations Between Israel and South Africa . . . ," United Nations General Assembly, A/AC.115/L.383, April 29, 1974, 1/8/3, vol. 2.

91. DFA, "Abdul Minty to Chairman of the UN Special Committee Against Apartheid," September 9, 1974, 1/8/3, vol. 2.

5 BROTHERS IN ARMS

1. Aaron S. Klieman, *Israel's Global Reach: Arms Sales as Diplomacy* (Oxford: Pergamon, 1985), 29.

2. Interview by author, Magnus Malan, Pretoria, February 9, 2006.

3. Sachar, 787.

4. Philip H. Frankel, *Pretoria's Praetorians: Civil-Military Relations in South Africa* (Cambridge: Cambridge University Press, 1984), 65.

5. Magnus Malan, interview by author.

6. Alex Mintz and Michael D. Ward, "Dynamics of Military Spending in Israel: A Computer Simulation," *Journal of Conflict Resolution* 31, no. 1 (1987): 87–88.

7. Shlaim, 323.

8. Gorenberg, *The Accidental Empire,* 272–74. Rabin was also untainted, having never before served in an Israeli cabinet.

9. Yitzhak Rabin, *The Rabin Memoirs* (Berkeley: University of California Press, 1996), 241, 307–9.

10. Binyamin Telem, interview by author, Beit Yehoshuah, September 20, 2005.

11. Stewart Reiser, *The Israeli Arms Industry: Foreign Policy, Arms Transfers, and Military Doctrine of a Small State* (New York: Holmes & Meier, 1989), 112–13.

12. Ibid., xiii; Klieman, 58.

13. Reiser, 114.

14. Ibid., 111–23. Exports increased from $39 million in 1968 to $70 million in 1973.

15. Ibid., 111–12. This occurred thanks largely to South African contracts.
16. Alex Mintz and Michael D. Ward, "The Political Economy of Military Spending in Israel," *American Political Science Review* 83, no. 2 (1989): 526.
17. Klieman, 124–27.
18. Ibid., 114–17.
19. Oren Barak and Gabriel Sheffer, "Israel's 'Security Network' and Its Impact: An Exploration of a New Approach," *International Journal of Middle East Studies* 38, no. 2 (2006): 235–61.
20. Klieman, 143.
21. Witney W. Schneidman, *Engaging Africa: Washington and the Fall of Portugal's Colonial Empire* (Lanham, MD: University Press of America, 2004), 136–39.
22. *South Africa: Defence and Strategic Value,* (London: South African Embassy Department of Information, 1977), 13.
23. Sparks, 183. Although pass laws briefly slowed the pace of black population growth in cities during the 1960s, separate development did not achieve its aim of deurbanization and the creation of white cities.
24. This meant South Africa was willing to pay a premium. There is no evidence of Israeli price gouging, but interviews with several retired SADF officials imply that Pretoria paid more than the market price for many weapons given that Israel was violating the U.N. embargo by selling to them after 1977.
25. To an extent the gold and mineral boom masked underlying stagnation in other sectors such as manufacturing. At this point the arms industry was still in its infancy.
26. See SANDF, HSI/AMI Z/23/6/1, vol. 3; SANDF, "SECMENT Agreement," April 3, 1975.
27. As reproduced in Eschel Rhoodie, *The Real Information Scandal* (Pretoria: Orbis, 1983), 117.
28. Magnus Malan, interview by author.
29. Dieter Gerhardt, interview by author, Noordhoek, March 8, 2006. The dates given to me in this interview contradict those in a 2000 article. Gerhardt claims the dates cited in that article were incorrect. See Ronen Bergman, "Treasons of Conscience," *Haaretz Magazine* (English edition), April 7, 2000.
30. Ibid.
31. For a brief history of the ISSACOM and strategic intelligence cooperation meetings, see SANDF, "Buitelandse Besoek: H.W.S.: ISSAKOM- en SICOPS Vergaderings: Israel," May 10, 1993, AFD INL 520/3/4/6, vol. 53, 66.
32. SANDF, "Proceedings of Discussions Held at Chief of Staff Intelligence . . . ," January 25, 1975, AMI/HSI MI/LIA/1/5/9, vol. 1, 214.
33. SANDF, "Uitruil van Info met Israel," May 17, 1973, AMI/HSI MI/LIA/1/5/9, vol. 1, 77–84.
34. Liberman, "Israel and the South African Bomb"; SAHA, "The Jericho Weapon System," March 31, 1975. The original Jericho memorandum is reproduced in an appendix to Liberman's article.
35. See SANDF, HSI/AMI Z/23/6/1, vol. 3, especially the notes regarding the third ISSA meeting. Because the offer of Jericho missiles, potentially armed with nuclear warheads, was discussed at two subsequent meetings in June, it appears that the offer first surfaced during the March 31 meeting, prompting Armstrong's memo and a series of decisions for the matter to be "held in abeyance" until June and then, again, until July 1975.

36. SAHA, "The Jericho Weapon System," March 31, 1975.

37. SANDF, "SECMENT Agreement," 2.

38. Indeed, it is still in effect. On April 23, 2006, the Directorate of Security of the Defense Establishment (Malmab) wrote to Armscor urging that they not release the 1975 document to the author. The SANDF archive released it in mildly redacted form, despite Israeli objections. See SANDF, "Pini Chen to Richardt du Toit: Security Agreement (MLMB/3311–06)," April 23, 2006.

39. The project's code name is corroborated by Dieter Gerhardt in his interview with the author and in other documents contained in SANDF, HSI/AMI Z/23/6/1, vol. 3.

40. SANDF, "Notes on a Meeting Between Minister S Peres and Minister P W Botha . . . ," June 4, 1975, HSI/AMI Z/23/6/1, vol. 3.

41. South Africa's costly clandestine efforts to develop its own indigenous nuclear capability in the following years would have been unnecessary if the Jericho deal had gone through in 1975. Dieter Gerhardt, interview by author.

42. SANDF, "Rules of Procedure (Annexure B)," June 30, 1975, HSI/AMI Z/23/6/1, vol. 3., states, "Requests by A.B. [Armaments Board] for purchases from other sources (non Israeli) will be processed directly by the M.O.D./Defence Sales Office in response to A.B. specific request."

43. SANDF, "State of Israel: Ministry of Defence: Directorate of Procurement and Production: Ref No. Mh/L/150.3/319," 1975 (undated), HSI/AMI Z/23/6/1, vol. 3.

44. "Notes on a Meeting Between Minister S Peres and Minister P W Botha . . ."

45. Trita Parsi, *Treacherous Alliance: The Secret Dealings of Israel, Iran, and the U.S.* (New Haven: Yale University Press, 2007), 74–78.

46. SANDF, HSI/AMI Z/23/6/1, vol. 3.

47. This claim is based on the data provided by Klieman and Reiser that approximates Israeli arms exports as well as IMI's exports during the 1970s (the ballpark figure for 1975 is $270 million). Klieman, 77–88; Reiser, 111–12. In fact, the IMI deal alone exceeds the annual total provided by Klieman.

48. Schneidman, 199–200.

49. Piero Gleijeses, *Conflicting Missions: Havana, Washington, and Africa, 1959–1976* (Chapel Hill: University of North Carolina Press, 2002), 276; Chester A. Crocker, *High Noon in Southern Africa: Making Peace in a Rough Neighborhood* (New York: W. W. Norton, 1992), 49.

50. Gleijeses, 259.

51. SANDF, "Planning Procedures: Operational Research . . . ," September 15, 1975, HSI/AMI Z/7/3/4/1, 35.

52. Gleijeses, 243. The Soviets had in fact cut back aid to Angola after 1972 and the bulk of assistance came from Tito's Yugoslavia. Soviet aid resumed in 1974, but it was Cuba that became the most influential force in the region.

53. For details of the Cuban intervention in Algeria from 1961 to 1962 and the Cuban military mission to Zaire—led by Che Guevara—in 1965, see Gleijeses, 30–56, 101–3.

54. NSA, "Conversacion Con El Embajador Sovietico," January 13, 1976; NSA, "Cuban Military Intervention in Angola: Report," January 6, 1976.

55. Schneidman, 208.

56. Ibid., 218.

57. Dick Clark, interview by author, Washington, November 15, 2005.

58. Gleijeses, 332.

59. William G. Howell and Jon C. Pevehouse, *While Dangers Gather: Congressional Checks on Presidential War Powers* (Princeton: Princeton University Press, 2007), 15.

60. In addition to Crocker, *High Noon in Southern Africa*, see Richard Leonard, *South Africa at War: White Power and the Crisis in Southern Africa* (Westport, CT: Lawrence Hill, 1983), 77–79; John Stockwell, *In Search of Enemies: A CIA Story* (New York: W. W. Norton, 1978).

61. Deon Geldenhuys, *The Diplomacy of Isolation: South African Foreign Policy Making* (Johannesburg: Macmillan, 1984), 76–77, describes Pretoria as feeling the United States had "pulled the carpet" from under them. See also Robert S. Jaster, "South African Defense Strategy and the Growing Influence of the Military," in *Arms and the African: Military Influences on Africa's International Relations*, William J. Foltz and Henry Bienen, eds. (New Haven: Yale University Press, 1985), 30.

62. Gleijeses, 299.

63. Mintz and Ward, "The Political Economy of Military Spending in Israel," 529; Reiser, 136.

64. Abraham A. Ben-Zvi, *Alliance Politics and the Limits of Influence: The Case of the US and Israel, 1975–1983* (Boulder: Westview, 1984), 16. For a detailed analysis of the reassessment crisis of 1975, see Abraham A. Ben-Zvi, *The United States and Israel: The Limits of the Special Relationship* (New York: Columbia University Press, 1993), 77–102.

65. "The Israeli Connection," *The Economist*, November 5, 1977.

66. Reiser, 130.

67. Rabin, 261. Rabin's views on the causes and consequences of the reassessment crisis are discussed on pages 253–75. Not surprisingly, he does not mention South Africa, given the secrecy surrounding those ties.

68. Dieter Gerhardt, interview by author.

69. Iran was involved in developing missiles with Israel prior to 1979. After the fall of the Shah, Israel looked to South Africa to help fund and jointly develop a missile system. See William E. Burrows and Robert Windrem, *Critical Mass: The Dangerous Race for Superweapons in a Fragmenting World* (New York: Simon & Schuster, 1994), 452–53; Bergman, "Treasons of Conscience."

70. Bergman, "Treasons of Conscience."

71. For a discussion of this hardening, see Rabin, 256; Ben-Zvi, *The United States and Israel*, 98–99.

72. See SANDF, HSI/AMI Z/23/6/1, vol. 3.

73. Andrew J. Pierre, "Arms Sales: The New Diplomacy," *Foreign Affairs* 60, no. 2 (Winter 1981–1982): 269.

74. Gleijeses, 231.

75. Klieman, 35.

76. Reiser, 214; Klieman, 40–41.

77. James Sanders, *Apartheid's Friends: The Rise and Fall of South Africa's Secret Service* (London: John Murray, 2006), 94–99.

78. Rhoodie, 113. Rhoodie used Oscar Hurwitz, a prominent Pretoria Jewish businessman, and contacts in the United States to forge connections in Israel.

79. Ibid., 110–11.

80. Ibid., 118.

81. Ibid., 115–16.

82. Unna, 127. "I was rather surprised when I got to know about it. It was decided at [a] very high level in Israel," recalls Unna.

83. According to most sources, Rhoodie, Mulder, and van den Bergh were the masterminds of the visit. However, Rhoodie's autobiography and a 1983 article suggest that Oscar Hurwitz played a major role in pushing Vorster to go to Israel. See David Braun, "Propaganda War Aimed at Israel and Black States: Prominent Jewish Lawyer Played a Major Role in Softening Attitudes Towards S.A.," *The Star,* December 1, 1983.

84. See, for example, Naomi Chazan, "Israel's 'Shortsighted' Policy on South Africa," *Jerusalem Post Weekly,* April 20, 1976.

85. Editorial, *Jerusalem Post,* April 11, 1976.

86. Arthur Goldreich, interview by author.

87. Joseph, 26.

88. John Scott, "Vorster: No Arms Deal," *Cape Times,* April 10, 1976.

89. "Bold Move," *Cape Times,* April 14, 1976; John Scott, "Visit Triumph for Vorster," *Cape Times,* April 12, 1976.

90. Mervyn Smith, interview by author, Cape Town, February 22, 2005.

91. "Historic Pact: Joint Cabinet Is World First," *Zionist Record & SA Jewish Chronicle,* April 14, 1976.

92. Benjamin Pogrund, interview by author.

93. Dennis Diamond, interview by author, Jerusalem, December 19, 2004.

94. JBOD, "Address Delivered by Mr. D. K. Mann . . . ," May 10, 1976, D. K. Mann Biography File.

95. Dennis Diamond, interview by author.

96. Mendel Kaplan, interview by author, Johannesburg, March 7, 2005.

97. Dennis Davis, interview by author, Cape Town, February 28, 2005; Dennis Davis, "Guess Who Came to Dinner?," *Strike,* May 1976.

98. Ibid.

99. Mervyn Smith, interview by author.

100. For an example of Israeli coverage, see Landau, "Vorster Denies Arms Deal . . . ," *Jerusalem Post,* April 11, 1976.

101. John Scott, "Vorster: No Arms Deal," *Cape Times,* April 10, 1976; John Scott, "Vorster Signs Pact with Israel," *Cape Times,* April 13, 1976.

102. "Israel and South Africa; Just Looking," *The Economist,* April 17, 1976; Terence Smith, "Vorster Visit to Israel Arouses Criticism," *New York Times,* April 18, 1976; Binyamin Telem, interview by author.

103. Moshe Decter, "Israel and South Africa," *New York Times,* November 11, 1976.

104. Klieman, 86.

105. See SANDF, HSI/AMI Z/7/3/4/1, 43–51.

106. Binyamin Telem, interview by author.

107. Ibid.

108. Ibid.

109. Klieman, 102–3; Oren Barak and Chanan Kahan, *Misrad Ha'chutz-Li'an?* (Jerusalem: Leonard Davis Institute for International Relations, 2006), 14–15.

110. Amos Baram, interview by author, Netanya, September 22, 2005.

111. Leonard, 11.

112. John Carlin, *Playing the Enemy: Nelson Mandela and the Game That Made a Nation* (New York: Penguin, 2008), 96–102.

113. Binyamin Telem, interview by author.

114. SANDF, "Provision of Transport: Visit of Maj General Holtzhausen and Group," November 28, 1977, AMI 520/3/4/6, vol. 2, 94.

115. Binyamin Telem, interview by author.

116. Richardt van der Walt, Hannes Steyn, and Jan van Loggerenberg, *Armament and Disarmament: South Africa's Nuclear Experience* (Lincoln, NE: iUniverse 2005), 48.

117. Binyamin Telem, interview by author.

118. Amos Baram, interview by author.

119. Unna, 110–16; Yitzhak Unna, interview by author, Netanya, August 24, 2005.

120. Van den Bergh arrested Protter and, seemingly inexplicably, drove him and Unna to the van den Bergh home in Pretoria before taking Protter to jail. South Africa's intelligence chief considered Protter clinically insane and insisted on affording him the dignity of breakfast before he began a life sentence in jail. Protter was released in 1995 and now runs a private security company called Rescue 911 in Mpumalanga Province. Protter spoke with me by phone on two occasions but declined to meet due to his busy schedule and did not respond to written questions regarding his motivations for the Fox Street hostage crisis.

121. Unna, 125.

122. Ibid., 120.

123. Ibid., 122.

124. "Pass Raid Arrests Made Envoy Feel Sick," *The Star*, March 15, 1979; "A Sick-Making Law," *Cape Times*, March 16, 1979; Unna, 137–38.

125. Yitzhak Unna, interview by author.

126. Magnus Malan, interview by author.

127. Yitzhak Unna, interview by author. It is also possible that Unna felt it necessary to compensate for Israel's material aid to the apartheid state with moral denunciations. Nevertheless, his abhorrence of apartheid seems genuine and unstaged even today.

128. SANDF, "C S.A.D.F. (Cape) to C Army," March 4, 1977, HSAW 520/3/4/6, vol. 1, 1d.

129. SANDF, "Verslag oor besoek aan Israeli Weermag deur Hoofleer en Direkteur Beplanning, Leerhoofkwartier," March 18, 1977, HSAW 520/3/4/6, vol. 1.

130. SANDF, "Visit to Argus: Members of the SA Army," July 22, 1977, AMI 520/3/4/6, vol. 1, 61.

131. SANDF, "Visit to Cane: Hoedspruit Communications System," July 29, 1977, AMI 520/3/4/6, vol. 1, 115; SANDF, "Visit to Israel: Air Force Planning Team," July 1977, AMI 520/3/4/6, vol. 1, 47.

132. SANDF, "Drop Tests—Proj Limbo," June 24–July 8, 1977, AMI 520/3/4/6, vol. 1, 102–5; Tienie Groenewald, interview by author (#2), Pretoria, July 6, 2006.

133. SANDF, "Verslag oor Besoek aan Argus oor die periode 18 Tot 28 Julie 1977," July 1977, AMI 520/3/4/6, vol. 1, 133. This disparity can be discerned by comparing data from the IMF Department of Trade Statistics, at http://www.esds.ac.uk/international/support/user_guides/imf/dots.asp, with the much higher annual totals totals from AFD, "Armscor Confidential Information: Bestel/Verskaffer Report," July 11, 2006.

134. Ibid., 130.

135. Barry Schweid, Associated Press, February 17, 1977.
136. SANDF, "Israeli Reaction to U.N. Arms Embargo Against South Africa," November 17, 1977, AMI/MI 204/3/I7, 19.
137. "Verslag Oor Besoek aan Argus oor die Periode 18 Tot 28 Julie 1977," 129.
138. Ibid.

6 A COMMON LOT

1. "Begin Urges Friendship with S.A.," *Jewish Herald*, November 2, 1971; Shindler, *Israel, Likud and the Zionist Dream*, 56.
2. SANDF, "Evaluasie: Tenkafkeerwapens en Outomatiese Teikenstelsels," October 26, 1977, AMI 520/3/4/6, vol. 2, 82.
3. Shindler, *The Triumph of Military Zionism: Nationalism and the Origins of the Israeli Right* (London: I. B. Tauris, 2005), 206.
4. Known alternately as the Irgun or by its Hebrew acronym, Etzel.
5. Shavit, 227.
6. Shimoni, *The Zionist Ideology*, 249.
7. Shavit, 365.
8. Ibid.
9. Shindler, *Israel, Likud and the Zionist Dream*, 21.
10. For an insider's perspective of the split, see Lankin, 43–45. Lehi was initially known as the Irgun Tzvai Leumi b'Yisrael.
11. Shavit, 232–33; Sasson Sofer, *Zionism and the Foundations of Israeli Diplomacy* (Cambridge: Cambridge University Press, 1998), 252–54, 263–64. Indeed, Lehi turned to Stalin after World War II, seeing the Soviet Union as the most reliable anti-British power in the postwar world.
12. Shavit, 231.
13. Ibid., 231–33; Sofer, 265. The borders of the British Mandate territory of Transjordan are roughly the same as those of present-day Jordan.
14. Shindler, *Israel, Likud and the Zionist Dream*, 28. Begin's comment also revealed his low regard for black South Africans and it suggests that he deemed their liberation struggle less legitimate than his own.
15. Lankin disputes the view that this turned Churchill against the Zionist movement. See Lankin, 93.
16. Michael Makovsky, *Churchill's Promised Land: Zionism and Statecraft* (New Haven: Yale University Press, 2007), 216–17.
17. For a detailed account of the Hunting Season, see Lankin, 97–110. Lankin also provides documentary evidence that World Zionist Organization leader Chaim Weizmann boasted of the successes of the Season to his friends in the British government. At the time of the Season, Weizmann's WZO was lobbying for support in Western capitals; Ben-Gurion's Jewish Agency for Palestine, which acted as a government for Palestine's Jews prior to Israeli statehood, had encouraged Jews to join the British war effort against the Nazis. The more moderate Revisionist movement, still hewing to Jabotinsky's line, condemned Lehi and Irgun violence against Britain.
18. Lankin, 224–25.
19. Shavit, 335.
20. Ehud Sprinzak, *Brother Against Brother: Violence and Extremism in Israeli Politics from Altalena to the Rabin Assassination* (New York: Free Press, 1999), 27.

21. Sofer, 236–37. Begin allegedly followed the advice of his operations officer, Amichai Paglin. One of the IDF officers commanding forces on the beach and lobbing grenades at the Irgun men was a young colonel named Yitzhak Rabin.

22. For a detailed first-person account, see Lankin, 335–44. For its part, Lehi protested partition by assassinating Swedish U.N. mediator Folke Bernadotte in September 1948. For a riveting account of the assassination, see Kati Marton, *A Death in Jerusalem* (New York: Arcade, 1996).

23. Ilan Peleg, *Begin's Foreign Policy, 1977–1983: Israel's Move to the Right* (New York: Greenwood, 1987), 5.

24. Begin did not simply seek to resettle West Bank areas surrounding Jerusalem that Jews had occupied prior to the War of Independence in 1948, but all of biblical Judea and Samaria. This area covered the entire West Bank and included many areas populated almost exclusively by Palestinians. Although Begin's settlement push represented a confluence of interests among secular Revisionist-inspired ideologues and messianic religious Zionists, there were also a number of prominent Labor Party intellectuals and politicians who advocated settlement. See Gorenberg, *The Accidental Empire*.

25. See Avineri, 171–80. Here, Avineri discusses Jabotinsky's praise for the Ukrainian nationalist poet Taras Shevchenko. Jabotinsky excused the poet's "explosions of wild fury against the Poles, the Jews and other neighbours" in appreciation of the larger nationalist project.

26. Ofira Seliktar, *New Zionism and the Foreign Policy System of Israel* (London: Croom Helm, 1986), 182; Barak and Sheffer, 235–61.

27. David Hacohen, "Partition for South Africa," *Jerusalem Post*, July 8, 1977.

28. Dennis Diamond, interview by author.

29. A caveat to this interpretation should be noted. Revisionism, in its post-1944 incarnation, was an explicitly revolutionary movement calling for armed revolt. This particular element of its message was understandably admired by some on the revolutionary left. In South Africa, Menachem Begin's memoir *The Revolt* appealed to Nelson Mandela, who read it in prison, while Begin was supporting the government of his captors.

30. Van der Walt, Steyn, and van Loggerenberg, 41.

31. Reiss, 9–10, 36n16–17.

32. The conflicting claims between Buys's account and that found in Reiss likely arise from the projected date of highly enriched uranium output from South Africa's "Y-Plant." Some HEU was produced in early 1978 but later that year there was a "massive catalytic in-process gas reaction between the UF6 and the hydrogen carrier gas" that resulted in the Y-Plant's closure until April 1980 and a delay in its next significant HEU production until July 1981. This set back the construction of the next bombs until 1982. See Waldo Stumpf, "South Africa's Nuclear Weapons Program: From Deterrence to Dismantlement," *Arms Control Today* 25 (December 1995–January 1996): 4–5. The Y-Plant's closure is disputed without substantiating evidence in Nicholas Badenhorst and Pierre Victor, *Those Who Had the Power* (Pretoria: Pierre Victor, 2006), 30.

33. Murrey Marder and Don Oberdorfer, "How West, Soviets Acted to Defuse S. African A-Test, Keeping S. Africa Out of the Nuclear Armaments Club," *Washington Post*, August 28, 1977.

34. Bergman, "Treasons of Conscience."

35. Van der Walt, Steyn, and van Loggerenberg, 40. The embassy officials using this

plane were expelled from the country by Botha the following year after reportedly photographing other strategic installations such as the Valindaba Y-Plant. The story of their expulsion is told in detail in Sanders, *Apartheid's Friends*, 127.

36. Richelson, 278–79.

37. Marder and Oberdorfer, "How West, Soviets Acted to Defuse S. Africa A-Test," A1.

38. Van der Walt, Steyn, and van Loggerenberg, 41.

39. Jim Hoagland, "Paris Warns South Africa on A-Testing . . . ," *Washington Post*, August 22, 1977.

40. Vorster denied making any such promise to Carter in a later interview, prompting Washington to release his written pledge not to develop nuclear weapons. Murrey Marder, "Carter Says S. Africa Denies Intent to Develop Any Nuclear Explosives," *Washington Post*, August 24, 1977; Warren Brown, "Vorster: No Promise to U.S. on A-Weapons," *Washington Post*, August 24, 1977; Edward Walsh, "Vorster Pledge on A-Testing Made Public by White House," *Washington Post*, October 26, 1977.

41. NSA, "Your Meeting with Gromyko: South Africa Nuclear Issue," September 21, 1977, 1–2.

42. Liberman, "The Rise and Fall of the South African Bomb," 53.

43. André Buys, interview by author, Pretoria, March 18, 2005. Though Vorster's 1974 decision envisioned building a weapon, it was not until 1977 that this message was formally relayed to the scientists working on the nuclear explosives program.

44. Van der Walt, Steyn, and van Loggerenberg, 41. The scientists assumed they could abandon the sophisticated scientific measurement preparations if deterrence was the only goal.

45. The debate surrounding the actual date of the decision to "go nuclear" hinges on differing bureaucratic interpretations of what a "nuclear weapon" is. Armscor's claim that the military nuclear program did not begin until 1978 is likely due to the fact that the defense industry did not consider it a credible deterrent unless the SADF could "fly it," and the plans for airplane-carried bombs and delivery systems did not begin until 1978. See Reiss, 9; Liberman, "The Rise and Fall of the South African Bomb," 53; Albright, "South Africa and the Affordable Bomb," 43; Purkitt and Burgess, 249n71.

46. *South Africa: Defence and Strategic Value* (London: South African Embassy Department of Information, 1977), 3–5, 17.

47. William F. Gutteridge, ed., *South Africa's Defence and Security into the 21st Century* (Aldershot: Dartmouth, 1996), 62–67.

48. Chester A. Crocker, *South Africa's Defense Posture: Coping with Vulnerability* (Beverly Hills, CA: Center for Strategic and International Studies, 1981), 83.

49. Klieman, 43–44. Also see John Prados, "Sealanes, Western Strategy and South Africa," in *U.S. Military Involvement in Southern Africa*, ed. Western Massachusetts Association of Concerned African Scholars (Boston: South End, 1978).

50. Mervyn Rees and Chris Day, *Muldergate: The Story of the Info Scandal* (Johannesburg: Macmillan, 1980), 163.

51. Ibid., 164.

52. Paul Blackstock, *The Strategy of Subversion: Manipulating the Politics of Other Nations* (Chicago: Quadrangle, 1964).

53. Rees and Day, 171.
54. For details of the propaganda efforts in the United States and South Africa's attempt to buy *The Washington Star*, see Sanders, 100–101.
55. Elaine Dutka and Alan Citron, "A Mogul's Bankroll, and Past . . . ," *Los Angeles Times*, February 28, 1992, A1.
56. Burrows and Windrem, 462–64. Smyth was captured in Spain in 2001, after sixteen years on the run, and extradited to the United States.
57. Sanders, 419n.
58. See Rees and Day for an exhaustive account.
59. Ibid., 212–22.

7 THE BACK CHANNEL

1. Supreme Court of South Africa (Cape of Good Hope), *The State v. Johann Philip Derk Blaauw*, September 9, 1988, 32.
2. James Adams, *The Unnatural Alliance* (London: Quartet, 1984), 171.
3. Cohen, *Israel and the Bomb*, 27; Karpin, 31–35.
4. Philip H. Frankel, *Pretoria's Praetorians*, 80.
5. Kenneth M. Grundy, *The Militarization of South African Politics* (London: I. B. Tauris, 1986), 45.
6. Annette Seegers, *The Military in the Making of Modern South Africa* (London: I. B. Tauris, 1996), 226. It lent its name to the notorious South African police vehicles, known as CASSPIRs, used in counterinsurgency operations in Namibia as well as by riot police dispersing demonstrators in black townships. The name was derived by combining the acronyms of its creator (CSIR) and its user (SAP).
7. NSA, "D.I.A.: Armscor and the South African Defense Industry (U)," December 1980, 11–12.
8. Hannes Steyn, interview by author, Pretoria, March 24, 2005.
9. Ibid.
10. For a lengthy profile of Ne'eman and a detailed account of his career at the helm of the Israeli nuclear program, see Ronen Bergman, "B'shvilo, Zeh Garinim," *Yediot Ahronot* (7 Yamim), March 18, 2005.
11. Louw Alberts, interview by author.
12. DFA, "C.V.D.M Brink to W. S. Hugo: Scientific Co-operation Between Israel and South Africa," January 20, 1975, 1/8/4, vol. 2. The military nature of the visits is further confirmed by the American Defense Intelligence Agency's interest in CSIR activities. See NSA, "U.S.D.A.O. Pretoria S.F. to D.I.A. Washington D.C.," September 10, 1987.
13. DFA, "Visit to Israel of Scientific Mission from South Africa: March 1975," July 9, 1975, 1/8/4, vol. 2.
14. "C.V.D.M Brink to W. S. Hugo: Scientific Co-operation Between Israel and South Africa," 1–2.
15. SANDF, "Visit No. 19 . . . Scientific and Technical Intelligence Organization," April 2, 1976, 520/3/4/6, vol. 1.
16. DFA, "Scientific Co-operation . . . Exchange Agreement," October 1976, 1/8/4, vol. 2.
17. APC, "Ministry of Defence: Visit of Mr. S. P. Botha, Minister of Labour and Mines–S.A. 26–31 July 1976" (Exhibit B38 from *State v. Blaauw*).

18. "Israel voer dalk uit S.A. in," *Die Burger,* August 2, 1976.
19. Given Dimona's actual undeclared operating capacity of 70 to 100 megawatts, two hundred tons would not last more than a few years.
20. Written correspondence with André Buys and Israeli journalist Yossi Melman; Norris, 73–75.
21. *State v. Blaauw,* 20.
22. Ibid., 22.
23. Fanie Botha, interview by author, Pretoria, July 7, 2006. Although Botha claims that there was no debate within South Africa's nuclear establishment about his order to lift the safeguards, the AEB officials tell a different story. At the time, the AEB's chief was Ampie Roux. His protégé, Waldo Stumpf, remembers a pair of threatening letters from Fanie Botha to Roux ordering him to lift the safeguards. Roux was the only official with the authority to do so as head of the agency that sold the uranium and was responsible for inspecting it. "I saw that letter," recalls Stumpf. According to him, Ampie Roux insisted that South Africa "should not supply uranium to Israel that could then be used as weapon fuel." Stumpf recalls a second letter threatening Roux with his job if he didn't lift the safeguards. "I specifically remember those two letters because they vindicated Ampie Roux if anyone ever would like to point a finger at him; he strongly objected and he was just overruled." Today, the letters are nowhere to be found in the archives. "The idea was always that it [the yellowcake] would be strictly under safeguards. . . . [But] the politicians started playing and interfering," Stumpf complains. Whether or not Ampie Roux agreed, he eventually submitted to the pressure and lifted the safeguards. Waldo Stumpf, interview by author, Pretoria, March 18, 2005.
24. Ibid.
25. *State v. Blaauw,* 19.
26. Jan van Loggerenberg, interview by author, Pretoria, March 22, 2005.
27. Pieter John Roos, interview by author, Centurion, January 20, 2006.
28. George Meiring, interview by author, Pretoria, March 16, 2005; Tienie Groenwald, interview by author, Pretoria, March 21, 2005; Magnus Malan, interview by author.
29. *State v. Blaauw,* 20. These spare parts were no longer available from France after de Gaulle's 1967 decision to cease supplying Israel.
30. Fanie Botha, interview by author.
31. According to the trial record, the deal was "concluded between the accused [Blaauw], General van den Bergh and Fanie Botha on the South African side and Benjamine [Blumberg] on behalf of Israel." Due to numerous references to Blaauw meeting the head of the Israeli Council for Scientific Liaison (Lakam) and to the Lakam head's request to purchase yellowcake, it is clear that "Benjamine" (an Afrikaans phonetic spelling of the Hebrew "Binyamin") is without a doubt the Lakam head, Binyamin Blumberg. See Yossi Melman, "Ha'kesher ha'garini shel Yisrael v'D'rom Afrika," *Haaretz,* April 27, 1997.
32. According to the *Bulletin of the Atomic Scientists'* 2002 nuclear weapons appraisal, Israel today possesses a tritium production capability at Dimona. If this was not operational in the 1970s, then the material would have come from the Soviet Union or the United States.
33. *State v. Blaauw,* 24; APC, lawyer's handwritten trial notes, *State v. Blaauw,* 5.

34. *State v. Blaauw*, 24. Both Fanie Botha and Waldo Stumpf see the tritium as the quid pro quo in the deal. However, Stumpf claims it was not needed for the bombs that the AEB was designing at the time, a view shared by André Buys and the head of Armscor's research and development at the time, Hannes Steyn. Fanie Botha, interview by author; Waldo Stumpf, interview by author; André Buys, interview by author; Hannes Steyn, interview by author.

35. Construction even began on a plutonium reprocessing and lithium-6 facility at Gouriqua in the Western Cape Province. Had it been finished, the plant would have supplied South Africa with its own indigenous supply of tritium.

36. Fanie Botha, interview by author. Botha is open about the fact that the tritium-safeguards deal was a quid pro quo.

37. O'Meara, *Forty Lost Years*, 234–40.

38. *State v. Blaauw*, 34–35.

39. Ibid., 27.

40. Ibid.

41. Ibid., 28.

42. Ibid., 27.

43. Mike Hannon, interview by author (by telephone), April 26, 2006.

44. Epstein, 39–41, 74–75.

45. This was achieved by pooling diamonds from De Beers–owned mines throughout the world and sending them to London for distribution. There, on the fifth Monday of each year, leading diamond dealers—known as sightholders—were invited for "sights," during which each dealer was allocated a shoebox-sized portion of rough diamonds for a fixed price. Although the quality varied, none dared refuse their allocation for fear of being excluded in the future. See Kanfer, 3–4.

46. APC, "O'Kiepmarine Gold Fields Inc. Appraisal of Offshore Diamond Mining Concessions," 1986. Due to the declining value of the rand, these concessions were worth much less at the time of the trial. At 1979 exchange rates, the same R900 million appraisal was worth $1.1 billion.

47. *State v. Blaauw*, 126.

48. Ibid., 77; *Sunday Express*, November 13, 1983.

49. O'Meara, *Forty Lost Years*, 217.

50. Seegers, 130–32.

51. For a detailed discussion of this power shift, see Sanders, *Apartheid's Friends*, 145–73.

52. Grundy, *The Militarization of South African Politics*, 42–44; Sanders, *Apartheid's Friends*, 123.

53. Leonard, 15–16.

54. For a discussion of Botha's regional destabilization policy and the growing militarism of his government, see Robert Davies and Dan O'Meara, "Total Strategy in Southern Africa: An Analysis of South African Regional Policy Since 1978," *Journal of Southern African Studies* 11, no. 2 (April 1985): 183–211; Robert S. Jaster, *The Defence of White Power: South African Foreign Policy Under Pressure* (Basingstoke: Macmillan, 1988), 79–91.

55. Adam and Giliomee, 135.

56. Grundy, *The Militarization of South African Politics*, 38; Seegers, 165–66.

57. Seegers, 163.

58. Ibid., 165.

59. Philip H. Frankel, *Pretoria's Praetorians*, 46.
60. Ibid., 260–62.
61. Magnus Malan, interview by author.
62. Kenneth W. Grundy, *The Rise of the South African Security Establishment* (Johannesburg: Bradlow Series, no. 1), 5.
63. For a critique of South African total strategy and a discussion of Brazil's 1964 military coup as an example of effective employment of Beaufre's ideas, see Philip H. Frankel, *Pretoria's Praetorians*, 52–53.
64. Jannie Geldenhuys, interview by author, Pretoria, March 8, 2005. The team was led by the commander of the Entebbe raid, Dan Shomron. The Entebbe raid took place after members of the Popular Front for the Liberation of Palestine and their German sympathizers hijacked an Air France flight from Tel Aviv to Paris, diverting it to Libya and then Uganda. Israeli commandos conducted a daring raid at the Entebbe airport and rescued all hostages except one. Future prime minister Benjamin Netanyahu's brother was killed in the operation.
65. Leonard, 17.
66. Jaster, "South African Defense Strategy and the Growing Influence of the Military," 123. U.S. officials were never convinced that Soviet interdiction of the Cape Route posed a dire threat.
67. Jaster, *South Africa's Narrowing Security Options*, 16; Philip H. Frankel, *Pretoria's Praetorians*, 72.
68. Ibid., 84. Armscor itself employed 29,000 in 1981, the remaining 70,000 worked with its affiliates and contractors; see also NSA, "D.I.A.: Armscor and the South African Defense Industry (U)," December 1980.
69. Jaster, "South African Defense Strategy and the Growing Influence of the Military," 144.
70. Although other countries were involved with South Africa after the U.N. embargo, none of these relationships approached the formal state-to-state alliance forged at the highest levels of government between Israel and South Africa. Britain provided spare parts for the SAAF's Buccaneer bombers and Japan sold missile components over the years, according to Gerhardt. Dieter Gerhardt, interview by author.
71. Peter L. Bunce, "The Growth of South Africa's Defence Industry and Its Israeli Connection," *Royal United Services Institute Journal* 129, no. 2 (1984): 44; Klieman, 152; AFD, "Armscor Confidential Information: Bestel/Verskaffer Report," July 11, 2006.
72. Ronnie Edwards, interview by author, Springs, July 1, 2006.
73. Robert E. Harkavy, "The Pariah State Syndrome," *Orbis* 21, no. 3 (1977): 626–27.
74. For a general discussion of the benefits of joint production for Israel, see Gerald Steinberg, "Israel: Case Study for International Missile Trade and Nonproliferation Project," in *The International Missile Bazaar*; eds. William Potter and Harlan Jencks (Boulder: Westview, 1993). Steinberg acknowledges the many reports of Israeli–South African cooperation but seems eager to dismiss them as speculative and possibly inaccurate. See also Jaster, *South Africa's Narrowing Security Options*, 44. While Israel was the most important fellow pariah, Taiwan and Chile also had limited military ties to Pretoria.
75. SANDF, "Verslag oor spesiale besoek aan Israel ivm missielprojek . . . ," March 13, 1979, HSAW 520/3/4/6, vol. 1.

76. Eitan, 9–22.
77. Ibid., 378–85.
78. "Magnus Malan to Rafael Eitan (Draft Letter)," March 1979, HSAW 520/3/4/6, vol. 1. Rafael (Raful) Eitan is not to be confused with Rafael (Rafi) Eitan, a former Mossad official who served in the Knesset until 2009.
79. SANDF, "Verslag oor spesiale besoek aan Israel ivm missielprojek . . . ," March 13, 1979, HSAW 520/3/4/6, vol. 1.
80. SANDF, "Rafael Eitan to Magnus Malan," May 11, 1979, AMI 520/3/4/6, vol. 4, 77.
81. SANDF, "Telegram: Hopper to C S.A.D.F. PTA," November 2, 1979, AMI 520/3/4/6, vol. 6, 34; SANDF, "Message From: H.S.A.W. 2 to G.G.," October 25, 1979, AMI 520/3/4/6, vol. 6, 30; SANDF, "Besoek aan Taper: 67200360PE Maj. W. Basson, S.A.G.D.," October 18, 1979, AMI 520/3/4/6, vol. 6, 5.
82. See Purkitt and Burgess, 326–27.
83. Pabian, 4–5.
84. Stumpf, 4.
85. Richard K. Betts, "A Diplomatic Bomb for South Africa?," *International Security* 4, no. 2 (1979): 113.
86. Stumpf, 8.
87. Robert S. Jaster, "Politics and the 'Afrikaner Bomb,' " *Orbis* (Winter 1984): 846.
88. Pabian, 3.
89. Ibid., 15–16.
90. Harkavy, "The Pariah State Syndrome," 642; Robert E. Harkavy, "Pariah States and Nuclear Proliferation," *International Organization* 35, no. 1 (1981): 153–60; Jaster, *South Africa's Narrowing Security Options*, 44.
91. Richard K. Betts, "Paranoids, Pygmies, Pariahs and Nonproliferation," *Foreign Policy* 26 (Spring 1977): 178.

8 OVER THE EDGE

1. Richelson, 285. The pattern is produced by the initial detonation's flash, which is then blacked out by an opaque shock wave of compressed air that dissipates over a larger area, eventually allowing a second emission of light from the explosion.
2. Thomas O'Toole and Milton Benjamin, "Officials Hotly Debate Whether African Event Was Atom Blast," *Washington Post*, January 17, 1980.
3. André Buys, interview by author. Buys maintains that it could not have possibly been a South African bomb because the one he was working on was not finished due to the Y-Plant's shutdown and a lack of weapons-grade uranium. Furthermore, the yield of the explosion detected by VELA was much lower (2 to 4 kilotons) than the most likely yield of the basic Hiroshima-type device being built at Kentron in 1979, which would have been in the range of 10 to 20 kilotons.
4. Ibid.
5. Hersh, 274.
6. Ibid., 275.
7. NSA, "Director of Central Intelligence, the 22 September 1979 Event," December 1979. According to Dieter Gerhardt, the South African naval base at Simonstown had been shuttered from September 17 to 23 and the SADF's Saldanha naval facility on South Africa's west coast had been placed on alert from September 21 to 23, the period when the flash occurred. In an interview, Gerhardt, a

former commander of the Simonstown dockyards, claimed this closure was unique: "The dockyard was sealed—never before had there been such a thing, never again." Gerhardt was not informed of the reason but had the sense that there was "something going on that's more secret than top secret . . . everything took place at night." Dieter Gerhardt, interview by author.

8. NSA, "Los Alamos Scientific Laboratory, Light Flash Produced by an Atmospheric Nuclear Explosion," November 1979. The Mission Research Corporation, a private government contractor, also examined and dismissed alternative sources but was bothered by the discrepancy between the two VELA sensors' readings of the second flash. This they attributed to malfunctioning of one of the sensors, which, while unlikely, was "much higher than the probability of any non-nuclear explanation." Richelson, 297–98.

9. Richelson, 301.

10. NSA, "Ad Hoc Panel Report on the September 22 Event," May 23, 1980, 9.

11. Ibid., 14–15.

12. NSA, "Defense Intelligence Agency, the South Atlantic Mystery Flash: Nuclear or Not?," June 26, 1980.

13. Richelson, 305.

14. NSA, "South Atlantic Nuclear Event (S): (State Department Memo to National Security Council)," October 22, 1979.

15. Waldo Stumpf, interview by author, Pretoria, March 18, 2005.

16. "South Atlantic Nuclear Event (S)," 3.

17. The significance of Scali's role has recently been called into question. See Richard Holbrooke, "Real W.M.D.'s," New York Times Book Review, June 22, 2008.

18. "South Atlantic Nuclear Event," 9.

19. Richelson, 309.

20. NSA, "Alan Berman to John Marcum: Evidence of the Possible Detection of Fission Products . . . ," November 3, 1980.

21. Richelson, 309.

22. "Alan Berman to John Marcum: Evidence of the Possible Detection of Fission Products . . ."

23. Richelson, 311.

24. NSA, "Memorandum: Report of Conversation Between Alan Berman and John Fialka of the Washington Star," August 7, 1980.

25. NSA, "Alan Berman to John Marcum," December 11, 1980.

26. The VELA flash was detected at 12:52 A.M. GMT. Local time at the presumed detonation point was then 3:52 A.M.

27. "Alan Berman to John Marcum," 2.

28. Ibid., 5.

29. Hersh, 280–81.

30. Richelson, 314. The most recent word comes from Israeli journalist Ronen Bergman. On the basis of new disclosures, Bergman argues that the September 1979 event was an Israeli test with some South African observers and that the obsessive secrecy surrounding it to this day stems in part from the involvement of Yechiel Horev, the head of Israel's feared Malmab until 2007. See Ronen Bergman, "Hapes b'Antarktika," Yediot Ahronot (7 Yamim), May 19, 2006.

31. Hersh, 280–81. Even Ruina himself had contact with an Israeli colleague at MIT

who had worked on the Israeli nuclear missile design and suggested VELA had picked up an Israeli–South African test. The information was forwarded to the White House but kept from the panel.

32. Ibid., 281.

33. "Director of Central Intelligence, the 22 September 1979 Event," 10.

34. Ibid., 9.

35. Magnus Malan, interview by author.

36. NSA, "South Africa: Defense Strategy in an Increasingly Hostile World," December 1980, 3.

37. Ibid., 3.

38. Albright, "South Africa and the Affordable Bomb," 37–38.

39. Bob Campbell, interview by author, McLean, VA, June 16, 2007.

40. SANDF, "Besoek van Genl. Ivri: Feb 80," February 28, 1980, AMI 520/2/5/6, vol. 3, 47.

41. Tienie Groenewald, interview by author (#1).

42. David Ivry, interview by author, Tel Aviv, September 19, 2005.

43. SANDF, "Magnus Malan to Rafael Eitan," May 22, 1980, AMI 520/2/5/6, vol. 5, 41–42.

44. SANDF, "Yonah Efrat to Margot and Magnus Malan," October 9, 1980, MV/UG/56/17, vol. 3.

45. Gorenberg, *The Accidental Empire*, 331–32.

46. SANDF, "Constand Viljoen to Yona Efrat," October 31, 1980, AMI 520/2/5/6, vol. 6, 34; SANDF, "Visit to RSA of General Yona Efrat, Israel Defence Force Reserve," November 12, 1980, AMI 520/2/5/6, vol. 6, 33.

47. SANDF, "Yonah Efrat to Magnus Malan," September 1981 (undated), MV/UG/56/17, vol. 3.

48. SANDF, "Telegram to C S.A.D.F. 1," March 26, 1980, AMI 520/3/4/6, vol. 6, 21.

49. SANDF, "Rafael Eitan to Magnus Malan, August 21, 1980," AMI 520/2/5/6, vol. 6, 134.

50. Black and Morris, 332–36; Burrows and Windrem, 275–79.

51. SANDF, "Rafael Eitan to Magnus Malan, June 10, 1981," MV 56/17, vol. 3.

52. SANDF, "Magnus Malan to Rafael Eitan, July 16, 1981," MV 56/17, vol. 3, 10.

53. See SANDF, AMI 520/2/5/6, vol. 6, and MV 56/17, vol. 3.

54. Drew Middleton, "South Africa Needs More Arms, Israeli Says," *New York Times*, December 14, 1981.

55. SANDF, "Magnus Malan to Ariel Sharon," April 26, 1982, MV 56/17, vol. 3, 16.

56. Eitan, 234.

57. SANDF, "Verslag oor besoek van H S.A.W. en Mev Viljoen . . . ," September 21, 1981, MV 56/17/1, vol. 2, Aanhangsel A, Byvoegsel 3.

58. SANDF, "Verslag oor besoek van H S.A.W. en Mev Viljoen aan Taper: 16 tot 24 Julie 1981," September 21, 1981, MV 56/17/1, vol. 2, Aanhangsel D. Viljoen came bearing gifts: Krugerrands and wine for the prime minister and defense officials and six packs of biltong—a form of cured meat beloved by South Africans—for his officers training in Israel.

59. Ibid., Aanhaengsel A, Byvoegsel 7.

60. Goodman, 171–81.

61. Thomas Friedman, "The Beirut Massacre: The Four Days," *New York Times*, September 26, 1982, A1.

62. Robert Fisk, *Pity the Nation* (New York: Atheneum, 1990), 360–61.
63. SANDF, "Verslag aan Minister van Verdediging tov Operasie 'Peace for Galilee,' " July 26, 1982, MV 56/17, vol. 3, 25.
64. SANDF, "Magnus Malan to Ariel Sharon, March 2, 1983," MV 56/17, vol. 3, 31.
65. Larry Gordon, "Occidental Recalls 'Barry Obama,' " *Los Angeles Times*, January 29, 2007, B1; http://www.wavenewspapers.com/special-sections/inauguration-2009/37903139.html.
66. SANDF, "Telegram: Tel Aviv to Secextern Pretoria," November 16, 1981, AMI 105/11/16, vol. 3, 117.
67. SANDF, "Telegram: Hopper to C S.A.D.F. 2," March 31, 1981, AMI 105/11/16, vol. 3, 7.
68. Van der Walt, Steyn, and van Loggerenberg, 13.
69. DFA, "J. P. Hugo to B. G. Walters: Recruitment of Scientific Staff in Israel," January 28, 1980, 1/8/6, vol. 8.
70. SANDF, "Sekerheid: Verhoudings Metro/RSA soos gepubliseer in 'Unnatural Alliance' deur James Adams," May 3, 1984, MI 203/2/16, vol. 26, 65.
71. Both Ivry and Telem claimed in interviews that Israeli arms sold to South Africa were not used domestically. David Ivry, interview by author; Binyamin Telem, interview by author. This argument was also a hallmark of Israeli diplomats' denials at the U.N. and in the press. However, the following document belies the claim that the weapons they sold and attempted to sell were never intended for use against black South Africans: SANDF, "Request: Viewing of New Equipment," December 1, 1983, MI 203/2/16, vol. 24, 71.
72. Ibid.
73. SANDF, "Outstanding Requests as at 29 February 1984," March 1984, MI 203/2/16/1, vol. 5, 38.
74. SANDF, "Register of Exchange Material Passed," March 1985, MI 203/2/16/1, vol. 5, 125–27.
75. Hannes Steyn, interview by author.
76. Jan van Loggerenberg, interview by author.
77. SANDF, "Verslag oor besoek aan Metro: 28 Oktober tot 20 November 1983," January 11, 1984, AMI 520/3/4/6, vol. 20, 142–43. IAI's Bedek division was the primary subcontractor for the massive project to overhaul South Africa's fighter jets.
78. SANDF, "Overseas Visit: Project Boerbok," March 15, 1984, AMI 520/3/4/6, vol. 20, 21–23.
79. Pieter John Roos, interview by author.
80. DFA, "Oorsese Projekbesoek aan Lanvin: Projek Kobalt," March 17, 1986, 1/8/3, vol. 30; Jaster, *The Defence of White Power*, 155; Deon Geldenhuys, *Isolated States: A Comparative Analysis* (Cambridge: Cambridge University Press, 1990), 523.
81. Jan van Loggerenberg, interview by author.
82. SANDF, "Project Brahman Training in Lanvin . . . ," May 13, 1985, AMI/DPO 103/3/4, vol. 12, 89–90.
83. NSA, "D.I.A.: South Africa: The Effect of Economic Sanctions on the Defense Industry (U)," December 1986.
84. CIA, "New Information on South Africa's Nuclear Program and South African–Israeli Nuclear and Military Cooperation," March 30, 1983.

85. David Albright, "A Curious Conversion," *Bulletin of the Atomic Scientists* 49, no. 5 (June 1993): 9.

86. Albright, "South Africa and the Affordable Bomb," 45–46. South African nuclear scientists also began to investigate the production of plutonium and lithium-6, which, in turn, could have one day produced South Africa's own supply of tritium. According to André Buys, the idea was to keep scientists busy with research and development and stop them from resigning, which would have been a major security risk. At the time there was no approval to actually build more advanced warheads or delivery systems. André Buys, interview by author.

87. Although Armscor claims that work on these high-tech weapons was only theoretical, the IAEA did find tritium in the South African inventory when they conducted inspections in the early 1990s. Tritium and deuterium react to increase the number of neutrons and boost the fission reaction with the enriched uranium core.

88. Dieter Gerhardt, interview by author; Tienie Groenewald, interview by author (#2). André Buys disputes these accounts and insists that "Kerktoring" referred exclusively to the missile program. André Buys, interview by author.

89. Badenhorst and Victor, 127–31; Norris et al., 73–75. There is some debate over the range of the system Israel and South Africa were testing at Overberg, which is probably due to uncertainty regarding the size of the payload it would carry if used as a ballistic missile. The Lawrence Livermore National Laboratory calculated that if Israel's Shavit satellite launch vehicle—a three-stage, solid-propellant launcher, the first two stages of which are identical to the Jericho 2—were deployed as a missile, it could travel 3,300 miles, the Pentagon estimated 4,500 miles, and the University of Maryland nuclear expert Steve Fetter calculated a range of 2,500 miles. See http://www.fas.org/nuke/guide/israel/missile/jericho-2.htm; http://www.nti.org/e_research/profiles/Israel/Missile/index.html.

90. SANDF, "Oorsese Besoek: Projek Kerktoring," November 8, 1984, 520/3/4/6, vol. 22.

91. Albright, "South Africa and the Affordable Bomb," 45; "I.A.E.A.: The Agency's Verification Activities in South Africa: Report by the Director General," 7.

92. Purkitt and Burgess, 76.

93. CIA, "New Information on South Africa's Nuclear Program and South African–Israeli Nuclear and Military Cooperation," March 30, 1983.

9 MASTERS OF SPIN

1. DFA, "Discussion Between J. J. Becker and Aharon Shamir," October 3, 1985, 1/8/3, vol. 26. Shamir was the editor of the *Yediot Ahronot* weekly magazine. Becker was the chief director of South Africa's Department of Foreign Affairs.

2. DFA, Miri Paz, "So Long as the State Cultivates Relations with South Africa—Who Are We to Oppose?" (translated), *Davar*, April 29, 1983.

3. DFA, Miri Paz, "Protest in a Colonial Suit" (translated), *Davar*, May 3, 1983.

4. DFA, Nili Nandler, "Sarid Against the Hosting . . . ," (translated), *Haaretz*, June 3, 1983.

5. DFA, Anat Sergoati, "A School Which Was a Center for Socialist Education in Israel Celebrated Friendship with the Fascist Regime in South Africa" (trans-

lated), *Ha'olam ha'zeh*, May 4, 1983; DFA, "Israel Radio 2 Transcript," May 3, 1983, 1/8/3, vol. 16.

6. DFA, "Tamar Mariaz to Shimon Peres," June 1983, 1/8/3, vol. 16.

7. DFA, "Shlomo Lahat to David du Buisson," May 3, 1983, 1/8/3, vol. 17.

8. DFA, "Talk with Professor Marcus Arkin," July 8, 1983, 1/8/3, vol. 17; DFA, "D. S. Franklin to Hertzel Katz," July 13, 1983, 1/8/3, vol. 17.

9. Ted Levite, "Bophuthatswana smee sterk bande met Israel," *Beeld*, November 12, 1981, 2.

10. Roy Isacowitz, "Home Sweet Homeland for Israeli Businessmen," *Rand Daily Mail*, December 3, 1983.

11. "Israel Can't Stop Flag Flying," *Citizen*, May 6, 1985.

12. Isacowitz, "Home Sweet Homeland for Israeli Businessmen"; "Ciskei's Link with Israel Worries Diplomats," *The Star*, October 31, 1984.

13. David Kimche, interview by author (by telephone), Tel Aviv, multiple occasions, December 2004.

14. Isacowitz, "Home Sweet Homeland for Israeli Businessmen."

15. Klieman, 119.

16. Isacowitz, "Home Sweet Homeland for Israeli Businessmen"; "R2m Israeli Factory for Ciskei," *Daily Dispatch*, December 2, 1983. When fifteen Knesset members made plans to attend the opening of the Ciskeian parliament in 1985, it led to a major debate in Israel. In the end, under pressure from their own government, the majority canceled their trip to Ciskei. Nevertheless, the South African Foreign Ministry made a point of meeting with this group of "influential Israelis" before they left the country. Keith Ross, "Israelis to Attend Opening of Ciskei Assembly," *Weekend Post*; "Relief as Israeli MPs Cancel Trip to Ciskei," *Citizen*, April 17, 1985; DFA, "Besoek aan Ciskei en RSA deur 'n groep Knessetlede van Israel," April 10, 1985, 1/8/3, vol. 24.

17. "Exorbitant Israeli Profit by Israeli Firm Is Alleged," *Business Day*, July 11, 1985; "Ciskei's Israelis 'Costly,' " *Citizen*, July 10, 1985; "Commission: Defects in Buildings," *Citizen*, November 12, 1985; "Ciskei Halts Israeli Trade," *Zionist Record*, August 9, 1985.

18. "Bank Hapoalim Jilts South Africans," *Jerusalem Post*, June 6, 1983.

19. DFA, "MK Aloni to Question Minister Shamir on Arms Sales to South Africa," July 1, 1983, 1/8/3, vol. 17.

20. Chazan, "The Fallacies of Pragmatism," 171. Israel was actually getting much more out of the relationship in economic terms. That same year, South African defense minister Magnus Malan wrote a testy letter to his Israeli counterpart, Moshe Arens, telling him, "The imbalance of purchases between our two countries in the military field, is perhaps one of the biggest problems for the continuation of cooperation." He noted that South Africa had poured billions into the Israeli defense industries while only selling $10 million of products. The imbalance was "of such a proportion, that my government must . . . consider alternatives." He proposed the sale of military metals and strategic raw materials to rectify the trade deficit. See SANDF, "Magnus Malan to Moshe Arens," May 18, 1983, MV 56/17, vol. 3.

21. Denis Goldberg, interview by author, Hout Bay, March 8, 2006.

22. Ibid.

23. Jonathan Broder, "Apartheid Fight Still His Passion," *Chicago Tribune*, March 21, 1985, C29.

24. Denis Goldberg, interview by author.
25. Broder, "Apartheid Fight Still His Passion," C29.
26. Denis Goldberg, interview by author.
27. See SANDF, MI 203/2/16/1, vol. 5, 137.
28. Denis Goldberg, interview by author. Goldberg was suspicious of any Israeli overtures and warned his superiors to be cautious, until noted anti-apartheid rabbi Selwyn Franklin asked him to meet with anti-apartheid Israeli government officials.
29. Herbert Rosenberg, the chairman of the Israel–South Africa Friendship League, approached the South African government for money. DFA, "Finansiele hulp aan die Israel-Suid Afrika Vriendskapsliga," June 3, 1986, 1/8/3, vol. 31.
30. See DFA, 1/8/3, vols. 27 and 28.
31. DFA, "Avigdor Eskin and Pinhas Gil to P. W. Botha," July 1, 1986, 1/8/3, vol. 32.
32. DFA, "Telegram: P.F.T. Serfontein to R. Des Marais," July 21, 1986, 1/8/3, vol. 32.
33. "Discussion Between J. J. Becker and Aharon Shamir," 4. The advice of Harvard political scientist Samuel Huntington ("Within limits, reform and repression may proceed hand-in-hand") was also taken as gospel by the South African government. Samuel P. Huntington, "Reform and Stability in South Africa," *International Security* 6, no. 4 (Spring 1982): 19. Huntington's article is adapted from a speech given to the Political Science Association of South Africa in September 1981.
34. "Discussion Between J. J. Becker and Aharon Shamir."
35. Ibid.
36. DFA, "Discussions Between the Chief Director . . . and Mr Ariel Weinstein," March 7, 1986, 1/8/3, vol. 29.
37. Weinstein was right. As former assistant secretary of state for Africa Herman Cohen recalled, there were only a few people left arguing to "leave them alone on apartheid" in 1986, namely White House Communications Director Pat Buchanan and officials at the Pentagon's Defense Intelligence Agency. Herman Cohen, interview by author, Washington, D.C., November 21, 2005.
38. "Discussions between the Chief Director . . . and Mr Ariel Weinstein," 3–4.
39. Adam and Giliomee, 141–42.
40. DFA, "J. J. Becker to J. F. Pretorius," May 21, 1986, 1/8/3, vol. 31. In May 1986, the South African Foreign Ministry decided to use Herbert Rosenberg, executive director of the South African Zionist Federation and a long-standing supporter of close ties with Israel, to lobby British prime minister Margaret Thatcher while she was visiting Ben-Gurion University in Israel. While it may have been preaching to the converted, Israeli Foreign Ministry officials told Rosenberg to "impress upon Mrs. Thatcher the futility and possible disastrous effects of sanctions" in the hope that it would strengthen her opposition to international calls for action against South Africa. The key argument, the diplomats stressed, was that Western leaders "don't recognize the ANC for what they are— a terrorist organization." They believed that Rosenberg, as a Zionist leader, would be the ideal messenger; DFA, "J. F. Pretorius to J. J. Becker," May 22, 1986, 1/8/3, vol. 31.
41. Herman Cohen, interview by author. His predecessor, Chester Crocker, was a leading advocate of the anti-sanctions, constructive-engagement approach. Crocker attributes the failure to ward off sanctions to a speech written by Pat

Buchanan, who, as Cohen mentioned, was one of the last holdouts in believing that South Africa deserved support as a bulwark against communism. Crocker claims, "We had a speech written for [Reagan] that would convey a sense of leadership, of holding hands with the victims of apartheid oppression." Instead, Buchanan wrote the speech. It was a coup for the South African propaganda machine. "There were actually phrases in the president's speech . . . written by South African officials." Chester Crocker, interview by author, Washington, D.C., November 15, 2005.

42. DFA, "J. J. Becker to Director General," January 24, 1986, 1/8/3, vol. 28.
43. DFA, "Press Release, Embassy of Israel, Vienna," July 4, 1983, 1/8/3, vol. 32.
44. The intense tension and ideological disagreement between Israel's Foreign and Defense Ministries, as well as the Defense Ministry's habit of running foreign policy in certain countries without the knowledge of the Foreign Ministry, is discussed elsewhere.
45. DFA, "South African Ambassador, Vienna to Director General, Pretoria," July 15, 1983, 1/8/3, vol. 17.
46. DFA, "C.B.C. Sunday Morning: Israel and South Africa" (transcript), July 31, 1983, 1/8/3, vol. 17.
47. DFA, "The Battle Against Apartheid (Statement in the General Assembly by Benjamin Netanyahu)," November 6, 1986, 1/8/3, vol. 33, 2.
48. Ibid., 3.
49. Ibid., 7.
50. The ANC leadership in exile initially preferred to avoid pointing fingers that would expose the hypocrisy of some of their professed allies in the Arab world. And so it was decided that the names of certain countries would not be specified. Finally, the ANC relented. By 1985, the Shipping Research Bureau felt its credibility was endangered due to the incomplete reporting, and it began publishing the full lists with the consent of the ANC. Richard Hengeveld and Jaap Rodenburg, eds., *Embargo: Apartheid's Oil Secrets Revealed* (Amsterdam: University of Amsterdam, 1995), 98–99.
51. Ibid., 105.
52. Paul Aarts and Tom de Quaasteniet, "Putting Money over Mouth, Profit over Principle: Arab and Iranian Oil Sales to South Africa, 1973–1993," in Hengeveld and Rodenburg, eds., 274–77. See also Arthur Jay Klinghoffer, *Oiling the Wheels of Apartheid: Exposing South Africa's Secret Oil Trade* (Boulder: Lynne Rienner, 1989).
53. DFA, "The Battle Against Apartheid" (Statement in the General Assembly by Benjamin Netanyahu), 10.
54. Hengeveld and Rodenburg, eds., 98.
55. See Resolution 35/206 D, adopted by the United Nations General Assembly on December 16, 1980, at http://www.anc.org.za/un/reddy/oilembargo.html.
56. Yosef Abramowitz, *Jews, Zionism and South Africa* (Washington, D.C.: B'nai B'rith Hillel Foundations, 1985), 6.
57. Yosef Abramowitz, e-mail correspondence with author, March 2009.
58. Yosef Abramowitz, 6.
59. Ibid., 18.
60. "Israeli Links with South Africa," *Intelligence Digest*, September 1, 1984.
61. AFD, "Armscor Confidential Information: Bestel/Verskaffer Report," July 11,

2006. Also see graphs based on Armscor data and IMF Direction of Trade Statistics data in Sasha Polakow-Suransky, "The Unspoken Alliance: Israel and Apartheid South Africa, 1960–1994" (Ph.D. diss., University of Oxford, 2007), 220–22.

62. Marcus Arkin, "Rejecting Apartheid," *South African Jewish Times*, July 5, 1985.

63. Mervyn Smith, interview by author. According to Smith, a liberal member of the Cape Town Board of Deputies at the time, many of his colleagues were paranoid and argued that "anything the Jewish community says in this country against the apartheid regime will result in damage to Israel. . . . They'll stop the money going out, they'll stop the special relationship . . . they'll stop everything."

64. SANDF, "Request: Viewing of New Equipment," December 1, 1983, MI 203/2/16, vol. 24, 71.

65. George E. Gruen and Kenneth Bandler, *Israel and South Africa* (New York: American Jewish Committee, 1985), 4–5.

66. Suzanne Golubski, "Koch Flunks Out," *New York Daily News*, May 14, 1985.

67. Dr. Vitenberg, "Israel et l'Afrique du Sud," *France-Israel Information*, Juin/Juillet 1987.

68. DFA, "S.A.W. Besoek aan Israel," September 27, 1988, 1/8/3, vol. 38.

10 LOSING THE LEFT

1. Jonathan Kaufman, *Broken Alliance: The Turbulent Times Between Blacks and Jews in America* (New York: Touchstone, 1995), 2–3. See also "Jews and Blacks in America, 1909–2009," *Moment*, January–February 2009, 34–44.

2. Glenda Elizabeth Gilmore, *Defying Dixie: The Radical Roots of Civil Rights, 1919–1950* (New York: W. W. Norton, 2008), 168–69.

3. Walter Russell Mead, "The New Israel and the Old," *Foreign Affairs* (July–August 2008), 41; Adam Clayton Powell Jr., *Adam by Adam: The Autobiography of Adam Clayton Powell, Jr.* (New York: Kensington, 1971). Powell says the amount was $150,000; Mead says it was $15,000.

4. Ronald Radosh and Allis Radosh, "Righteous Among the Editors: When the Left Loved Israel," *World Affairs*, Summer 2008, 65–75.

5. Kaufman, 202.

6. For a fuller scholarly treatment of this debate, see Penslar, 90–111.

7. Lipset, " 'The Socialism of Fools': The Left, the Jews, and Israel," in Chertoff, ed., *The New Left and the Jew*.

8. Ibid., 128.

9. Michael Feher, "The Schisms of '67," in *Blacks and Jews: Alliances and Arguments*, ed. Paul Berman (New York: Delacorte, 1994), 268, 278.

10. Kaufman, 207.

11. Ibid., 208–9.

12. Renata Adler, "Letter from the Palmer House," *The New Yorker*, September 23, 1967.

13. Kaufman, 209.

14. Berman, *A Tale of Two Utopias*, 93–95.

15. Berman, ed., *Blacks and Jews*, 16–17.

16. Leonard Fein, "The New Left and Israel," in Chertoff, *The New Left and the Jews*, 179.

17. Devin W. Carbado and Donald Weise, eds., *Time on Two Crosses: The Collected Writings of Bayard Rustin* (San Francisco: Cleis, 2003), 319. Writing in 1974, Rustin was wrong to state that Israel was "a consistent supporter of the freedom movements in Angola and Mozambique." By then, the alliance with South Africa was well under way.

18. Ibid., 321–25.

19. James Zogby, interview by author, Washington, D.C., September 20, 2007.

20. Lipset, 122.

21. Carbado and Weise, eds., 321; Berman, *A Tale of Two Utopias*, 271–73.

22. Kaufman, 214–17.

23. Ibid., 246.

24. Ibid., 272–73.

25. Ibid., 232.

26. James Zogby and Jack O'Dell, eds., *Afro-Americans Stand Up for Middle East Peace* (Palestine Human Rights Campaign, 1979), 13.

27. Ibid., 8–9.

28. JBOD, "B'nai B'rith International Resolution No. 83–106: Opposition to Apartheid," December 6, 1983, Public Relations Files, 1980–1990.

29. JBOD, "Telegram from Charles Glick to Warren Eisenberg," December 21, 1983, Public Relations Files, 1980–1990.

30. Diana Aviv, interview by author (by telephone), February 22, 2008.

31. Kaufman, 248–49.

32. James Zogby, interview by author.

33. Kaufman, 250–51.

34. Ibid., 256–57.

35. Ibid., 256–61.

36. See Glenn Frankel and David Ottaway, "Emergency Shatters Botha's Vision," *Washington Post*, July 28, 1985, A1.

37. For an early formulation of the constructive engagement policy, see Chester Crocker, "South Africa: Strategy for Change," *Foreign Affairs* (Winter 1980–1981). Crocker was named assistant secretary of state for Africa a few months after his article was published.

38. NSA, "Meeting with the National Security Council," September 5, 1985.

39. Ibid., 3.

40. DFA, "Connections Between South Africa and Israel" (PBS transcript), March 18, 1986, 1/8/3, vol. 30.

41. Ibid., 8.

42. Thomas Friedman, "Israel Will Curb Arms to Pretoria," *New York Times*, March 18, 1987. Friedman's numbers exceed the 1986 amount from Armscor's financial data because that amount excludes joint ventures.

43. AFD, "Armscor Confidential Information: Bestel/Verskaffer Report," July 11, 2006.

44. SANDF, "Anton van Graan to Constand Viljoen," March 12, 1985, AMI 520/3/4/6, vol. 24, 21–22.

45. Reliable IMF data for South Africa prior to 1994 does not exist. I have therefore attempted to illustrate the financial dimensions of the relationship through Israeli import-export data amended with the Armscor data. See graphs based on Armscor data and IMF Direction of Trade Statistics data in Polakow-Suransky,

283

220–22. It should be noted that the dollar amounts between 1980–1990 are distorted due to the precipitous devaluation of the rand during that period, from a value of more than $1.25 to less than $0.40 against the dollar. Therefore, the actual rand outlays did not drop significantly between 1980 and 1983 as the dollar amounts suggest and they increased far more dramatically between 1984 and 1987 than the dollar figures indicate. Due to the volatility of the South African rand over the course of the period in question, all values have been converted to U.S. dollars, on an annual basis, using the historical exchange rate tables of the South African Reserve Bank available at: http://www.resbank.co.za/economics/histdownload/histdownload.htm.

46. Hayden has since retracted, claiming, "I was Israel's dupe." See http://www.counterpunch.org/hayden07202006.html.
47. Tom Tugend, "Centre Forward," *Jerusalem Post Magazine*, April 18, 1986, 8.
48. Shlaim, 426–27.
49. Shimshon Zelniker, interview by author, Jerusalem, December 2, 2004.
50. Ibid.
51. David Ariel, interview by author, Jerusalem, December 22, 2004.
52. DFA, "National Intelligence Service Document No. 86005340," January 31, 1986, 1/8/3, vol. 28.
53. DFA, "Colonel J. M. Barnard to the Director General, Foreign Affairs," January 30, 1986, 1/8/3, vol. 28. This flatly contradicts the thesis put forward by Jane Hunter and other left-wing critics who regarded the Histadrut program as helpful to the South African government. See Jane Hunter, *Israeli Foreign Policy: South Africa and Central America* (Nottingham: Bertrand Russell Peace Foundation, 1987), 81–84.
54. DFA, "Collaboration Between the Afro-Asian Institute of Tel Aviv and South African Black Organisations," December 17, 1985, 1/8/3, vol. 27.
55. Howard Wolpe, interview by author, Washington D.C., September 24, 2007.
56. "Buthelezi Calls for Bridge Between Zulus and Jews," *S.A. Jewish Times*, September 13, 1985.
57. Dan Fisher, "Israeli Project Aims at Ties to S. Africa Blacks," *Los Angeles Times*, March 30, 1986.
58. Michael Precker, "Israel Cultivating Ties with Black S. Africans," *Dallas Morning News*, April 7, 1986.
59. JBOD, "Kenneth Jacobson to A.D.L. Regional Offices," April 16, 1986, International Relations Files.
60. DFA, "Press Conference Held at the Afro-Asian Institute" April 7, 1986, 1/8/3, vol. 30, 4.
61. Dan Fisher, "S. African Blacks See Israel Training as Aid for Future," *Los Angeles Times*, April 8, 1986.
62. "Press Conference Held at the Afro-Asian Institute," 16. Yehuda Paz, the Afro-Asian Institute director, attempted to cool things down by incorrectly telling the audience that "Israel's share in the arms supply to South Africa is small," assuring them that France's contribution to arming the apartheid state was "20 times as great." Even though their numbers were wildly off, Paz and Zelniker stressed their commitment to changing Israeli policy and ending military ties.
63. SANDF, "Verslag oor die inligtingskonferensie . . . ," February 7–14, 1986, MI 205/17/208/TK, 145.

64. SANDF, "Biologiese en Chemiese Oorlogvoering (BCO): SAW Beleid," September 29, 1987, MI 306/3, vol. 1, 45.

65. Thomas Friedman, "In Cameroon, Scenes from a Valley of Death," *New York Times*, August 26, 1986, A1. In Cameroon, there is a widely accepted conspiracy theory that Israel tested a neutron bomb in Lake Nyos, killing living organisms in the area and leaving structures intact. The rapid response by Israeli doctors and Peres's arrival soon after the disaster—after thirteen years of silence—is taken as evidence that Israel conducted a clandestine test and sought to repay Cameroon with aid and medical assistance. Geologists and ecologists who have studied the incident have found ample scientific evidence of a toxic gas eruption. See George Kling et al., "The 1986 Lake Nyos Gas Disaster in Cameroon, West Africa," *Science* 236, no. 4798 (1987): 169–75.

66. DFA, "J. Kilian to R. Desmarais," August 25, 1986, 1/8/3, vol. 32, 3.

67. DFA, "Sanksies Teen die R.S.A. in die Amerikaanse Senaat," August 26, 1986, 1/8/3, vol. 32.

68. "Cameroonians Greet Israelis in Exuberant Hebrew," *New York Times*, August 25, 1986, A2.

69. Dan Fisher, "Visit to Cameroon Underscores Israeli Gains," *Los Angeles Times*, August 26, 1986, A1.

70. DFA, "Sanksies teen die R.S.A. in die Amerikaanse Senaat"; Fisher, "Visit to Cameroon Underscores Israeli Gains," A1.

71. As reproduced in Rhoodie, 117.

11 FORKED TONGUES

1. DFA, "Press Conference Held at the Afro-Asian Institute" (transcript), April 7, 1986, 1/8/3, vol. 30, 11.

2. DFA, "Knesset Session 215: The State of Emergency in South Africa" (translated transcript), June 18, 1986, 7.

3. Shlaim, 424–25.

4. "Knesset Session 215: The State of Emergency in South Africa," 8, 12.

5. Ibid., 17.

6. Ibid., 16.

7. Ibid., 28.

8. *Divrei Ha'Knesset* (Jerusalem: The Knesset), October 11, 1986.

9. "Knesset Session 215: The State of Emergency in South Africa," 43.

10. Ibid., 26.

11. Yossi Beilin, interview by author, Tel Aviv, December 15, 2004.

12. Ibid.

13. For an excellent summary of the debate as it began to unfold in early 1987, see Thomas Friedman, "Israelis Reassess Supplying Arms to South Africa," *New York Times*, January 29, 1987.

14. David Ariel, interview by author.

15. Yossi Beilin, interview by author.

16. *Divrei Ha'Knesset* (Jerusalem: The Knesset), June 11, 1986.

17. AFD, "Armscor Confidential Information: Bestel/Verskaffer Report," July 11, 2006.

18. Thomas Friedman, "How Israel's Economy Got Hooked on Selling Arms Abroad," *New York Times*, December 7, 1986, C1.

19. Yonatan Sherman, "D'rom Afrika: Ha'heshbon ha'kalkali," *Haaretz*, March 20, 1987.

20. Gabriel Shtrasman, "Apartheid v'tzviyut," *Maariv*, March 22, 1987.

21. Akiva Eldar, "B'zchot ha'tzviyut," *Haaretz*, January 25, 1987; Akiva Eldar, "Rov ha'sarai ha'likud b'kabinet neged itzumim al D'rom Afrika," *Haaretz*, March 18, 1987.

22. Yoel Markus, "Inianim Katnunaim," *Haaretz*, March 20, 1987.

23. DFA, Amnon Abramovich, "Value Sensitivity and Adolescent Innocence" (translated), *Maariv*, January 30, 1987.

24. Alon Liel, interview by author, Tel Aviv, December 3, 2004.

25. These days, India has come to fill a similar role in buying large quantities of weapons and stimulating the Israeli arms industry. See Thomas Withington, "Israel and India Partner Up," *Bulletin of the Atomic Scientists* 57, no. 1 (2001): 18–19.

26. USNA, "Legislative Activities Report, Senate Committee on Foreign Relations, Report 100–28," March 31, 1987, 52–53.

27. USNA, "Mark-up of S. 2701, the Comprehensive Anti-Apartheid Act of 1986," August 1, 1986.

28. DFA, "V.S.A. aksies ten einde militere samewerking tussen Israel en Suid-Afrika . . . ," April 3, 1987, 1/8/3, vol. 34.

29. Douglas Bloomfield, interview by author (by telephone), February 14, 2008.

30. Ibid.

31. For an outline of Reagan's preferred policy, see NSA, "United States Policy Toward South Africa," September 7, 1985.

32. So did the Anti-Defamation League. When the National Jewish Community Relations Advisory Council proposed sending a letter to members of Congress, urging them to override President Reagan's veto of the South Africa sanctions bill, the ADL exercised its own veto power to stop the letter. The ADL's national chairman cited the wishes of the South African Jewish community as his motive. DFA, "Burton Levinson to Albert Chernin," September 26, 1986, 1/8/3, vol. 33.

33. Douglas Bloomfield, interview by author.

34. Roy Isacowitz, "Why Israel Is Unlikely to Opt for Sanctions," *Jerusalem Post*, July 26, 1986.

35. David Ariel, interview by author. Even former ambassador Yitzhak Unna, an outspoken critic of apartheid, told the press, "The Afrikaner feeling of isolation, the fear that comes from being an outnumbered and disliked minority, should certainly strike a chord in our own memories. . . . As Israelis and Jews we should feel a tie to them."

36. Alon Liel, interview by author; Dan Raviv and Yossi Melman, "Has Congress Doomed Israel's Affair with South Africa?," *Washington Post*, February 22, 1987.

37. Privately it was another matter; Rabin had assured the South Africans that the changes would be cosmetic. DFA, "Visit of Messrs Alon Liel and M Padan," February 18, 1987, 1/8/3, vol. 34.

38. JBOD, "Israel's Policy Toward South Africa. Cabinet Decisions 16 September 1987," September 16, 1987, Israel Correspondence Files, 1980–1990; Meron Medzini, ed., *Israel's Foreign Relations: Selected Documents, 1984–1988*, vol. 2 (Jerusalem: Ministry of Foreign Affairs, 1989), 696.

39. USNA, "Report to Congress Pursuant to Section 508 of the Comprehensive Anti-Apartheid Act of 1986: Compliance with the U.N. Arms Embargo," April 1,

1987. The report accuses France and Italy of violating the embargo after 1977 and names private companies in Germany, the United Kingdom, Switzerland, and the Netherlands of exporting prohibited items without the permission of their governments.

40. Ibid., 2.

41. Ibid., 3. Responding to questions in the Knesset two weeks after the congressional report, Defense Minister Rabin insisted that "there is no governmental decision in this spirit. From time to time, the industries themselves plan their manufacturing according to orders of the defense system and according to export feasibility." Faced with questions about arms exports from Amira Sartani, Rabin responded cryptically, telling members that "the criteria for receiving an arms trading permit are among others: The exported product, the destination countries, the purchaser's ties with the product and exporting country, and the marketing arrangement that he maintains with the export country, the reliability of the buyer and the security classification of the product." *Divrei Ha'Knesset* (Jerusalem: The Knesset), April 12, 1987.

42. Israel Radio interview with Yossi Beilin and Moshe Arens (translated transcript), April 3, 1987, 1–2. Former ambassador Yitzhak Unna also took to the airwaves to criticize the decision. For the other side of the debate, see an article by Katya Gibel-Azoulay, "Rather Than Curse the Darkness: A Call for Mobilization," *New Outlook*, March 1987. Gibel-Azoulay was then Naomi Chazan's research assistant.

43. Lili Galili, "Lo Shachor/Lavan," *Haaretz*, November 15, 1985; Begin had first tried to send his friend to London, but the British government made it clear that an erstwhile anti-British revolutionary like Lankin would never be welcome as ambassador.

44. Ibid.

45. Eliahu Lankin, "Unfair Pressure," *Jerusalem Post*, April 18, 1987.

46. Goodman 159–60; Eitan, 247–48.

47. "Raful: Anachnu c'mo ha'miyut ha'lavan b'D'rom Afrika," *Yediot Ahronot*, December 25, 1987.

48. Tehiya split from Likud in 1978 in opposition to the Camp David Accords. Tzomet refused to join Rabin's government in 1992 and became part of Likud in 1996.

49. DFA, "Rafael Eitan to E. Anton Loubser," May 29, 1987, 1/8/3, vol. 34.

50. A February 1987 *Newsweek* report that "Israeli Defense Minister Yitzhak Rabin made a brief, top-secret visit to South Africa recently, warning government leaders there that Israel would soon have to 'lower its profile' as a supplier of arms and military expertise to Pretoria" seems to confirm Ivry's version of events. Lucy Howard, "Lower Profile," *Newsweek*, February 2, 1987, 4.

51. David Ivry, interview by author. Ivry may be correct that the top brass recognized the need to cool off relations with South Africa, but it was Beilin who spearheaded the effort in the face of resistance from Moshe Arens and other military figures who did not wish to go as far. An alternative interpretation of Beilin's and Ivry's is that the United States was fed up with the capture of Israeli spy Jonathan Pollard and sensitive to Israeli arms-trade allegations, given Israel's role in funneling arms to Iran and the Nicaraguan contras during the Iran-contra scandal. Public statements attributing the 1987 decision on the Pollard

affair were made by former ambassador Yitzhak Unna after passage of the cabinet resolution. See also Reiser, 141.

52. Shlomo Gur, interview by author, Tel Aviv, December 7, 2004.

53. Princeton Lyman, interview by author, Washington, D.C., November 21, 2005.

54. DFA, "Notule van 'n interdepartementale vergadering," April 1, 1987, 1/8/3, vol. 34.

55. David Ariel, "The Future of SA-Israeli Relations," *Jewish Affairs* (May 1987): 15–17.

56. JBOD, "Proposed Framework for Memorandum . . . ," May 1987, Israel Correspondence Files, 1980–1990.

57. Yossi Beilin, interview by author. Kaplan claims he told Beilin, "Yossi, my interest is the Jewish community of South Africa. I've got to maintain strong relations between South Africa and Israel." Mendel Kaplan, interview by author.

58. Alon Liel, interview by author. They could not compete because the International Olympic Committee would exclude Israel if it didn't maintain a sports boycott of South Africa.

59. JBOD, "Aide Memoire," April 29, 1987, Israel Correspondence Files, 1980–1990.

60. Dennis Davis, "An Unholy Alliance," *Strike*, 1987 (undated); Shimoni, *Community and Conscience*, 211–12. Shimoni argues that "it may well be suggested that sheer cognitive dissonance placed them in a state of denial in this regard." Rabbi Selwyn Franklin of Cape Town's Sea Point congregation was one notable exception. Franklin openly spoke out against the cooperation between the two governments, especially its military aspects, which he feared would antagonize black South Africans and be detrimental to the Jewish community's and Israel's interests. When it came to military cooperation, South African Jewish leaders did not distinguish between normal trade and arms sales. Shimoni defends the board's opposition to Israeli sanctions as a natural reaction to global anti-Semitism, arguing that "precisely because denunciation of Israel's relations with South Africa was suffused with patently anti-Semitic motifs, Zionist counterpropaganda went a long way toward satisfying the almost existential need felt by Jews to justify these relations." While Shimoni is correct that certain critics of the Israeli–South African alliance were no doubt also anti-Semites, the Jewish community's enthusiastic support for the alliance and its resistance to sanctions had far more basic motives: it was simply a way to protect their own financial interests while denying the true basis of the relationship.

61. Trita Parsi, interview by author (by telephone), February 29, 2008. Even so, most Iranian Jews who remained did so willingly and their fate was never the overriding priority for the Israeli government. Much more important were strategic considerations and a desire to remain on good terms with a former ally.

62. Reiser, 214.

63. This is confirmed by Steven Weissman, who served on the staff of the House Foreign Affairs Committee at the time. Steven Weissman, interview by author, Washington, D.C., October 19, 2007.

64. Benny Morris, "D.C. Lobby Urges Sanctions Against SA," *Jerusalem Post*, July 18, 1987.

65. Medzini, ed., 696.

66. DFA, "Von Hirschberg to Du Buisson," August 10, 1987, 1/8/3, vol. 35. It

appears that officials in Pretoria were drawing on information provided by South Africans with close contacts in AIPAC or the Israeli government. See also DFA, "Visit of Messrs Alon Liel and M Padan," February 18, 1987, 1/8/3, vol. 34.

67. DFA, "South African Inventions Development Corporation Re: Israeli Trade Sanctions," March 23, 1987, 1/8/3, vol. 34.

68. DFA, "Reg Donner to F. G. Conradie," January 5, 1988, 1/8/3, vol. 36.

69. Chaim Even-Zohar, interview by author.

70. Chaim Even-Zohar, *From Mine to Mistress: Corporate Strategies and Government Policies in the International Diamond Industry* (Edenbridge, U.K.: Mining Journal Books, 2007), 167; Chaim Even-Zohar, correspondence with author, November 2006.

71. Eliahu Lankin, "Yachaso shel ha ma'arav l'D'rom Afrika . . . ," *Nativ* (May 1988): 33–34.

72. Ibid.; Rafael Medoff and Mordechai Haller, "South Africa in the Mind of Israel," *National Review*, April 15, 1988; DFA, "Book Proposal: South Africa: The Jewish Dilemma," June 10, 1988, 1/8/3, vol. 37. The South African Foreign Ministry was prepared to pay Medoff $15,000 to complete the book. According to a curt 2006 e-mail from Medoff to the author, the project never came to fruition.

73. DFA, "Ambassadeur Viljoen se gesprekke met Israeli Eerste Minister . . . ," August 24, 1988, 1/8/3, vol. 38.

74. Ibid., 3.

75. Ibid., 6.

76. DFA, "R.F. Botha to Magnus Malan," October 6, 1988, 1/8/3, vol. 38.

77. DFA, "Reserwebankgoedkeuring vir die oordrag van fondse geskenk deur sekere Joodse besigheidslui aan die Herut Party in Israel," July 19, 1988, 1/8/3, vol. 38.

78. DFA, "J.W.H. Meiring to B. J. du Plessis," October 1988, 1/8/3, vol. 38; DFA, "B. J. du Plessis to R.F. Botha," October 21, 1988, 1/8/3, vol. 38.

79. This pattern is remarkably similar to Israel's treatment of Iran prior to 1979. See Parsi, *Treacherous Alliance*.

80. Wolf Blitzer, "A Very Delicate Tightrope," *Jerusalem Post Magazine*, December 16, 1988.

81. Robert I. Friedman, "How the Anti-Defamation League Turned the Notion of Human Rights on Its Head, Spying on Progressives and Funneling Information to Law Enforcement," *Village Voice*, May 11, 1993, 28.

82. Eric Pace, "Irwin Suall, Fierce Fighter of Bias for A.D.L., Dies at 73," *New York Times*, August 20, 1998.

83. Robert I. Friedman, "How the Anti-Defamation League Turned the Notion of Human Rights on Its Head," 32.

84. Ibid., 27.

85. JBP, "S.F.P.D. Interview of Roy Bullock," January 25, 1993, 97.

86. Nathan Perlmutter and David Evanier, "The African National Congress: A Closer Look," *ADL Bulletin* (May 1986).

87. JBP, "F.B.I. Interview of Roy Bullock, January 22, 1993," 8.

88. JBP, "McCloskey Deposition of Roy Bullock," January 1993, 34.

89. Ibid., 35.

90. "F.B.I. Interview of Roy Bullock, January 22, 1993," 11–12.

91. "McCloskey Deposition of Roy Bullock"; JBP, "S.F.P.D. Interview of David Gurvitz," January 28, 1993, 352–53.

92. "F.B.I. Interview of Roy Bullock, January 22, 1993," 12. As his ADL colleague David Gurvitz told the San Francisco police, "He also mentioned to me, it wasn't any great effort . . . on his behalf because he was doing that kind of work anyway for the ADL." "S.F.P.D. Interview of David Gurvitz," 22.

93. "F.B.I. Interview of Roy Bullock, January 22, 1993," 15.

94. Ibid., 16.

95. JBP, "F.B.I. Interview of Roy Bullock, January 26, 1993," 7.

96. "F.B.I. Interview of Roy Bullock, January 26, 1993," 5; "S.F.P.D. Interview of Roy Bullock, January 25, 1993," 176.

97. Ibid., 177.

98. Ibid., 194.

99. "F.B.I. Interview of Roy Bullock, January 26, 1993," 17.

100. Howard Wolpe, interview by author.

101. Diana Aviv, interview by author; Alan Riding, "Mandela Moves to Reassure Visiting Group of U.S. Jews," *New York Times,* June 11, 1990.

102. Letter to the Editor, *New York Times,* June 24, 1990.

103. "S.F.P.D. Interview of Roy Bullock, January 25, 1993," 183-84.

12 THE END OF THE AFFAIR

1. Hugh Davies, "Israel Is Helping S Africa to Build Rockets, Says US," *Daily Telegraph*, October 28, 1989.

2. Seegers, 224-32.

3. Ibid., 259.

4. SANDF, "Visit to Defender by Mission Controllers," April 5, 1988, AMI 520/3/4/6, vol. 33, 10; SANDF, "Project Brahman: Project Team Visit to Defender 9–26 July 1988," April 22, 1988, AMI 520/3/4/6, vol. 33, 26–29.

5. SANDF, "Project Emblazon: Overseas Visit: Visit to Defender," May 25, 1988, AMI 520/3/4/6, vol. 33, 91–95.

6. Peres had authorized the project as a measure of pride and self-sufficiency. But by 1980 there was strong U.S. opposition. Washington was being lobbied by the Northrop Corporation not to allow American military aid to be used to fund the Lavi. They were developing the F-20 fighter at the time and the Lavi was seen as a direct competitive threat. Furthermore, the American arms industry wished to see defense aid from Washington reinjected into the U.S. economy rather than Israel's. This, coupled with ballooning research and development costs, dampened enthusiasm for the Lavi. Key Israeli hawks began to turn against the project as it consumed more and more of the national budget. Israel Military Industries employees were being laid off and Israel Aircraft Industries was losing other contracts. Professor Pinchas Zussman at the Defense Ministry called it "the lion that may eat all the other small animals." For an in-depth discussion of the Lavi's rise and fall, see Reiser, 171–85.

7. "U.S.D.A.O. Pretoria S.F. to D.I.A. Washington D.C." Reiser has also noted that many of the Lavi engineers opted for jobs in South Africa. Pentagon analysts were skeptical that the South African fighter jet would ever get off the ground. "Although some technology transfer will come this way as a result of the cancellation of the *Lavi* . . . do not expect to see the 'young lion' patrolling the Bushveldt any time soon," the analysts predicted. After all, the DIA argued, "If the *Lavi* was too expensive for the Israelis it would prove doubly so for the

South Africans since they often have to pay twice the normal price for high tech items." Still, for a few years, South Africa poured money into the project. In 1989, American intelligence picked up on Israel's involvement. "The SADF/ Armscor has recently taken delivery of an unknown number of Israeli manufactured J79 engines. It is assumed that the engines will be employed in some kind of upgrade program for the Cheetah," the DIA noted. General Tienie Groenewald claims the government spent billions of rand in the late 1980s trying to develop the Cava fighter. But in the end it went nowhere. The DIA had seen the writing on the wall. Given the new political circumstances, there was simply no need for such an advanced new aircraft. And so, like the Lavi, the Cava was scrapped. "U.S.D.A.O. Pretoria S.F. to D.I.A. Washington D.C."; NSA, "U.S.D.A.O. Harare to D.I.A.," February 1, 1989; Tienie Groenewald, interview by author (#1); Pieter John Roos, interview by author.

8. Warren Strobel, "U.S. Plans Talks with Israel on Project with S. Africa," *Washington Times*, October 31, 1989.

9. Burrows and Windrem, 445–48.

10. "D.I.A.: Special Assessment: South Africa: Missile Activity (U)," 1–2.

11. CIA, "South Africa: Igniting a Missile Race?," December 8, 1989, 7. Both reports remain heavily redacted so the full extent of American knowledge of the cooperation remains a mystery.

12. Michael R. Gordon, "U.S. Sees Israeli Help in Pretoria's Missile Work," *New York Times*, October 27, 1989.

13. David Albright and Mark Hibbs, "South Africa: The A.N.C. and the Atom Bomb," *Bulletin of the Atomic Scientists* 49, no. 3 (April 1993): 36. As André Buys notes, "We had a look at the rockets that were being developed for launching the satellites and these could also potentially be used as the means of delivery for a warhead." However, he adds, "it was never approved that we should equip those missiles, it was an R&D program and by the time the program was terminated that decision had still not been taken." André Buys, interview by author.

14. Some observers believe that Bush was angry about the transfer of American parts to South Africa by Israel. Purkitt and Burgess, 75. See also Burrows and Windrem, 448–49; Strobel, "U.S. Plans Talks with Israel on Project with S. Africa," A7. The Pentagon was angry, too, and publicly objected to the sale of two IBM supercomputers to the Haifa Technion (also known as the Israel Institute of Technology) allegedly because of their ability to simulate nuclear explosions.

15. Zvi Gov-Ari, interview by author, Yavne, December 21, 2004.

16. Shlomo Brom, interview by author, Tel Aviv, December 15, 2004.

17. See Rees and Day, 200.

18. *The Southern Africa Policy Forum* (Queenstown, MD: Aspen Institute, 1989). See also subsequent reports from 1990–1993; Dick Clark, interview by author. The NP refused to come when the ANC was present, hence the separate seminars.

19. Elazar Granot, interview by author, Kibbutz Shoval, December 15, 2004.

20. See Alon Liel, *Tzedek Shachor* (Tel Aviv: Ha'kibbutz ha'meuchad, 1999).

21. DFA, "Malcolm Ferguson to D. W. Auret: Israeli Assessment of Developments in South Africa, July 23, 1993, 1/8/3, vol. 44, 5.

22. Ibid., 3–4.

23. "Telegram: Malcolm Ferguson to D. W. Auret: Meeting with Prime Minister Rabin and David Ivri," August 19, 1993, July 23, 1993, 4.

24. Ibid.

25. Purkitt and Burgess, 120; André Buys, interview by author.

26. Princeton Lyman, interview by author.

27. Jackson Diehl, "Israel, Pressured by U.S., Puts Limits on Its Export of Missile Technology," *Washington Post*, October 3, 1991.

28. Harry Schwarz, interview by author.

29. NSA, "Telegram: Secretary of State Washington DC to American Embassy Pretoria," November 5, 1991.

30. Princeton Lyman, interview by author.

31. Van der Walt, Steyn, and van Loggerenberg, 102.

32. "Atoomgeheime: Kernmanne vra te veel, se Denel werkloses dreig hulle vertel alles," *Beeld*, March 28, 1994; "Wetenskaplikes Mag Nie Praat oor Kerngeheime," *Beeld*, March 30, 1994; also see Purkitt and Burgess, 76.

33. Peter Hounam and Steve McQuillan, *The Mini-Nuke Conspiracy: Mandela's Nuclear Nightmare* (New York: Viking, 1995), 268. More recently, similar allegations have emerged in Badenhorst and Victor, *Those Who Had the Bomb*.

34. Hounam and McQuillan, 134–49.

35. "I.A.E.A.: The Agency's Verification Activities in South Africa: Report by the Director General," 10–11.

36. Stumpf, 7.

37. F. W. de Klerk, "Speech on the Nonproliferation Treaty to a Joint Session of Parliament, March 24, 1993," in *Joint Publications Research Service* (Proliferation Issues), March 29, 1993.

38. Paul Stober, "De Klerk's Three Nuclear Lies," *Weekly Mail & Guardian*, February 11, 1994.

39. André Buys disputes the contention that de Klerk lied. He helped to draft the speech and claims that "this wording was very carefully considered." Equipment that could be used for both nuclear weapons and peaceful purposes (dual-use technology) was not defined as "nuclear weapons technology" for the purposes of the speech. Nor was yellowcake or components of delivery systems that could be used for either conventional or nuclear weapons. André Buys, interview by author. Buys is correct that by this extremely restrictive definition, de Klerk did not lie. However, it is my contention that de Klerk was fully aware of the cooperation and that his advisers sought to absolve other parties of responsibility by way of clever semantics.

40. SANDF, "Overseas Visit: S.A.A.F.: Project Tunny: Israel . . . ," April 25, 1994, AMI 520/3/4/6, vol. 55, 40.

41. Other analysts have linked the Cava project, discussed above, to Project Tunny. The archives confirm that Tunny was an Israeli update of Cheetah weapons and avionics but there is no reference to it prior to the early 1990s. If the Cava project was scrapped in the late 1980s as suggested by Groenewald and Roos, then Tunny was simply a less ambitious and less costly program of a related nature. See Badenhorst and Victor, 108.

42. SANDF, "Buitelandse Besoek: S.A.L.M.: Projek Tunny: Israel," May 12, 1993, AMI 520/3/4/6, vol. 53, 97.

43. SANDF, "Project Tunny: Visit to Israel: 1 Jun to 2 Jul 93," May 3, 1993, AMI 520/3/4/6, vol. 53, 79; SANDF, "Boxing Tour: Israel 16–23 January 1994," November 8, 1993, AMI 520/3/4/6, vol. 55, 1–4.

44. Stephen Ellis, "The Historical Significance of South Africa's Third Force," *Journal of Southern African Studies* 24, no. 2 (1998): 261–62.

45. Tienie Groenewald, interview by author; Carlin, 124.

46. Ibid., 123.

47. SANDF, "Besoekverslag: Bywoning van Issakom . . . ," July 6, 1993, AFD INL 520/3/4/6, vol. 53, 66.

48. Carlin, 128–30; "Report on the Inquiry into the Events at the World Trade Centre on 25 June 1993," Commission of Inquiry Regarding the Prevention of Public Violence and Intimidation, at http://www.hurisa.org.za/Goldstone/C1027.pdf.

49. Carlin, 133–137.

50. Ibid., 137–41.

51. Gershom Gorenberg, "Road Map to Grand Apartheid? Ariel Sharon's South African Inspiration," *American Prospect*, July 2003; Akiva Eldar, "People and Politics: Sharon's Bantustans Are Far from Copenhagen's Hope," *Haaretz*, May 13, 2003.

52. Carlin, 149.

53. Peter Stiff, *Warfare by Other Means* (Alberton, South Africa: Galago, 2001), 567.

54. SANDF, "Motivation for Overseas Visit: Israel: Project Kabeljou," May 28, 1993, AMI 520/3/4/6, vol. 54, 10–15.

55. SANDF, "Visit Report: Visit to Israel by Maj S. P. Morgan . . . ," July 29, 1993, AMI 520/3/4/6, vol. 54, 35–37.

56. DFA, "Re-location of Armscor Component in S.A. Embassy, Tel Aviv," July 28, 1993, 1/8/5, vol. 2. Armscor had been kicked out in 1991 "for disciplinary reasons relating to the handling of the Gulf War evacuation." Even so, Armscor's team proposed to move from covert to overt status and was allowed to move back into the embassy office. Ambassador Malcolm Ferguson also encouraged a "buy-back" program, whereby South African firms could provide goods and services to Israel to pay off Armscor's contractual debt of more than $300 million.

57. NSA, "William B. Robinson to Mr. McNamara," June 10, 1994. Even though the United Nations and the United States lifted their respective arms embargoes after Mandela's inauguration, sanctions against Armscor remained in effect well into the Clinton administration as a result of this case.

58. NSA, "American Consulate Cape Town to Secretary of State Washington DC," March 16, 1993.

59. Adams, *The Unnatural Alliance*, 38–71. Bull was also a vital asset to the Pentagon. In 1972, thanks to his contributions to American defense research, Bull was naturalized as a U.S. citizen at the urging of Senator Barry Goldwater.

60. James Adams, *Bull's Eye: The Assassination and Life of Supergun Inventor Gerald Bull* (New York: Times Books, 1992); William Lowther, *Arms and the Man: Dr. Gerald Bull, Iraq and the Supergun* (London: Macmillan, 1991).

61. DFA, "Weapon Sales to Syria/Iran: Israeli Demarche," February 8, 1994, 1/8/3, vol. 46.

62. China was a major purchaser of Israeli weapons for a brief period in the 1990s, and today India is a major customer. See Withington, 18–19; Bruce Riedel, "Israel and India: New Allies," *Brookings Institution Middle East Bulletin*, March 21, 2008, at http://www.brookings.edu/opinions/2008/0321_india_riedel.aspx; Pankaj Mishra, "Purification Rites," *The National* (Abu Dhabi), March 27, 2009.

For more amusing evidence of the current arms trade between Israel and India see the *New York Times* online video: http://thelede.blogs.nytimes.com/2009/03/10/israeli-arms-dealer-tries-bollywood-pitch.

63. These weapons were of dubious strategic value to a newborn nation at peace. See Andrew Feinstein, *After the Party: Corruption, the ANC and South Africa's Uncertain Future* (New York: Verso, 2009). These postapartheid arms deals planted the seeds of a massive corruption scandal that has poisoned South African politics for the last fifteen years and was the backdrop for the 2009 election campaign.

64. Granot was "very angry" when South Africa extended recognition to Palestine, and he made an official protest to Deputy President Thabo Mbeki.

65. Elazar Granot, interview by author.

66. David Ivry, interview by author.

67. AFD, "Armscor Confidential Information: Bestel/Verskaffer Report." These figures represent direct acquisitions from Israel and licensed local production of Israeli hardware. They do not include joint ventures and shared South African financing of Israeli projects. This data is not available but would undoubtedly make the $10 billion figure significantly greater.

68. Elazar Granot, interview by author.

69. There have been periodic flare-ups at times of violence between Israel and the Palestinians. The apartheid-era friendship between the ANC and the Palestinian leadership has not faded, and since Granot's time Israel has not received much affection from the ANC, although Pretoria has occasionally sponsored conflict resolution workshops for Israelis and Palestinians.

70. Elazar Granot, interview by author.

EPILOGUE

1. See, for example, Nancy Murray, "Dynamics of Resistance: The Apartheid Analogy," *MIT Electronic Journal of Middle East Studies* (Spring 2008): 133–36, at http://www.palestinejournal.net/gmh/MIT_journal.htm.

2. Perlmutter and Evanier, "The African National Congress: A Closer Look."

3. http://www.frontpagemag.com/Articles/ReadArticle.asp?ID=25653.

4. http://www.guardian.co.uk/world/2007/nov/30/israel.

5. Shulamit Aloni, "Yes, There Is Apartheid in Israel" (translated), *Yediot Ahronot*, December 31, 2006.

6. http://www.haaretz.com/hasen/pages/rosnerBlog.jhtml?itemNo=777128.

7. http://www.washingtonpost.com/wp-dyn/content/article/2006/12/11/AR2006121101225.html.

8. See http://www.nybooks.com/articles/14380; Dennis Ross, *The Missing Peace: The Inside Story of the Fight for Middle East Peace* (New York: Farrar, Straus & Giroux, 2004).

9. Akiva Eldar, "People and Politics: Sharon's Bantustans Are Far from Copenhagen's Hope," *Haaretz*, May 13, 2003. For a discussion of the "bantustanization" of the West Bank and Gaza Strip and a thoughtful analysis of the many similarities and differences between South African apartheid and contemporary Israel, see Leila Farsakh, "Israel: An Apartheid State," *Le Monde Diplomatique* (English edition) (November 2003).

10. Penslar, *Israel in History*, 96.

11. Hannah Arendt, *The Origins of Totalitarianism* (New York: Harcourt Brace, 1973), 185–221; Sparks, 180. Interestingly, Geoff Cronjé—one of the ideological fathers of apartheid—had foreseen this dilemma. Writing in 1945, Cronjé warned that whites would have to learn to live without blacks doing menial labor if his dream of total racial separation was to come true.

12. Farsakh, 2.

13. For two interesting analyses of the similarities and differences between the two liberation movements, see Mona N. Younis, *Liberation and Democratization: The South African and Palestinian National Movements* (Minneapolis: University of Minnesota Press, 2000); Heribert Adam and Kogila Moodley, *Seeking Mandela: Peacemaking Between Israelis and Palestinians* (Philadelphia: Temple University Press, 2005). It should be noted that the popularity of the two-state solution among Palestinians is waning; many are now calling for a binational state instead. See Ehud Yaari, "Armistice Now," *Foreign Affairs*, (March–April 2010): 50–62.

14. Shlomo Ben-Ami, "A War to Start All Wars," *Foreign Affairs* (September–October 2008): 156.

15. Joseph, 12.

16. Amiram Barkat, "For the First Time, Jews Are No Longer a Majority Between the Jordan, the Sea," *Haaretz* (English edition), August 11, 2005.

Bibliography

BOOKS, JOURNAL ARTICLES, AND OTHER SECONDARY SOURCES

Abizadeh, Arash. "Was Fichte an Ethnic Nationalist: On Cultural Nationalism and Its Double." *History of Political Thought* 26, no. 2 (2005): 334–59.

Abramovitz, Arnold. "Apartheid Injuries and Diaspora Privileges." *Jewish Affairs* (Autumn 1997): 19–26.

Abramovitz, Yosef. *Jews, Zionism and South Africa.* Washington, D.C.: B'nai B'rith Hillel Foundations, 1985.

Adam, Heribert, and Hermann Giliomee. *Ethnic Power Mobilized: Can South Africa Change?* New Haven: Yale University Press, 1979.

Adam, Heribert, and Kogila Moodley. *Seeking Mandela: Peacemaking Between Israelis and Palestinians.* Philadelphia: Temple University Press, 2005.

Adams, James. *Bull's Eye: The Assassination and Life of Supergun Inventor Gerald Bull.* New York: Times Books, 1992.

———. *The Unnatural Alliance.* London: Quartet, 1984.

Adelman, Kenneth. "The Club of Pariahs." *Africa Report* (November–December 1980): 8–11.

Adler, Renata. "Letter from the Palmer House." *The New Yorker,* September 23, 1967, 56.

Akenson, Donald H. *God's Peoples: Covenant and Land in South Africa, Israel and Ulster.* Ithaca: Cornell University Press, 1992.

Albright, David. "A Curious Conversion." *Bulletin of the Atomic Scientists* 49, no. 5 (1993): 8–11.

———. "South Africa and the Affordable Bomb." *Bulletin of the Atomic Scientists* 50, no. 4 (1994): 37–47.

Albright, David, and Mark Hibbs. "South Africa: The A.N.C. and the Atom Bomb." *Bulletin of the Atomic Scientists* 49, no. 3 (April 1993): 32–37.

Arendt, Hannah. *The Origins of Totalitarianism.* New York: Harcourt Brace, 1973.

Ariel, David. "The Future of SA-Israeli Relations." *Jewish Affairs* (May 1987): 15–21.

Auerbach, Franz. "Do We Apologise? South African Jewish Community Responses to Apartheid." *Jewish Affairs* (Autumn 1997): 31–35.

Avineri, Shlomo. *The Making of Modern Zionism: The Intellectual Origins of the Jewish State.* London: Weidenfeld & Nicolson, 1981.

Badenhorst, Nicholas, and Pierre Victor. *Those Who Had the Power.* Pretoria: Pierre Victor, 2006.

Bandler, Kenneth, and George E. Gruen. *Israel and South Africa: A Special Report of the*

International Relations Department. New York: American Jewish Committee, April 1985.

Barak, Oren, and Chanan Kahan. *Misrad ha'chutz—Li'an?* Jerusalem: Leonard Davis Institute for International Relations, 2006.

Barak, Oren, and Gabriel Sheffer. "Israel's 'Security Network' and Its Impact: An Exploration of a New Approach." *International Journal of Middle East Studies* 38, no. 2 (2006): 235–61

Bass, Warren. *Support Any Friend: Kennedy's Middle East and the Making of the U.S.-Israel Alliance.* New York: Oxford University Press, 2003.

Begin, Menachem. *The Revolt.* New York: Nash, 1972.

Beinart, Peter. "The Jews of South Africa." *Transition* 71 (1996): 60–79.

Beinart, William. *Twentieth Century South Africa.* Oxford: Oxford University Press, 2001.

Beinart, William, and Saul Dubow, eds. *Segregation and Apartheid in Twentieth Century South Africa.* London: Routledge, 1995.

Beit-Hallahmi, Benjamin. *The Israeli Connection: Who Israel Arms and Why.* New York: Pantheon, 1987.

Benvenisti, Meron. *Sacred Landscape: The Buried History of the Holy Land Since 1948.* Berkeley: University of California Press, 2000.

Ben-Zvi, Abraham A. *Alliance Politics and the Limits of Influence: The Case of the US and Israel, 1975–1983.* Boulder: Westview, 1984.

———. *The United States and Israel: The Limits of the Special Relationship.* New York: Columbia University Press, 1993.

Bergman, Ronen. "B'shvilo, zeh garinim." *Yediot Ahronot* (*7 Yamim*), March 18, 2005.

———. "Hapes b'Antarktika." *Yediot Ahronot* (*7 Yamim*), May 19, 2006.

———. "Treasons of Conscience." *Haaretz Magazine* (English edition), April 7, 2000, 7–13.

Berman, Paul. *A Tale of Two Utopias: The Political Journey of the Generation of 1968.* New York: W. W. Norton, 1996.

Berman, Paul, ed. *Blacks and Jews: Alliances and Arguments.* New York: Delacorte, 1994.

Bernhard, N. M. "Conscientising the Jewish Community: An Orthodox Rabbi Looks Back." *Jewish Affairs* (Autumn 1997): 71–73.

Betts, Richard K. "A Diplomatic Bomb for South Africa?" *International Security* 4, no. 2 (1979): 91–115.

———. "Paranoids, Pygmies, Pariahs and Nonproliferation." *Foreign Policy* 26 (Spring 1977): 157–83.

Black, Ian, and Benny Morris. *Israel's Secret Wars: A History of Israel's Intelligence Services.* New York: Grove, 1991.

Blackstock, Paul. *The Strategy of Subversion: Manipulating the Politics of Other Nations.* Chicago: Quadrangle, 1964.

Blechman, Barry, and Douglas Hart. "The Political Utility of Nuclear Weapons: The 1973 Middle East Crisis." *International Security* 7, no. 1 (1982): 132–56.

Blight, James. "Critical Oral History" *as a Scholarly Tool* [accessed May 23 2004]. At http://chronicle.com/colloquylive/2002/10/blight.

Bloomberg, Charles. *Christian-Nationalism and the Rise of the Afrikaner Broederbond in South Africa, 1918–48.* Basingstoke: Macmillan, 1990.

Blow, Desmond. *Take Now Thy Son: The Yom Kippur War: South Africa's Involvement.* Cape Town: Howard Timmins, 1974.

Borstelmann, Thomas. *Apartheid's Reluctant Uncle: The United States and Southern Africa in the Early Cold War*. Oxford: Oxford University Press, 1993.

Boyne, Walter J. *The Yom Kippur War and the Airlift That Saved Israel*. New York: Thomas Dunne, 2003.

Braude, Claudia. "From the Brotherhood of Man to the World to Come: The Denial of the Political in Rabbinic Writing Under Apartheid." In *Jewries at the Frontier: Accommodation, Identity, Conflict*, ed. Sander L. Gilman and Milton Shain. Chicago: University of Illinois Press, 1999.

Brecher, Michael T. *The Foreign Policy System of Israel: Setting, Images, Process*. Oxford: Oxford University Press, 1972.

Brubaker, Rogers. *Citizenship and Nationhood in France and Germany*. Cambridge: Harvard University Press, 1992.

Bunce, Peter L. "The Growth of South Africa's Defence Industry and Its Israeli Connection." *Royal United Services Institute Journal* 129, no. 2 (1984): 42–49.

Burrows, William E., and Robert Windrem. *Critical Mass: The Dangerous Race for Superweapons in a Fragmenting World*. New York: Simon & Schuster, 1994.

Carbado, Devin W., and Donald Weise, eds. *Time on Two Crosses: The Collected Writings of Bayard Rustin*. San Francisco: Cleis, 2003.

Carlin, John. *Playing the Enemy: Nelson Mandela and the Game That Made a Nation*. New York: Penguin, 2008.

Carus, W. S. "Israeli Ballistic Missile Developments." Commission to Assess the Ballistic Missile Threat to the United States, Unclassified Working Papers, Appendix III. At http://fas.org/irp/threat/missile/rumsfeld/pt2_carus2.htm.

Cervenka, Zdenek, and Barbara Rogers. *The Nuclear Axis: The Secret Collaboration Between West Germany and South Africa*. New York: Times Books, 1978.

Chazan, Naomi. "The Fallacies of Pragmatism: Israeli Foreign Policy Toward South Africa." *African Affairs* 82, no. 327 (1983): 169–99.

———. "Israel and South Africa: Some Preliminary Reflections." *New Outlook* 31, no. 6 (1988): 8–11.

———. "Israeli Perspectives on the Israel–South Africa Relationship." *IJA Research Reports* (1987): 1–45.

Chertoff, Mordecai S., ed. *The New Left and Israel*. New York: Pitman, 1971.

Christie, Renfrew. *Electricity, Industry, and Class in South Africa*. London: Macmillan, 1984.

Cohen, Avner. *Israel and the Bomb*. New York: Columbia University Press, 1999.

———. "Nuclear Arms in Crisis Under Secrecy: Israel and the Lessons of the 1967 and 1973 Wars." In *Planning the Unthinkable: How New Powers Will Use Nuclear, Biological, and Chemical Weapons*, eds. Peter R. Lavoy, Scott D. Sagan, and James T. Wirtz. Ithaca: Cornell University Press, 2000.

———. "Crossing the Threshold: The Untold Nuclear Dimension of the 1967 Arab-Israeli War and its Contemporary Lessons." *Arms Control Today* 37, no. 5 (2007): 12–16.

Coker, Christopher. *NATO, the Warsaw Pact and Africa*. Basingstoke: Macmillan, 1985.

———. *The United States and South Africa, 1968–1985: Constructive Engagement and Its Critics*. Durham, NC: Duke University Press, 1986.

"Community and Conscience: A Symposium." *Jewish Affairs* (Spring 2004): 17–27.

Connelly, Matthew. *A Diplomatic Revolution: Algeria's Fight for Independence and the Origins of the Post–Cold War Era*. New York: Oxford University Press, 2002.

Crocker, Chester A. *High Noon in Southern Africa: Making Peace in a Rough Neighborhood.* New York: W. W. Norton, 1992.

———. *South Africa's Defense Posture: Coping with Vulnerability.* Beverly Hills: Center for Strategic and International Studies, 1981.

———. "South Africa: Strategy for Change." *Foreign Affairs* (Winter 1980–81).

Curtis, Michael, and Susan Gitelson, eds. *Israel in the Third World.* New Brunswick, NJ: Transaction, 1976.

Dahbour, Omar, and Micheline Ishay, eds. *The Nationalism Reader.* Atlantic Highlands, NJ: Humanities Books, 1995.

Davenport, T.R.H., and Christopher C. Saunders. *South Africa: A Modern History.* Basingstoke: Macmillan, 2000.

David, Steven R. "Explaining Third World Alignment." *World Politics* 43, no. 2 (1991): 233–56.

Davies, Robert, and Dan O'Meara. "Total Strategy in Southern Africa: An Analysis of South African Regional Policy Since 1978." *Journal of Southern African Studies* 11, no. 2 (1985): 183–211.

Day, Chris, and Mervyn Rees. *Muldergate: The Story of the Info Scandal.* Johannesburg: Macmillan, 1980.

Diamond, Dennis. "To Chaim Bermant: An Open Letter." *Jewish Affairs* (May 1979): 24–26.

Dinerstein, Herbert S. "The Transformation of Alliance Systems." *American Political Science Review* 59, no. 3 (1965): 589–601.

Dubow, Saul. *Racial Segregation and the Origins of Apartheid in South Africa, 1919–36.* Basingstoke: Macmillan, 1989.

———. *Scientific Racism in Modern South Africa.* Cambridge: Cambridge University Press, 1995.

Du Toit, André. "No Chosen People: The Myth of the Calvinist Origins of Afrikaner Nationalism and Racial Ideology." *American Historical Review* 88, no. 4 (1983): 920–52.

Eban, Abba. *Abba Eban: An Autobiography.* New York: Random House, 1977.

Eitan, Raful. *A Soldier's Story.* New York: S.P.I., 1992.

Ellis, Stephen. "The Historical Significance of South Africa's Third Force." *Journal of Southern African Studies* 24, no. 2 (1998): 261–99.

Epstein, Edward Jay. *The Death of the Diamond.* London: Sphere, 1983.

Even-Zohar, Chaim. *From Mine to Mistress: Corporate Strategies and Government Policies in the International Diamond Industry.* Edenbridge: Mining Journal Books, 2007.

Evron, Yair. *Israel's Nuclear Dilemma.* Ithaca: Cornell University Press, 1994.

Farr, Warner D. *The Third Temple's Holy of Holies: Israel's Nuclear Weapons* [accessed January 1, 2006] at http://www.au.af.mil/au/awc/awcgate/cpc-pubs/farr.htm.

Farsakh, Leila. "Israel: An Apartheid State." *Le Monde Diplomatique* (English edition) (November 2003).

Fedder, Edwin H. "The Concept of Alliance." *International Studies Quarterly* 12, no. 1 (1968): 65–86.

Feinstein, Andrew. *After the Party: Corruption, the ANC, and South Africa's Uncertain Future.* New York: Verso, 2009.

Feldman, Shai. *Israeli Nuclear Deterrence: A Strategy for the 1980s.* New York: Columbia University Press, 1982.

Fisk, Robert. *Pity the Nation: The Abduction of Lebanon.* New York: Atheneum, 1990.

Frankel, Glenn. *Rivonia's Children: Three Families and the Cost of Conscience in White South Africa.* New York: Continuum, 1999.

Frankel, Philip H. *An Ordinary Atrocity: Sharpeville and Its Massacre.* Johannesburg: Witwatersrand University Press, 2001.

———. *Pretoria's Praetorians: Civil-Military Relations in South Africa.* Cambridge: Cambridge University Press, 1984.

Friedman, Steven. "Judaism, Apartheid and the Sojourner Myth." *Jewish Affairs* (Autumn 1997): 60–62.

Furlong, Patrick. *Between Crown and Swastika: The Impact of the Radical Right on the Afrikaner Nationalist Movement in the Fascist Era.* Johannesburg: Witwatersrand University Press, 1991.

Geldenhuys, Deon. *The Diplomacy of Isolation: South African Foreign Policy Making.* Johannesburg: Macmillan, 1984.

———. *Isolated States: A Comparative Analysis.* Cambridge: Cambridge University Press, 1990.

Gibel-Azoulay, Katya. "Rather Than Curse the Darkness: A Call for Mobilization." *New Outlook* (March 1987): 13–14.

Giliomee, Hermann Buhr. *The Afrikaners: Biography of a People.* London: C. Hurst, 2003.

Gilmore, Glenda E. *Defying Dixie: The Radical Roots of Civil Rights, 1919–1950.* New York: W. W. Norton, 2008.

Ginor, Isabella, and Gideon Remez. *Foxbats over Dimona: The Soviets' Nuclear Gamble in the Six-Day War.* New Haven: Yale University Press, 2007.

Gleijeses, Piero. *Conflicting Missions: Havana, Washington, and Africa, 1959–1976.* Chapel Hill: University of North Carolina Press, 2002.

Goldberg, Aleck. "Apartheid and the Board of Deputies." *Jewish Affairs* (Autumn 1997): 48–52.

———. "The S.A. Jewish Board of Deputies, 1958–1990: A Personal Overview." *Jewish Affairs* (Autumn 2003): 36–47.

Goodman, Hirsh. *Let Me Create a Paradise, God Said to Himself.* New York: Public-Affairs, 2005.

Gorenberg, Gershom. *The Accidental Empire: Israel and the Birth of the Settlements, 1967–1977.* New York: Times Books, 2006.

———. *The End of Days: Fundamentalism and the Struggle for the Temple Mount.* Oxford: Oxford University Press, 2002.

———. "Road Map to Grand Apartheid? Ariel Sharon's South African Inspiration." *American Prospect* (July 2003).

Greenstein, Ran. *Genealogies of Conflict: Class, Identity, and State in Palestine/Israel and South Africa.* Hanover, NH: University Press of New England, 1995.

Gruen, George E., and Kenneth Bandler. *Israel and South Africa.* New York: American Jewish Committee, 1985.

Grundy, Kenneth W. *The Militarization of South African Politics.* London: I. B. Tauris, 1986.

———. *The Rise of the South African Security Establishment.* Johannesburg: Bradlow Series, no. 1, 1983.

Gutteridge, William F., ed. *South Africa's Defence and Security into the 21st Century.* Aldershot: Dartmouth, 1996.

Hamann, Hilton. *Days of the Generals.* Cape Town: Struik, 1999.

Handel, Michael I. "The Yom Kippur War and the Inevitability of Surprise." *International Studies Quarterly* 21, no. 3 (1977): 461–502.

Hanks, Robert J. *Southern Africa and Western Security.* Washington, D.C.: Institute for Foreign Policy Analysis, 1983.

Harkavy, Robert E. "Pariah States and Nuclear Proliferation." *International Organization* 35, no. 1 (1981): 135–63.

———. "The Pariah State Syndrome." *Orbis* 21, no. 3 (1977): 623–50.

Harris, C. K. "The Moral Repudiation of Apartheid in Jewish Classical Sources." *Jewish Affairs* (Autumn 1997): 58–59.

Hengeveld, Richard, and Jaap Rodenburg, eds. *Embargo: Apartheid's Oil Secrets Revealed.* Amsterdam: University of Amsterdam, 1995.

Hersh, Seymour. *The Samson Option: Israel's Nuclear Arsenal and American Foreign Policy.* New York: Random House, 1991.

Houbert, Jean. "Settlers and Seaways in a Decolonized World." *Journal of Modern African Studies* 23, no. 1 (1985): 1–29.

Hounam, Peter, and Steve McQuillan. *The Mini-Nuke Conspiracy: Mandela's Nuclear Nightmare.* New York: Viking, 1995.

Howell, William G., and Jon C. Pevehouse. *While Dangers Gather: Congressional Checks on Presidential War Powers* (Princeton: Princeton University Press, 2007).

Hunter, Jane. "Israel and the Bantustans." *Journal of Palestine Studies* 15, no. 3 (1986): 53–89.

———. *Israeli Foreign Policy: South Africa and Central America.* Nottingham: Bertrand Russell Peace Foundation, 1987.

———. "Israel, South Africa and the Bomb." *MERIP Middle East Report* 143 (1986): 13.

Huntington, Samuel P. "Reform and Stability in South Africa." *International Security* 6, no. 4 (Spring 1982): 3–25.

Inbar, Efraim. *Outcast Countries in the World Community.* Denver: Graduate School of International Studies, University of Denver, 1985.

Jabbour, George. *Settler Colonialism in Southern Africa and the Middle East.* Khartoum: University of Khartoum, 1970.

Jacob, Abel. "Israel's Military Aid to Africa, 1960–1966." *Journal of Modern African Studies* (August 1971): 165–72.

Jaster, Robert S. *The Defence of White Power: South African Foreign Policy Under Pressure.* Basingstoke: Macmillan, 1988.

———. "Politics and the 'Afrikaner Bomb.' " *Orbis* 28 (Winter 1984): 825–51.

———. "South African Defense Strategy and the Growing Influence of the Military." In *Arms and the African: Military Influences on Africa's International Relations,* ed. William J. Foltz and Henry Bienen. New Haven: Yale University Press, 1985.

———. *South Africa's Narrowing Security Options.* London: International Institute for Strategic Studies, 1980.

Jeffrey, Jaclyn, and Glenace Edwall, eds. *Memory and History: Essays on Recalling and Interpreting Experience.* Lanham, MD: University Press of America, 1994.

Joseph, Benjamin. *Besieged Bedfellows: Israel and the Land of Apartheid.* Westport, CT: Greenwood, 1988.

Kanfer, Stefan. *The Last Empire: De Beers, Diamonds, and the World.* New York: Farrar, Straus & Giroux, 1993.

Kann, Robert A. "Alliances Versus Ententes." *World Politics* 28, no. 4 (1976): 614–16.

Karpin, Michael I. *The Bomb in the Basement: How Israel Went Nuclear and What That Means for the World*. New York: Simon & Schuster, 2006.

Kaufman, Jonathan. *Broken Alliance: The Turbulent Times Between Blacks and Jews in America*. New York: Touchstone, 1995.

Kedourie, Elie. *Nationalism*. 4th ed. Oxford: Blackwell, 1993.

Kimche, David. *The Afro-Asian Movement: Ideology and Foreign Policy of the Third World*. Jerusalem: Israel Universities Press, 1973.

———. *Israel and Africa*. African Geopolitics, 2003 [accessed December 10, 2004], at http://www.african-geopolitics.org/show.aspx?ArticleId=3097.

Kissinger, Henry. *Years of Upheaval*. Boston: Little, Brown, 1982.

Klieman, Aaron S. *Israel's Global Reach: Arms Sales as Diplomacy*. Oxford: Pergamon, 1985.

Kling, George, et al. "The 1986 Lake Nyos Gas Disaster in Cameroon, West Africa." *Science* 236, no. 4798 (April 10, 1987): 169–75.

Klinghoffer, Arthur Jay. *Oiling the Wheels of Apartheid: Exposing South Africa's Secret Oil Trade*. Boulder: Lynne Rienner, 1989.

Kreinin, Mordechai. *Israel and Africa: A Study in Technical Cooperation*. New York: Praeger, 1964.

Landgren, Signe. *Embargo Disimplemented: South Africa's Military Industry*. Oxford: Oxford University Press, 1989.

Lankin, Eliahu. *To Win the Promised Land: Story of a Freedom Fighter*. Walnut Creek, CA: Benmir, 1992.

———. "Yachaso shel ha ma'arav l'D'rom Afrika . . ." (Western Attitudes Toward South Africa . . .). *Nativ* (May 1988): 27–34.

Laskier, Michael M. "Israel and Algeria Amid French Colonialism and the Arab-Israeli Conflict, 1954–1978." *Israel Studies* 6, no. 2 (2001): 1–32.

Leonard, Richard. *South Africa at War: White Power and the Crisis in Southern Africa*. Westport, CT: Lawrence Hill, 1983.

Liberman, Peter. "Israel and the South African Bomb." *Nonproliferation Review* 11, no. 2 (2004): 46–80.

———. "The Rise and Fall of the South African Bomb." *International Security* 26, no. 2 (2001): 45–86.

Liel, Alon. *Tzedek Shachor*. Tel Aviv: Ha'kibbutz ha'meuchad, 1999.

Lipset, Seymour Martin. " 'The Socialism of Fouls': The Left, the Jews, and Israel." In *The New Left and the Jews*, ed. Mordechai S. Chertoff. New York: Pitman, 1971.

Liska, George. *Alliances and the Third World*. Baltimore: Johns Hopkins University Press, 1968.

———. *Nations in Alliance: The Limits of Interdependence*. Baltimore: Johns Hopkins University Press, 1962.

Lowther, William. *Arms and the Man: Dr. Gerald Bull, Iraq and the Supergun*. London: Macmillan, 1991.

Lustick, Ian. *Arabs in the Jewish State: Israel's Control of a National Minority*. Austin: University of Texas Press, 1980.

———. *For the Land and the Lord: Jewish Fundamentalism in Israel*. New York: Council on Foreign Relations, 1988.

———. *Unsettled States: Britain and Ireland, France and Algeria, Israel and the West Bank/Gaza*. Ithaca: Cornell University Press, 1993.

MacMillan, Margaret. *Paris 1919: Six Months That Changed the World*. New York: Random House, 2001.

Makovsky, Michael. *Churchill's Promised Land: Zionism and Statecraft*. New Haven: Yale University Press, 2007.

Mandela, Nelson. *Long Walk to Freedom*. Boston: Little, Brown, 1994.

Marks, Shula, and Stanley Trapido, eds. *The Politics of Race, Class and Nationalism in Twentieth Century South Africa*. Harlow: Longman, 1987.

Masiza, Zondi. "A Chronology of South Africa's Nuclear Program." *Nonproliferation Review* 1 (Fall 1993): 37.

Marton, Kati. *A Death in Jerusalem*. New York: Arcade, 1996.

Mazrui, Ali. "Black Africa and the Arab-Israeli Conflict." *Middle East International* (September 1978).

———. "Zionism and Apartheid: Strange Bedfellows or Natural Allies?" *Alternatives* 9 (Summer 1983).

Mead, Walter R. "The New Israel and the Old," *Foreign Affairs* (July–August 2008).

Medoff, Rafael, and Mordechai Haller. "South Africa in the Mind of Israel." *National Review*, April 15, 1988.

Medzini, Meron, ed. *Israel's Foreign Relations: Selected Documents, 1984–1988*, vol. 2. Jerusalem: Ministry of Foreign Affairs, 1989.

Meir, Golda. *My Life*. New York: Putnam, 1975.

Minty, Abdul S. *South Africa's Defence Strategy*. London: Anti-Apartheid Movement, 1969.

Mintz, Alex, and Michael D. Ward. "Dynamics of Military Spending in Israel: A Computer Simulation." *Journal of Conflict Resolution* 31, no. 1 (1987): 86–105.

———. "The Political Economy of Military Spending in Israel." *American Political Science Review* 83, no. 2 (1989): 521–33.

Modelski, George. "The Study of Alliances: A Review." *Journal of Conflict Resolution* 7, no. 4 (1963): 769–76.

Moodie, T. Dunbar. *The Rise of Afrikanerdom: Power, Apartheid, and the Afrikaner Civil Religion*. Berkeley: University of California Press, 1975.

Morgenthau, Hans J. "Alliances in Theory and Practice." In *Alliance Policy in the Cold War*, ed. Arnold Wolfers. Baltimore: Johns Hopkins University Press, 1959.

———. *Politics Among Nations: The Struggle for Power and Peace*. 5th ed. New York: Alfred A. Knopf, 1973.

Mugomba, Agrippah T. *The Foreign Policy of Despair: Africa and the Sale of Arms to South Africa*. Nairobi: East African Literature Bureau, 1977.

Murray, Nancy. "Dynamics of Resistance: The Apartheid Analogy. *MIT Electronic Journal of Middle East Studies* (Spring 2008): 132–148.

Norris, Robert S., Hans M. Kristensen, William Arkin, and Joshua Handler. "Israeli Nuclear Forces 2002." *Bulletin of the Atomic Scientists* 58, no. 5 (2002): 73–75.

Ojo, Olusola. *Africa and Israel: Relations in Perspective*. Boulder: Westview, 1988.

O'Meara, Dan. *Forty Lost Years: The Apartheid State and the Politics of the National Party, 1948–1994*. Athens: Ohio University Press, 1996.

———. *Volkskapitalisme: Class, Capital and Ideology in the Development of Afrikaner Nationalism, 1934–1948*. Cambridge: Cambridge University Press, 1983.

Oren, Michael. *Six Days of War: June 1967 and the Making of the Modern Middle East*. London: Penguin, 2003.

Osia, Kuniram. *Israel, South Africa and Black Africa: A Study in the Primacy of the Politics of Expediency*. New York: University Press of America, 1981.

Owen, David. *In Sickness and in Power: Illnesses in Heads of Government During the Last 100 Years.* Westport, CT: Praeger, 2008.

Pabian, Frank V. "South Africa's Nuclear Weapon Program: Lessons for U.S. Nonproliferation Policy." *Nonproliferation Review* 3, no. 1 (1995), 1–19.

Parsi, Trita. *Treacherous Alliance: The Secret Dealings of Israel, Iran, and the U.S.* New Haven: Yale University Press, 2007.

Paul, T. V. "Nuclear Taboo and War Initiation in Regional Conflicts." *Journal of Conflict Resolution* 39, no. 4 (1995): 696–717.

Péan, Pierre. *Les Deux Bombes: Ou Comment la Guerre du Golfe A Commencé le 18 Novembre 1975.* Paris: Fayard, 1991.

Peleg, Ilan. *Begin's Foreign Policy, 1977–1983: Israel's Move to the Right.* New York: Greenwood, 1987.

Penslar, Derek J. "Israel: A Colonial or Post-Colonial State." Paper presented at Oxford Center for Hebrew and Jewish Studies, May 2004.

———. *Israel in History: The Jewish State in Comparative Perspective.* New York: Routledge, 2007.

Peres, Shimon. *Battling for Peace: Memoirs.* London: Weidenfeld & Nicolson, 1995.

Perlmutter, Amos, Michael Handel, and Uri Bar-Joseph. *Two Minutes over Baghdad.* London: Frank Cass, 2003.

Perlmutter, Nathan, and David Evanier. "The African National Congress: A Closer Look." *ADL Bulletin* (May 1986).

Peters, Joel. *Israel and Africa: The Problematic Friendship.* London: British Academic Press, 1992.

Pierre, Andrew J. "Arms Sales: The New Diplomacy." *Foreign Affairs* 60, no. 2 (Winter 1981–82): 266–86.

Polakow-Suransky, Sasha. "The Unspoken Alliance: Israel and Apartheid South Africa, 1960–1994." Ph.D. diss., University of Oxford, 2007.

Powell, Adam Clayton, Jr. *Adam by Adam: The Autobiography of Adam Clayton Powell, Jr.* New York: Kensington, 1971.

Prados, John. "Sealanes, Western Strategy and South Africa." In *U.S. Military Involvement in Southern Africa,* ed. Western Massachusetts Association of Concerned African Scholars. Boston: South End, 1978.

Purkitt, Helen E., and Stephen F. Burgess. *South Africa's Weapons of Mass Destruction.* Bloomington: Indiana University Press, 2005.

Rabin, Yitzhak. *The Rabin Memoirs.* Berkeley: University of California Press, 1979; reprinted 1996.

Rabinovich, Abraham. *The Boats of Cherbourg.* New York: Seaver, 1988.

Radosh, Ronald, and Allis Radosh. "Righteous Among the Editors: When the Left Loved Israel." *World Affairs* (Summer 2008), 65–75.

Rafael, Gideon. *Destination Peace: Three Decades of Israeli Foreign Policy, a Personal Memoir.* London: Weidenfeld & Nicolson, 1981.

Ravitzky, Aviezer. *Messianism, Zionism, and Jewish Religious Radicalism.* Chicago: University of Chicago Press, 1996.

Ray, Ellen, et al., eds. *Dirty Work: The CIA in Africa.* London: Zed, 1980.

Rees, Mervyn, and Chris Day. *Muldergate: The Story of the Info Scandal.* Johannesburg: Macmillan, 1980.

Reich, Bernard. "Israel's Policy in Africa." *Middle East Journal* 18, no. 1 (1964): 14–26.

Reiser, Stewart. *The Israeli Arms Industry: Foreign Policy, Arms Transfers, and Military Doctrine of a Small State.* New York: Holmes & Meier, 1989.

Reiss, Mitchell. *Bridled Ambition: Why Countries Constrain Their Nuclear Capabilities.* Washington, D.C.: Woodrow Wilson Center Press, 1995.

"Report on the Inquiry into the Events at the World Trade Centre on 25 June 1993." Commission of Inquiry Regarding the Prevention of Public Violence and Intimidation, at: http://www.hurisa.org.za/Goldstone/C1027.pdf.

Rhoodie, Eschel. *The Real Information Scandal.* Pretoria: Orbis, 1983.

Richelson, Jeffrey T. *Spying on the Bomb: American Nuclear Intelligence from Nazi Germany to Iran and North Korea.* New York: W. W. Norton, 2006.

Riedel, Bruce. "Israel and India: New Allies." *Brookings Institution Middle East Bulletin,* March 21, 2008, at http://www.brookings.edu/opinions/2008/0321_india_riedel .aspx.

Ron, James. *Frontiers and Ghettos: State Violence in Serbia and Israel.* Berkeley: University of California Press, 2003.

Ross, Dennis. *The Missing Peace: The Inside Story of the Fight for Middle East Peace.* New York: Farrar, Straus & Giroux, 2004.

Rothstein, Robert L. *Alliances and Small Powers.* New York: Columbia University Press, 1968.

Rudolph, Harold. *Security, Terrorism and Torture: Detainees' Rights in South Africa and Israel, a Comparative Study.* Cape Town: Juta, 1984.

Sachar, Howard M. *A History of Israel.* 3rd ed. New York: Alfred A. Knopf, 2007.

Sadeh, Sharon. "Israel's Beleaguered Defense Industry." *Middle East Review of International Affairs* 5, no. 1 (2001): 64–77.

Sagan, Scott D. "Lessons of the Yom Kippur Alert." *Foreign Policy* 36 (Autumn 1979): 160–77.

Sanders, James. *Apartheid's Friends: The Rise and Fall of South Africa's Secret Service.* London: John Murray, 2006.

———. *South Africa and the International Media, 1972–1979: A Struggle for Representation.* London: Frank Cass, 2000.

Sarig, Mordechai, ed. *The Political and Social Philosophy of Ze'ev Jabotinsky: Selected Writings.* London: Vallentine Mitchell, 1999.

Sayigh, Yezid, and Avi Shlaim, eds. *The Cold War and the Middle East.* Oxford: Clarendon Press, 1997.

Schechtman, Joseph B. *Rebel and Statesman: The Vladimir Jabotinsky Story.* New York: Thomas Yoseloff, 1956.

Schneidman, Witney W. *Engaging Africa: Washington and the Fall of Portugal's Colonial Empire.* Lanham, MD: University Press of America, 2004.

Schwarz, Harry. "Jewish Modes of Opposition." *Jewish Affairs* (Autumn 1997): 27–30.

Schweller, Randall L. *Deadly Imbalances: Tripolarity and Hitler's Strategy of World Conquest.* New York: Columbia University Press, 1998.

Seegers, Annette. *The Military in the Making of Modern South Africa.* London: I. B. Tauris, 1996.

Seliktar, Ofira. *New Zionism and the Foreign Policy System of Israel.* London: Croom Helm, 1986.

Shain, Milton, and Sally Frankental. "Accommodation, Activism and Apathy: Reflections on Jewish Political Behaviour During the Apartheid Era." *Jewish Affairs* (Autumn 1997): 53–57.

Shavit, Jacob. *Jabotinsky and the Revisionist Movement, 1925–1948.* London: Frank Cass, 1988.

Sherman, David. "My Encounter with Apartheid: A Reform Rabbi Looks Back." *Jewish Affairs* (Autumn 1997): 74–75.

Shimoni, Gideon. *Community and Conscience: The Jews in Apartheid South Africa.* Hanover, NH: University Press of New England, 2003.

———. *Jews and Zionism: The South African Experience, 1910–1967.* Cape Town: Oxford University Press, 1980.

———. "Zionism and the Apartheid Dilemma of South African Jewry." *Jewish Affairs* (Autumn 1997): 41–42.

———. *The Zionist Ideology.* Hanover, NH: University Press of New England, 1995.

Shindler, Colin. *Israel, Likud and the Zionist Dream: Power, Politics and Ideology from Begin to Netanyahu.* London: I. B. Tauris, 1995.

———. *The Triumph of Military Zionism: Nationalism and the Origins of the Israeli Right.* London: I. B. Tauris, 2005.

Shlaim, Avi. *The Iron Wall: Israel and the Arab World.* London: Penguin, 2000.

Smith, Mervyn. "Apartheid and South African Jewry." *Jewish Affairs* (Spring 2003): 21–23.

Snyder, Glenn H. *Alliance Politics.* Ithaca: Cornell University Press, 1997.

Sofer, Sasson. *Zionism and the Foundations of Israeli Diplomacy.* Cambridge: Cambridge University Press, 1998.

Sparks, Allister. *The Mind of South Africa: The Story of the Rise and Fall of Apartheid.* London: Mandarin, 1991.

Sprinzak, Ehud. *Brother Against Brother: Violence and Extremism in Israeli Politics from Altalena to the Rabin Assassination.* New York: Free Press, 1999.

Stanislawski, Michael. *Zionism and the Fin de Siècle: Cosmopolitanism and Nationalism from Nordau to Jabotinsky.* Berkeley: University of California Press, 2001.

Steinberg, Gerald M. "Israel: Case Study for International Missile Trade and Nonproliferation Project." In *The International Missile Bazaar,* eds. William Potter and Harlan Jencks. Boulder: Westview, 1993.

———. "The Mythology of Israel–South African Nuclear Cooperation." *Middle East Review* 19, no. 3 (1987): 31–38.

Stevens, Richard P. *Weizmann and Smuts: A Study in Zionist–South African Cooperation.* Beirut: Institute for Palestine Studies, 1975.

Stiff, Peter. *Warfare by Other Means.* Alberton, South Africa: Galago, 2001.

Stockwell, John. *In Search of Enemies: A CIA Story.* New York: W. W. Norton, 1978.

Stumpf, Waldo. "South Africa's Nuclear Weapons Program: From Deterrence to Dismantlement." *Arms Control Today* 25 (December 1995–January 1996): 3–8.

Suzman, Mark. *Ethnic Nationalism and State Power: The Rise of Irish Nationalism, Afrikaner Nationalism and Zionism.* Basingstoke: Macmillan, 1999.

Thompson, Leonard M. *The Political Mythology of Apartheid.* New Haven: Yale University Press, 1985.

Unna, Yitzhak D. "As I Remember It" (unpublished manuscript).

Van der Walt, Richardt, Hannes Steyn, and Jan van Loggerenberg. *Armament and Disarmament: South Africa's Nuclear Experience.* Lincoln, NE: iUniverse, 2005.

Vatcher, William Henry. *White Laager: The Rise of Afrikaner Nationalism.* London: Pall Mall, 1965.

Vitenberg, Dr. "Israel et l'Afrique du Sud." *France-Israel Information* (Juin–Juillet 1987).

Walt, Stephen. *The Origins of Alliances.* Ithaca: Cornell University Press, 1987.

Waltz, Kenneth. *Theory of International Politics*. New York: McGraw-Hill, 1979.

Weber, Max. *From Max Weber: Essays in Sociology*. Eds. Hans Heinrich Gerth and C. Wright Mills. New York: Oxford University Press, 1958.

Withington, Thomas. "Israel and India Partner Up." *Bulletin of the Atomic Scientists* 57, no. 1 (2001): 18–19.

Younis, Mona N. *Liberation and Democratization: The South African and Palestinian National Movements*. Minneapolis: University of Minnesota Press, 2000.

Zogby, James, and Jack O'Dell, eds. *Afro-Americans Stand Up for Middle East Peace*. Palestine Human Rights Campaign, 1979.

AUTHOR INTERVIEWS

Israel (Boomie) Abramowitz. Johannesburg, March 14, 2005.

Louw Alberts. Pretoria, February 27, 2006.

David Ariel. Jerusalem, December 22, 2004.

Diana Aviv (telephone). February 22, 2008.

Amos Baram. Netanya, September 22, 2005.

Yossi Beilin. Tel Aviv, December 15, 2004.

Chris Bennett. Cape Town, February 28, 2005.

Douglas Bloomfield (telephone). February 14, 2008.

Fanie Botha. Pretoria, July 7, 2006.

Shlomo Brom. Tel Aviv, December 15, 2004.

André Buys. Pretoria, March 18, 2005.

Bob Campbell. McLean, VA, June 16, 2007.

Dick Clark. Washington, D.C., November 15, 2005.

Herman Cohen. Washington, D.C., November 21, 2005.

Chester Crocker. Washington, D.C., November 15, 2005.

Dennis Davis. Cape Town, February 28, 2005.

Dennis Diamond. Jerusalem, December 19, 2004.

Ronnie Edwards. Springs, July 1, 2006.

Chaim Even-Zohar. Washington, D.C., October 18, 2007.

Malcolm Ferguson. Johannesburg, March 5, 2005.

Jannie Geldenhuys. Pretoria, March 8, 2005.

Dieter Gerhardt. Noordhoek, March 8, 2006.

Aleck Goldberg. Johannesburg, March 7, 2005.

Denis Goldberg. Hout Bay, March 8, 2006.

Arthur Goldreich. Herzliya, December 16, 2004.

Zvi Gov-Ari. Yavne, December 21, 2004.

Elazar Granot. Kibbutz Shoval, December 15, 2004.

Tienie Groenewald (#1). Pretoria, March 21, 2005.

Tienie Groenewald (#2). Pretoria, July 6, 2006.

Shlomo Gur. Tel Aviv, December 7, 2004.

Mike Hannon (telephone). April 26, 2006.

J. P. Hugo. Pretoria, March 1, 2006.

Harry Hurwitz (#1). Jerusalem, December 20, 2004.

Harry Hurwitz (#2). Jerusalem, July 24, 2006.

David Ivry. Tel Aviv, September 19, 2005.
Mendel Kaplan. Johannesburg, March 7, 2005.
David Kimche (telephone). December 20, 2004.
Alon Liel. Tel Aviv, December 3, 2004.
Bertie Lubner (telephone). August 14, 2006.
Princeton Lyman. Washington, D.C., November 21, 2005.
Magnus Malan. Pretoria, February 9, 2006.
George Meiring. Pretoria, March 16, 2005.
Trita Parsi (telephone). February 29, 2008.
Benjamin Pogrund. Jerusalem, December 12, 2004.
Kenneth Prendini (telephone). July 5, 2006.
Pieter John Roos. Centurion, January 20, 2006.
Harry Schwarz. Johannesburg, March 18, 2005.
Mervyn Smith. Cape Town, February 22, 2005.
Hannes Steyn. Pretoria, March 24, 2005.
Waldo Stumpf. Pretoria, March 18, 2005.
Binyamin Telem. Beit Yehoshuah, September 20, 2005.
Chris Thirion. Pretoria, March 16, 2005.
Yitzhak Unna. Netanya, August 24, 2005.
Jan van Loggerenberg. Pretoria, March 22, 2005.
Julius Weinstein. Tel Aviv, September 6, 2005.
Steven Weissman. Washington, D.C., October 19, 2007.
Howard Wolpe. Washington, D.C., September 24, 2007.
Shimshon Zelniker. Jerusalem, December 2, 2004.
James Zogby. Washington, D.C., September 20, 2007.

Index

Page numbers in *italics* refer to illustrations.

Printed in the United States
by Baker & Taylor Publisher Services